"Ferrante's writing seems to say something that hasn't been said before—it isn't easy to specify what this is—in a way so compelling its readers forget where they are, abandon friends and disdain sleep."

—Joanna Biggs, *The London Review of Books*

"Ferrante has written about female identity with a heft and sharpness unmatched by anyone since Doris Lessing."

—Elizabeth Lowry, *The Wall Street Journal*

"Ferrante, in her unflinching willingness to lead us toward 'the mutable fury of things,' places the readers inside intimate relations between women and men with an irresistible and urgent immediacy."

—Roger Cohen, *The New York Review of Books*

"Elena Ferrante's decision to remain biographically unavailable is her greatest gift to readers, and maybe her boldest creative gesture."   —David Kurnick, *Public Books*

"Reading Ferrante is an extraordinary experience. There's a powerful and unsettling candor in her writing."

—Nick Romeo, *The Boston Globe*

"To the uninitiated, the Italian novelist Elena Ferrante is best described as Balzac meets *The Sopranos* and rewrites feminist theory."   —*The Times of London*

"Ferrante writes with the kind of power saved for weather systems with female names."   —*The Los Angeles Times*

FRANTUMAGLIA

Elena Ferrante

FRANTUMAGLIA

PAPERS: 1991-2003
TESSERAE: 2003-2007
LETTERS: 2011-2016

Europa
editions

Europa Editions
214 West 29th Street
New York, N.Y. 10001
www.europaeditions.com
info@europaeditions.com

All translations by Ann Goldstein unless otherwise noted.
Original title: *La frantumaglia*
Translation copyright © 2016 by Europa Editions

The author and the publishers are grateful to the journalists and all those
whose questions have contributed to the publication of this book.

Library of Congress Cataloguing in Publication Data is available
ISBN 978-1-60945-292-6

Ferrante, Elena
Frantumaglia

Book design by Emanuele Ragnisco
www.mekkanografici.com

Cover photo: Francesca Woodman, *House #3*, Providence, Rhode Island
Copyright © George and Betty Woodman

Prepress by Grafica Punto Print – Rome

Printed in the USA

CONTENTS

FRANTUMAGLIA

I

PAPERS: 1991-2003

THESE LETTERS

T hese letters are intended for those who have read, loved, and talked about *Troubling Love* and *The Days of Abandonment*, Elena Ferrante's first two novels. Over the years, the first became a cult book, and in 1995 Mario Martone made a film based on it; meanwhile, questions about the author's public reticence multiplied. The second novel further broadened her audience; she gained passionate readers, both male and female; and questions about the person of Elena Ferrante became pressing.

To satisfy the curiosity of this exacting yet generous audience, we decided to collect here some letters from the author to Edizioni E/O; the few interviews she has given; and her correspondence with particular readers. Among other things, these writings should clarify, we hope conclusively, the writer's motives for remaining outside, the media circus and its demands, as she has for ten years.

> Sandra Ozzola and Sandro Ferri,
> publishers of Edizioni E/O
> and Europa Editions.

NOTE
This introduction was included in an earlier edition of *La Frantumaglia*, released in Italy in September, 2003.

All the notes that follow have been added by the editors of this unabridged and updated edition of *Frantumaglia*.

1.

THE GIFT OF THE BEFANA

Dear Sandra,

During the meeting I had recently with you and your husband, which was very enjoyable, you asked me what I intend to do for the promotion of *Troubling Love* (it's good that you're getting me used to calling the book by its final title). You asked the question ironically, with one of your bemused expressions. There and then, I didn't have the courage to answer you: I thought I had already been clear with Sandro; he had said that he absolutely agreed with my decision, and I hoped that he wouldn't return to the subject, even jokingly. Now I'm answering in writing, which eliminates awkward pauses, hesitations, any possibility of compliance.

I do not intend to do anything for *Troubling Love*, anything that might involve the public engagement of me personally. I've already done enough for this long story: I wrote it. If the book is worth anything, that should be sufficient. I won't participate in discussions and conferences, if I'm invited. I won't go and accept prizes, if any are awarded to me. I will never promote the book, especially on television, not in Italy or, as the case may be, abroad. I will be interviewed only in writing, but I would prefer to limit even that to the indispensable minimum. I am absolutely committed in this sense to myself and my family. I hope not to be forced to change my mind. I understand that this may cause some difficulties at the publishing house. I have great respect for your work, I liked you both immediately, and I don't want to cause trouble. If you no longer mean to support me, tell me right away, I'll understand. It's not at all necessary for me to publish this book. To explain all the reasons for my decision, is, as you know, hard for me. I will only tell you that it's a small wager with myself, with my convictions. I believe that books, once they are written, have no need of their authors. If they have something to say, they will sooner or later find readers; if not, they won't. There are plenty of examples. I very much love those mysterious volumes, both ancient and modern, that have no definite author but have had and continue to have an intense life of their own. They seem to me a sort of nighttime miracle, like the gifts of the Befana, which I waited for as a child. I went to bed in great excitement and in the morning I woke up and the gifts were there, but no one had seen the Befana. True miracles are the ones whose makers will never be known; they are the very small miracles of the secret spirits of the home or the great miracles that leave us truly astonished. I still have this childish wish for marvels, large or small, I still believe in them.

Therefore, dear Sandra, I will say to you clearly: if *Troubling Love* does not have, in itself, thread enough to weave, well, it means that you and I were mistaken; if, on the other hand, it does, the thread will be woven where it can be, and we will have only to thank the readers for their patience in taking it by the end and pulling.

Besides, isn't it true that promotion is expensive? I will be the publishing house's least expensive author. I'll spare you even my presence.

Warmly,

Elena

NOTE

Letter dated September 21, 1991

The Befana is an ugly old woman who brings gifts to good children—somewhat in the manner of Santa Claus—on the eve of Epiphany, January 6.

2.
MOTHERS' DRESSMAKERS

Dear Sandra,
     This business of the prize is very upsetting to me. I must say that what has most perturbed me isn't that my book is being given a prize but that the prize has the name of Elsa Morante. In order to write a few lines of thanks that would be essentially an homage to a writer I love, I began to look through her books for suitable passages. I discovered that anxiety plays dirty tricks. I leafed through book after book, and I couldn't track down even a word that would do for my situation, when in fact I clearly remembered many. How and when words escape from books and the books end up seeming like empty graves is something to think about.

     What veiled my mind in these circumstances? I was searching for an unequivocally female passage on the mother figure, but the male narrative voices invented by Morante clouded my view. I knew that maternal passages existed, yet to find them I would have to regain the impression of my first reading, when I had been able to hear the male voices as disguised versions of female voices and feelings. But to achieve something like that the worst thing you can do is read with the urgent need to find a passage to quote. Books are complex organisms, and the lines that affected us deeply are the most intense moments of an earthquake that the text provokes in us as readers from the first pages: either one tracks down the fault, and becomes the fault, or the words that seemed written just for us can't be found, and, if they are, they seem banal, even a cliché.

In the end I resorted to the quotation you know; I wanted to use it as an epigraph for *Troubling Love,* but it's hard to use because when I read it today it seems obvious, merely a humorous passage on how the southern male dematerializes the body of the mother. Therefore, in case you consider it necessary to quote that passage to make the reading of my thank-you text more comprehensible, I transcribe here the entire page. Morante summarizes freely what her character, Giuditta, will say to her son, commenting on the Sicilian attitude the boy has adopted to mark the end of his mother's theater career, after she has been humiliated, and her return to a less disturbing figure.

Giuditta seized his hand and covered it with kisses. At that moment (she said to him later), he had assumed the expression of a Sicilian: of those severe Sicilians, men of honor, always watchful of their sisters, making sure they didn't go out alone at night, didn't attract suitors, didn't wear lipstick! And for whom "mother" means two things: old and holy. The proper color for a mother's clothes is black, or, at most, gray or brown. The clothes are shapeless, since no one, starting with the mother's dressmaker, must think that a mother has a woman's body. Her age is a mystery with no importance, because her only age is old age. That shapeless old age has holy eyes that weep not for herself but for her children; it has holy lips, that recite prayers not for herself but for her children. And woe to those who utter in vain, in front of those children, the holy name of their mother! Woe! It's a mortal offense!

This passage, I would insist, should be read without emphasis, in a normal voice, with no attempt at the declamatory tones of a bad actor. Whoever reads should emphasize only, and slightly, *shapeless, mothers' dressmakers, woman's body, mystery with no importance.*

And here at last is my letter for the prize jury. I hope it's clear that Morante's words are not at all a cliché.

I apologize again for the trouble I cause you.

Dear President, Dear Jurors,

I deeply love the works of Elsa Morante, and I have many of her words in my mind. Before writing to you, I tried to find some to hold on to and extract their meaning. I found almost none where I remembered them. Many were concealed. Others I recognized as I paged through the books, even though I wasn't looking for them, and they fascinated me more than the ones I was looking for. Words make unpredictable journeys in the reader's mind. Among other things, I was looking for words about the mother figure, which is central in Morante's work, and I searched in *House of Liars*, in *Arturo's Island*, in *History*, in *Aracoeli*. I finally found some in *The Andalusian Shawl*, the ones that after all, perhaps, I was seeking.

You certainly know them better than I do and it's pointless for me to repeat them here. They describe the way sons imagine their mothers: in a state of perennial old age, with holy eyes, with holy lips, dressed in black or gray or at most brown. At first the author speaks of particular sons: "those severe Sicilians, honorable, always watchful of their sisters." But, within a few sentences, she has set aside Sicily and moves instead—it seems to me—to a less local maternal image. This happens with the appearance of the adjective "shapeless." The mother's clothes are shapeless and her only age, old age, is also "shapeless," "since," Elsa Morante writes, "no one, starting with the mother's dressmaker, must think that a mother has a woman's body."

That "no one must think" seems very significant. It means that shapelessness is so powerful, in conditioning the word "mother," that sons and daughters, when they think of the body to which the word should refer, cannot give it its proper shapes without revulsion. Not even the mother's dressmaker, who is also a woman, daughter, mother, can do so. She, in fact, out of habit, heedlessly, cuts out clothes for the mother that eliminate the woman, as if the latter were a leprosy of the former. They do this, and so the mother's age becomes a mystery with no importance, and old age becomes her only age.

I thought of these "mothers' dressmakers" in a conscious way only now, as I write. But they have a great attraction for me, in particular if I associate them with an expression that has intrigued me since I was a child. The expression is: "cut out the clothes on"—that is, "cut down," or "gossip." I imagined that it hid a spiteful meaning: a malicious aggression, a violence that ruins the clothes and indecently exposes the wearer; or, even worse, a magic art capable of molding a body to the point of obscenity. Today the expression seems to me neither spiteful nor indecent. Rather, the connection between cut, clothe, speak excites me. And it seems to me fascinating that that connection gave rise to a metaphor of gossip. If the mother's dressmaker learned to cut out her clothes and expose her, or if she cut the clothes in such a way as to recover the woman's body that the mother has, that she had, in clothing her the dressmaker would undress her, and her body, her age, would no longer be a mystery with no importance.

Perhaps when Elsa Morante spoke of mothers and their dressmakers she was also speaking about the need to find the mother's true clothes and tear up the habits that weigh on the word "mother." Or maybe not. In any case I remember other images (the reference to a "maternal shroud," for example, described as the "weave of fresh love on the leper's body") within which it would be nice to lose oneself in order to rise again as a new dressmaker ready to fight the error of the Shapeless.

NOTE

Troubling Love was awarded a prize for a first novel by the 1992 Procida Prize, Arturo's Island—Elsa Morante. The author did not attend the ceremony but instead sent the publishers this letter to the jurors, which was read during the ceremony. The text was published in *Cahiers Elsa Morante*, edited by Jeal-Noël Schifano and Tjuna Notarbartolo, Edizioni Scientifiche Italiane 1993, and it is reprinted here with slight modifications. The passage cited is from the story collection *Lo Scialle Andaluso* (*The Andalusian Shawl*).

3.
WRITING ON COMMAND

Dear Sandra,
What a terrible thing you've done: when I happily agreed to write something for the anniversary of your publishing venture, I discovered that the slope of writing to order is a slippery one, and that the descent is in fact pleasurable. What is next?

Now that you've made me pull out the plug, will all the water flow out through the drain? At this moment I feel ready to write about anything.

Will you ask me to celebrate the new car you've just bought? I'll fish out from somewhere a memory of my first ride in a car and, line by line, end up congratulating you on yours. Will you ask me to compliment your cat on the kittens she's given birth to? I will resurrect the cat that my father first gave me and then, exasperated by its meowing, took away, abandoning her on the road to Secondigliano. You'll ask me to contribute an essay to a book you're doing on the Naples of today? I'll start from a time when I was afraid to go out for fear of meeting a busybody neighbor whom my mother had thrown out of the house, and, word by word, bring out the fear of violence that reaches us on the rebound today, while the old politics touches up its makeup and we don't know where to find the new that we ought to support. Should I make an offering to the feminine need to learn to love one's mother? I will recount how my mother held my hand on the street when I was little: I'll start from there—actually, thinking about it, I'd really like to do this. I preserve a distant sensation of skin against skin, as she held tight to my hand, out of anxiety that I would slip away and run along the uneven, dangerous street: I felt her fear and was afraid. And then I'll find a way to develop my theme to the point where I can cite Luce Irigaray[1] and Luisa Muraro.[2] Words draw out words: one can always write a banal, elegant, heartfelt, amusing coherent page on any subject, low or high, simple or complex, frivolous or fundamental.

What to do, then, say no to people whom we love and trust? It's not my way. So I've written some commemorative lines, trying to communicate a true feeling of admiration for the noble battle that you've been fighting all these years, and that today, I think, is even more difficult to win.

Here, then, is my message: good wishes. For the time being, I'll settle for beginning with a caper bush. Beyond that, I don't know. I could inundate you with recollections, thoughts, universalizing sketches. What does it take? I feel capable of writing to order on the youth of today, the abominations of TV, Di Giacomo,[3] Francesco Iovine,[4] the art of the yawn, an ashtray. Chekhov, the great Chekhov, talking to a journalist who wanted to know how his stories originated, picked up the first object he happened on—an ashtray, in fact—and said to him: You see this? Come by tomorrow and I'll give you a story entitled "The Ashtray." A wonderful anecdote.

But how and when does the opportunity to write become necessity? I don't know. I know only that writing has a depressing side, when the sinews of the occasion are visible.

---

[1] Luce Irigaray (1932, Belgium) is a Belgian feminist, philosopher, linguist, psychoanalyst, sociologist, and cultural theorist.
[2] Luisa Muraro (1940, Italy) is an Italian feminist, philosopher, and historian.
[3] Salvatore Di Giacomo (1860-1934) was a Neapolitan poet, songwriter, and playwright.
[4] Francesco Jovine (1902-1950) was an Italian novelist, journalist, and essayist.

Then even the truth can seem artificial. So, to avoid any mis-understandings, I will add in the margin, without capers or anything else of the sort, without literature, that my congratulations are true and heartfelt.

Until next time,
Elena

In one of the many houses where I lived as a child, a caper bush grew, in all seasons, on the wall facing east. It was a rough, bare stone wall, riddled with chinks, and every seed could find a bit of earth. But that caper bush, especially, grew and flourished so proudly, and yet with colors so delicate, that it has remained in my mind as an image of just force, of gentle energy. The farmer who rented us the house cut down the plants every year, but in vain. When he decided to fix up the wall, he spread a uniform coat of plaster over it and then painted it an unbearable blue. I waited a long time, trustfully, for the roots of the caper to win out and suddenly fracture the flat calm of that wall.

Today, as I search for a way to congratulate my publisher, I feel that it has happened. The plaster cracked, the caper exploded anew with its first shoots. So I hope that Edizioni E/O continues to struggle against the plaster, against all that creates harmony by elimination.

May it do so by stubbornly opening up, season upon season, books like the flowers of the caper.

NOTE
Letter to Sandra Ozzola on the occasion of Edizioni E/O's fifteenth anniversary, in September, 1994.

4.
THE ADAPTED BOOK

D ear Sandro,
    Of course I'm curious, I can't wait to read Martone's screenplay, please send it to me right away, as soon as you get it. I'm afraid, however, that reading it won't satisfy my curiosity, which to me means understanding what in my book nourished and is nourishing Martone's film project, what nerve of his the text touched, how it set off his imagination. Further, in thinking about it, I foresee that I will find myself in a situation that is partly funny, partly embarrassing: I will become the reader of someone else's text that is telling me a story written by me; I will imagine on the basis of his words what I've already imagined, *seen*, put down in my own words, and this second image will, like it or not, have to reckon—humorously? tragically?—with the first; I will, in other words, be the reader of a reader of mine who will describe in his way, with his means, with his intelligence and sensibility, what he read in my book. How I might take it I can't say. I'm afraid of discovering that I know little about my own book. I'm afraid of seeing in someone else's writing (a screenplay is specialist writing, I imagine, but still writing to tell a story) what I *really* wrote and of being disgusted with myself; or of discovering instead its weakness; or even just realizing what it lacks, what I should have told and—through lack of ability, fear, self-limiting literary choices, superficiality of view—did not tell.

But enough, I don't want to drag this out. I have to admit that the taste for a new experience prevails over small anxieties and worries. I think I'll proceed like this: I'll read Martone's screenplay disregarding the fact that it's a way of arriving at his film; I'll read it as an occasion for going deeper, through the work, the invention of someone else, not into my book, which now is on its own, but into the material that I touched on in writing it. Tell him in fact, if you see or talk to him, that he shouldn't expect a contribution that is technically useful.

Thank you for the trouble you've taken.

Elena

NOTE
The letter is from April, 1994, and refers to the screenplay adapted by Mario Martone from *Troubling Love*. The director sent the text to Ferrante with a letter.

5.

THE REINVENTION OF *TROUBLING LOVE*
Correspondence with Mario Martone

Campagnano, April 18, 1994

Dear Signora Ferrante,
What I've sent you is the third draft of the screenplay I'm working on. As you can imagine, there will be others, which will gradually incorporate new ideas, changes having to do with the development of characters or the choice of settings, and other adjustments. A screenplay in fact is a little like a map: the more precise it is, the freer the journey that begins with shooting the film. Until that moment, you never stop working on it.

I tried to understand and respect the book, and at the same time filter it through my experiences, my memories, my perception of Naples. I'm trying to give life to a Delia who may be different from the one you know: it has to be done, precisely because in the novel you decided to conceal her image. You reveal her thoughts, throw the reader some definite hooks, but you never describe her to us through the evidence given by the other characters. That extraordinary process of writing, which creates the mystery of the relationship between Delia and Amalia, for me inevitably has to dissolve, in order to then, I hope, be re-created cinematographically: from the start of the film, in fact, we have to see Delia. I'm trying to give Delia a personality that is at the intersection of the character of your novel and the actress who will play her, Anna Bonaiuto, following a process I'm very attached to (if by chance you've seen the film *Death of a Neapolitan Mathematician*, think of the character of Renato Caccioppoli and the actor Carlo Cecchi). It's a way of trying to adhere to the story with cinematic concreteness: you mustn't forget that the camera will be shooting that face, that body, that look.

The flashbacks, like the intrusions of the offscreen voice, are perhaps too numerous, but consider that the material can be very freely edited later, and it seems to me better to keep for now. I've changed some settings, in particular you'll see that I changed the hotel room to a spa. These changes, and there will likely be others, are due mainly to the fact that I'm going to try to find real places that are close to the spirit of the novel and not re-create the settings scenically; and in the second place because sometimes (as with the hotel room) seeing on the screen is inevitably different from seeing with the imagination. For that same reason I prefer, for example, that Uncle Filippo have both his arms: otherwise, I'm afraid that the spectator sits there wondering where the trick is.

As for the period when the film takes place and the electoral climate that I've sketched in the background, I would like to know what you think: I don't want it to seem gratuitous. I'm sending a photocopy of an article that appeared in *Il Manifesto* that I think captures well the relationship between the femininity of Alessandra Mussolini and Fascism as an "anthropological" fact in Naples: a relationship, it seems to me, not completely irrelevant to the story of *Troubling Love*.

I ask you, therefore, not to hesitate, if you'd like, to give me directions and suggestions, even in detail: they will be incredibly valuable for me. I truly hope that the screenplay doesn't disappoint you: as I start work on the film, I would like to be able to count on your faith in it.

With affection and gratitude,
Mario Martone

Dear Martone,

Your screenplay has excited me so much that, although I've tried several times to write to you, I haven't managed to get beyond the first lines stating my esteem and admiration for your work. I'm sincerely afraid that I don't know how to contribute to your project. I've decided therefore to do the following: I will indicate below, pedantically and with some embarrassment, a few marginal points, at times completely irrelevant, where one might intervene, as I noted them while I was reading, without too much insistence. Many of the notes will seem to you unjustified, dictated more by the way the event and the characters remain in my mind than by the way they are now in the writing. Furthermore, maybe they don't take into account sufficiently your effort to reinvent the character of Delia in a cinematographic mode. I apologize in advance.

p. 10 The reference to Augusto: Delia is a person who is constricted in every muscle, in every word; kind and cold, affectionate and distant. Her relationships with men are not experiences but experiments intended to test a choked-off body: failed experiments. She can't, I think, enjoy solitude. Solitude isn't a break for her, a vacation in a busy life: it's an entrenched defense transformed into a way of life. Every gesture or word of hers is a knot. It will be these events which loosen her. I don't think it's useful to refer to her having a normal life, made up of common phrases and feelings. If there were an Augusto, Delia wouldn't talk about him. In other words I would eliminate that name and the reference to solitude, as well as the "Let's tell each other a few things."

p. 14 Maria Rosaria's remark seems excessive. I would replace it with one that gives an immediate, precise indication of the father's jealousy. I will take advantage of this to tell you that it should perhaps be made clearer that the father has *always* been jealous. In fact, it's starting from that paternal jealousy that Delia has constructed an image of the *unreliable mother*. She was convinced, as a child, that Amalia brought her into the world only to project her outside herself, to separate from Delia and give herself wantonly to others. That specter of Amalia—not the real Amalia—is the intersection between the father's obsessions and the sense of abandonment experienced by Delia as a child (reference to the storeroom, in the first pages).

pp. 16-17 Maria Rosaria's second line and the line of Wanda's that follows don't seem justified. They say things that all three sisters already know. They're formulated as rhetorical questions, useful perhaps to the audience but not to the characters. Furthermore, doesn't Maria Rosaria's tone contradict what she's saying about her husband and her? If the theme is the flight from Naples and from their family situation, maybe it would be suitable for the three sisters to confront it with statements that reveal to each something about the others.

p. 18 The body of the old sewing machines and the child's exploration of them could lead to the mother's work at home to the theme of clothes (putting on the clothes that she imagines to be her mother's and that will turn out to have been chosen for her) to the injured finger. They are the signs (machine, needle, plaster, thimble, pincushion, and gloves and fabrics and clothes) that indicate how Amalia hid or empowered her disobedient body, deserving punishment. But I would also like to emphasize that Amalia's work recalls the struggle, in certain milieus, in the forties and fifties, to move from pure survival to a more comfortable way of life (Caserta's blue suit and camel-hair overcoat were, in the eyes of the child Delia, the proof of the mother's *other life*, a secret life). At the root of what happens in *Troubling Love* is the great waste of energy in moving from a state of working-class precariousness to possessing the symbols of some para-bourgeois comfort. We have to imagine that Nicola Polledro's activities have supported his father's pastry shop on the outskirts; that Nicola Polledro had an economically successful phase by exploiting "the art" of Delia's father; that he then slid into small illegal enterprises, to the point where as an old man he scrapes by on the edges of his son's illegal Camorrist activities. We have to imagine that Delia's father originally had a crude talent—perhaps the painting of the Vossi sisters really is his—deflected first by the need to get by and then by the need not to keep up with Caserta (the prosperity that Caserta flaunts has made him envious, mean). We have to imagine that the effort directed toward a change of status has released in him tensions and violence fused with jealousy, sexual terror, revenge for his wasted talent, for the exploitation suffered. That scheming seems to Delia herself a thing that men do. But the moments when she realizes for the first time that her mother's work produced money for the family are important; that her mother's body was the *nude* model on which the image of the Gypsy is based; that the break between Caserta and her father (and Amalia's being mixed up in it) happened around the economic use of the image of that body.

p. 19 Why is the voice-over that prepares for the episode of the elevator placed here? Wouldn't it be better to see Amalia, on the landing, calling Delia, and then return to the episode?

p. 33 Delia's first remark seems to me unjustified. Further, in my mind the father's violent jealousy has always been there. At this point, simply, his reasons for jealousy become more complex and his fury increases.

p. 34 The figure of Nicola Polledro's father—Antonio's

grandfather—doesn't seem very vivid to me (but perhaps I'm wrong). Yet it should be clearly defined, because of the role he plays. Caserta doesn't sell the bar but pushes his pastry-maker father to sell it. The old man should be imagined as having been "put up to it" by Nicola, who meanwhile *acts the gentleman.*

p. 38 The theme of the painting could be enhanced, beyond my book: it's the only moment when Delia's father can effectively waver between boasting and talent betrayed.

p. 53 The change of setting (the baths in place of the hotel) I don't mind. I'm only afraid, as I've already said, that one loses an aspect of Delia's character: her body is blocked in a sort of programmatic reversal of the sexually intense figure that she has attributed to her mother. The scene has to communicate the sensation of Delia's body choking between repulsion and desire, and at the same time her suffering, or it risks being an erotic gift to the spectator.

p. 68 I would eliminate that "look, look, look." It doesn't seem to me the right tone for Delia.

p. 69 The theme of the painting—I would insist—perhaps needs one more touch. The aspect of the search for economic, social, and cultural emancipation through the mythicizing of art could be a "positive" trait of the father, who has a socially disadvantaged talent, not cultivated but ambitious. But I don't think it's a question of adding: maybe it's only something to be visualized, when you work with the actor who plays that character.

p. 74 Delia's line is difficult. It should be thought of not as a discovery (it's a discovery for the audience, not for her) but as the effort of expressing a truth that is known yet only in that moment is about to become words.

Finally: I don't dislike the electoral updating, provided it remains "landscape," distant sound, not indispensable detail.

I hope you will be lenient with me. I know almost nothing about how to read a screenplay, and probably I've noted with some rudeness things that were already clear to you, that were already present in your mind, or that have little to do with a story in images. In that case throw it all away and keep only my admiration for your research, for your work. What is important to me (and flatters me) about my book is that it has served to inspire imagination and creativity, which fully belong to you.

With respect,

Elena Ferrante

Dear Martone,

This last draft is more convincing to me than the preceding, but it's hard to explain clearly why. All I know is that I read your text with an intensity and an engagement that my own for now denies me. The more you reinvent *Troubling Love*, the more I find it again, I see it, I feel what it carries with it. It's a sensation I ought to reflect on. For now, I'm pleased with the result, both for you and for me.

I have almost no objections to placing Delia in Bologna. Rome has no role in the story: at most it conferred on Delia a more anonymous place, as a single woman, with a small talent that enables her to earn a living, a woman hard enough on herself and others to protect her precarious equilibrium; but fragile, anxious, in some ways childish when her mother's visits impose on her a regression to her native city. Bologna, on the other hand, as far as I know, suggests a bit more of the "artistic" and the "alternative" that, at least in my intentions, isn't in the character. But if you think that that city will be more useful for the construction of the working profile of the character and for its verisimilitude, that's fine.

I'm more excited about your decision to put Amalia's apartment in one of the palazzos of the Galleria. I know those buildings. It seems to me a good choice, and even more promising because of your sensitivity to the story and to the anthropological changes in that space. I had imagined a narrow street in a less expensive area. But I very much liked the image of Delia looking out into the Galleria and hit by the echo of voices in dialect.

Also, the changes you've brought to the night scene in the building—I suppose suggested by the choice of place—are convincing, although I was attached to Delia's moving from the high toward the low. (Her adolescent refuge is *high up*, something that in my mind—perhaps a bit mechanically—was opposed to the *low* of the childhood cellar. Delia has drawn her mother to that refuge, there Caserta should ascend; but both encounters fail and Delia is forced to go *downward*, a slide that is faintly present in the whole plan of the story, and which you—it seems to me—have summarized well by accentuating the passage from the center to the periphery. But these are subtleties: the scene as it is now seems very tense, sharp, effective.)

The meeting with the mother in the elevator remains a problem, in my opinion. It's an important moment, in which the mother-daughter relationship plunges openly into jealousy for the first time and into an embarrassing physicality (an embarrassment represented, in the book, by a gesture: Delia pulls her hand away, places it on her heart, then opens the door and asks her mother to leave). I think that this is one of the cases in which the narrator's voice, anticipating Delia's jealous question, diminishes the scene and confuses the issue, rather than clarifying it. I don't know how to keep the audience from seeing it as a vision rather than as a memory: but you've resolved a lot of problems, you'll resolve this one, too.

Speaking of the voice-over, I'm convinced, reading this last draft and admiring the result, that the first-person story must have been an irksome cage for you (the first person, once it's there, can't resign itself to becoming the third). Yet you've come out of it very creatively, now enhancing the child Delia's gaze, now inventing the device of the glasses. However— besides the difficulties having to do with the elevator scene— I'd like to encourage you to make a last effort to eliminate completely, or almost completely, the voice of the narrator.

In my book, it's the voice of a Delia who is already outside the story; it belongs not to the woman who is living her days in Naples but to the woman who has emerged from those days changed and *now*, again far from Naples, can describe the change, internal and external, that she has undergone. You, on the other hand, from the moment you could (as you did) construct a Delia whom it's possible to see "inside" and "outside" just as the action is happening (the finale, which is very beautiful, is the best proof of your fine result), no longer have a need for a retrospective summary. Thus the fragments of voice-over that remain in your text now seem superfluous and in a certain sense contradictory to their origin. Originating as bits from a voice that is telling a story after it's over, they can't function as "current thoughts" of a third person who doesn't yet know what will happen to her—the person whom we see acting on the screen and who already has, among other things, an inner world effectively visualized in parallel.

Yes, if possible abolish what remains of the voice-over: it shouldn't be difficult for you, at this point. Perhaps, if you don't find anything better, you could keep only the beginning, without the adjustments there are now but, rather, displaying the literary articulation.

Now I would like to move on to some notes on the reading. Out of necessity you have fully occupied the verbal space left empty by my story: the dialect. You have done it with such naturalness that—I think—it's one of the elements that contribute to the emotion with which I read your work. I imagine that the background noises, the unwritten lines, will also contribute to the creation of that dialectal tide that Delia feels as a threatening sign, a recall to the language of the obsessions and violence of childhood (in this sense I very much like that in scene 17 you avoid ascribing directly to Caserta the burst of obscenity, but have it flow out of the sounds of the city; similarly, I appreciated the insistence on the roar of voices in the lunch scene).

I am not very convinced, on the other hand, by Delia reporting to Giovanna (scene 6) *the phrase* that is partly (not alone) at the origin of her verbal block. I'll tell you why: it seems to me wrong that Delia should resort to dialect in the first scenes of the film, in a setting distant from Naples in every way, when, instead, her cadence and her definitely dialect phrases should emerge either as an instinctive reaction (*"strunz"*—shit—she'll cry later to the troublesome young man) or as a step in her approach to Amalia; but above all it seems wrong that we hear that sentence—from her mouth—immediately. It has a story that we have to traverse backward: we'll start with Amalia; we'll hear a mysterious hint on the part of Uncle Filippo; we'll place it clearly in the mouth of the child Delia; we'll learn that she heard it from old Polledro; and only at the end will we understand how she readjusted it, and hear it pronounced in a liberating way by the adult Delia.

In other words it doesn't persuade me that the phrase is repeated, at the start of the film, by Delia (she wouldn't do it, among other things; she would skip it; or she would use a

generic formula, in embarrassment, unable to tolerate the irritation at the mother's obscenity). I tend to believe that the phrase
should appear clearly in the mouth of Amalia, which is unbearable for Delia. It will be the rest of the story that makes us think
those words were uttered by Amalia, maybe in a state of anxiety
and mental instability, as a signal of danger (with me is Caserta;
your father still wants to hurt me, etc.) or as the outburst of a
tipsy old woman or as a disoriented act of reconciliation.

In short, those words, in my opinion, should be heard by
the audience, clearly, at the end of scene 5, among other muf-
fled obscenities uttered by Amalia on the telephone, and
immediately afterward collide with Delia's bewildered expression: the first time her expression indicates to us inner richness
and knowledge derived from suffering. "Mamma, who are you
with?" could be uttered by Delia after that phrase of Amalia's,
as a kind of jolt of memory.

As for the phrase itself, I would like to cautiously observe (I
don't have clear ideas about it) that either it is really, intolerably obscene (and it isn't) or it suggests the obscene through a
total indeterminacy. Your phrase is of the second type; therefore I would favor the elimination of that "under," which, precisely because it specifies, might lead the audience to think that
it specifies too little.

Finally, still on this point, as I was reading I had the impression that at the conclusion of scene 44, when Polledro gets up
and leaves, we could already see the father and hear the voice
of the child Delia who reports old Polledro's phrase as if
Caserta had addressed it to Amalia. Then one could move to
Delia, who says: "And then if I'm sick..."; then start with 12.
This to clarify the story, because I've noted the need to know
directly what use the child Delia has made of the old man
Caserta's words. But maybe I'm wrong. I'm writing in a hurry,
without the time necessary to refine senseless suggestions.

There is another theme that has puzzled me somewhat: the economic exploitation of Delia's father's work.

To characterize the trafficking among the three men, I would aim, yes, at a Caserta who, as it says in the book, does business with "the Americans," but I would give more details. From the way you've constructed the beginning of the scene of the slap (another good solution), we know little about what those three men really did: the exultant cry of Uncle Filippo doesn't tell us much. If you develop, instead, the few lines in the book in which there is a mention of "portraits for the Americans" Uncle Filippo could—let's say—arrive, in scene 4, with some photos and say something like: "Now make four more American portraits. Caserta says he wants them right away. I've brought the photographs" (forgive this ridiculous pseudo dialect sketch). And we could see in detail the photos brought by Uncle Filippo (there are some descriptive hints in the book), a last one attached to the edge of the easel and in a corner the portrait that has just been made from it, other portraits ready, mixed with seascapes and country scenes. Delia then could say, on page 31: "He's the one who did business with American sailors in the Galleria, he got them to take out family photographs and persuaded them to have oil portraits done of their mother, their fiancée, their wife. He exploited homesickness and allowed us all to eat, including you…" Caserta's scheming, at least in regard to Delia's father, would consist, in that case, in getting in touch with the sailors and transforming them into commissioners of oil portraits made from photos (their photos, of fiancées, of distant mothers, etc.). The other middleman, Migliaro, would intervene later to get Delia's father out of a market that was probably in decline and place him in another, completely different market, expanding along with the petit-bourgeois expansion of the fifties.

I suggest these things because I'm afraid that visually the

weakest point of your text is precisely the definition of the activities of Caserta and Delia's father. If you refer to these not at all unlikely "artistic" dealings with the Americans, you gain a concreteness (the photos, the portraits scattered through the room) that—it seems to me—is at the moment missing from Uncle Filippo's irruption (very effective, besides: it shouldn't be touched), which is completely focused on the Gypsy.

I have nothing else to suggest, except for some small annotations that I will list here below by page number. But note: I realize that I have already let myself get out of hand. I've discovered that because of certain, scarcely rational idiosyncrasies of mine I've even eliminated that "no?" in Delia's remark on page 5: "Your father is still at the police station, no?" Take out the no. Be merciful, please.

p. 13 The dialogue between the sisters is better, but there are still things that I would change. Especially Delia's "very many": it seems vague and mournful, I would replace it with an approximate number (but there is the scene in which Delia has revealed to her mother her refuge in the elevator, on the top floor. When did it happen? Two years earlier? Three? Can't Delia answer, without contradiction: "Yes. Two or three years"?); or I would leave only the "yes"; or replace it with a "yes, many."

Maria Rosaria's answer also continues to bother me: maybe I feel a danger implicit in all the lines in dialect, the lurking stereotype of the recitation in a Neapolitan cadence, complaining, maudlin, tremulous, overdone, with a display of sentimentality that doesn't communicate sentiments. It's true that there is a type of communication in Neapolitan that has these characteristics (and in the text the echoes are heard here and there in Uncle Filippo and in Signora De Riso); but I wouldn't exaggerate it in the writing with a disparaging imitation of a theatrical or film performance, etc. I would make a Maria Rosaria who tries to contain her emotion with a blunter: "It was mamma who was supposed to get on the train and go to visit you in Bologna," a half reproach: then the weeping, which Wanda joins with a certain irritation.

p. 25 In Signora De Riso's line, at the bottom of the page: wouldn't "this apartment" be better, eliminating "in the Galleria"?

p. 28 It occurred to me that in the old, yellowed photograph, shown after the identity card (which Delia naturally doesn't examine), it would be good if Amalia were also there and we could see her face, her hair. The audience has to match the identity card with a distinct photographic image of Amalia, so that it can be a bigger surprise when Delia, after the quarrel with Polledro, checks the identity card and discovers that the photograph (an old one) has been touched up. But any other invention that would allow us to see Amalia in a photograph *before* we get to the scene with Polledro and the surprise of the identity card would be fine.

p. 32 I feel something unnatural in this important line but I don't know what. Maybe it's that "half naked" that seems redundant, especially if otherwise the actress's tone—and expression—are the right ones. It occurred to me, further, that this might be one of the points where Delia lets a little dialect escape, calmly, without overemphasis, as if suddenly she heard the voices of that time. Something like: "He did good. He didn't want hundreds of copies of that Gypsy to end up in country fairs…" But I don't want to overdo it: am I stupidly interfering in your work too much?

p. 54 I wanted to tell you that the erasure of a too powerful mother by breathing on the glass is very beautiful; even more beautiful is the way the mother and Caserta return, having aged, as the glass clears, amid the crowd in the Camorrist-electoral dining room.

p. 56 I would take the "Delia" out of Polledro's line at the bottom of the page. He addresses her and that's all: he is thinking of his own troubles, he doesn't want to establish a real contact with that particular person who is called Delia; it's why she is ironic in the following line.

p. 57 Polledro's line doesn't seem clear to me. Maybe it's better: "You came to the shop. It wasn't that I went looking for you."

p. 65 Shouldn't Delia dial a telephone number at the end of 48? Isn't there confusion in ending on a ring, opening on a ring?

p. 69 I'd like the father to be more yielding and say at the bottom of the page: "…What did she think: she loved me, she never loved me. She was a liar," etc.

For this character I would like—beyond my book and as if to counterbalance a scene that I feel as terrible—a good moment before. For example, at the end of 4, the child could wind up with her father, who has now gone back to the easel, and the Gypsy, or while he's already sketching one of the new commissioned portraits. The man would take her on his knees, perhaps distractedly, and she wouldn't willingly accept that contact and he would ask her: "What happened to you? Who made you cry?" and she would wriggle free, sullen: "No one," and he would go back to painting. But I don't know if you can do that, since there's already the really fine scene with the assistants.

p. 71 Isn't the father's second line, "What was she doing," too little? Wouldn't it be better "What was she doing with Caserta?" And then Delia's line, too, should perhaps be harsher: "Yes, it was a lie, but what did you start making a child believe? For you she was a whore if she just said hello to another man! You didn't think twice about believing me. Not twice! You believed me the way I believed you when I saw that she was going there and I thought: If she goes, it means she really is a whore." Or something like that. Anyway it's here that Delia could slip again into dialect.

p. 72 The father's third line: better to be specific. "I had done it already when I was twenty-five. I sold it…" etc.

p. 75 I don't like the line "Look." From "Where are you" we perceive that Delia believes she's being observed.

p. 76 Delia's third line: I would eliminate "disgusting"; it's a redundant comment, what we are seeing is already repulsive. Furthermore, I would add: "I told my father…" or (in my view preferable) the "Come here etc." could be uttered by Caserta as an old man, and the adult Delia, after repeating it to herself, could finally admit: "I told my father that Caserta had said and done to Amalia what instead that old man had said and done to me."

I'm finished, I hope I have done diligently what you asked of me. I foresee that these notes of mine will reach you when you have already started shooting and will be of no use. Ah well. It gave me pleasure just the same to focus on your text and imagine what might help it: at certain moments it was like being able to put my hand again to mine. I've been happy about this involvement, which I didn't expect or pretended not to expect, because I was afraid of it. I ask you not to take account of my poorly controlled narcissism, drools of pride, immodest intrusions.

With friendship, with gratitude,
Elena Ferrante

Rome, January 29, 1995

Dear Elena,

The film is now ready. Some phases of the editing (sound editing and mixing, photographic correction of the final print) are still to come, but the working copy that we are now able to project contains essentially everything. *Troubling Love* will be in the theaters in April.

The last time I wrote to you was August, and we were a month away from starting to shoot: the following months were so intense that it's hard for me to try to describe now, in a letter, the whole combination of emotions and reflections during this exciting and exhausting period. I can only try to tell you how grateful I am to you for having given me the chance to make this film, which I absolutely and completely love independently of whatever success it may have. The trust that I would be truly happy not to have betrayed is yours.

Your last letter was very precious to me. I kept it with me during the shooting, and it helped me confront decisively the more obscure areas, besides polishing and perfecting the screenplay. Elena, would you like to come to Rome to see the film? I know your reserve, and I don't mean to violate in any way your wish not to appear. You choose the time and the means, or, if you don't want to, tell me no, I will understand very well. But know that Anna and I, and all my collaborators, loved and respected you, and we always thought we were making the film with you.

With affection, and I hope to have an answer from you soon,
Mario

Dear Mario,

Your invitation has complicated my life. It's pointless to tell you how much I wish to see the results of your work, it's very important to me in a particular way. But in this period every day is a risk for me. I'm working intensely on a new book—it's hard to call it a novel: I don't know exactly what it is—and every morning I start writing with the anxiety of being unable to go forward. I know from experience (a very bad experience) that any accident can weaken the impression of necessity in the pages I'm writing; and when that impression fades, it's the work of months that vanishes, all I can do is to wait for another opportunity.

Seeing your film is, obviously, anything but an accident. Although I've tried, in these months, to think of it as an artistic activity independent in substance not so much of *Troubling Love* as of the feeling I preserve of it, I doubt that I would be an indifferent viewer. The idea I've formed of you—of the passion and intelligence with which you threw yourself into this work—keeps me from fooling myself. I can very well foresee the effects of a work that, I imagine, will strike me with an energy far greater than what I needed for the book. I'm sure, in other words, that your film will leave a deep impression, and that for a while I will have to reopen accounts with myself, with what I've done up to now, with what I intend to do in the future. This is why, after much hesitation, I've decided to concentrate on this new work and try to finish it without risking interruptions that could be definitive.

It distressed me to make this decision. The desire to be

knocked over by your film (of whose success I've had no doubts from the moment I read the screenplay) is at least as strong as that of seeking a sturdy shelter. Naturally I will not resist for long and in the end I will not find any adequate protection. But I'm sure that until then you will understand not so much my reserve (I'm hardly reserved) but my fears.

With great affection,

Elena Ferrante

NOTE

The Martone-Ferrante correspondence on *Troubling Love* was published in the magazine *Linea d'ombra*, double issue 106, July/August 1995.

6.
MEDIA HIERARCHIES

D ear Erbani,
Your letter impressed me with its terse frankness, a quality that only the writing of clear-minded people has. If I were sure of being able to respond with equal transparency to the questions you intend to ask, I would say all right, let's do the interview. But I look for ideas by running after words, and it takes me many sentences—real, confusing, jumbled speeches—to arrive at an answer. This doesn't mean that I wouldn't like to chat with you. Your letter, thanks precisely to the clean exposition that distinguishes it, provoked in me the wish to ask you a question in turn. The question is the following: Why, although you read my book a year ago, although you admire it as you say, did you get the idea of communicating with me only now, after learning that a film is being made from *Troubling Love*?

If we were to have, let's say, not an interview but a friendly conversation, I would discuss with you in particular the reasons for this long delay, starting, for example, from an observation of yours. You write, but less brutally than in my summary: your book says something to me, but your name says nothing. Question: if my book had said nothing to you and my name had said something, would it have taken you less time to ask for an interview?

Don't take it as a bitter remark, it isn't; I'm just exploiting the fact that you've written plainly to bring up plainly a problem that is important to me. I want to ask you this: Is a book, from the media point of view, above all the name of the person who writes it? Is the fame of the author or, rather, the author personality who takes the stage thanks to the media, a crucial support for the book? Isn't it newsworthy, for the cultural pages, that a good book has been published? Is it newsworthy, instead, that a name able to say something to editorial offices is on the cover of some book or other?

I think the good news is always: a book worth reading has come out. I also think that, for real readers, who wrote it isn't important. I think that readers of a good book hope at most that the author of a good book will continue to work conscientiously and make other good books. I think, finally, that even the authors of the classics are only a pile of dead letters alongside the life that flares up in their pages as soon as one begins to read them. That's all. To put it another way: even Tolstoy is an insignificant shadow if he takes a stroll with Anna Karenina.

You will say: What do you want from me, it's the unwritten law of journalism that imposes such procedures; if one is no one I can't give him space; if not even in Naples is there a dog who's ever heard of the author of *Troubling Love*, why in the world should it be necessary to talk about her book, interview her in the pages of a big newspaper? Merely because she has written a decent book?

You're right, you have acted in the only way that is journalistically possible today. You have waited for an event that could justify an article, a headline, on a book that you didn't dislike. A year later, the event arrived: a film is being made from that book, the director has a not unimportant name, it's now possible to ask for an interview with this woman, who doesn't have even a tiny local reputation. Finally, you explained to me clearly, politely, perhaps sadly, that it is the film-event that makes my book a worthy interview subject.

Well, I won't complain. I'm pleased that a film is being made from *Troubling Love*, I hope that this brings the book more readers. But must I also be happy to observe that a book becomes important for the cultural pages only because a film is being made from it? Must I also be happy to be promoted to an interviewed author only thanks to the good name of another author, Martone, who works in theater and cinema, fields more loudly acclaimed by the media? Must I also be happy that it is the film of *Troubling Love* that indicates the existence of the book *Troubling Love*? Don't you think that accepting hierarchies of this type, taking them as natural, encourages the idea that literature, in the lists of cultural products, occupies the lowest position? Don't you think that it would be nice to provide a journalistic initiative that risked everything by saying to the public: read books, see movies, go to the theater, hear music, and construct your own preferences based on the works and not on the editorial pecking order displayed by the dailies, by the Sunday supplements, by TV?

I will stop here and thank you for your kind request.

NOTE
The letter is undated but is probably from 1995. It wasn't sent. It originated as a response to the following letter from Francesco Erbani:

Dear Signora Ferrante,
A year ago your novel fell into my hands. I opened it with curiosity, I read the beginning and found it breathtaking. I was born in Naples in the late fifties and I have a certain familiarity with Neapolitan writers, those of the generation that came right after the war, those active in the sixties, the youngest. But your name said nothing to me. And then that scorching beginning. I read *Troubling Love* in a couple of days, at times eagerly, seduced by the colors that the city seemed to me to emanate. Then I left it there, to float in memory. Some time ago I discovered that a film would be made from your book and I developed the idea of getting in touch with you.

I am a journalist, I work for the cultural pages of the *Repubblica*, and I would be very pleased if I could interview you. I've been told of your reserve, and I'm afraid you'll refuse, but at the same time I nourish a hope that a conversation with you published in a newspaper would be only a small break in a rule that I admire.

If you agree, I could come and see you, but if you prefer I could let you have the questions in writing.

I await your response confidently.

Cordially,

Francesco Erbani

After reading the letter in the first edition of *La Frantumaglia*, Erbani wrote to the author:

. . . The arguments that you raise are real . . . : I, too . . . suffer greatly from certain requirements imposed by show business and from the reduction of literary work to goods. And you are right when you maintain that often in the newspapers books are not discussed for their value and that authors are neglected because "they are no one." But the point is another: I didn't write to you when I had read the book, I believe in the summer of 1993, and did not ask you for an interview, for the very simple reason that at the time I worked not at *la Repubblica* but in a press agency, where I was employed in the foreign news department. I spoke of it two years later, as soon as I could, taking Martone's film as the occasion.

7.
YES, NO, I DON'T KNOW
Hypothetical laconic interview

Dear Sandra,

I'm sorry to say that I can't answer the questions from Annamaria Guadagni. It's a limitation not of the questions, which in fact are good and profound, but of mine. Let's resign ourselves and from now on avoid promising interviews that I won't give. Maybe in time I'll learn, but I take it for granted that in time no one will have the desire to interview me, and so the problem will be resolved at its root.

The fact remains that every question makes me want to gather ideas, rummage in favorite books, use old notes, annotate, digress, relate, confess, argue. All things that I like doing and that in fact I do: they are the best part of my days. But in the end I realize that I put together material not for an interview, not for an article (as Guadagni also, politely, proposes) but for a story-essay, and naturally I lose heart. What does a newspaper do with at least ten dense pages for every question of the interview?

So, since I'm stubborn, I put everything aside and try to find a few brilliant sentences that clearly express the meaning of the pages I've accumulated in the meantime. Soon, however, the sentences seem to me not at all brilliant but at times fatuous, at times pretentious, for the most part stupid. As I result I let it go, very depressed.

Maybe interviews should be of this type:

Q. Is it wrong to think that the mother in *Troubling Love* is one with Naples?

A. I don't think so.

Q. Did you flee Naples?

A. Yes.

Q. For you is the imperfect the true dimension of writing?

A. Yes.

Q. Does confusing oneself with one's mother in fact mean losing one's identity as a woman, losing oneself?

A. No.

Q. Is *Troubling Love* the need to possess the mother?

A. Yes.

Q. Is it your distorted gaze that gives us the impression of traveling in a hallucination, amid unreal bodies?

A. I don't know.

Q. Doesn't it seem to you that your book, once on the screen, might generate something between a mystery film and a horror film?

A. Yes.

Q. Did you help Martone with the screenplay of his film?

A. No.

Q. Will you go to see it?

A. Yes.

But what would Annamaria Guadagni make of an interview of this type? And then it is enough for me to reread the yeses, the nos, the I don't knows to start again from the beginning. For example the I don't knows, if you dug deep enough, might reveal that I know a lot or even too much. And some yeses, by force of argument, might become I don't knows. In other words, dear Sandra, let's drop it, and in such a way that Guadagni will forgive me and I apologize, to you and Sandro, for the way I complicate your editorial life.

Until next time,

Elena

NOTE
Letter of March, 1995. Below are the questions from Annamaria Guadagni.

Dear Elena,

I'm very pleased that you've agreed to answer my questions. But, given that we will speak only in writing, we could also work in another way: for example, you could write an article that follows the course of my questions. See what you think, I leave the choice up to you. I would ask you also to let me have some information on your life and current profession. Naturally, what you consider suitable: all that is known of you is that you live in Greece. In fact, maybe I would start there, at a distance, to ask my questions.

1. In my imagination the mother who kills herself in *Troubling Love* is confused with the city. A livid, vulgar, and vital Naples, hated and loved. Is it a mistaken impression? And did you escape from Naples?

2. Childhood is a tissue of lies that endure in the imperfect. The imperfect is the tense of stories and fables. How long does it last? Forever? Is it the dimension where one can be Amalia but also her husband, Caserta but also his son Antonio? In short, for you is it the dimension of writing?

3. Femininity is defined around the mother-daughter relationship. But the battle of identity is to find oneself, detaching oneself from the other, the mother. One of the most disturbing aspects of your book is that it seems to achieve this journey backward: in the beginning there are two women and in the course of the novel they become confused with one another. I think that the daughter therefore loses herself, but do you agree? Is she lost or found?

4. At the end of the novel there is a sort of revelation: the jealousy of Amalia's husband is the jealousy of Delia, who furthermore discovers or recalls that she set it off with a childish act of informing. A confusion in which fantasies about the mother's lover are confused with those of a seduction of the child Delia by Antonio's grandfather. But what is the troubling love, the engine of everything? The need to possess the mother?

5. The bodies in your novel seem unreal. Is it that somewhat distorted gaze that gives us so to speak the sensation of traveling in a hallucination?

6. Imagining this story on the movie screen evokes famous changes of identity. Alfred Hitchcock's *Psycho* or Roman Polanski's *The Tenant*. Something between a mystery and horror. What do you think?

7. Did you help Martone with the screenplay of the film? Will you see it?

I would ask you to send a text that is not longer than four pages as soon as possible. It will appear in *l'Unità* very likely with an interview with Martone on the film. I would like to meet you.

Meanwhile thank you for everything, fondly,
Annamaria Guadagni

8.
CLOTHES, BODIES
Troubling Love on the screen

Dear Mario,
I've seen the film again and again, and it's really beautiful—it seemed to me a very important work. More than that I can't tell you, because my situation as a not disinterested viewer won't let me. So I will try to write to you not about the artistic results that you achieved but about the feelings that your work aroused in me. I doubt, however, that I will be able to finish this letter; my ideas are very confused, and I'm afraid I won't find a thread that satisfies me.

The film, I'll tell you immediately, caused a violent uneasiness in me. You, rightly, in order to realize your work, gave the book a sharp tug that deprived it of its literary clothing. The places, the people, and the acts are shown in their very concrete definition and, to my eyes, in their naked recognizability. Right away, the disquiet that Naples, with its sounds, its words, has always provoked in me reached me directly from the screen. Almost all the characters in my story again became living persons, bodies moving in well-known settings, individuals often miraculously resembling the inhabitants of my memory. I saw clearly for the first time what a disturbing story I had told. I was very upset, I struggled not to withdraw. In the moment I couldn't understand what had really happened to my book, how it could be that I who had written the story could *see it* only now, exposed in all its extreme consequences. Evidently, although I often said it to myself, I hadn't taken into account that if the director is very good, as you are, everything that on the page is disguised or invented to make the story function becomes, on the screen, emotionally irrelevant, one barely sees it, while the living nucleus that animates everything is revealed with an intolerable disruptiveness.

Don't misunderstand me, I haven't changed my mind, I'm pleased with your work and that of your colleagues, pleased and moved. But I'm also upset by it. Deep down I hoped that, of my book, one would see on the screen the way in which an adult woman, Delia, was capable of telling herself how she had used her childhood hostility toward her mother in a murky male game aimed at the use, the control, the violent protection of a woman's body that was too seductive. I counted on the fact that the rest would remain in the background and surface only here and there, outside the actions of the plot, like a luminous signal. I was in other words more or less prepared to see Delia, determined as a detective in a thriller, traveling through a male city ungovernable in both its public and its private behavior. But she didn't do that, or rather she didn't do *only* that. You skillfully directed the woman's investigation of men whose movements can't be ordered, who are guided by the worst aspects of the Neapolitan past—those which are unredeemable. You showed the bodies of Caserta, of the uncle, of Antonio, of the father, and also, I would say, of the candidate, caught in a tangled mass of hatreds and complicity and weaknesses, a network of misery and power and hierarchically institutionalized subjection. And you put in Delia's eyes a mocking, aggressive, sexually disgusted or distracted, at times compassionate gaze. But you didn't stop here. Rather, you almost immediately obscured the mechanics of the plot and distinguished with an astuteness of vision, from the first scenes, the junctions of the mother-daughter relationship. That is what upset me. I don't know how to tell you what a violent emotional shock Delia's gaze upon the nursing mother and the movement of Amalia among children-work-husband gave me: Licia Maglietta is a perfect *young mother*, with a piercing truthfulness. During the entire arc of the film there is not a single moment in which the image of the mother's body—which Delia loves and rejects with an insistent childish passion that is still urgent in the half-sleep of the adult—isn't true, almost unbearably so.

I felt a painful unease as I watched Delia wake up, when the old mother—what a disturbing appearance Angela Luce's is—brings her coffee and talks to her in that affectionately annoying voice and touches her and sits beside her and Delia barely moves, her voice reaches us languidly from sleep, from affection and hostility. But the most effective and most disturbing moments came as I watched the hallucinatory movement of the elevator: the contact between bodies, the attraction-repulsion, the mother with the swollen belly, the whole with those tonalities which seem to capture psychic rather than physical reality. What in the film is for me true and thus difficult to see is there, in that *obsession* of the daughter with her mother. The strongest moments for me are those in which you find great visual solutions for showing Delia's emotions on the screen. I'm referring to what you've done with the scene on the bus, how you transfer it to the hallucination of the tram, to the use you make of that extraordinary actor who plays the uncle. I'm referring to the concreteness of the half-naked women in the Vossi store, the embarrassment-ostentatiousness with which Delia changes her clothes. I'm referring to Bonaiuto in the rain in an anguished Naples, to how her body slides into the cavelike environment of the sauna, up to the scene, beautiful both for its visual qualities and for its symbolic ones, of masturbating in the water (a scene much more dazzling than in my book: the change of place for the sexual encounter between Delia and Antonio is effective, and then also there the image of the actor on the screen is astonishing, it sweeps away invention and sinks into the reality I know).

But the most effective proof of your great achievement, and

the deepest point of what disturbs me, has to do with your staging of the game of clothes. You have made visible the fact that
Caserta's hypothetical fetishism has no value in itself but in reality is the engine that allows Delia to *move* from the *masculine*
clothes in which she arrives in Naples to the *feminine* ones that
in an obscure exchange Amalia intended to bring her as a gift,
and then to the empty dress in the cellar. You've shown that
clothes for Delia are always and only a semblance of the body:
the body of the mother, a body finally unwearable, a dead body,
and yet perhaps precisely for that reason now alive in her forever, impelled to develop autonomously in the future. And in
doing so you have created memorable moments, which for me
contain the truly emotional part of the film: Delia who looks for
the smell of her mother in the only garment she had on when she
drowned, the new bra from the Vossi sisters; Delia who, when
she takes Amalia's clothes out of the garbage bag, wipes her
hands on the material of her pants with a gesture that seemed to
me beautiful; Delia who as she puts on the clothes that were
intended for her gradually discovers that they had already been
worn by her mother before dying; not to mention the red dress
that Delia puts on for the first time in the Vossi sisters' store.

On the screen at that point an extraordinary image explodes,
which, despite the shock it gave my heart, I hope has a long
future. That body in red that, devoured by an obscure and troubling passion, conducts its investigation in a sometimes expressionistic Naples is, I believe, an important moment for the
iconography of the female body today, a summary of the woman
in search of herself, a movement that for Delia goes from the
cold masculinity of covering to the retrieval of the original body
of the mother in the depths of the cellar, to the knowledge that
the bond with Amalia has been accepted, that the historic flow
from mother to daughter has been reconstructed, and that,
meanwhile, the unconfessable has been uttered.

I very much love your finale, with the red disappearing from

Delia's body, to then reappear on the large body of Amalia; the blue-red, red-blue exchange; the movement of expressions of understanding, of satisfaction, of contentment, of acceptance, of grief on Delia's face as she imagines what could have happened to her mother on the beach; the conclusiveness that is also subtly disquieting as Delia—now in clothes that are definitely hers—calls herself, to the boys on the train, by Amalia's name.

It is in this visual explicitness of a more than arduous psychic articulation that your result is for me marvelous and, in its piercing physical recognizability, painful. The finale alone is reason enough to congratulate you again: you have moved me, I'm moved even as I write to you. You've given a visual form and found an intelligent dialogue solution to the two sentences that end my book: "Amalia had been. I was Amalia." The pluperfect had to definitively end the unique, unrepeatable story of Amalia. The imperfect tended instead to reopen her, suggesting a nuance of disturbing incompleteness and yet allowing it to endure in Delia, who now could consciously accept her mother in herself and represent her. And in what direction did you go? You staged a part of Delia's return train journey. From the visual perspective of leaving Naples, you gave a visionary summary of the end of Amalia's life. Then you brought in Delia's identity card, you showed how she skillfully grafts onto her features her mother's old-fashioned hairstyle. Finally you inserted the boy's question about the identity card: "Is it expired?" And you did it in such a way that Delia introduced herself to the youth with the name of Amalia. With this skillful visual transposition of the play of verb tenses you not only increased my admiration for you but rid me of a series of prejudices I had concerning the limits of a filmed story.

NOTE
Letter of May, 1995, incomplete, not sent.

9.

D
ear Fofi,
     I'm sorry to have to tell you that I don't know how to
     give concise answers to the questions you sent me.
Evidently I haven't reflected enough on many of the issues you
raise, and to find comprehensive expression is difficult or even
impossible. So I'll try to sketch some answers just to converse
with you outside the pale of journalistic requirements. I apologize in advance for the confusing or contradictory passages you
may encounter.

I will begin at the end, mainly because your concluding
questions allow me to start from facts. No, I've never been in
analysis, even though in certain phases I've been very curious
about the analytic experience. Nor do I have what you call an
education of a psychoanalytic type, if by that expression you
mean a sort of cultural imprint, a dominant point of view, a spe-
cialization. Also, to assert that I have a feminist mindset seems
to me exaggerated. Owing in particular to limitations of character, which I've struggled to accept, and within which I live
today without too many cravings or too many regrets, I've never
exposed myself publicly, or taken sides: I don't have the physical courage that, in general, is required for these things. So it's
difficult today to give myself a personal story that is not completely private (a reading list, bookish sympathies) and hence
uninteresting. I grew up, in addition, on things seen or heard or
read or scribbled, nothing else. Within this timid frame, like a
mute listener, I can say that I am slightly interested in psycho-

analysis, and fairly interested in feminism, and that I am sympathetic to the ideas of difference feminism. But I've been attracted by many other things that have little to do with psychoanalysis or feminism or with current ideas about women. I am pleased that in *Troubling Love* they do not appear openly.

A discussion of what you call "staying away from the means of mass communication" is more complicated. I think that at its root, apart from the aspects of character I've already mentioned, is a somewhat neurotic desire for intangibility. In my experience, the difficulty-pleasure of writing touches every point of the body. When you've finished the book, it's as if your innermost self had been ransacked, and all you want is to regain distance, return to being whole. I've discovered, by publishing, that there is a certain relief in the fact that the moment the text becomes a printed book it goes elsewhere. Before, it was the text that was pestering me; now I'd have to run after it. I decided not to. I would like to think that, while my book enters the marketplace, nothing can oblige me to make the same journey. But maybe I would also like to believe, at certain moments, if not always, that that "my" which I refer to is in substance a convention, so that those who are disgusted by the story that is told and those who are excited by it cannot, in a mistaken logical step, be disgusted or excited by me as well. Perhaps the old myths about inspiration spoke at least one truth: when one makes a creative work, one is inhabited by others—in some measure becomes another. But when one stops writing one becomes oneself again, the person one usually is, in terms of occupations, thoughts, language. Thus I am now me again, I am here, I go about my ordinary business, I have nothing to do with the book, or, to be exact, I entered it, but I can no longer enter it. Nor, on the other hand, can the book re-enter me. So what's left is to protect myself from its effects, and that is what I try to do. I wrote my book to free myself from it, not to be its prisoner.

There is obviously more. As a girl, I had an idea of literature as all-absorbing. To write was to aim for the maximum, not to be content with intermediate results, to devote oneself to the page without half measures. Over the years, I've fought against this overestimation of literary writing with an obstinate underestimation ("There are many other things that deserve unlimited dedication"), and, having reached an equilibrium—I have a life that I consider satisfying, both on the private and on the public level—I don't wish to go back, I would like to hold on to what I consider a small victory. I am pleased, of course, that *Troubling Love* has admirers, I'm pleased that it inspired an important film. But I don't want to accept an idea of life where the success of the self is measured by the success of the written page.

Then there is the problem of my creative choices, which I am not capable of explaining clearly, especially to those who might pick out of the text phrases and situations and feel wounded by them. I am used to writing as if it were a matter of dividing up the booty. To one character I give a trait of Tom's, to another a phrase of Dick's; I reproduce situations in which people I know and have known have actually been. I draw on real situations and events but not as they really happened; rather, I assume as having "really happened" only the impressions or fantasies that originated in the years when that experience was lived. So what I write is full of references to situations and events that are real and verifiable but reorganized and reinvented as if they had never happened. The farther I am from my writing, then, the more it becomes what it wants to be: a novelistic invention. The closer I get, and am inside it, the more overwhelmed the novel is by real details, and the book stops being a novel, and risks wounding me, above all, as the malicious account of a disrespectful ingrate. Thus I want my novel to go as far as possible precisely so that it can present its novelistic truth and not the accidental scraps—which it nevertheless contains—of autobiography.

But the media, especially in linking photographs of the author with the book, media appearances by the writer with its cover, goes precisely in the opposite direction: it abolishes the distance between author and book, operates in such a way that the one is spent in favor of the other, mixes the first with the materials of the second and vice versa. In the face of these types of intervention, I feel exactly what you correctly define as "private timidity." I worked for a long time, plunging headlong into the material that I wanted to narrate, to distill from my own experience and that of others whatever "public" material could be distilled, whatever appeared to me extractable from voices, facts, persons near and far, to construct characters and a narrative organism of some public coherence. Now that that organism has, for good or ill, its own self-sufficient equilibrium, why should I entrust myself to the media? Why continue to mix its breath with mine? I have a well-founded fear that the media, which, because of its current nature, that is, lacking a true vocation for "public interest," would be inclined, carelessly, to restore a private quality to an object that originated precisely to give a less circumscribed meaning to individual experience.

Perhaps this last part of the subject, in particular, merits discussion. Is there a way of safeguarding the right of an author to choose to establish, once and for all, through his writing alone, what of himself should become public? The editorial marketplace is in particular preoccupied with finding out if the author can be used as an engaging character and thus assist the journey of his work through the marketplace. If one yields, one accepts, at least in theory, that the entire person, with all his experiences and his affections, is placed for sale along with the book. But the nerves of the private person are too sensitive. If they are out in the open, all they offer is a spectacle of suffering or joy or malice or resentment (sometimes even generosity, but, like it or not, on display); certainly I cannot add anything to the work.

I would conclude this subject by saying, finally, that writing with the knowledge that I don't have to appear produces a space of absolute creative freedom. It's a corner of my own that I intend to defend, now that I've tried it. If I were deprived of it, I would feel abruptly impoverished.

We come now to Elsa Morante. I never met her; I've never been able to get to know people who provoked intense emotions in me. If I had met her, I would have been paralyzed, I would have become so stupid that I would have been incapable of establishing any meaningful contact with her. You ask me about influences, a question I find so appealing that frankly I risk telling lies just to confirm your hypothesis. The problem presented itself for the first time when *Troubling Love* won the Procida Prize. Was it possible that my book had a connection, however tenuous, with that author? I began to search through Morante's pages to find even a line that might justify, above all to myself, in a thank-you letter to the prize givers, the legitimacy of such an award. I searched mainly in *Aracoeli*, but I searched unsuccessfully, I didn't find anything that would allow me to establish a modest connection. On the other hand, I'm not a conscientious reader, with a good memory. I read a lot but in a disorderly way, and I forget what I read. Rather, to put it more precisely, I have a distorted memory of what I read. At the time, because I was in a hurry and maybe a bit opportunistic, I seized on a single sentence in *The Andalusian Shawl*: "No one, starting with the mother's dressmaker, must think that a mother has a woman's body." It was an easy quotation that I'd had in mind for years, annotated in various ways. I'd often rooted around in the sense of anxiety instilled by the idea contained in that passage. It said that women who were expert in dressing women's bodies nevertheless were unable to do their job when it was a matter of sewing fabric on the body of the mother. I had imagined scissors that refused to cut, measuring sticks that lied about length, basting that didn't hold, chalk that didn't leave a mark. The mother's body produced a revolt among the dressmaker's tools, an annihilation of her skills. Dressing oneself and dressing other women was easy; but dressing the mother was to lose the war with the shapeless, was to "bundle"—another Morantian word.

This failure of dressmakers faced with the problem of dressing the maternal body stayed with me for a long time. It was accompanied by a much earlier impression, that of a careless reader, inclined to fantasize on a few lines and not very attentive to true meanings. This impression was connected to reading *Arturo's Island*, which I did for the first time twenty years ago. I was overwhelmed by it but for reasons that at the time I was ashamed of. As I read, I thought, through the whole arc of the story, that Arturo's real sex was female. Arturo was a girl, it had to be. And although Morante wrote as a male "I," I couldn't help imagining her as a mask of herself, of her feelings, of her emotions. It wasn't a matter of "being transported," in an ordinary literary way. I perceived—and the same thing happened later with all Morante's male characters, who go shamelessly into the depths of their relation with their mother—a disguise aimed at doing, in literature, precisely what the mothers' dressmakers couldn't do: removing the maternal figure (dead mother—Nunziatina—homosexual father) from her shapeless wrapping; using the limbo of a male adolescence—freer as in many other things—to not muffle her, to tell what otherwise, in the female experience, has no shape.

I also thought for a long time about the epigraph, from Saba, to reinforce that impression. Saba writes, "If I remember myself in him, it seems clear to me . . . " In whatever direction you take "Il fanciullo appassionato" ("The Passionate Boy") in its entirety, somewhere in me, where *Arturo's Island* is concerned, all that counts is that line and that *in him,* placed under the title to say: "It seems to me a good thing that I can remember myself writing from inside him, Arturo."

On the other hand—I think—the moment has to come when we'll truly be able to write *outside of him*, not from an ideological claim but because, like Platonic souls, we'll truly remember ourselves without need of the comfort, the habit, the distancing of having to represent ourselves *in him*. I imagine that the mothers' dressmakers have been studying for a long time. Sooner or later we'll all learn not to bundle up everything, not to bundle ourselves.

What to tell you, in conclusion? I'd like it if even a weak connection existed between *Troubling Love* and Morante's books. But I have to confess that many of Morante's stylistic traits are alien to me; that I feel incapable of conceiving stories of such breadth; that for a long time I haven't valued a life in which Literature counts more than anything else. There are, rather, certain low levels of storytelling that appeal to me. Over the years, for example, I've become less ashamed of how much I like the stories in the women's magazines I find around the house: trash about love and betrayal, which has produced in me indelible emotions, a desire for not necessarily logical plots, a taste for strong, slightly vulgar passions. It seems to me that this cellar of writing, a fund of pleasure that for years I repressed in the name of Literature, should also be put to work, because it was not only with the classics but there, too, that the desire for storytelling developed, and so does it make sense to throw away the key?

As for Naples, today I feel drawn above all by the Anna Maria Ortese of "The Involuntary City." If I managed again to write about this city, I would try to craft a text that explores the direction indicated there, a story of wretched petty acts of violence, a precipice of voices and events, small, terrible gestures. But, to do so, I would have to return there to live, something that for family and work reasons is impossible.

With Naples, though, accounts are never closed, even at a distance. I've lived for quite a while in other places, but that city is not an ordinary place, it's an extension of the body, a matrix of perception, the term of comparison of every experience. Everything that has been permanently meaningful for me has Naples as its backdrop and is expressed in its dialect.

This emphasis, however, is recent and is the product of repeated visits at a distance. For a long time, I experienced the city I grew up in as a place where I continually felt at risk. It was a city of sudden quarrels, of blows, of easy tears, of minor arguments that ended in curses, unrepeatable obscenities, and irreparable breaks, of emotions so extreme as to become intolerably false. My Naples is the "vulgar" Naples of people who are "settled" but still terrified by the need to go back to earning a living through temporary odd jobs; ostentatiously honest but, in the event, ready for petty crimes in order not to make a bad impression; noisy, loud-voiced, monarchist, but also, in certain ramifications, Stalinist; drowned in the thorniest dialect; coarse and sensual, still without petit-bourgeois decorum but impelled to give at least superficial signs of it; respectable and potentially criminal, ready to sacrifice themselves to the occasion, or the necessity, not to appear more fool than others.

I felt different from that Naples, I experienced it with revulsion, I ran away as soon as I could. I brought it with me as a synthesis, a surrogate, that would always remind me that the power of life is damaged, humiliated by unjust modes of existence. But for a long time I've looked at it under a microscope. I isolate fragments, I descend into them, I discover good things that as a child I didn't see and others that appear to me even more wretched than they did then. But not even for these do I feel the old bitterness. In the end it's an experience of a city that can't be erased even if you wanted to, and turns out to be useful everywhere. I can wander through streets and alleys simply by lying in bed with my eyes closed: when I return I have initial moments of uncontainable enthusiasm; then, in the space of an afternoon, I move on to hating it, I regress, I'm mute again, I feel a sense of suffocation, a diffuse anxiety. I seem to have grasped as a child not a phase limited in time and space but the signs of a degeneration that has now spread, so that ultimately the city, with its calls of a lost time to find again, or sudden remembrances, acts like a perverse siren, using streets, alleys, this ascent, that descent, the poisoned beauty of the bay, but remaining a place of decomposition, of disloca-tion, of panic; and, outside of it, I struggled to learn to make it function a little. And yet it's my experience, and contains a lot of meaningful emotions; I feel its human richness, the complex layers of its cultures. I've stopped avoiding it.

I don't know how to answer the questions you ask about Delia and Amalia. It doesn't seem to me that I consciously established a metaphorical connection between Amalia and Naples. Naples, in my book and in my intentions when I wrote it, is thought of as pressure, a dark force of the world that weighs on its subjects, the sum total of what we call the threat-ening reality of today, engulfing, through violence, every space of mediation and civil relationship around and within the char-acters. But, that said, in my book Delia must simply manage to tell herself a story, which she knows well from beginning to end—which she has never repressed. The story has remained entangled in certain spaces of the city, in the dialectal voices through which it took shape. This woman comes into the labyrinth of Naples to capture it, put it in order, arrange space and time, finally tell her own story out loud. She tries and in doing so understands that, if she succeeds, she will also suc-ceed in finally adding to herself her mother, her mother's world, her wrongs, struggles, passions consummated or imag-ined, inhibited energies and those which expanded within the few accessible channels. That's all. Even the mystery of Amalia's death slowly becomes irrelevant for Delia; or rather it becomes a minor part of her and her mother's story.

Naturally it's true, Naples isn't purely background. As I was writing, I realized clearly that there was not a place or a gesture in the story that was not marked by a certain Neapolitanness, unredeemed and unredeemable, lacking narrative value, irritating. On the other hand Delia's effort consisted mainly in telling what had for a long time seemed to her not worth telling, and going down that road was useful to me. It's possible that in the end the most elusive, hardest to grasp, most densely ambiguous person, this Amalia who absorbs difficulties and beatings but doesn't give in, was charged with the least definable Neapolitanness, and so is a sort of woman-city who is tugged, trapped, shaken, pursued, humiliated, desired, and yet endowed with an extraordinary capacity to endure. If it were so, I would be happy about it. But I don't know how to confirm that for you.

Besides, I confess that I don't like a narrative that tells me programmatically what Naples is like today, what its young people are like today, what the women have become, how the family is in crisis, what ills Italy suffers from. I have the impression that such works are almost always the staging of media clichés, the poeticizing of a magazine article, of a television segment, of sociological research, of a party position. What I expect, instead, from a good story is that it will tell me about today what I can't know from any other source but that story, from its unique way of putting something into words, from the feeling that it implies.

I don't have the right tools to talk about Mario Martone's film and so I will say nothing. I wrote to him, but then I didn't send the letter: it seemed to me that I could tell him only things he already knew. I can, on the other hand, talk to you about the screenplay, which at the time I read and reread. In my book, the weave of past and present is entrusted to the alternation between the said and the not said, an alternation determined in absolute autonomy *within* the narrator. Delia, that is, on the page, is a literary first person, the only source of speech and the only source of the truth of the story; no one will ever really intervene from *outside* her narrator's voice. In the cinema, instead, the narrator's voice, when it's there, has to reckon with its own body-object displayed on the screen; it has a surface that is dominant, and so it's always a pale semblance of the literary voice. Thus it seemed to me natural that Martone would have to go in other directions and probably set other goals.

For example, the story of Delia, once it was embodied, had to be inscribed within the *real* city and its *real* dialect. As a result, once Delia was fixed outside the narrator, it was obvious that, even using her silences and her half-sentences, she had to be represented from the outside, in search of something that she doesn't know and has to discover, a journey that requires the overexplaining you allude to, and that, if it wants to exploit fully the possible margins of ambiguity, has of necessity to place, show, state, deny, clarify more than the first-person literary narrative does.

To me, especially when I read the final version of the screenplay, it seemed that Martone had found intelligent and creative solutions. I'll give you just one example, in order not to drag this out too much. In the few words of the final scene, I worked more or less consciously on a play of tenses: "Amalia had been there. I was Amalia." The pluperfect of the first sentence was meant to imply that Amalia's story concluded not with her death but with the transfer, now completed, of the truth of her experience to her daughter. The imperfect of the second sentence, and the transformation of the subject of the first into the predicate, was intended to revive Amalia's life, to let it be fulfilled again in Delia, to transform it into a *more* that, if it doesn't say anything about Amalia, now can help her daughter to fully *be*. I didn't intend the *I was* to have a pathological function. It's not—at least as far as what I had in mind, while I was writing—a loss of identity. It is, rather, a recovery of the little Delia's childish game in the cellar, when she played with Antonio and pretended she was Amalia, but it's a recovery whose function is reversed. That game now helps her tell herself that a terrible side of herself as a child has become adult, has been accepted, can share with others its time as a grown woman. The solution invented by Martone—the simple answer ("Amalia") to the young man who asks her her name—seemed to me as good as could be done, within a film, to hold together all the things that I tried to put into those two sentences. For that and other inventions I'm very glad that Martone took on *Troubling Love*.

I hope that, as far as possible, I've been thorough, and I'm happy to have had a chance to speak to you with a certain freedom. I'd like you to consider these pages, which cost me some effort, a sort of thank you to a person who, by calling himself my affectionate admirer, made me happy for a whole day.

NOTE
Unsent letter (1995). The critic and magazine editor Goffredo Fofi sent Ferrante a number of questions through her publishers. The letter that appears above is the author's reply to his questions:

1. Mario Martone's film is very respectful toward your novel, but he chooses to make a clear distinction between the present and the past (through flashbacks), while in the novel everything happens in the present, in Delia's reflections. The other difference between the novel and the film lies in the fact that the film explains a lot, including what in the novel was unsaid or implicit. The third, finally, is a kind of greater modesty (male?) on the part of Martone in accepting Delia's sexuality in the past, in adhering, one might say, to the

psychology of the child Delia. In that part, in the film, Amalia is only a victim. What do you think of these interventions, and do you attribute the differences to Martone's different sensibility or, rather, to the need for cinema to be, in itself, in its obligation to show, more didactic?

2. The Naples you describe with extreme precision and decisiveness (places and neighborhoods, besides human environments, behavior) has not been described much in cinema, as literature has not described the passage from the still proletarian peasant periphery to the city of the lowest bourgeoisie, to which Delia's family belongs. What impact does this Naples have, and what do you think has changed in the city's current process of renewal? Have you followed this process? Do you still feel involved in Naples and by Naples? Is your geographical distance from the city a definite choice (like Delia's) or is it due to other factors? Would you go back to living in Naples today? And will Delia return to live in Naples? In other words, can one consider the reconciliation of Delia and Amalia a reconciliation with a Neapolitan identity—irksome and pathological, but nevertheless one from which one must start again? In still other words, Amalia is a mother-Naples: can she be seen as a metaphor of Naples?

3. When the novel came out, you won the Procida Prize—Elsa Morante, and critics saw a sort of connection between your novel and certain of Morante's works (especially *Aracoeli*). Do you accept this connection? And how does one become disconnected from it? (Like Delia from Amalia?) Did you ever meet Morante? And what other female writers—and in what way—have influenced your development (Ortese, for example)?

4. What is your new novel about, if I may ask?

5. Did you imagine that the main characters of your novel would look like Angela Luce and Anna Bonaiuto? In what way do they seem to you to have best captured the character of the protagonist? And in what are they distant from it?

6. What is the underlying reason for keeping your distance from the media: is it a feeling of distrust (vis-à-vis the society of the spectacle)? A form of reserve? Today, when the tendency is to personalize works as the products of recognizable authors who regularly appear in the pages of the newspapers and on the television screen, as if these appearances were indispensable, your situation is truly anomalous. Even without wanting to make it too much of an exam-

ple, one has the temptation to take it as a model. What do you think of this possibility?

7. Have you ever been in analysis? Have you had a psychoanalytic type of education? A feminist type?

Thank you, and warm regards from your affectionate admirer,
Goffredo Fofi

10.
WORKING WOMEN

D ear Sandra,
I owe you an explanation. The manuscript I promised to give you to read will not reach you. I see that you've already tried to find a title (I like *Working Women*; I rule out *Women Workers*), but I've changed my mind, the story doesn't seem ready to be read yet. In the past week I myself couldn't read even a line without feeling disgusted. I need time to return to it calmly and understand what to do with it. But as soon as I've made a decision I'll let you know.

Now, don't think it's your fault, you were right to insist. In all these years every time you've pressed me to let you read something I've begun to write with greater motivation; I was glad that at least one person—you—was waiting for my new book. In this case maybe it was a mistake to summarize the contents of the book. I must have perceived your editorial disappointment; or I became worried because of the length of the manuscript—you've always said that, except for thrillers stuffed with adventures, books that are too long put readers to flight. But, even if that were the case, my decision not to keep my promise has other motives.

I wrote this story because it has to do with me. I was inside it for a long time. I kept shortening the distance between the protagonist and me, I occupied all her cavities, and there is nothing about her, today, that I wouldn't do. So I'm exhausted, and now that the story is finished I have to catch my breath. How? I don't know, maybe by starting to write another book.

Or reading as many as possible on the subject of this story, and so remaining nearby, on the sidelines, and testing it the way you test a cake to see if it's baked, poking it with a toothpick, pricking the text to see if it's done.

I think of writing now as a long, tiring, pleasant seduction. The stories that you tell, the words that you use and refine, the characters you try to give life to are merely tools with which you circle around the elusive, unnamed, shapeless thing that belongs to you alone, and which nevertheless is a sort of key to all the doors, the real reason that you spend so much of your life sitting at a table tapping away, filling pages. The question in every story is the same: is this the right story to seize what lies silent in my depths, that living thing which, if captured, spreads through all the pages and gives them life? The answer is uncertain, even when you get to the end. What happened in the lines, between the lines? Often, after struggles and joys, on the pages there is nothing—events, dialogues, dramatic turns, only that—and you're frightened by your very desperation.

To me it happens like this: I always struggle at first, it's hard to get started, no opening seems really convincing; then the story gets going, the bits already written gain power and suddenly find a way of fitting together; then writing becomes a pleasure, the hours are a time of intense enjoyment, the characters never leave you, they have a space-time of their own in which they are alive and increasingly vivid, they are inside and outside you, they exist solidly in the streets, in the houses, in the places where the story must unfold; the endless possibilities of the plot select themselves and the choices seem inevitable, definitive. You begin every day by rereading to get energized, and rereading is pleasant, it means perfecting, enhancing, touching up the past to make it fit with the story's future. Then this happy period comes to an end. The story is finished. You have to reread not the work of the day before but the entire narrative. You're afraid. You test it here and there, nothing is written as you had imagined it. The beginning is insignificant, the development seems crude, the linguistic forms inadequate. It's the moment when you need help, to find a way to draw the ground the book rests on and understand what substance it is truly made of.

Now I'm just at that anguished point. So, if you can, help me. What do you know about novels that tell a story of women's work obsessively observed by an idle, malicious, sometimes fierce gaze? Are there any? I'm interested in anything that focuses on the female body at work. If you have any title in mind—it doesn't matter if it's a good book or junk—write to me. I doubt that work ennobles man and I am absolutely certain that it does not ennoble woman. So the novel is centered on the hardships of working, on the horror implicit in the necessity of earning a living, an expression in itself abominable. But don't worry: I assure you that, although I've used all the jobs I am thoroughly familiar with because I've done them myself, and also those I'm familiar with thanks to people I know well and trust, I haven't written an investigation into women's labor: the story has great tension, all kinds of things happen. But I don't know what to say about the result. Now that the book seems to me finished I have to find reasons to calm myself. Eventually, in all serenity, I will tell you if the novel can be read or not, if it can be published or should be added to my writing exercises. In the latter case I would be truly sorry to have disappointed you again. On the other hand, I believe that, for those who love to write, time spent writing is never wasted. And then isn't it from book to book that we approach the book that we really want to write?

Until next time,

Elena

NOTE
Letter of May 18, 1998. The publisher never received the novel under discussion.

11.
LIES THAT ALWAYS TELL THE TRUTH

Dear Sandro,

You say it's necessary to do interviews, at least, and that's fine, you're right. Tell Fofi to send me the questions, I'll answer. In these ten years I hope I've grown up.

In my own defense, however, I will say only this: in the games with newspapers one always ends up lying and at the root of the lie is the need to offer oneself to the public in the best form, with thoughts suitable to the role, with the makeup we imagine is suitable.

Well, I don't at all hate lies, in life I find them useful and I resort to them when necessary to shield my person, feelings, pressures. But lying about books makes me suffer, literary fiction seems to me made purposely to always tell the truth.

Therefore I care deeply about the truth of *The Days of Abandonment*, I wouldn't want to talk about it meekly, complying with the expectations implicit in the interviewer's questions. The ideal for me would be to obtain, through short answers, the same effect as literature, that is, to orchestrate lies that always tell, strictly, the truth. Let's see, in other words, what I'm capable of, I feel I'm in good shape, I tend to tell true lies even if I'm writing a note of congratulations. As soon as you have the questions send them to me.

NOTE

Letter of January, 2002. Between 2002 and 2003, after the publication of *The Days of Abandonment* in Italy, Elena Ferrante gave three interviews. The questions were sent to her through the publisher. The interviews follow.

12.
THE CITY WITHOUT LOVE
Answers to questions from Goffredo Fofi

Fofi: *Naples, Turin: two very different settings, and, frenzied as the Neapolitan atmosphere was (or so we remember it, thanks to Martone's film, which exaggerated its characteristics), so the Turinese is cold and, besides, in summer, sparsely inhabited and fairly quiet. Was it necessary to further detach the character of the protagonist, in her crisis of abandonment and near madness? Of Turin one "sees" little, it's only a background. Why? Is the "ghost" of the abandoned Neapolitan woman, a memory that becomes an obsession, what ties this novel most closely to the previous one?*

Ferrante: Olga is a woman not alone but isolated. I wanted to tell the story of her isolation, it was what interested me most. I wished to follow moment by moment the contraction around her of spaces both real and metaphorical. I wanted Turin and Naples, although distant and different, to coincide as places without community, backdrops for individuals stunned by grief. Delia, in *Troubling Love*, still manages to find in Naples a story of her own that is gripping, and places in the city that have an enveloping power. Olga, on the other hand, in Naples as elsewhere, today finds only names that are increasingly incapable of retaining warmth and meaning. It's this growing failure of the cities that flings her out of the background.

Fofi: *As the background fades, the crisis that the novel narrates becomes more invasive and explosive, central. Do the protagonist's references to* Anna Karenina *and to de Beauvoir's* The

Woman Destroyed also indicate the perpetuity of a situation: abandonment is abandonment, the crisis that follows from it is inevitable, and it recurs outside of time and culture?

Ferrante: No, I don't think Olga starts from that sequence of ideas. She is combative, she doesn't want to be Anna Karenina or a broken woman. Above all she doesn't want to be like the abandoned woman of Naples who made an impression on her as a child, she feels that she is the product of a different culture, a different female story, she thinks that nothing is inevitable. Of course, she feels deeply that every abandonment is a vortex and an annihilation, maybe also an indication of the desert that has expanded around us. But she reacts, she recovers, she lives.

Fofi: Olga, a woman of middle age, has not found in writing any sublimation or fulfillment. Do feelings remain the keystone of every human experience, in particular that of women?

Ferrante: For Olga, writing is enduring and understanding. Writing has no magical or mystical coloration, at most it's the need for style. As a girl she claimed from writing much more; now it's useful only as a means of keeping under control the problem she's encountered—can one continue to live if one loses love? It seems like a pretty much discredited subject; in reality it's the question most crudely posed by female existence. The loss of love is a failure, it causes an absence of sense. The city without love is an unjust and cruel city.

Fofi: To what degree have you been influenced by feminism (Italian, of the seventies), and did you think about the achievements of feminism in writing your novel?

Ferrante: I've read a fair amount of feminist writing, and passionately, yet I have no militant experience. I have a lot of sympathy for the thinking of difference feminism, but it's something that has more to do with me than with the story of Delia or of Olga. A story takes its own path, it's the receptacle of everything and the opposite of everything, it functions only if we allow it to take what it needs to seek its truth. I don't think one can know more about a work by having information about the reading habits and the tastes of the one who wrote it.

Fofi: Olga seems to reject every "transcendence," every dimension of existence that is not "secular" and earthly, except in the dimension of hallucination; and yet there are in the novel hidden threads, strange correspondences, echoes of presences, and central to it is the relationship (which has something of a primary identification) with an animal, the dog Otto—true scapegoat in the structure of the story. Is it a contradiction?

Ferrante: Olga is strictly secular. But the experience of abandonment consumes her in her convictions, in her way of being, in her expressive register, even in her emotional reactions. That coming apart lets filter in fantasies, beliefs, emotions, and buried feelings, a physical primitivism that, yes, weaves its own strands, difficult to control, but without transcendent results. Olga in the end discovers that suffering won't sink us or raise us up and concludes that there is nothing either high or low that can console her. As for the dog Otto, I don't want nor do I know how to tell you anything, except that he is the character, if I can put it like this, who caused me the most suffering.

Fofi: This novel comes out at a particular moment in Italian history, dominated by a return to a "private" utilitarian boorishness and a sort of collective public hypocrisy, as in a television show. Your first novel came out many years ago, and one assumes that The Days of Abandonment *was written in the course of many years. Were you thinking about the "Italian background" of those years: do you recognize it as the background of Olga's story?*

Ferrante: Yes, that background you speak of shows, I think, especially through the new features that Olga's husband slowly reveals, through some of his references to a disillusioned political realism. But I don't think that the time in which a story originates and is conceived is revealed through imitation of the repulsive features of the contemporary world. Not even a detailed anthology of our present extremely vulgar times would be enough to make a story. When one writes, one hopes, rather, that the particularity of the era is caught in the workings of the text; in the actions of the abandoned Olga, for example, a prisoner in her apartment, isolated in the heart of the absent city.

Fofi: Is Olga's acceptance of Carrano, the musician neighbor, also acceptance of a fragility common to men and women? What can it be a prelude to in Olga's life? The question is stupid but necessary. Thank you.

Ferrante: Olga is helped by Carrano to draw close to men again after every feeling has dried up, after the loss of love has demonstrated to her the naked brutality of relations between the sexes and not only between the sexes. Carrano is not a linear character; he even has some repulsive aspects, but Olga prefers him to the veterinarian, for example, to his flaunted, put-on pleasantness. It's Carrano who at the end moves her and gives her a new emotional persepective. I think that the men we choose say, like many other important choices, what sort of women we are, what women we are becoming.

NOTE
The interview appeared in *Il Messaggero*, January 24, 2002, preceded by an introduction by Goffredo Fofi and entitled "Ferrante: Journey to the Center of the Planet Woman."

13

WITHOUT KEEPING A SAFE DISTANCE
Answers to questions from Stefania Scateni

Scateni: The Days of Abandonment *describes a terrible moment in a woman's life and does so with a naked sincerity, especially regarding the protagonist. Do you think your anonymity was helpful?*

Ferrante: I don't know. I've always had a tendency to separate everyday life from writing. To tolerate existence, we lie, and we lie above all to ourselves. Sometimes we tell ourselves lovely tales, sometimes petty lies. Falsehoods protect us, mitigate suffering, allow us to avoid the terrifying moment of serious reflection, they dilute the horrors of our time, they even save us from ourselves. Instead, when one writes one must never lie. In literary fiction you have to be sincere to the point where it's unbearable, where you suffer the emptiness of the pages. It seems likely that making a clear separation between what we are in life and what we are when we write helps keep self-censorship at bay.

Scateni: Why did you choose not to become a public personage?

Ferrante: From a somewhat neurotic desire for intangibility. The labor of writing touches every point of the body. When the book is finished, it's as if you had been rudely searched, and you desire only to regain integrity, to return to being the person you usually are, in occupations, in thoughts, in language, in relationships. The work is public: in it, there is everything we have to say. Today, who really cares about the person who wrote it? What's essential is the finished work.

Scateni: Your writing does not seem to be written for readers; rather, it seems to have originated as private writing, without any interlocutor but the page (or the computer) or yourself. Is that true?

Ferrante: No, I don't think so. I write so that my books will be read. But while I'm writing that isn't what counts; what counts is finding the energy to dig deeply into the story I'm telling. The only moment of my life in which I don't let myself be disturbed by anyone is when I'm searching to find the words to go beyond the surface of an obvious gesture, a banal phrase. It doesn't even frighten me to discover that the digging is futile, and under the surface there's nothing.

Scateni: Reading your book, I thought of the life that makes writing, that the tempo of living is that of writing. Is that why you've written two books in ten years?

Ferrante: I have to admit with some embarrassment that I haven't written two books in ten years, I've written and rewritten many. But *Troubling Love* and *The Days of Abandonment* seemed to me the ones that most decisively stuck a finger in certain wounds I have that are still infected, and did so without keeping a safe distance. At other times, I've written about clean or happily healed wounds with the obligatory detachment and the right words. But then I discovered that that is not my path.

Scateni: On the same subject, your writing is very concrete, physical, as if the body had become the carrier of words. It's a writing composed of gestures, the daily gestures made fluent by habit, which are shed at the moment of the "illness." In short, it's female writing. Are there women writers (or male writers) to whom you feel close?

Ferrante: When I was very young, my goal was to write with a masculine tone. It seemed to me that all the great writers were male, and hence it was necessary to write like a real man. Later, I began to read women's literature attentively and I embraced the theory that every little fragment that revealed a feminine literary specificity should be studied and put to use. Some time ago, however, I shook off theoretical preoccupations and readings, and began to write without asking myself what I should be: masculine, feminine, neuter. While I'm writing, I confine myself to occasionally reading books that keep me company not as entertainment but as solid companions. I have a modest list, I call them books of encouragement: *Adele*, by Federico Tozzi, *The Best of Husbands*, by Alba de Cespedes, Morante's *House of Liars* and *Arturo's Island*, etc. Incongruous as it might seem, the book that was my closest companion while I was working on *The Days of Abandonment* was *The Princess of Clèves*, by Madame de La Fayette.

Scateni: Olga, the protagonist of The Days of Abandonment, *had found a meaning for her existence in a relationship, in the rituals of a relationship. Left alone, she has to start again from zero, realizing her mistake, and she approaches another relationship, with Carrano, armed with a great deal of skepticism. What do you think of love?*

Ferrante: The need for love is the central experience of our existence. However foolish it may seem, we feel truly alive only when we have an arrow in our side that we drag around night and day, everywhere we go. The need for love sweeps away every other need and, on the other hand, motivates all our actions. Read Book 4 of the *Aeneid*. The construction of Carthage stops when Dido falls in love. The city would continue to grow powerful and happy if Aeneas stayed. But he goes away, Dido kills herself, and Carthage, potentially a city of love, becomes a city with a mission of hatred. Individuals and cities without love are a danger to themselves and to others.

Scateni: The Days of Abandonment *might seem to be a "feminist" novel . . . Do you feel in agreement with Simone de Beauvoir and her book* The Woman Destroyed?

Ferrante: No, not anymore. I used that book, in the story of Olga, just as I could have used Dido, who, having been abandoned, wanders through the city beside herself, and stabs herself with Aeneas' sword, one of the "souvenirs" he has left her. In reality, Olga is a woman of today who knows that she can't react to abandonment by breaking down. In life, as in writing, the effect of this new knowledge interests me: how she acts, what resistance she offers, how she fights against the wish to die and gains the time necessary to learn to bear her suffering, what stratagems or fictions she employs in order to accept life again.

Scateni: What do you think of Roberto Faenza's plan to adapt The Days of Abandonment *into a film? Are you involved in the project?*

Ferrante: No, for the moment no. I love the cinema but I don't know anything about the language of film. I hope that his *Days of Abandonment* turns out better than mine.

NOTE
The interview with an introduction by Stefania Scateni, appeared in *l'Unità* on September 8, 2002, under the title "Elena Ferrante, la scrittura e la carne" ("Elena Ferrante, Writing and the Flesh").

14.
A STORY OF DISINTEGRATION
Answers to Questions from Jesper Storgaard Jensen

J *ensen: Thanks to the success of* The Days of Abandonment, *you could have had the sort of fame that many people seek. Why, instead, have you chosen not to appear?*
Ferrante: In *Totem and Taboo* Freud tells of a woman who had forced herself not to write her own name anymore. She was afraid that someone would use it to take possession of her personality. The woman began by refusing to write her own name and then, by extension, she stopped writing completely. I am not at that point: I write and intend to continue to write. But I have to confess that when I read that story of illness it right away seemed wholly meaningful. What I choose to put outside myself can't and shouldn't become a magnet that sucks me up entirely. An individual has the right to keep his person separate, if he wants, even his image, from the public effects of his work. But it's not only that. I don't think that the author ever has anything decisive to add to his work: I consider the text a self-sufficient body, which has in itself, in its makeup, all the questions and all the answers. And then real books are written only to be read. Increasingly, the promotional activity of authors tends, instead, to cancel out the works and the need to read them. In many cases the name of the writer, his image, his opinions are better known than his works, and that goes not only for contemporary writers but unfortunately, by now, also for classics. Finally, I have a life, both private and public, that is quite satisfying. I don't feel the need for new equilibriums. I prefer that the corner for

writing remain a hidden place, without surveillance or urgency of any type.

Jensen: Although you've chosen anonymity yourself, don't you miss direct contact with your readers?

Ferrante: Readers, if they want, can write to the publisher. I'm happy with that. I respond more or less punctually.

Jensen: Are you willing to give a brief description—and, if you like physical, as well—of yourself?

Ferrante: No. And allow me to cite, for this somewhat abrupt answer, Italo Calvino, who, convinced that only the works of an author count, in 1964 wrote to a scholar of his books: "I don't give biographical facts, or I give false ones, or anyway I always try to change them from one time to the next. Ask me what you want to know, but I won't tell you the truth, of that you can be sure." I've always liked that passage, and I've made it at least partly mine. I could tell you that I am as beautiful and athletic as a star, or that I've been in a wheelchair since adolescence, or that I'm a woman afraid even of her own shadow, or that I adore begonias, or that I write only between two and five in the morning, and other nonsense. The problem is that, unlike Calvino, I hate answering a question with a chain of lies.

Jensen: Surely you must have followed the attempts on the part of certain persons in the Italian press to discover your identity. Have you gotten any amusement out of the theories according to which you are a well-known critic (Goffredo Fofi), a Neapolitan writer (Fabrizia Ramondino), or a Neapolitan homosexual?

Ferrante: I very much respect the writers you've mentioned, and the idea that my books could be attributed to them is flattering. I even rather like the gay hypothesis. It's the evidence that a text can accommodate more than what the writer knows about himself.

Jensen: Could you tell us the origin of the book's plot?

Ferrante: At its origin there is certainly a German shepherd, a German shepherd I loved. The rest came slowly, accumulating over the years.

Jensen: Is there an autobiographical component to the book, given the expressive form that renders so effectively the sense of disgust and disaffection that Olga feels for herself and for sex, among other things?

Ferrante: There is no story that doesn't have roots in the feeling that the writer has about life. The more that feeling filters into the story, into the characters, the more distinctly the page gives form to an incisive effect of truth. But what counts, in the end, is what I would call the graphic quality of that effect, the ways in which the writing achieves it and enhances it.

Jensen: What is the theme that you were interested in investigating through Olga's story?

Ferrante: I wanted to tell a story of disintegration. Someone who takes love away from us devastates the cultural structure we've worked on all our lives, deprives us of that sort of Eden that until that moment had made us appear innocent and lovable. Human beings give the worst of themselves when their cultural clothes are torn off, and they find themselves facing the nakedness of their bodies, they feel the shame of them. In a certain sense the loss of love is the common experience closest to the myth of the expulsion from the earthly paradise: it's the violent end of the illusion of having a heavenly body, it's the discovery of one's own dispensability and perishability.

Jensen: The Days of Abandonment *communicates powerful emotions to the reader. How do you manage to obtain such a "clean" writing style that is able to communicate those emotions? What is your method of writing?*

Ferrante: I work by contrast: clarity of facts and low emotional reaction alternating with a sort of storm of blood, of frenzied writing. However, I try to avoid dividing lines between the two moments. I tend to make them slide into one another without a break.

Jensen: Today, in your opinion, is it important to be capable of communicating strong feelings in order to sell books, as Andrea De Carlo, among others, maintains?

Ferrante: A writer seeks above all a form for his world. Naturally it's an interior world, hence private, not yet public or only partly public. In that sense "publishing a book" means deciding to offer to others, in the form that seems to us most fitting, what intimately belongs to us. Asking instead what the public wants (strong feelings or weak ones or something else) seems to me to go in a completely different direction. In this second case it's no longer my individual world seeking a public dimension through literary form but the public dimension of the consumer imposing on me and my writing. I don't say that it's wrong to work in that manner, the roads to a good book are infinite. But it's not my way of looking at the creative process.

Jensen: Would you call The Days of Abandonment *a feminist novel?*

Ferrante: Yes, because it's sustained by the female reaction to abandonment, from Medea and Dido on. No, because it doesn't aim at telling what is the theoretically and practically correct reaction of the contemporary woman faced with the loss of the beloved man nor does it brand male behaviors as vile. When I write I construct a story. I make it with my experience, my feelings, my readings, my convictions, and above all with my most secret and uncontrolled depths, even though these often fight with good readings and just beliefs. I never worry about constructing a story that illustrates, demonstrates, spreads some conviction, even if it's a conviction that counted and counts for me.

Jensen: The Days of Abandonment *is the story of a person who loses love. Forgive the banal question, but what does love represent for you?*

Ferrante: A living and benevolent force both for the individual and for the community. When love abandons the individual and, even worse, the community, the actions of human beings become deathlike, and both stories and history take the route of wholesale slaughter.

Jensen: Ten years passed between your first book and this recent one. Would you call yourself a perfectionist?

Ferrante: No, only someone who writes when she wants to and publishes when she's not too ashamed of the result.

Jensen: After the success of The Days of Abandonment, *are you not tempted to strike while the iron is hot, to try to finish a book in a shorter time?*

Ferrante: A bit of success warms the heart and provokes a desire to start work again right away. It also happened ten years ago. If the books that I tried to write in that time had seemed suitable for publication, I would have printed one with no trouble even every six months. But it didn't go like that.

Jensen: Are you pleased that some consider you "the greatest female Italian writer since the time of Morante"?

Ferrante: Of course, I love the works of Morante. But I know perfectly well that it's a journalistic exaggeration.

Jensen: I find it odd that in the two books that have had perhaps the greatest success in Italy in the past year (besides yours, Don't Move, *by Margaret Mazzantini) the male protagonists have the role of the coward, the scoundrel. They're stories in which the men are weak and the women strong. What do you think?*

Ferrante: In my intentions Mario, Olga's husband, is neither cowardly nor a scoundrel. He's just a man who has stopped loving the woman he lives with and comes up against the impossibility of breaking that bond without humiliating her, without hurting her. His behavior is that of a human being who deprives another human being of his love. He knows it's a terrible action, but his need for love has taken other pathways, and he can't do anything but fulfill it. Meanwhile he takes time, he tries to slow down the effects of the wound that he has inflicted. Mario is an ordinary person who is facing the discovery that to do harm is often painfully inevitable.

Jensen: In a male chauvinist society like Italy's, is the female in reality the stronger sex, in that women are forced to develop special talents and a strong character in order to survive or make it?

Ferrante: I dismiss the idea that women have become the strong sex. I think, rather, that we are increasingly constrained, in our actions, to subject ourselves to punishing trials involving the reorganization of our private life and admission to public life. It's not a choice, it's not the effect of a transformation: it's a necessity. To avoid these trials would mean a return to being swallowed up by subordination, to giving up ourselves and our specificity, to being absorbed again by the universal Man.

Jensen: You wrote a short story on the theme of conflict of interest in which you tell the tale of a negative character of your childhood? At the end of the story there is an open reference to

Berlusconi as another negative character. What do you think of the governing political class in Italy today?

Ferrante: I am repulsed by it.

Jensen: On the cover of your book there is a painting by a Danish artist, Christoffer Eckersberg ("Nude from Behind, Morning Toilet"), and in the novel the male protagonist goes to Denmark. Do you have a connection with Denmark, and, if so, what is it?

Ferrante: I've been to Denmark only a few times. On the other hand as a child I loved the stories of Andersen and as an adult I adored those of Karen Blixen. The connections that I have with places are almost always those which I establish through books that tell me about them.

NOTE
The interview appeared August 17, 2003, in the Danish weekly *Weekendavisen*, on the occasion of the publication of *The Days of Abandonment* in Denmark.

15.
SUSPENSION OF DISBELIEF

Dear Sandro,
I wrote the story reluctantly and instead of hiding my reluctance I inserted it directly into the text. I'm afraid you won't like this, so I'll try to explain why I did it.

To tell you the truth, I don't believe that political stories have a decisive function, especially when freedom of opinion and of the press are still well protected and the writer certainly may risk something but not prison or his life. Indignation at how badly the government is run frequently stimulates the imagination and can inspire memorable invective, great allegories, fables that satisfy the aesthetic sense of adults and even of children. But what of any real political effect? In general it seems to me disappointing: a rhetorically complicit nudge given to a public that is already convinced, already in agreement, and whose agreement, beyond a guarantee of success, is also one of the many safeguards against harassment, retaliation, insults, lawsuits, work restrictions, and other common misfortunes that those who express themselves in black and white against the opposing party are exposed to.

To be more explicit, but also to justify myself to you, I will list the questions I asked myself while I was writing. Who is hurt, in the fierce dark political theater of today, by the allusions of a minor story about grandmothers and apartment buildings, like mine? Why, when the newspapers and the essay collections in bookstores are full of misdeeds clearly attributed to the head of the government, do I choose to express my anti-

Berlusconi-ism in a coded way, telling a small family story from years ago? And even if I had invented some other more effective, stinging, amusing, grotesque, anguished, satirical parable, would it make political sense, today, to express oneself obliquely, by apparently talking about something else?

Just to get out of these self-critical convulsions I tried, as you'll see, to write the name of Silvio Berlusconi at the end of the story. Beware, though, I did it not to say that a political story, in the current portrait of our civil society, has the duty to emerge from metaphor (literature, good or bad, is always metaphor) but, rather, to indicate that narratives that can state more directly, even if through literature, the reasons for our repugnance as citizens are necessary. In other words, blunt questions of the following type should be transformed into novels: Is it true that Berlusconi *can be* a great statesman because *he is* a great entrepreneur? How did we become convinced that there is a connection between the two things? Was it the great and good works of that grand entrepreneur that convinced us? What are those works? What is the meritorious work that persuaded us of his capacities as a great statesman? Maybe it's his bad television empire, created by his highly prized and highly paid employees? Hence, does one become a great statesman by being the great entrepreneur of a bad television company that has vulgarized all the other television companies and also, out of a crossover attraction, cinema, newspapers, supplements, publicity, the supporting literature, the entire Italy of TV ratings? Is it possible? If the great work of the entrepreneur Berlusconi is what we have before our eyes every evening, how could it happen that half of Italy *believed* that he really could, as he says, fix the nation? And, besides, what Italy does this man want to fix, if he governs alongside someone who would rather dismantle Italy, in the name of a good and very pure geographical area that he has christened Padania?

It's this credulity not of *citizens* but of the *audience* that I find narratively interesting. If I were capable of writing about our Berlusconian Italy not through allegories, parables, and satires, I would like to find a plot and characters that could represent the mythology within which the symbol Berlusconi is dangerously encysted. I say symbol because the man will disappear, his personal troubles and those of his management have their power, one way or another the political struggle will remove him from the scene, but his ascent as supreme leader within democratic institutions, the construction of his figure as a democratically elected economic-political-television *duce*, will remain a perfectible, repeatable model.

A model that naturally has a history (and if one day you have the desire and the time we'll squabble about this, you, Sandra, and I, to understand how big a part the left itself had in this transformation of citizens into an enthusiastically credulous audience). Berlusconi, for me, is the most garish expression (for now) of the traditional illusionism of politicians, of their capacity to pretend, even within the democratic institutions of which they should be the willing servants, that they are benevolent divinities on some Olympus from which they govern the fates of wretched mortals. That illusionism (which has fed both democracies and totalitarianisms: I think among other things of the *invention* of the body of the leader, of the macho, of the best, the body like a saint's reliquary, of a heavenly nature) unfortunately for us has been definitively welded, thanks to a bold proprietary relationship, to the fictions of what is today the most powerful means of mass communication: television, that factory of *characters and protagonists*, as the media call them, justly adopting the terminology of products of the imagination. And the characters, the protagonists of social-television mythology, are experienced by the audience just as characters are in novels, by *suspending disbelief*, accepting, that is, an agreement on the basis of which you are willing to take as true everything you are told.

Berlusconi the statesman is possible only thanks to his tendentious monopoly of the medium that best realizes and imposes that suspension of disbelief. The *great protagonist* (what an abuse of greatness the media have accustomed us to) in effect has completed the transformation of citizens into an audience and is for now the most unprincipled exponent of the reduction of democracy to imaginary participation in an imaginary game. His money, his television channels, his market surveys have practically demonstrated that the interests of an individual can be installed overnight, thanks to a business group (not a party), on top of the political dissatisfaction of half of Italy, higher classes and lower classes, passed off as a heroic story of national salvation and, above all, without extinguishing democratic assurances.

It's not a nice thing, especially for true liberals. A novel about today that is engaging and full of characters and events should be a novel about and against the suspension of disbelief—here's a nice paradox I'd like to work on. It would describe the political dangers of today but also ask if it's still possible that from a credulous audience critical citizens can emerge, so as to knock the great characters and great protagonists off the media Olympus, reducing them to the measure of people among people.

But for now read my little story; after so much talk, it's all that I really have to offer you, for your initiative. I apologize meanwhile for the pointless outburst: if I don't have an outburst with you with whom would I?

Fondly,

Elena

Beautiful Form

I don't know what to write, I don't know if I can write.

Reluctant, I have in mind only Matteo Carraccio, a dark figure of twenty years ago. For years I sent Carraccio letters, written by me and signed by my grandmother: her name, her surname, her address. She lived in Camaldoli.

Carraccio was a man in his fifties, jovial, always slightly excessive in his voice, his gestures, his clothes—everything he wore was expensive. My grandmother told me his misdeeds on the telephone, I put pen to paper, but in vain.

They were small wrongs, quarrels about the apartment building up in Cappella Cangiani, amid the asphalt and concrete of the hill in Naples, four hundred meters above sea level. Carraccio didn't want her to use a certain passageway in the building. Carraccio extracted money for repairs that were never done. Carraccio maintained that he alone could park in the courtyard or have parties on the building's terrace. Carraccio claimed contributions for expenses necessary only for maintaining his own property. And although at the time I was overwhelmed by brutal university exams, I was forced to attend the building meetings to raise my voice in place of my grandmother, or write beautifully formulated, vainly threatening letters of protest.

A waste of time: powers great or small do not fear fine words, or even harsh ones. In fact they often make books of them through their publishing firms, and with concise arguments, with similes and metaphors, they gain advantage. Property appropriates for itself commas, periods, signs, bitterness, pale memories.

Carraccio was the owner of a great number of the apartments in the building; he himself occupied a very large one with all his numerous family. An engineer who was the son of an engineer, he had houses scattered over the Vomero hill. When the weather was good he sat on the terrace amid little trees and flowers of every type chatting with his wife and children; when it rained he was nervous, he was afraid, I think, that a chasm somewhere would swallow up his bricks. He had sold my grandmother her two-bedroom apartment. He hadn't wanted checks, he had insisted on cash. We grandchildren shouldn't have agreed, but my grandmother was so fond of the apartment, she was in love with it, and besides everyone said that paying in cash was normal; the notary himself was neither opposed nor surprised, he said merely: I, however, mustn't know anything about what you're doing. I had crossed Naples, I remember, with my heart racing, fearful that I would be robbed. I was young, however, and doing things that involved some risk also excited me. Less exciting was dealing with a man who respected no rule, while pretending to respect them all.

I've had a cup of tea. Now I'm writing again, but I can't wait to get to an ending and stop making a memory into a metaphor. Real names would be useful, nouns without adjectives, to describe how the rules of civic cohabitation come undone.

Carraccio, empowered because of the enormous number of square meters he possessed, had been named president, secretary, and administrator of the condominium. He always had a majority for every question and if someone challenged him he turned bitter and said he was the only one who had the good of the building at heart.

The worst fight with my poor grandmother exploded because of some small plants that, because she didn't have balconies, she kept on iron supports that she had had attached to the external wall, under the windowsills. My grandmother was very fond of those plants, some of which she had nurtured for years, some even for decades. But Carraccio found the iron supports illegal; he ordered her to get rid of them and have the damage done to the building wall repaired.

In response to my letters of protest he held a meeting of the condominium at which he proposed a new article in the rules which strictly forbade iron supports for plants under the windowsills, and had it voted on and approved. He succeeded not because he had the right but because he had the force.

Sometimes a memory is a tremor of resentment. I worked all afternoon to make a story out of something I detest, but I'm not pleased. It depresses me that the truth of an abuse of power seems an effect of rhetoric.

When the plants began to die, my grandmother, too, declined.

I drink another cup of tea, leaving on the monitor a long white space, then I began again from the beginning, still reluctantly. I wrote "Silvio Berlu," tapping the keys with one finger. "Sconi" I added later and felt annoyed.

NOTE
The letter is from April, 2002, and refers to an initiative of Edizioni E/O, which had asked its Italian authors to write a short story on conflict of interest. "Beautiful Form," reprinted here with some small corrections, appeared first in *Sette*, a supplement to *Corriere della Sera*, May 3, 2002, and then in *Micromega*, issue 3, 2002.

16

La Frantumaglia

Dear Sandra,

Here we go again. I thought I had gotten good at this after *The Days of Abandonment*, and instead look what I've done with the questions from the women at *Indice*.

I'm a little embarrassed, but I ended up in a sort of organizational frenzy, I opened drawers, I looked through books, and here we are.

I could keep all these pages for myself, but it was a pleasure to write them, and the passionate writer always needs an audience of at least one reader. Therefore I send you this endless letter and ask you to forward it to my interviewers, making it clear that I have no desire to make a shorter, publishable version.

If, when you have time, you, too, would read this ramble through the pages of the two books that I imagine—yes, imagine—I've written (real books take their own path and no longer belong to me), you would do me a great favor.

If you would then let me know what you think, I would be grateful.

Here is the letter.

Dear Giuliana Olivero, dear Camilla Valletti,

Thank you for your request for an interview. I tried to write clear, concise answers, but since you ask complex questions and do so with intelligence, the result seemed to me inadequate. So I dropped the hypothesis of the interview and began to write simply for the pleasure of answering you.

Vortexes

You ask me about suffering in my two books. You even come up with a hypothesis. You say that although Delia in *Troubling Love* and Olga in *The Days of Abandonment* are modern women, their suffering derives from the need to come to terms with their own origins, with archaic female models, with Mediterranean cultural myths still active within them. It may be. I have to think about it, but in order to do so I can't start with the lexicon that you propose: the word "origin" is overloaded; and the adjectives you use ("archaic," "Mediterranean") have an echo that confuses me. I would prefer, if you don't mind, to reflect on a word having to do with suffering that comes from my childhood and accompanied me during the writing of both books.

My mother left me a word in her dialect that she used to describe how she felt when she was racked by contradictory sensations that were tearing her apart. She said that inside her she had a *frantumaglia*, a jumble of fragments. The *frantumaglia* (she pronounced it *frantummàglia*) depressed her. Sometimes it made her dizzy, sometimes it made her mouth taste like iron. It was the word for a disquiet not otherwise definable, it referred to a miscellaneous crowd of things in her head, debris in a muddy water of the brain. The *frantumaglia* was mysterious, it provoked mysterious actions, it was the source of all suffering not traceable to a single obvious cause. When she was no longer young, the *frantumaglia* woke her in the middle of the night, led her to talk to herself and then feel ashamed, suggested some indecipherable tune to sing under her breath that soon faded into a sigh, drove her suddenly out of the house, leaving the stove on, the sauce burning in the pot. Often it made her weep, and since childhood the word has stayed in my mind to describe, in particular, a sudden fit of weeping for no evident reason: *frantumaglia* tears.

It's impossible now to ask my mother what she really meant

by the word. Interpreting in my own way the meaning she gave it, I thought as a child that the *frantumaglia* made you sick, and that, on the other hand, someone who was sick was fated sooner or later to become *frantumaglia*. What in fact *frantumaglia* was I didn't know and don't. Today I have in my mind a catalogue of images, but they have more to do with my problems than with hers. The *frantumaglia* is an unstable landscape, an infinite aerial or aquatic mass of debris that appears to the I, brutally, as its true and unique inner self. The *frantumaglia* is the storehouse of time without the orderliness of a history, a story. The *frantumaglia* is an effect of the sense of loss, when we're sure that everything that seems to us stable, lasting, an anchor for our life, will soon join that landscape of debris that we seem to see. The *frantumaglia* is to perceive with excruciating anguish the heterogeneous crowd from which we, living, raise our voice, and the heterogeneous crowd into which it is fated to vanish. I, who sometimes suffer from the illness of Olga, the protagonist of *The Days of Abandonment*, represent it to myself mainly as a hum growing louder and a vortex-like fracturing of material living and dead: a swarm of bees approaching above the motionless treetops; the sudden eddy in a slow body of water. But it's also the right word for what I'm convinced I saw as a child—or, anyway, during that time invented by adults that we call childhood—shortly before language entered me and instilled speech: a bright-colored explosion of sounds, thousands and thousands of butterflies with sonorous wings. Or it's only my way of describing the anguish of death, the fear that the capacity to express myself would get stuck—as if the organs of speech had been paralyzed—and everything I'd learned to control, from the first year of life until now, would start fluctuating on its own, dripping or hissing out of a body becoming a thing, a leather sack leaking air and liquids.

I could continue with the list: it's one of four or five words in my family lexicon into which I stuff everything I need. But in this case it's useful mainly for explaining that, if I had to say what suffering is for my two characters, I would say only: it's looking onto the *frantumaglia,* the jumble of fragments inside. I've kept a passage from *Troubling Love* that I didn't use, but I offer it here to talk about this looking onto. The episode has to do with the quality of Amalia's black hair and is narrated, naturally, by Delia as she investigates the death of her mother.

I had my father's fine hair. It was very thin and fragile, it had neither air nor light, it wouldn't obey, settling on my head any which way, and so I hated it. Styling it like my mother's—the chignon, the wave swelling over her forehead, the rebellious curl that sometimes grazed her eyebrow—was impossible. I looked angrily at myself in the mirror, Amalia had been treacherous, she hadn't given me her hair. She had kept for herself the luxuriant locks, she hadn't wanted me ever to be as beautiful as she was. She had given me inferior hair, pasted smoothly to my skull like a dull patina, of an uncertain color that seemed a mockery, brown weakly tending toward black—not the shiny pitch of her hair, not the dark shimmering molten glass into which all those who said to her how beautiful it is blew breath. No one said that to me. No matter that I left it loose and grew it long, so long, I dreamed, that it would reach my feet, longer, perhaps, than hers had ever been, for I can't remember her with her hair loose—no matter what, my hair remained an inelegant flutter in the air, buds that didn't burgeon profusely into beautiful hairdos, that had not even a trace of the power that gave her hair the energy of a rare plant in spring. So, once, I don't know how it began: I was twelve. Maybe I wanted an opportunity to withdraw into an indisputable reason for suffering; maybe I felt irremediably ugly and was tired of looking for beauty in myself; maybe I just wanted to challenge my mother, silently shout my hostility. Anyway, I stole her dressmaker's scissors, crossed the hall, locked myself in the bath-room, and determinedly cut my hair, dry-eyed, feeling a fierce joy. In the mirror a stranger appeared, an unknown visitor with a thin face, long, narrow eyes, a pale forehead, a wild misery in the moss covering the skull. I thought: I'm someone else. Immediately afterward I thought: my mother, too, under her hair is someone else. Other, then, and others, others, others. My heart pounding in my chest, I stared at the tufts of hair in the sink, on the floor. I felt a double urge: first I cleaned everything up carefully, I didn't want my mother to be upset by seeing the scattered hair; then I went to show her, to make her suffer, I wanted to tell her, Look, I no longer need to make my hair like yours. Amalia was sit-ting at her sewing machine, working. She heard me, she turned, what have you done, a breath. Her eyes were bright with tears, and the sockets turned purple. She didn't shout, she didn't beat me, she avoided the usual paths of a punish-ing mother. She saw something that wounded or frightened her. She began to cry.

I know why, ten years ago, I left that passage out of the book. The episode seemed to say too much about that mother-daughter relationship, and weakened other important moments; rereading it now, I haven't changed my mind, the symbolism of the hair is obvious, too exaggerated, evidently only modesty kept me from alluding to Samson and Delilah, or to Iris, who tears a lock of Dido's fair hair, freeing her from life, or to who knows what else in the confusion of material that crowds around the writer asking to be used, reused, remade, cited. Yet I find here passages that interest me now more than they did then: for example, Delia's insistence on eliminating from her body the image of the mother, as if her own develop-ment as a woman would be possible only by removing Amalia from herself; and Amalia's weeping at the end, weeping that we can't fully account for, it's out of place, excessive. Daughter and mother, child and adult see something; they see that merely putting a hand to the hair can shift everything, as in an earthquake. Delia looks through the window of the mirror and perceives a throng of others, beyond her own shorn head. Amalia looks beyond her daughter's ruined hair and glimpses something that not even she can describe but that is there and makes her dissolve in tears: my daughter is hostile to me, I won't expand in my daughter, her development will reject me, will shatter me. Suffering is in this act, which touches a deep chord: a wished-for hairstyle, a rejected hairstyle, the present that is crowded with many others, a gesture that burns bridges, breaks a chain, sets off an eddy that breaks up and causes tears. My two characters, Delia and Olga, originated in that act: women who hold on to their I, strengthen it, become hardened, and then discover that cutting your hair is enough to cause a collapse and lose solidity, to feel yourself a chaotic flow of debris that is still useful and of no use, polluted or reclaimed.

To see if this was true, I looked through the two books. I wanted to see how I constructed Delia, but I reread only some twenty pages. In the case of Olga a few lines were enough—I still had in my mind all the words for her. Finally I decided to reflect on them apart from the books, and I discovered that they have in common at least one trait: they are women who practice a conscious surveillance on themselves. Women of the preceding generations were closely watched over by parents, by brothers, by husbands, by the community, but they did not watch over themselves, or, if they did, they did so in imitation of their watchers, like jailers of themselves. Delia and Olga are, rather, the product of a new, yet very ancient sort of surveillance, a surveillance that has to do with the need to expand their lives. I'll try to explain in what sense.

The word "surveillance" has been badly tarnished by its

police use, but it's not an ugly word. It contains the opposite of the body dulled by sleep, a metaphor counter to opacity, to death. Instead, it displays watchfulness, vigilance, invoking not the gaze but, rather, an eagerness for feeling alive. Men have transformed surveillance into a sentinel's activity, a jailer's, a spy's. Surveillance is, if well understood, more an emotional tendency of the whole body, an expansion and an inflorescence on and around it.

This is an idea from long ago, a trace of which I found in the ugly *vigere* that I noticed with surprise in the passage of the hair cited above—I had forgotten it. But ugly writing often seems denser than beautiful writing. *Vigere*, burgeon or expand—a verb that indicates the spread of life—is in the root of *vigile*, watchful or vigilant, of *veglia*, wakefulness, and, it seems to me, illuminates the meaning of "surveillance." I think of the surveillance of the pregnant woman, of the mother over her children: the body feels a swelling wave all over, and every sense is affectionately active. I think also of women's age-old surveillance over all the activities that allow life to flourish. And I don't have in mind an idyllic condition: *vigere* is also to impose, to oppose, to expand with all one's forces. I am not among those who believe that the line along which vital female energy spreads is better than that of vital male energy; I believe only that it's different. And I'm happy to note that this differ-ence is increasingly visible. I think, then—to return to the par-ticular meaning of surveillance that I'm trying to define—of the relatively new fact of surveillance of oneself, of one's own specificity. The female body has learned the need to watch over itself, to take care of its own expansion, its own vigor. Yes, vigor. Today this noun may seem suitable only for the male body. But I suspect that at first it was mainly a female virtue, that the vigor of the woman was like that of plants, invasive life, rampant life, or, to take a word that makes a bad impres-sion, *vigenza*, force. I'm very attached to forceful women who practice surveillance on themselves and others in precisely the sense that I'm trying to explain. I like writing about them. I feel that they are heroines of our time. That's how I invented Delia and Olga.

Olga, for example, who has exercised over herself a "masculine" surveillance, who has learned self-control, and has trained herself to the prescribed reactions, emerges from the crisis of abandonment only by virtue of the close surveillance of herself that she manages to achieve: to remain vigilant, that is, to recover the desire for wakefulness, to mobilize for this purpose little Ilaria, entrust to her the paper cutter, tell her, if you see me distracted, if you see that I don't hear you, if I don't answer you, prick me—as if to say, hurt me, use your hostile feelings, but remind me of the need to live.

You see, for me the child armed with the paper cutter, ready to strike the mother to bring her back to wakefulness and keep her from losing herself, is an important image. In an earlier version Olga, shut in her apartment, increasingly unstable, reached the decision to arm her daughter and use childish hostility after yet another hallucination. The Neapolitan woman who, decades earlier, drowned herself in the waters of Capo Miseno because she couldn't tolerate abandonment—the *poverella*, as she was now called in the neighborhood, because she had killed herself, like Dido after the departure of Aeneas—had just appeared to her in the kitchen.

I have to make a cup of coffee, the coffee will take away my drowsiness. I went to the kitchen, I unscrewed the moka, I filled it with black powder, I screwed the top back on. Pay attention, I said to myself: attention even to how you breathe. When I was about to light the gas, I was afraid: what if I didn't turn it off afterward? That moment put in chronological order all the actions I had performed to prepare the moka, actions that until that moment had been sloppy, disorderly, not in sequence. I suspected that I hadn't put water in the bottom. You don't know how to be in the world, you can't be trusted. I unscrewed the top part, but I got my fingers wet, the water was there. Of course it was there, everything had been done as it was supposed to be done. I realized instead that I had filled the moka not with coffee but with a black dust that perhaps was tea. I was discouraged, I didn't have time to remedy it, I couldn't find the energy. I heard a rustling and saw that the woman of Piazza Mazzini was sweeping the kitchen with great concentration. She stopped a moment, she showed me her ring finger, she didn't have a wedding ring.

"The worst is taking it off," she said. "Mine wouldn't slide off, I had to have it cut. If I had known that I would get so withered I would have waited. It would have fallen off my finger, look what ugly hands I've got, the life went out of my fingers."

I realized that I didn't have a ring, either, I clenched my fingers into a fist to feel their strength. The woman smiled at me, she murmured:

"You'll see, if someone sweeps the broom over your feet you'll no longer be married. And if you're no longer married, see what happens."

As if to give me a demonstration, she began to sweep her feet insistently. I felt disgusted because that action was crushing them. Her feet were of a friable material that under the sweeps of the broom was flaking into bloody scales.

I cried: Ilaria.

Relations between Ilaria and Olga aren't good; they resemble those between Delia and Amalia. But, unlike Amalia, Olga, the woman of today, completes a journey that allows her to accept Ilaria's hostile love as a vital feeling, which can be used against the fascination with death that comes from the past, from the *poverella*. Together—mother and daughter—they will declare a right to the life outside, outside the model of broken women.

Now perhaps I can get to the heart of your question. The passage I've cited here—and others, not dissimilar, which I will spare you—went more or less explicitly in the direction you indicated. The *poverella* of Naples was, in the early versions of the story, loaded with symbols, a sort of synthesis of the abandoned woman, from Ariadne on. The wedding ring that has to be cut off the ring finger, the loss of vital energy, the broom as a condition of domestic slavery and as a sexual allusion, the anguish of not being married or remarried or of no longer finding men, the reduction to *frantumaglia*: Olga sees in that ghost all the female anguish of the patriarchal epoch and recognizes it in herself. But I didn't like that. I eliminated all of it, except the Virgilian allusion to Capo Miseno. I eliminated it because it didn't seem to me the right narrative path, I was afraid that there was a break between the before—archaic models and myths, precisely—and the after, Olga the new woman, and that Olga would seem to be an expression of the progressive fates of the female gender. I decided instead to deepen the confusion of time, as in *Troubling Love,* where what was Amalia is never different from what is Delia, and so only at the end can Delia state as a goal, as the high point of her own vital expansion, the positive result of her whole journey: Amalia had been, I was Amalia. I wanted the past not to be overcome but to be redeemed, precisely as a storehouse of sufferings, of rejected ways of being.

Here, for a better understanding, we should speak of how suffering modifies the image of time. The eruption of suffering cancels out linear time, breaks it, makes it into whirling squiggles. The night of time crouches at the edges of the dawn of today and tomorrow. Suffering casts us down among our single-celled ancestors, among the quarrelsome or terrorized muttering in the caves, among the female divinities expelled into the darkness of the earth, even as we keep ourselves anchored—let's say—to the computer we're writing on. Strong feelings are like that: they explode chronology. An emotion is a somersault, a tumble, a dizzying pirouette. When suffering hits Delia and Olga, the past stops being past and the future stops being future, the order of before and after ceases. Even writing about it has that movement of confusion. The "I" calmly tells a story, creates clear accounts, makes events go slowly. But when the wave of a feeling arrives the writing arches, becomes excited, spins around breathlessly absorbing everything, putting into circulation memories, desires. Delia and Olga have to gradually calm down so that their narrating "I" can return to the slow course of the story. The return is of brief duration. The pace that puts events in order is only the moment of gathering energy before a new tornado. This is an image that is useful to me: it allows me to think of a period of suffering that hits us advancing like a whirlwind; but also of a writing about emotions that has the sonority of breath, a wind from the lungs that, producing music, swirls the debris of different epochs and finally, whirling, passes.

Delia and Olga tell their stories from within that whirling. Even when they slow down they don't distance themselves, they don't contemplate, they don't carve out external spaces for reflection. They are women who tell their story from the middle of a dizzy spell. So they don't suffer because of the conflict between what they would like to be and what their mothers were, they are not the painful end result of a female genealogy that moves, in chronological order, from the ancient world, from the great myths of the Mediterranean, to end up at them as a visible peak of progress. Suffering derives, instead, from the fact that crowding around them, simultaneously, in a sort of achrony, is the past of their ancestors and the future of what they seek to be, the shades, the ghosts: up to the point, for example, where Delia, after taking off her clothes of the present, can put on her mother's old dress as the definitive garment; and Olga can recognize in the mirror, in her own face, as a constituent part of her, the figure of the *poverella*-mother who has killed herself.

The Beast in the Storeroom

I move on to your second question. It's true that I don't know how to trace a sharp line between guilt and innocence—I think it's clear from my books that these are concepts that confuse me. For example, the religious axe that separates the guilty from the innocent doesn't convince me. Nor does the distinction between those who are legally innocent and those who are legally guilty: there are people innocent according to the law who are stained with blackest guilt and people guilty before the law for whom I've felt sympathy, sometimes friendship. No, legal guilt and innocence don't help much. According to legal truth Adriano Sofri[5] commissioned a vile political murder, but his behavior as a man guilty according to the law has proved his innocence against every reasonable doubt, and the fact that he remains in prison is an abomination. Instead, if the present head of the government (I don't even want to name him), after founding a party with his wealth and his television stations, after entering parliament by means of his money and his company, after making laws that put him above the law, thanks to his countless billions and his media power—in other words, after devoting the major part of his political activity to manufacturing loaded dice for himself and

[5] Adriano Sofri: (b. 1942, Trieste) is a journalist, writer, and former leader of the left-wing militant movement Lotta Continua. He was sentenced in 1988 to twenty-two years in prison for instigating the murder of the police officer Luigi Calabresi. Sofri was released in 2012.

his friends—should one day be declared legally innocent, I would consider that path to innocence his greatest crime, the crime of one who makes arrogant use of economic and political power by demonstrating to the weakest citizens, between one stupid joke and the next, how cleverly democracy can be manipulated. As a result, today, as I write, justice has an admirable witness in jail while, precisely where it should be embodied by exemplary behavior, it is fatuously humiliated or flaunts moralists with a double or triple life. Besides, the entire political class that governs us, which has no culture, no brain, no sense of justice, ironically considers itself innocent and declares with a nauseating sly little smile that the crimes, if they exist, were committed by others. I hate the tone of voice in which these obtuse and blustering power brokers manipulate guilt and innocence. I don't trust their declarations of intent, their defenses, their proud and immodest self-definitions. I prefer people who are aware of the moral ambiguity of every gesture and try persistently to understand what they really do, both good and bad, to themselves and others.

For me, the so-called ethical problem began some decades ago, in a little room. There I had a desire to kill, and to punish myself for that desire; it was the secret location of a long conflict with my mother. But let's go in order, as far as possible. That little room—it appears in a few lines in *Troubling Love*—was a place without windows, without electric light, in my childhood home, in Naples. It was used as a storeroom and was so crammed with things that it was hard to enter; just passing by made me die of fear. Sometimes the door was left ajar, and a cold breath came out that smelled of DDT. I knew that it was the breath of a large beast, ugly as the yellowish larva of a cicada, ready to devour me. It was lying in ambush in there, amid old furniture, broken chairs, chests, lamps, an anti-gas mask, but I didn't tell anyone, maybe I was afraid of not being believed. The perils of the little room remained my secret.

When I was around nine or ten that room became for the first time a place of primary importance. My youngest sister, whom I will call Gina, was then four, and she was an annoying obstacle to the games of my other sister, who was seven, and me. No matter how often we said that Gina had passed through the sieve or under the bridge—slang expressions that meant: she's not in the game; she thinks she is but she isn't really, she runs through it, she's useless in it—she continued to bother us. If we chased her away, she went crying to our mother. If we threatened her, she became even whinier. If we hit her, she threw herself on the floor, screaming and kicking as if we had cut off an arm or a leg. She often asked, anxiously, with a friendly little smile: I'm playing, am I playing?

Once, in exasperation, I said in dialect: We need a rope, there's one in the storeroom. Note: I didn't say to Gina, We need a rope, it's in the storeroom, go get it. Instead, I expressed a need and indicated the place where, if you wanted, it could be fulfilled, nothing else. I was exasperated, I wanted my sister to die. I thought that she deserved it, because she disrupted our game and had done so from birth. Killing her wasn't a simple wish; it seemed to me a necessity, even though I knew that sisters don't kill each other. So I was satisfied with that phrase, which came to me naturally, and which I'll always remember, as the conscious beginning of my relationship with words: We need a rope, there's one in the storeroom. The syntax apparently let the child decide if she would go and die in the jaws of the beast or not. But I knew that she would go, she was too happy to have, at last, a precise task. The sentence pushed her and yet covered me, hid my murderous wish. In fact, she started off immediately, she needed a role, she couldn't believe she'd suddenly grabbed one. From that moment time stood still and I stopped breathing.

Here, then, the small child heads toward the place of horrors, she's running, afraid that my other sister will go in her place and she'll miss her chance. The ugly dwarf, the walking stink. Even my mother can't bear her, sometimes she shouts I can't take you anymore; so if the yellow beast eats her we're all happy. The monster is waiting, now he's an enormous fly with long transparent wings. He's eager to fill his stomach, but he's also furious because he, in turn, fills the black belly of the little room. He has big antennae and is constantly working his jaws. In his large belly there is room for at least two little sisters the size of mine, but chewed thoroughly, ground up. The image makes a wave in my stomach. The wave swells, it makes me dizzy and nauseous, it eats at my guts. I can't help it, I decide to stop my sister. I run, faster than Gina. I pass her, I enter the storeroom, I close the door behind me. I'm all sweaty, she shouts furiously that she wants to come in, terror freezes my hearing, the beast advances, who will save me. I heard my mother's voice saying Open that door immediately, and the beast retracted its claws.

I emerged. Gina saw me and began to scream even louder, she bit her knuckles, she threw herself kicking on the floor. Then my mother lost patience; she was a very anxious woman at the time. She tried to calm the child, but she couldn't and got angry with me: why had I shut myself in there, why didn't I want Gina to come in? Because, I said stupidly, it's our game and she shouldn't disrupt it. I got a slap.

Later, I thought a lot about that slap, bitterly; I was a meticulously reflective child. I couldn't understand: I had kept my sister from being devoured by the beast even though she deserved it, and my mother treated me as if I were the guilty one? Guilty of what? Of not wanting the little girl to ruin our games? So, to be innocent, I had to willingly accept that the third sister should make the first two unhappy? And didn't it count that I had intervened to save from death the cause of my unhappiness, of the whole family's unhappiness?

It took time to get beyond that; it required that games be

replaced by soliloquy, a ghost-packed mental theater that lasted through the years, question and answer.

Was I not guilty anyway, guilty of words designed to be a fatal trap?

Yes, but on the other hand who had made me guilty?

She, the little girl.

And how?

With her intrusive behavior.

So was she the guilty one, before I became the guilty one?

No. But she wasn't innocent.

What would she have had to do to be innocent—exclude herself from the game, not disturb the alliance between the other sister and me, exist elsewhere or not exist at all?

Yes, certainly yes.

Innocence—I began to convince myself—is never to get into the situation of arousing malicious reactions in others. Difficult but possible. So I taught myself to be silent, I apologized for everything, I reined in my tongue, I was polite and compliant. Yet secretly I was bad. I didn't know how to calm the blood that made me potentially a fury, I was seething, and for that I tortured myself. I knew that I was the child who had been able to find the sentence that would send the little girl to her death without taking her there in person. I knew I possessed the capacity to do harm through words without being seen, without bearing the responsibility. I hated myself. My innocence was really a talent for shunting: I hid ferocity behind an appearance of kindness and then I shifted it into words that seemed innocuous but could induce in people who injured me thoughts and actions that could hurt them.

Soon it seemed to me that I was a beast who pretends to be tame; in every human relationship I saw only chains of guilt, an infinite number of reasons to respond to evil with evil—I saw no innocence. Yet often I argued about redemption. When I felt discouraged and sought a less sinister image of myself, I

pointed out that I had run to keep my little sister from entering the room. In reality, I reassured myself, I have a good heart.
I felt redeemed.

But then I tended to complicate everything again. Didn't
redemption mean that there was a sin to redeem? How could
redemption cancel out the fact of guilt? Isn't it hypocritical, I
thought, to inject first the poison of fury and then the antidote? So why did I rush to keep Gina from falling into the
trap? Why had I hurried to die in her place? Was it possible,
with that change of mind, to cancel out my wish for her death?

I pressed on, gnawed by a sense of guilt, especially when my
youngest sister, growing up, infuriated her teachers, did badly
in school, complicated in every possible way the life of our
family, told lies about herself so as to seem a model girl, and
then confessed her wrongdoing in front of all of us with intolerable humiliation. I went back to the little room. I thought:
she's like that because I excluded her from our games, she'll
end up excluded from everything, it would have been better to
let her die. I had never seriously rid myself of that desire to kill
her. Rushing to keep her from ending up in the mouth of the
beast hadn't signaled a change at all. The negative feelings of
before had returned afterward. What then had that moment of
devotion been?

The answer at a certain point was brutal: that moment had
been purely a reaction to physical disgust. The image of my sister's body reduced to a bloody pulp had created in me an
unendurable anxiety. And I had run to the door of the little
room solely to rid my body of the disgust. But then what was
redemption? A way of silencing the anxiety of one's own body
when it had acted out of anxiety about someone else's body?

Now I was grown up, and the more I hated any opportunism the more I discovered it in my own actions, my own
words. So eventually, in the end, I appreciated my mother's
slap. That senseless punishment seemed like the reality of all

punishments. It served to balance the accounts of the wrong I had already done, justifiably restoring my hatred for my sister and the legitimacy of the desire to kill her. And so later—I remember clearly—I planned other, less repugnant ways to eliminate her: poison her, push her out the window, hang her, in a way not to arouse reactions that would then force me to redeem myself. And so? Was I made to do evil? Or was it not my nature but the wrongs of others that led me to evil and did that evil then lead my mother to wrong me and that wrong reinvigorate the desire for murder, in a chain that would never end?

I was blocked. I found a way out only when at eighteen I swallowed two thousand years of Christianity in Kantian pills. I concentrated obsessively on giving myself a will that was good in itself and I began a wearying struggle to keep external objects from adjusting my will to their requirements. In that daily battle it seemed to me that I resolved all my moral problems and for a while, as long as the effort lasted, I forgot the day that, thanks to a skillful formulation, I had sent my sister to die in the storeroom.

But the journey isn't that orderly; it's writing that makes it so. From that little room to the room in which I'm writing now the way is long and much more twisted, with more detours. The road that at the time seemed secondary later acquired force and became primary. That disgust, for example. And the arrival of my mother. Later I often closed myself in the storeroom, just to test her, to see if she cared about me, if she loved me more than anyone else. So allow me to go back, to when I was about ten, and start again from the moment when I shut myself in the storeroom to keep my sister from entering. Had I really decided to let myself be torn to pieces in her place? I don't know. I preserve distant emotions, confused with feelings that came later. I kick at the darkness, I overturn objects, I break things, a destructive activity that should keep away not only the yellow beast but also my revulsion. I make noise, I shout, against Gina, against fear, and I even feel a slight pleasure, because in the effort to create a racket the disgust passes, the fury of the body diminishes, the evil that I do and that I fear is done to me is a warm, vivifying fluid. Most important, I feel that my mother hears me and will come.

I'm glad she's coming and yet I fear her, sometimes she's worse than the yellow beast, she frightens me when she's nervous, I have the impression that she's returning from the blackness of the black of the storeroom like a ghost. But when she's not nervous she's very kind; for example, when she nursed Gina she would let us sit beside her. My sister and I watched, lost, as the infant greedily attached herself to Mamma's flesh and sucked without stopping. We waited for her to get tired but she never did, she remained attached until she fell asleep. And when she slid unwillingly into sleep and her pale, milky lips slowly gave up the nipple, our mother smiled at us with her dark eyes and let white drops from her breasts drip into our mouths, a warm, sweet taste that stunned us.

She had a miraculous and cruel body, our mother, she did wonderful things but granted us only a small taste, otherwise she was devoted only to Gina. I harassed her, I was always calling her, I insisted that she hurry immediately whenever I wanted her. She became mean, especially if the call was only a whim. But to me every whim seemed a necessity: that day in the storeroom the necessity seemed undeniable. When my mother came running she seemed good, I thought that putting myself in danger would bring her to me more quickly, in some way more justly, as if my being at risk restored me to her and her to me after a guilty absence. The slap not only seemed unjust but, when I thought about it, gave the injustice deep roots, seemed a disappointing response to a cry of fear.

It's here, starting from that disappointment, that the storeroom stops being the place of a deathly ambush for my sister and becomes something more elusive, a space permanently inhabited in memory by my mother and me alone, the sort of place where, as in certain dreams, always the same action, always the same need is repeated.

But in order to understand I should first tell you what happened to me in those years. My father, like Delia's, was very jealous. It was a jealousy that was based on the pure and simple fact that my mother was beautiful. What made my father jealous wasn't that my mother might betray him with a particular man, a neighbor, a friend, a relative. If he had thought such a thing, he would have killed her instantly, her and her putative lover. My father's jealousy was preventive. He was jealous of the pleasure that other men might feel in looking at her, being near her, talking to her, touching I won't say her, something inconceivable, but by chance the edge of her dress. He was jealous of the possible, he was even more jealous of my mother's power than of any acts she could have committed. He was jealous from the beginning, without selectivity, he was jealous of the fact that my mother, being a living body, exposed herself to life. As a result it wasn't in other men that my father saw the source of every threat, not at all. The likely rivals were there, on the other shore, and couldn't do anything but be dazzled by the vital flow of which my mother was the origin. Instead it was her body, in every gesture, that was guilty of that dazzlement. My mother had the naked guilt of being a source of possible pleasures for others.

I believed in that guilt, it was a secret conviction I'd always had; even today it returns in dreams at dawn. As a child I hoped that my father would lock her in the house and not let her go out. I hoped that he would order her to stay in one room, without even breathing, whenever friends or relatives visited. I was sure that she would do terrible things if she merely appeared, and so I hoped that she would be forbidden to expose herself. But contradictorily that didn't happen. My father in fact couldn't bear her to be ugly, he got angry if a sentence, a word seemed to restrict his wife's beauty, he was the first to encourage the care of her looks. He once gave her a lipstick, and I often unscrewed the top of the container to smell its exciting fragrance. When they were going out together I looked apprehensively at my mother, I saw her touch the surface of the lipstick with one finger, and she was immediately even more beautiful than she had been. My father, too, looked at her enchanted and anxious, aggressive and lost. He was dizzy with the pleasure of feeling that he was the unique beneficiary of all that beauty, and yet, at the same time, his anxiety at having to expose her to the lust of the world increased. I didn't understand him, I became silently angry, frightened. His anguish was mine, I was as alert as he was. Yes, I would have liked him to be more determined, not to punish her with angry quarrels after the sin of exposing herself but simply to forbid her to expose herself.

All that was the norm of my childhood. The abnormal moment, instead, the most terrible, happened when my father wasn't home and my mother decided to go out alone, without his consent.

I studied her, then, while she got ready with her usual care. It was useless to hope that in that circumstance she would decide to go out looking slovenly, unkempt—in other words, less visible. My mother never set foot outside the house without attending to every detail of her appearance, and that threw me into a state of growing anxiety. Every gesture in front of the mirror seemed to me an excess: an excess of danger, a further offering of herself to the rapacity of the streets, of the buses and trams, of the shops. I followed her step by step through the house, I was angry with her, I hated her. I thought: she'll be stolen, that's what she wants, she makes herself beautiful in order to leave us and never return. When the door of the house closed behind her elegant body, I was gripped by panic, I trembled, I couldn't calm down.

The time of her absence was interminable. In my mind I

imagined abominable things, and what I imagined made me vile in my own eyes. Yet the fantasies became an unbearable reality, I considered my mother guilty of confused but repulsive crimes, I hoped she would never return. Soon, however, that wish seemed intolerable, I was disgusted with myself for having conceived it, anything—I said to myself—provided she returns. She didn't return. Then I stopped playing with my sisters and went almost on tiptoe into the storeroom.

I opened the door, I entered the darkness, I closed the door knowing that only my mother's voice in the house would have the magical power to let me out. I didn't move, I breathed in the odor of DDT, I wept silently. The beast moved cautiously in the dark but didn't attack me, it was there together with many other colored shapes of the horror, which licked me and retreated. Time was suspended, my body itself lost its dimensions, it was as if something were breathing inside, inflating me: I was afraid I would burst, I touched my skin and it felt smooth and tense as a bladder.

I daydreamed. I imagined that my mother had only pretended to go out and instead was here and was now spying on me to find out if I truly loved her. I thought that she didn't like me, so inflated in the darkness, and I pressed my chest and stomach with my hands, but I felt like sobbing and the more I pressed the more I cried. I thought that, wherever she was, she could truly feel me in danger, and I let the terror grow like a summons, so that far away she would be touched by my dilated body and with a start would leave the repulsive things she was doing and return. How terrible that internal tension was, a noise, words, the very voice of my mother that was blowing inside me as if into a balloon.

Until I heard her footsteps in the house. Then my mood changed, I became sharp and bitter. I resisted joy, I didn't come out, I wanted to hear my name in her worried voice, I wanted her to look for me without finding me. I imagined that she would open the door of the little room and I would pull her in unexpectedly and barricade myself there with her and give her to the beast, who now was my friend, and he would devour her in a corner. But she didn't look for me, she didn't call me or even come to look in the storeroom. Then I emerged. I circled around her, her body set off a wave of revulsion in me, I examined her to discern the traces of the crimes my father would have attributed to her if he had known that she had left the house. I did it fearing I really would discover those signs. I did it hoping to find them before he did, to help her eliminate them in time, so that they wouldn't be seen.

Of this self-seclusion in the storeroom I've written many times but unsuccessfully. Over the years it's become a difficult object to arrange on a plain page. Yet surely my two books start from there. The closed door, the imagining of evil, the fear: why did I shut myself in there? The most linear answer I've found is the following: the fear that the little room inspired kept at bay the anguish about my mother's fate. But I know it's a lazy response. Being in the dark, in the most feared place in the house, was perhaps a form of expiation and at the same time a desperate cry of love. I eliminated the spaces of the apartment, I eliminated the window that looked out on the street at the end of which my mother had disappeared and on which she had to return. I abolished my body, I gave it to the forces of darkness, I let it expand until it was reduced to a tightly stretched skin. I immolated myself, I delivered myself to terror to gain her salvation in exchange. Was I then the innocent who sacrifices herself to redeem the guilty? Or was I the guilty one who punishes herself to restore innocence to the victim? I don't know. At ten I felt I was in an intolerable situation: I feared that whenever my mother went out she would betray us, abandon our just path for that of others, and that crime of hers made me detest her, I couldn't forgive the lightness with which she wounded my love, made it insufficient, humiliated it, took away faith in it; on the other hand I felt that she was incapable of abandoning us, I felt it in her body, in her eyes, and, instead, the fact that I had thought it, had imagined it, assumed an intolerable weight.

To conclude: today I believe that the degree of our innocence derives not from the absence of guilt but from the capacity to feel true loathing for our daily, recurring, private guilt. The feeling of what is right is rooted in the shudder of revulsion that makes our skin crawl, in the expression of disgust that crosses the face of the murderer as he kills his victim. Women have a memory of that expression, of that shudder, they know how many specters they harbor, and—I believe—they have always frequented shadowy storerooms more than men.

From within these rooms the religious or legal order of the male city appears a simplification, an enclosure where the miscellaneous crowd of ghosts can be chased to the edges. And perhaps, to get to the bottom of your question, it's really this which makes the difference. Women still entertain ghosts, we have long experience with exhausting secret negotiations with *revenants* that sink their teeth into you as they caress you, and we don't avoid them, we know that they are true inhabitants of that tangle of veins, blood, liquids, flesh that is our body. Men instead have long since retreated, they rule broad territories in the light of the sun, in the light of the sun they slaughter the helpless, bomb, humiliate, destroy, but at night with the blades of spotlights they cut through knots that are too tangled, and if they meet their ghosts they get frightened and right away call a doctor, a policeman, a lawyer, some godsend who will draw a line of demarcation between good and evil.

The Image of the Mother

I have to confess that when, around the age of sixteen, I learned something about psychoanalysis, it frightened me, and it still frightens me. I know why. It induces us to cast a long gaze, beyond every established order, and when our visual range returns to normal nothing is as it was before, every conversation seems a mask of words that is worn to hide our anguish. Not surprisingly, it's a fear that attracts me, and I especially like the visionary boldness in psychoanalytic discourse, the corrosive power concealed behind the therapeutic promise. Otherwise I belong to the crowd of the dubious. Is it therapy, is it thaumaturgy? I've never been in analysis. But it's rare that one saves oneself from a rickety landing at the top of a building by throwing oneself down the stairwell.

I love Freud, and I've read a fair amount of him: it seems to me that he knew better than his followers that psychoanalysis is the lexicon of the precipice. I scarcely know Jung. I read Melanie Klein passionately. I know almost nothing of Lacan, I know a lot about Luce Irigaray, I've followed the confrontation and the battles in Italy between the different lines of feminist thought. How much those readings and others and the speeches and discussions have influenced my books is a mystery to me; I'm a reader who quickly forgets everything she reads. I hope, however, that the debts I've contracted are of little importance, I don't like stories that are a programmatic enactment of the theory of the group one belongs to.

On the other hand, how to deny that *Troubling Love* comes in part from what, at the end of the eighties, I knew about the research and the debate on female childhood and on girls' attachment to the mother? The very title of the book, for example, preserves traces of a passage of Freud's essay "Female Sexuality" (1931) concerning the girl's pre-Oedipal phase: "In reality during that phase," Freud writes, "the father is for the girl only a troublesome rival." Troublesome rival, a "*rivale molesto*" in Italian. At the time, Edizioni E/O was proposing titles for my first book like *Il molestatore* (*The Troublesome Man*), *Molestie sessuali* (*Sexual Harassments*), and

I remembered that phrase of Freud's, which I thought would be a good title: *Rivale molesto* (*The Troublesome Rival*). But then the reference to the paternal image seemed misleading, and, in what for me was an important shift, I finally chose *Amore molesto* (*Troubling Love*). It seemed in keeping with the story that love should be troubling, the love that makes the father the daughter's rival, the exclusive love for the mother, the single great tremendous original love, the matrix of all loves, which cannot be abolished.

It was a theme that interested me at the time and still does today; women analysts and women philosophers have done work on the pre-Oedipal phase in girls with fascinating results, and literary writing can only make use of it. But I would insist that I don't like repeating and reinforcing the lexicon of some orthodoxy. I prefer stories that, if they are really stories, plunge down the path of suffering without paying attention to the "right way." I always read stories by women with trepidation: novels, diaries, narratives of women's lives that touch dark depths. I expect something that seemed unsayable to appear miraculously on the page, and miracles are possible, sometimes they happen. But when I feel that the story, whether invented or real, is concerned with being "correct," I pull back unhappily, I sense a flaw in the excavation that women in particular should not allow themselves. We have to watch ourselves, attend to our very individual expansion into the internal lands that are ours, and drill, searching beyond the tested vocabulary. Better to make a mistake with the incandescent lava we have inside, better to provoke disgust with that, than to assure ourselves success by resorting to murky, cold finds.

Psychoanalytic theory is, like all the objects of this world, of ambivalent usefulness. It names psychic reality, takes credit for it, in short organizes into universalizing representations what in the individual, beyond any system, beyond any analysis, remains pure specific inner disorder, irreducible flashes of ectoplasm, a jumble of fragments without any chronology. If the storyteller resorts to that inventory lazily he has no hope of making a true story. Psychoanalysis is a powerful stimulus for those who want to dig inside, it can't be disregarded, it conditions us even when we reject it, it's the map for any treasure hunt amid the shadows of our body. A map, however, is only a map. Neither a cross, nor a tall tree, nor Skeleton Island is enough to make *Treasure Island*. It's a matter of insuring that the story, even if it starts with named and studied psychic objects, has sufficient inventive force to continue on where there are no reassuring signposts or recognizably commendable tones.

As far as I'm concerned, when I write I hate all the clichés of analysis and I confess that I put aside many pages of both *Troubling Love* and *The Days of Abandonment* precisely because they seemed like a textbook. It was frequently painful, because what I was narrating was mine, I had struggled to dig it out and find a form for it, I was sorry to waste it because I had been unable to avoid the influx of soothing formulas. Here is an example from my second book; the unpublished passages give me a melancholy satisfaction.

Suddenly I had before me two beings in one, bodies of different times now superimposed. Ilaria is three, maybe younger. I saw her as she was now, at seven, hateful and beloved at the front door, and as she had been only four years earlier in the living room, a tormenting doll, two Ilarias and a single one.

The child of before is on the couch, stomach down, but her legs aren't stretched out, she's on her knees. She's wearing a red dress, white underpants, it's summer. I stop in the doorway, she doesn't seem to notice me. Her chin sinks into the green pillow, there is a veiled look in her round, wide-open eyes, her cheeks are red, her hair pasted to her sweaty forehead. Her arms are crossed, they disappear under her stomach, they go up and down with effort, she's panting. I intuit that she is working with both hands on her sex. She's moving like a reddish spider, wounded, last gasps. I'm ashamed of her, I know that children masturbate, I'm a mother who has done her reading. But just the same I'm ashamed. Did the blond babysitter with the reddened skin teach her? Did she do it to gain the child's affection and hear her say don't go, I love you, and so be sure of keeping the job? Did I teach her without wanting to, out of the need to be loved by that always hostile child? And how did it happen, when? Little machine of rosy flesh, she touches herself frantically, as I must have done at her age.

That thought was enough. Yes, that thought was enough to see three children now, three Ilarias, but the smallest was me, I was masturbating as I pretended to wash myself, I felt the soap on my fingers, a sensation that remains, and I like it, I often dream that I'm washing my hands and I use up the whole bar of soap, I washed for hours with the motion that my mother had taught me.

I looked and was afraid. We were three, Ilaria at seven, who was staring at me, I who resembled her but was as young as I appeared in a picture of many years earlier on a beach, Ilaria at three lying on the couch masturbating and wetting the green cushion with saliva. All in the same time but in no time, I no longer knew if the time was now or then or a vortex of hot wind. I knew only that Ilaria in her red dress had looked up, had seen me, but hadn't stopped touching herself, in fact she had smiled at me with a child-ish smile that was also an expression of weariness. And I had thought I shouldn't reproach her. But maybe I should have, and uttered a prohibition, as is always done, shouted at her what are you looking at, stop it, and don't laugh, what's behind that look and that smile, I know you, I know everything about everything, beloved child, spiteful child, I know that if you had the strength and the malice you would twist my neck and then you would fuck my corpse. As she is dreaming of doing now, I saw it in her eyes. It's a dream that's already vanishing, and yet she will cultivate the feeling as long as she lives.

Texts like that seem to me missed opportunities. I remember that as I was writing my heart was racing and that rapid heartbeat frightened me, pushing me back toward known terrain, I felt it was urgent to get to the end quickly and calm down. But that is precisely the wrong way to tell a story. If your heart accelerates you have to let it accelerate, and run the risk of letting it burst. On the page I cited I know that something came to the surface, the living tail of a reptile that is darting off. I even know where the something is: it's in Olga's look at little Ilaria who is masturbating. I should have stayed there and kept the wriggling material from slipping away. But I couldn't do it, I let go and retreated into illustrative writing, into cryptic citations, to expel the bitterness from my blood.

That is the worst sin the writer can commit. And also the worst sin of someone who reflects on what he has written. You ask, for example, if, in writing about betrayals, I kept in mind the original betrayal of the parental images. I am inclined to answer, with the slight agitation of someone who fears she will be coming out into the open when she wishes to remain sheltered: yes, of course, I had them in mind. But it's not true, it's not true in those words: I wanted to avoid the slightest allusion to such formulas, they would be ice for the writing, saying everything and nothing. So I aspired to go beyond, forget the formulas, tell a story that I knew well and that as a writer I wanted literally to get to the bottom of. When we tell a story, the only thing that should matter is to find a cascade of our words that will flood all the marked-out territory with the persistence—even if devastating—of a mucilage. In the case of abandonment, I tried to tell what a destabilizing force is released even today, even when the abandoned woman has considerable tools for defense, resistance, counterattack. Often, the narration of the crisis seemed to rest on quicksand; I thought it was necessary to give Olga more story, more past, more motivations. I worked a lot to that end. But when I realized that I risked either normalizing her tragedy or confusing the abandoned woman with the cold investigating Delia of the preceding book—whose literary sister she is in any case—when, especially, I realized that, by dint of looking for motivations, I was about to return somewhat pedantically to the theme of attachment to the mother, I let it go. Of that journey into the past I kept only a few essential passages, the rest ended up in a drawer. From which I'm now pulling out a few pages for you, those (deleted from the book) which relate to how Olga makes an effort to understand Mario's betrayal by resorting to a reexamination of her own erotic experience, occasions when she planned to betray him.

This sleeping together, what a mistake: a habit that casts out the foundations of solitude and prepares one for the chill of when the other opens the door and leaves.

I remained in the dark all night, in the bed, besieged by a parade of pale shades. Mario talking, Mario laughing, Mario in each of his charming gestures. My sisters and my mother had immediately liked him. My father hadn't, my father merely said a few cold words. For a while I was afraid that he was really hostile, but he was only timidly aloof, then he seemed to get used to him, as if to an annoying obstacle that you automatically avoid in order not to bump your forehead.

I wasn't sorry about that indifference; I didn't much love my father, ever since I was a child I had felt him as an intruder who gave off a heavy odor of the fish market, sordidly alien to the good smells of the family. Better that he should have little to do with Mario. Better, in fact, that Mario should have nothing to do with any of my relatives. I didn't like that my mother, in emotional tones, often praised his blue-green eyes, and she began to talk about the identical color of her father's eyes, her older brother's, her grandfather's. I liked Mario's eyes a lot, but it irritated me that she brought them back to herself, to her own family. I had hazel eyes and sometimes, when I saw Mario coddled by all the women in the house, I felt excluded, I feared that, starting with my eyes, he, too, would feel that I was repulsively alien to my mother's attractive lineage. I decided to keep him away from my house, in fact I planned to leave it soon; it was a plan I had harbored for a long time, ever since I'd dreamed of abandoning the whole family one night and going to live with the dark-eyed Gypsies.

We had our first sexual relations at his parents' house, in silence, in his room, which in its disorder resembled a storeroom. We were both inexperienced. He couldn't penetrate me, I pretended it was nothing but I felt only that it hurt. At a certain point he knelt on the bed, gently spread my legs, and examined my sex like an engineer, as if he were making calculations. Afterward he lay down again and began to push the tip of his sex against mine, helping with his hand and asking, in an always polite whisper: Am I hurting you? I said no and suffered. When finally he entered me, I hugged him hard so that he would feel my gratitude. He never got angry, he didn't blame me, and for that, I realized, I truly loved him and would love him my whole life.

We married two years later, and in time we gained sufficient experience with our genitals. I taught him to caress me for a long time, he was patient and skillful. Reflecting on it now, I loved—more than his thin, adolescent body with its pale skin, more than his slender sex, elegantly erect—his obedient willingness, the domestic flavor he had, the odor. I yielded to his arms as if they were a garment of early childhood and I had become a girl again while remaining miraculously adult, without even the annoying obligation to act like a child. I contributed diligently to his pleasure, I welcomed him inside me, I let him heave with his unexpectedly fierce thrusts. But what truly bound me to that tense body, eagerly desiring me, was the impression of sweet drowning that it gave me, as if his thrusts had propelled me into the hot blood inside my own veins.

For three years I took little notice of the attentions of men of any age, they were like the indecipherable gestures of shadows on walls, there was only Mario. Then I met the brother of a woman I knew, someone who worked at a newspaper. He generally expressed himself with a cultured sarcasm, but in my presence he became abruptly distracted. Knowing he liked me made me like him, yet I never thought of him as a possible lover. Still, I began to want him to want me. I made no effort to see him more often, but when I knew I might see him I took special pains with my appearance, and to run into him, to feel his silent passion, provoked in me an ill-contained joy. I had coffee with him and noticed his unease if he barely grazed me or his pleasure if he made me laugh. Once he tried to kiss me, I pushed him away with disgust. He said he loved me, he seemed to have understood that I felt something for him. I answered that I felt nothing, and he became depressed, he mumbled that I had led him on. For a while he continued to insist, I continued to dress up for him; I didn't like giving up that game. Then he got tired of it, he made a point of not running into me, I forgot his existence. Sometimes, however, I went back to the café where that attempt at a kiss had taken place, tasting a melancholy residue of emotion.

In bed now, in the vast marriage bed, I said to myself that if I wanted to understand why Mario had left me I should think back to the pleasure of slight flirtations like that, with no consequences, a harmless, frivolous pleasure that lightened the days. Maybe for him, too, it had begun like that, I should accept the fact, understand the normality of his betrayal from the norm of my games of seduction. But why had he crossed the line whereas I hadn't? I reflected. There are those who stop and those who don't, and we can't understand what sets us off down the slope and what blocks us. Over the years my occasions for little flirtations multiplied, and they became a secret vice, I knowingly sought them in order to repeat the sensation they gave me of a full life. When they began, I got from them greater con- sideration for myself, I suffered less from my duties as a wife and mother who no longer worked, they made me feel like reading, studying, writing again. Above all, I suddenly marveled at what I looked like, my mouth, eyes, breasts; I went to the hairdresser more often, bought new underwear and clothes. Time was marked by occasional encounters with my current admirer, men who were charming and so charmed me, never sought out, at most encouraged by the sum of circumstances—the presentation of a book, a party I decided to go to only because I knew he would be there. In those circumstances even sensitivity was as if heightened. If in the course of a walk or a drive a passionate phrase crossed the smell of burned stubble or simply of gas in the traffic, the burning, the gas that ran from the pump to fill up the tank began to excite me even when the possible lover had ended in nothing, without real events.

Once only I let myself be kissed and during the kiss I didn't push away the hand that pressed on my shirt, sought me under my skirt. I crossed that threshold not out of desire but because I felt sorry for the man. He was the owner of a big bookstore in the center. He had the sly, complacent eyes of one who is always joking with the clerks, and it was clear that he considered them happy recipients of his good humor as the boss. But in a short time his passion for me made him serious, he was constantly trying to achieve a depth of feeling and thought for which he had no aptitude. That evening he seemed worn out by the unfulfilled desire that I roused in him. We were in the car, on a street not far from my house, and I was afraid that Mario would come back from work, that some neighbor might see me. I didn't feel well, I had a sore throat, maybe the flu. His rough tongue in my mouth disgusted me, it seemed salty, acid with tobacco. I asked myself why I was with him, a stranger, why what was happening was happening, my whole body felt empty, empty of words and feelings. Yet, incongruously, in perceiving that dispiriting emptiness, I felt a pleasant excitement that embarrassed me. I said in a hurry that I had to go, I opened the door and ran off. When I came in Mario was already home, dinner wasn't ready, I began cooking. I had in my mouth the repulsive taste of that man, in my nostrils his odor of tobacco, and I was angry because the revulsion clashed with a lasting sexual excitement. As soon as I could I went to the bathroom to wash off the nicotine, Mario didn't smoke, nor did I. I rubbed my teeth with a lot of toothpaste, over and over. I took a shower, I went to bed, but the excitement didn't pass. I wasn't even lying down when Mario put his hand under my nightgown to touch my sex. I had a rash reaction, I jumped up, I began attacking him with harsh words of disdain for that lack of respect. I stared into his blue-green eyes, which usually filled me with emotion. Instead I felt a sudden revulsion for that family color, as if he belonged to the genealogy of my blood and that made him repugnant. Mario was stunned, he didn't understand, I didn't understand, either. I was wrong, I knew it, and yet I felt absolutely certain that I was right. I felt a fierce rage at his attempt to touch me with that invasive gesture, and the fact that it was a long-standing habit, that he did it every night before going to sleep, like a kind of good night, made me even angrier. I had no privacy, then, I was exposed to a sort of permanent control of emotions. It was intolerable, I couldn't calm down. It seemed to me that he had no right to intrude, I was sure in that moment that it was right to defend the secrecy of the body's reactions, my life was my life.

Mario said nothing, he withdrew in confusion. I went furiously into the kitchen to make a tisane. The next day the bookseller looked for me, he was no longer on the verge of profound thoughts, he joked and laughed lightheartedly, he seemed sure that after that kiss, after his hands on my shirt, under my skirt, everything was clear between us, now he had only to find a way of giving a satisfying outlet to our passion. He was amazed, he smiled, incredulous, when I told him that I didn't feel that need and coldly said that I hadn't liked his kiss, I didn't really like anything about him. He didn't believe me, he harassed me for days, for months. I stopped seeking opportunities to meet, and finally he resigned himself. I didn't see him again.

But the yearning to be courted soon returned. The darkest story was recent, it had involved the husband of a colleague of Mario's. It happened a year after our first marital crisis. I was depressed, I despised my mediocrity, the children especially were exhausting. Since I went around the house with a mournful air that was unbearable to me especially, Mario, maybe to distract me, maybe to avoid staying alone with me, began a crowded program of dinners to which he invited methodically all his colleagues at the university. He cooked, he had the children help him, making it a game, I confined myself to the role of mistress of the house and at most I cleared the table with an empty head, reluctantly putting pots and plates in the dishwasher late at night.

Everything changed the night Cecilia came. She was a very cultured, stylish woman in her fifties, she wore beautiful lapis-lazuli earrings, and had deep eyes, a woman for whom Mario had so much respect that he became tongue-tied. I didn't know her except through the devoted stories of my husband, but just seeing her I felt a great emotion. I liked everything about her, I was moved that she immediately talked to me in a tone of genuine interest, so that, surprised at myself, I began to talk to her easily about the work I had done in the past, the book I had written, how I felt trapped, hopeless.

Her husband arrived later. He was an architect from Ferrara transplanted to Turin and worn down by endless obligations. The same age as Cecilia, he was tall and very thin, with a thick blond beard that must once have been red, brusque manners, words that verged on the offensive. Ernesto—his wife said in a low tone as soon as he began to laugh too loudly—the children are sleeping. And he recomposed himself immediately, turned to me as if he suddenly really saw me, gave me the look of someone thinking, Who gives a damn about the children, smiled and apologized with a hint of mockery—just enough to let me imagine a phantom showing the false respect of a male who is amused by feigning women's gestures.

For a little while, the evening progressed haltingly. Mario in Cecilia's presence lost his brilliance, and everything he said sounded stupid or ingenuous, becoming an occasion for Ernesto's teasing. As for me, encouraged by Cecilia's serene indulgence, and perhaps to make a good impression on her and feel her approval, I began to express opinions that I didn't even know I had but that her engaging manner drew gently to the surface. A sentence, two, three, and the climate changed. Ernesto began to be interested in everything I said, he laughed, shaking his narrow chest, he was moved to tears if an idea seemed clever to him, he kept repeating to Mario, with the clear intention of humiliating him: You don't know what you're saying, your wife has a fine mind, you don't. Cecilia smiled and murmured, Ernesto.

Our dinner was followed by a dinner at their house. I had no desire to go, I was afraid that Ernesto with his exaggerated compliments would make fun of me. But that evening I took a long shower, and under the thick, aggressive needles of water I found that I wanted to put an end to the mysterious melancholy I had been feeling. As I dried my hair I felt again the sudden desire to choose a dress, a pair of shoes, a new way of doing my makeup. Ernesto paid little attention to my beauty, but his wife was full of compliments, and I discovered that I had dressed up just for that praise, the praise of a refined woman, whose sparely furnished house was utterly suited to her cultivated taste.

All evening I talked only to her, in a low voice. Her husband persisted in humiliating Mario, fiercely, tactlessly; then, abruptly, he offered him well-paying work as a consultant on a job he was doing. We toasted it. I noticed for the first time Ernesto's figure next to Cecilia's. It seemed to me that that closeness cast him in the proper light, as it did the clothes she wore, the furniture she surrounded herself with, the books she talked about. Suddenly I found myself thinking that if Cecilia had been with that man for so many years, that man must possess a hidden refinement, a way of being that fit hers. I observed him more closely, secretly. He had a naturally elegant bearing, long hands, his lean face had managed to hold off the years. As a couple they seemed like the pair of pans on an old scale: he very lively and aggressive, always up, she tolerant, maternally watchful, pushing down.

From then on the two appeared more frequently at our house; Ernesto always had something about the job to discuss with Mario. He would come in and immediately start shouting something derisory at him, he kissed me on the cheeks, sometimes on the neck, as if because of a poorly controlled movement of the lips, then he paid no attention to me and instead angrily, bitterly quarreled with my husband. I willingly talked to Cecilia, but I soon felt that Ernesto's lack of attention, and the fact that, even in the middle of the most heated discussion, he was quick to pick up the slightest signal given by his wife, irritated me, wounded me, made me feel insignificant. I came to hate that indifference, I was afraid that it undermined me in the eyes of that serene woman I wanted to please, whose respect I sought. I felt better only when he took up something I had said and, interrupting his discussion with Mario, looked at me with curiosity, exclaiming: Here is a beautiful woman who knows how to think.

I decided to react. I began to look through the papers to find public occasions at which Ernesto and his wife might possibly be present. Suddenly it became indispensable to me that that man should notice me, be aware of my virtues, realize that I had interests and thoughts no different from those of him and his wife. Gradually, following a practice that was by now familiar, I began to go to the places where I might meet them, taking great care with how I looked, in case of that eventuality. Sometimes they were there, sometimes not. When they were, he greeted me with an ostentatious gesture, pointed to where his wife was seated, shouted my name in the midst of a speech by one of the presenters without caring that he embarrassed me. If, instead, they weren't there, I sat down, listened to boring programs, scanned the entrance and the audience, left in disappointment.

Then Mario had to go to a conference on Lake Garda with Cecilia. He asked halfheartedly if I would go with him, and I decided to only when he said that Cecilia hoped I would, that Ernesto was busy, and couldn't come. I was flattered by that request, we made an arrangement for the children, we left. But soon that decision seemed a mistake. Mario and Cecilia were full of engagements, surrounded as they were by an aura of admiration. Cecilia especially was constantly the center of attention, she spoke in calm authoritative tones, always winning approval. I soon felt like a shadow, a houseplant.

The second day, to our surprise, Ernesto appeared; he was very cheerful, and his good humor made him seem younger. He had gotten rid of his obligations, he declared that he would not spend a single minute in the conference hall, not even to listen to Cecilia's report or Mario's speech, and he carried me off, to the café, the restaurant, insisting: the two of us are not made for that foolishness. Unlike Mario, he was curious about everything, entertained by opposition, the enemy of silence and dead time. I felt in the two days that followed an intense pleasure in dressing and making myself up for him, crossing my legs under his gaze, feeling his arm under my arm. I quickly saw that he liked me, that he had come not for his wife but purposely for me. I got a sensation of power, more violent than in those paltry previous affairs.

After that our relations intensified. When we were with people we knew and went for a walk or to the movies or a restaurant, I always managed to place myself next to Ernesto, worrying every time that I would end up walking with Cecilia and see him talking to other women; often I grabbed Mario by the arm and, without him noticing it, pushed him toward Ernesto so that he would see me and remember me. I maneuvered, in short, to attract his attention, to meet his gaze, to sit next to him, and the fact that he never visibly did the same, that in fact he often indulged in raucous laughter with very complacent women, made me suffer. Then I was excessively attentive to how I looked, sometimes I forced myself to be brazen. Mario never noticed anything. Only at a certain point Cecilia began to treat me with polite coolness and that grieved me, as if there had been a misunderstanding. Once she seemed to look at me even when her gaze was turned elsewhere, not with her eyes but with her earrings, pupils under the fleshy lobes of her ears. She's jealous, I said to myself with sincere regret and an embarrassing hint of satisfaction, is it possible that a woman experienced in the world, so refined, could be jealous of me?

The work with Mario ended in disagreements, Ernesto's visits and phone calls diminished, I was again stricken by ill humor. Not seeing him made me sad. Several times I thought of calling him, of a meeting without Mario and Cecilia, in some way confirming our friendship. I gave it up out of prudence, modesty, virtues of mine that I detested. Then there was another conference, this time an important international conference in Erice. Mario asked me to go with him, he insisted, Cecilia was also going, Cecilia, too, insisted, and I accepted. But when I found out that Ernesto was busy and would remain in Turin for his own work, I cautiously found a way of getting out of it. Mario left, the children went to stay overnight with some friends, I was alone.

I spent a long time beside the telephone, waiting until it was dark. What could be wrong with telephoning him? He was my friend now, surely more my friend than Mario's. And we were both alone in the city, it was a pleasant way to spend the evening, that's all. But I was lying and I knew it. I had crossed the boundaries of the game almost without realizing it. If he had invited me to dinner, I would have accepted. If he had said come have dinner at my house, I would have accepted. If he had asked me to cook something for him, I would have done it—, let's meet at my house I would have proposed. I dialed the number with trepidation, knowing that I was performing an act that would be decisive for my life. Because if he kissed me I would kiss him. If he wanted to make love I would have done it. If he had asked me to leave Mario and the children, I wouldn't have hesitated. If he had insisted that I go away with him, change cities, even though I was thirty-four and he was sixteen years older, I would have followed him.

He answered on the second ring, his voice nervous. I tried some humorous phrase about how did he feel, shut in the house alone, in boring Turin. He said he was fine and he wasn't alone. Cecilia at the last minute had decided not to go, too many things to do at the university, they were working. I flushed with shame, my voice choked. He abruptly handed the phone to Cecilia, who insisted that I should come to dinner at their house. I refused, hating myself. I had revealed to her, I had revealed to myself that I wanted to take her husband away. A desire more than a plan, a desire born equally from the admiration I had for her. Would I have liked Ernesto if he hadn't gone to bed with her every night for decades? Occupying her place, taking myself out of mine, now seemed to me a mistake. Would I have fantasized about that man if he hadn't been the husband of that distant woman, so obviously better than me, the woman I would have liked to become, by studying, writing? I hung up with a terrible feeling in the pit of my stomach, a desire for laceration.

Now, years later, as the furious song of the birds began, I thought: if I was like that, why am I surprised at Mario? What is destroying me? His journey is known to me, I know how it began, how it continued. I only have to be quiet, accept, wait. But I wasn't convinced, I said to myself no. I jumped out of bed furiously, I pulled up the blinds sharply to see the dawn. There was a difference between him and me: I had dreamed of betrayal, he had betrayed; I didn't even know if those men scarcely touched were shadows of old desires, lies that I was now telling myself at dawn to pretend I had a life that was independent of his, while he for years really had hidden himself in the flesh of another. That difference counted. He hadn't recognized anything indispensable in me. Nothing in the entire parade of semblances that in his eyes I ought to represent had been able to restrain him. I, on the other hand, bore invisible chains that had kept me from humiliating him, as if reality couldn't accept the insult imagined in those small insubstantial love affairs, except by insulting me.

It's a long passage; I hope you'll forgive me for imposing it on you. I cut it from the book for many reasons that it's pointless to list here (for example, a boring, superficial Bovary-ism that didn't really fit Olga). I will point out here the one reason that has to do with your question: Olga's little love affairs, as you will have noted, are woven together by her need to betray yet remain faithful to the man whom, symbolically, her mother liked, and who therefore comes with a sort of parental seal; and that framing device, its obviousness, seemed a mistake.

The inspiration for the long erotic digression further derived, consciously, from a couple of passages in "Female Sexuality," the essay I cited above in regard to *Troubling Love*. There Freud speaks at least twice about marriage, and in a curious manner. First, he says that a woman, even when she chooses her husband based on a paternal model, "yet in her married life repeats with her husband her bad relations with her mother." Then he hypothesizes that "the attachment to the mother must inevitably perish just because it is the first and most intense, similarly to what we so often find in the first marriages of young women, entered into when they were most passionately in love." In both cases, he says, "the love-relation probably comes to grief by reason of the unavoidable disappointments and an accumulation of occasions for aggression." And he concludes, "As a rule second marriages turn out much better."

Now, in telling the story of Olga's sexuality and what I know about sexuality, I wanted at least three basic things to be perceived, all inspired by those passages, even if critically: first, that for women every love relationship, in marriage or not, is based not only in its bad aspects *but also in the good ones* on the reactivation of the primitive bond with the mother; second, that marriage—whether first, second, or third, heterosexual or homosexual—can't expel from a woman's life the troubling love for the maternal image, the *only* love-conflict that in every case lasts forever; third, that what keeps Olga from betraying Mario is the fact that Mario from the beginning inadvertently became for her the cocoon of fantasies tied to the mother, and it is this above all that makes the abandonment so devastating.

The convictions remain, obviously; they are now part of my way of seeing. But I wanted the story of Olga, although it might accommodate that mode, to do it silently, not to be strangled by it. When you begin a story, you have to be the sole source of the story, you have to get lost in it, because there are no predetermined maps; and if perceptible traces of what you have learned from books remain, they have to be eliminated without indulgence, assuming it's possible. Because it's not always possible, nor is it good: writing is also the story of what we have read and are reading, of the quality of our reading, and a good story, finally, is one written from the depths of our life, from the heart of our relations with others, from the heights of the books we've liked.

Cities

One morning—it was summer, a very hot Neapolitan summer, I was eleven—two boys who were scarcely older, playmates who were silently in love, invited my sister and me to get an ice cream. Our mother had absolutely forbidden us to leave the courtyard of the building where we lived. But we were tempted by the ice cream, by the prospect of love, and decided to disobey. One act of disobedience led to another. We didn't limit ourselves to going to the café at the end of the street, but, absorbed by the pleasure of acting as uninhibited women, we kept going, all the way to the gardens of Piazza Cavour, to the Museum.

At a certain point the air turned black. It began to rain, with thunder and lightning, the liquid sky dripped down on us and ran in torrents toward the sewers. Our escorts looked for shelter, my sister and I didn't: I already saw my mother anxiously shouting our names from the balcony.

We felt abandoned in the rain, and we ran, lashed by the heavy water. I held my sister by the hand, shouting at her to hurry, the rain was soaking us, my heart was pounding. It was a long overexcited moment of disorder. The boys had left us to our fate; the home we were running toward was surely a place of punishment, anything could happen there. I was aware of the city for the first time. I felt it on my back and under my feet, it was running along with us, panting with its dirty breath, horns honking madly, it was alien and known at the same time, limited and boundless, dangerous and exciting, I recognized it by getting lost.

That impression remained. Ever since, every city has existed only when it abruptly enters the blood that moves the legs and blinds the eyes. I took the wrong street many times not because I didn't know the way home but because the known space also felt my anxiety and opened up before me in erroneous routes, and the erroneous routes were also a desire for error, possibilities of flight from my mother, of never returning home but wickedly getting lost in the streets, in all my most secret thoughts.

I had to stop, tug on my sister so that she wouldn't run away, grasp the thread of orientation, which is a magic thread, to tie one street to the next, making tight knots, so that the streets would calmly settle down and I could find the way home. At first our mother was overcome by emotion, because we were alive, then, just because we were alive, she punished us by spanking us with a trowel.

As for your question about the cities of Delia, of Olga, I want to try to answer by starting with that run in the rain. I soon left Naples, and, as it happened, I lived in various and distant places. I rarely got along well with the cities I lived in. Now cities all seem to me merely prostheses, but with different effects: either they remain dead material, forever alien, or they become one with your body and you feel them as an active part of what you feel. Only in that second case do cities count for me, for better or worse. Otherwise they are meaningless topographies. Even if they have beautiful, evocative names and fascinating traces of the past, they don't excite me even as a tourist; I have little interest in being a tourist with my nose stuck in a Touring Club guide. Starting with that experience of late childhood, the true model of urban involvement is Naples pressing in on me and confusing me as I run in the storm.

I must tell you, however, that the aftermath of that run was crucial. I mean the calming down, regaining eyes and ears, seeing the city as if I had redrawn it with anxieties and its pleasures. I mean the resorting to a thread that reconnects the places shattered by emotions and allows us not only to get lost but to govern our getting lost.

In this regard there is a passage by Walter Benjamin that I am very fond of. Over the years I've found everything I need there: the descent to the Mothers of an urban area seen through the eyes of a child, the city-labyrinth, the role of love, the troublesome governess, even the rain that falls on childhood. I'm referring to the opening chapter of *Berlin Childhood Around 1900*, entitled "Tiergarten."

I'm not going to talk here about Benjamin's gaze, the extraordinary gaze of eyeballs that are pupils in their entire spherical surface, and which therefore see not only before, not only outside, not the afterward that is in store but the ahead-behind, the inside-outside, the after in the then-now, without chronological order. I wish to emphasize, rather, the marvelous opening that goes: "Not to find one's way around a city does not mean much. But to lose one's way, as one loses one's way in a forest, requires some schooling."[6]

Learning to get lost in a city, precisely: hearing the names of the streets like the snapping of dry twigs, like mountain gullies that reflect the time of day. Benjamin talks about it in an anomalous sort of writing, a vortex-like writing that seeks to reach the *difficult to express*, what is deep down and barely visible. When does the city become the city of being lost? Where is the origin of the labyrinth, when is one schooled in the art of getting lost? "This art I acquired rather late in life; it fulfilled a dream, of which the first traces were labyrinths on the blotting papers in my school notebooks. No, not the first, for there was one earlier that has outlasted the others. The way into this labyrinth, which was not without its Ariadne, led over the Bendler Bridge, whose gentle arch became my first hillside."

The dizzying velocity of the writing is beautiful, the going back, in just a few lines, to the ink marks on the blotting paper of childhood, in search of the primary labyrinth. Is the intuition of the art of getting lost in the city in that swirl of ink? No, the valley goes deeper, there's an *even before*, a before that comes before the squiggles on the blotting paper. One has to

---

[6] Harvard University Press, 2006. Trans. Howard Eiland

go back. The original urban labyrinth is in childhood. It's the labyrinth that in the form of the park at the zoo in Berlin in which the child Benjamin navigated a mysterious corner where "in fact must have lain the couch of that Ariadne in whose proximity I first experienced what only later I had a word for: love. Unfortunately the Fraulein intervenes at its earliest budding to overspread her icy shadow. And so this park, which, unlike every other, seemed open to children, was for me, as a rule, distorted by difficulties and impracticalities."

The primary labyrinth is sketched by the child's gaze as it wanders in the mystery outside the house, far from his guardian divinities, and encounters love for the first time. It is *difficulties and impracticalities* that the child Benjamin experiences when the icy shadow of the governess is cast over his Ariadne (there is not a city-labyrinth, therefore, without a Pasiphae who gives birth to the Beast-Minotaur, without an Ariadne and love), disturbing the apparition. The adult Benjamin will dream forever of that getting lost which began when he crossed the Bendler Bridge, and will seek the thread enabling him to return to that experience and transform it into art that can be expressed, apprehended.

Of Benjamin's Ariadne we know nothing, of course, he tells us not about her but about the childhood of a small Berlin Theseus; it's only natural. But for me the faint apparition of the girl, immediately covered by the icy shadow of another woman, the governess-mother-monster, is unforgettable. If Theseus is stopped at the incapacity to orient himself, it's little Ariadne who preserves the art of getting lost, it's she who possesses the thread that can control it. I've loved this myth since I was a child. It's very possible that that day in Naples, in the storm, I thought of Ariadne, and that I thought of her many years later, describing Delia who, wandering through the city, gets lost in her childhood. As a very studious and dreamy middle-school adolescent I often had fantasies of guiding the hand of Theseus as he killed the Beast, my blood relation, leading the hero to safety, abandoning for him the city-prison and my terrible family, sailing to another city, discovering him ungrateful behind the appearance of the fine curly-haired youth, and finally winning for myself wild and vengeful joys, perdition with Dionysus, perdition that at fifteen I desired more than I did later, as an adult.

With myths there is always something that shifts within. Years afterward—by then grown up and in a completely different frame of mind—I returned to Naples for several months; I had my own problems. I retraced many of the routes of my childhood, including the one I had taken with my sister in the rain. I rediscovered the anguish of that breathless run, but also the pleasing impression of a city that was mine and no one else's, hostile and seductive, which I had taken possession of for the first time on that long-ago day. I recalled the image of the labyrinth as an ordinary space, a known place that, with oneself, is suddenly disrupted by a strong emotion. I got some books (including that vast captivating hodgepodge that is Graves's *The Greek Myths*), I wanted to see if the myth would help me describe, by giving me distance, a story of intolerance, flight, love, and abandonment: not the abandonment experienced by Olga—that came much later, when I had understood that to write well you have to do the opposite of what the handbooks prescribe, get close, shorten the distance, abolish it, feel the pulsing veins of living bodies on the page.

A variation of the Ariadne story fascinated me. It's the story of the Cretan girl who is now pregnant, and worn out by seasickness, and whom Theseus puts ashore in Amathus for fear she'll miscarry. The girl has just set foot on land when a strong wind forces the hero's fleet to put out to sea. Ariadne is desperate, about to give birth, suffering because of her lover's abandonment. Then the women of Amathus intervene, and, to console her, take turns writing her love letters, pretending they're from Theseus. The lie lasts until Ariadne dies in childbirth.

I worked on this story for a while, during those months in Naples. I invented in detail a sort of Campanian city of today, an Amathus that was like a town on the Amalfi coast. It was a city of female friendship and solidarity, but free in its thoughts and in its conflicts. I imagined a community of modern women writing consoling love letters to a modern Ariadne, the abandoned foreigner, attributing them to the traitorous lover. I was drawn to the possibility of describing how women dream of being loved, and so I applied myself mainly to four things: the women's effort to enter the head, the words of a man; the women's collaboration—a true, harmonious group project—to feign a man's psychic and lexical makeup; questioning themselves, on the other hand, to find out what they would have liked to hear from a man in love; the search-confession of what they would have said to the desperate Ariadne if, as was happening to some, amid endless contradictions, they had been hopelessly in love.

I remember that I liked imagining the arguments that preceded the drafting of the letters. But when I began to actually draft them, everything got complicated; in the end they seemed pointless effort—I wrote two and stopped. Evidently the idea was weak, the letters tended to sketch an ideal male in whose reality no Ariadne, however desperate in her abandonment, would have believed, especially today; the city was too perfect; the community of women, even in its vivacity, seemed sentimentally full of good feelings and thus inauthentic. No, even in the case of cities dominated by women one can and must write only of city-labyrinths, the repositories of our complex and contradictory emotions, where the Beast is lying in ambush and it's dangerous to get lost without having first learned to do so.

The problem—and here I'm expanding slightly on the subject of your question—is that one has trouble imagining what sort of polis women could construct, if they sought to do so in their image and likeness. Where is the image-model, what female traits would it resemble? As far as I know the city, for women, always belongs to others, even when it's their native city. It's true that for a long time now women representatives have actively taken part in the management of the polis but only on the condition that they don't take over, immediately, to try to really reinvent it. Those who try are disappointed, leaving behind a wake of bitter discourse or adapting to the clichéd phrases of contemporary politics.

Evidently the female city will be a long time coming and doesn't yet have true words. To look for them we have to descend beyond the squiggles of our blotting paper, into the labyrinth of our childhood, into the unredeemed chaos of fragments of our past and our remote past. An arduous undertaking. The heroines of myths are in general solitary, individuals without affiliation, in search of a small transient sovereignty, which, however, when it is achieved is paid for with shame, with their lives. Often they commit actions that deviate from the male order, at times they rebel against the laws of their native city. It's rare that they found a city. Only once, as far as I remember at the moment, does a woman decide to plan a polis of her own, oversee its construction, be *dux femina facti*. Obviously I'm talking about Dido, a character it took me a long time to love completely.

As a girl I was annoyed by her suicide. In high school the story fascinated me not for what Virgil describes at length but for what Virgil barely hints at: the bloody story the woman has behind her, the brother who killed her husband, the flight from Tyre, the skill she displayed in Africa, the way she got the land on which to establish, with her sister, a new city. At the time I liked women who fled. For Dido I had at hand domestic inspirations with which to give her body. And here I should tell you that my mother was a dressmaker for a long period of her life, and that was important for me. With needle, thread, scissors, fabrics she could do anything. She altered old clothes, made new ones, sewed, unsewed, let out, took in, made tears invisible with skillful mending. Because I had grown up in the middle of all that cutting and sewing, the way Dido tricks the king of the Gaetuli immediately convinced me. Iarbas had said to her mockingly: I'll give you as much land as the skin of a bull can go around. Little, very little, an ironic male insult. The king—I was sure, not for nothing was he the son of Amon—must have thought that even if the bull's hide was cut into strips it would never surround enough land for the construction of a city. But I had seen the fair-haired Dido in the same concentrated pose as my mother when she worked—beautiful, her black hair carefully combed, her skilled hands scarred by wounds from the needle or the scissors—and I had understood that the story was plausible. All night (crucial labors are carried out at night), Dido had been bent over the hide of the beast, reducing it into almost invisible strips, which were then sewed together in such a way that the seams couldn't even be guessed at, a very long Ariadne's thread, a ball of animal skin that would unroll to enclose a vast piece of African land and, at the same time, the boundaries of a new city. That seemed to me true and had excited me.

Later, at university, I still found things to dislike about Dido, I preferred the woman who was at the head of a great enterprise, the woman who was directing the construction of the enormous walls and the fortress of the new Carthage. I was especially struck by the fact that Virgil has her enter just as pious Aeneas, in the temple dedicated to Juno, is contemplating a bas-relief depicting a raging (*furens*) Penthesilea engaged in battle. I've always been disturbed by stories that introduce an almost imperceptible sign of future imbalances into a happy scene, that take your breath away with the specter of an abrupt reversal of fate. When she first appears, Dido, who is very beautiful, and escorted by young suitors, is serenely active, vigilantly governing the progress of works in the city, and I, as a student-reader-translator who already knew what would happen, from that moment on suffered at every word: I was sorry that that woman, in the fullness of her female vigor, would be consumed by a mad love, and would be transformed from happy, *lieta*—Virgil's *laeta*, the adjective suited to her—to furious, like the other, losing female model, Penthesilea *furens*. I was sorry for her and for the city, which was also rising auspiciously.

Only when I reread Virgil, to help me write the story of Olga, did I suddenly like Dido in every aspect. I have to say that I also liked Aeneas; his dull piety no longer seemed to me mannered—well brought up men of today have some resemblance to him, with that same hesitant yet fierce *pietas*. This time I felt that the course of the story was true and agonizing, there was no hint of the faults I had found as a girl. But what made the strongest impression was Virgil's use of the city. Carthage isn't a background, isn't an urban landscape for people and events. Carthage is what it has not yet become but is about to be, material that is being worked, stone exploded at times by the internal movements of the two characters. Not coincidentally, even before Aeneas admires the beautiful Dido, he admires the bustling activity of the work of building, the construction of the walls, the fortress, the port, the theater, the columns. His first comment is a sigh: How lucky the Tyrians are, their walls are already rising. Into those walls he puts his feelings as a founder. They accommodate simultaneously the memory of his destroyed fatherland, the hope and yearning for the future city, and the desire of the nomad to camp in the middle of the foreign city, which is also a city-beautiful woman, to be possessed.

Cities are this, stone made suddenly alive by our emotions, by our desires, as we can see above all in the relationship between Carthage and Dido. The work is actively proceeding under the direction of this woman who has fled the horror of Tyre, the city that had abused her, the city where her brother shed the blood of his brother-in-law, and every feeling was forever polluted by the desire for murder. The queen doesn't want to repeat Tyre and organizes the great urban construction site according to what is just and lawful. She welcomes the foreign exile, she has taken care that the walls of the temple of Juno, goddess of marriage and childbirth, should display the horrors of war and murder, a sort of memento. And she is a woman in her full splendor, the youths who crowd around her say so. It's evident that under her direction Carthage aspires to be completed, amid endless difficulties, not as an enclosure for the Beast but as a polis of love.

Then passion explodes, absorbs all energy, turns into mad love. Immediately the city, too, reacts. What had been started stops, the work breaks off. Like Dido, the stones wait to decide their fate. If the love between Aeneas and her is happily fulfilled, becoming a joyful long-lasting connection, Carthage will gain power from it, the work will start up again, the stones will welcome the positive feeling of the human beings who are shaping it. Instead, Aeneas abandons her. Dido, the happy woman, becomes furious, raging. The past is joined to the future, Tyre virtually reaches Carthage, every street becomes a labyrinth, a place to get lost without art, and the blood that Dido has left behind returns to stain the new city. It is no longer unfinished. In the words of the dying Dido, Carthage is suddenly a city distinguished by hatred and revenge, and her final curse conclusively dismisses the hypothesis of a just polis: *Nullus amor populis nec foedera sunto* is her bitter cry.

This is the result of getting lost in the urban labyrinth without art, without a thread: *No love, no accords.* The Virgilian connection between love and the constitution of civic life is significant. Certainly the wars between Rome and Carthage had economic and political causes, not the abandonment of Dido by Aeneas, not the removal of love, which is only a poetic

cause. But why "only"? I—like anyone who loves literature—
believe that the poetic causes say more than the political and
economic causes, in fact they go to the heart of the political
and economic causes. I'm one of those who believe that it's
precisely the exile of love from cities that leaves them open to
economic and political oppression. Until there is a widespread
culture of love—and I mean solidarity, respect, a movement
toward a good life for all, the antidote, in other words, to the
furies and to the easy impulse to annihilate the enemy—the
reality of war, of devastation, means that the accords of com-
munal life will always be provisional, truces for catching one's
breath and recovering weapons and renewing the desire for
destruction.

No love between peoples, then, no accords: the two things
go together. One line says more than a thousand ponderous
readings. And there's nothing to be surprised at. Writers of stories know that the poetic causes are not moths with transparent wings. They have flesh and blood, passions, complex feelings: poetry is digging around in one's belly with movements
that are never predictable. Dido is nourished on sweat and
saliva, she's not a crust of caramel on the top of a crème brûlée.
She can curse the person she still loves; she can kill herself with
a gift from the beloved.

As a girl, as I said, I detested that suicide. I thought that as
a woman you go into labyrinths with a magic thread that can
control getting lost. And yet I'm convinced that the mistake of
every new city lies at its roots, is in its claim to be a city of love
while leaving no possibility for labyrinths, a place neither difficult nor impractical, a space of joy, with no furies lying in wait.
Even a feminine city—a future that redeems the past—risks
not knowing how to completely reckon with itself. It's a shortcut to set aside what is formidable about women, to imagine us
merely as organisms with good feelings, skilled masters of gen-
tility. Maybe that's useful for encouraging us, for political

growth, but those who create literature have to make hostility, aversion, and fury visible, along with generous sentiments. It's their task, they have to dig inside, describe women from close up, feel that they are there, Aeneas or no Aeneas, Theseus or no Theseus.

I don't like to think, as we often tend to do, that the tremendous actions of the heroines of myths are merely the product of a pernicious male racket, of a patriarchal plot: in the end it's like attributing to women a lack of humanity, and that isn't useful. We have to learn, rather, to speak with pride of our complexity, of how in itself it informs our citizenship, whether in joy or in rage. To do this we have to learn the art of getting lost in the difficulties and impracticalities, there is no Ariadne who doesn't cultivate somewhere a troubling love, the image of a beloved mother who nevertheless gives birth to suicidal dolls and minotaurs.

Listen to us, see us. Sometimes in the urban labyrinths we fearlessly ask burial for our brother, sometimes we collaborate in the killing of our stepbrother and flee with his murderer, in certain cases we kill our children, more often we utter terrible curses before falling victim to the furies ourselves. The story of Virgilian Carthage expresses well how consumingly the polis lives on the feelings of its citizens. It also expresses what happens when love—the thread both for getting lost and for finding our way—is banished, each breath becomes fire, the accords of civic life dissolve.

But that's enough, what counts is to try and keep trying to sew for ourselves with needle and thread the perimeter of the city. As a diligent student I was never bored by winter afternoons spent on the lines of the Aeneid. It was wonderful to see the queen on the throne as she managed equitably the enormous work site, a rare occasion to dream of founding a city. I tried out endings different from the one in which she stabs herself with the sword that was a gift from Aeneas. I imagined that she expelled the furies, found love again, learned the art of getting lost and finding the way out. Every so often I would get up and go to the window; my cold feet prevented me from studying. Often when Naples comes to my mind, it's a cold city in a storm.

Women's Clothes

I know I'm in danger of overdoing it, but, if I'm going to talk to you about clothes and makeup, as you asked, you'll have to endure my telling you yet again something about my mother.

Her work as a dressmaker began—for me, naturally—in the fabric stores. I liked going with her. I would look at the clerk spellbound—or at the owner himself if the shop didn't have clerks—as he moved with a sort of cheerful lightness. He took the rectangular rolls of fabric down from the shelves and, facing my mother, began unfolding them in waves even before they had touched the counter, making the block of fabric jump, leap, turn rapidly over itself as if it were alive. She touched the fabrics, rubbing an edge between thumb and index finger, meanwhile staring straight ahead, as if not looking at the material increased the sensitivity of her fingers. I inhaled the odor of the new fabric, a sharp smell that normally lay stagnant in the shop but that the rapid unrolling of the material had blown directly in my face. I stood beside my mother, my head reaching her waist, the material of her dress just touching me. I looked at the fabrics that piled up on the counter, I felt that she was choosing the right one on which to weave her spell. It was a spell I was deeply familiar with but it enchanted me anyway, always. The new fabric that she was about to buy would be marked with chalk, the scissors would cut it, shreds would cover the floor. My mother, with pins, with needle and thread, would give it a shape, the precise shape of a body, she was able to make bodies of fabric. The smell of the new fabric would be released for the last time, an alien wild fragrance, which, once tamed in our house, would then be lost.

This was how it always happened. I clearly remembered when the dress she now wore, which had her smell, had been in its turn a fabric in the shop. When she decided to buy it, she would tell the clerk in a cordial voice how many meters she needed. The clerk performed broad, swift gestures that made the fabric flow along a short section of the counter's edge. That dance was followed by a precise strike of scissors, a sharp tug, an agonizing whiff of another bitter smell. I was an expert, the art of clothes began there.

As for ending, it ended on my parents' bed. The oldest memory I have of a dress just finished—at least the one that seems to me the oldest—is of a black dress, or maybe dark blue, spread on the red quilt of the double bed. There my mother laid the freshly ironed dresses, there was no other place in the house—she said—where they wouldn't get wrinkled. We were forbidden to enter that room when there were clothes ready to be delivered. I must have gone in once, I can't fix a date, certainly I wasn't that young. It was a phase when I felt sudden gusts behind me, presences at my back even when there was no one in the room, shadowy things, which, however, didn't frighten me; in fact I was glad for them, because I could describe them to my sisters who, unlike me, were afraid. I opened the door, I looked into the room. The dress was lying in the middle of the bed, the waist narrow, the sleeves spread, the skirt arranged in a trapezoid. Nothing happened except a puff of air that inflated the dress, a brief swelling as if for a breath. Afterward, one edge of the skirt was rumpled, just lifted. I was afraid that my mother would blame me, as she usually did for everything. So I went to smooth it down. Instead, for no reason, I lifted it up and looked under the dress. There was the naked body of a woman, with the legs cut off, the hands cut off, the head cut off, violet but bloodless: a body of a material without veins. I retreated, left the room. I was reprimanded when she discovered—and scolded me, because she was already anxious—that the dress was in disarray.

I've always felt that dresses aren't empty, that they are human beings who at times stand empty in a corner, desolately lost. When I was a child I tried on my mother's dresses. I found inside them beautiful women of great renown, but dead. Then I put them on, wore them, and gave life to their adventures. They all had the smell of my mother, I imagined I had it, too. They had no husband but many lovers. I felt their pleasures intensely, their adventurous bodies released mine. As soon as I felt the material on my chest, my legs, it warmed my stomach, my imagination. I knew the fabrics well, they had been in my mother's hands for a long time, in her fingers, on her lap.

As a small child I saw the dresses come into being, before my mother stopped working as a dressmaker. She didn't teach me anything about it, but at a certain point I helped take out a basting, or she taught me a stitch she called a whipstitch, and one that she called a hemstitch. But her work remained in my eyes: the gestures, especially, and the tools fascinated and preoccupied me, a fascination that contained a hint of fear. I didn't like the material to be cut, the cutting made me uneasy, the shreds of material that ended up on the floor under the table repelled me. When I learned the expression "to cut the clothes on," to gossip, I endowed it with that ambiguous childhood feeling. Was the material shaped by the scissors on the living body, to cover it? Or was the living body denuded by the action of the scissors? I went back and forth between those two fantasies and watched my mother.

She, yes, she cut the clothes on the body, and at times she did it just as Licia Maglietta does in Mario Martone's film: the cutting and sewing was accompanied by talk, by smiles and laughter, by gossip and stories, the pleasure of storytelling among women, stories about other women, stories about clients and neighbors. Meanwhile the words fell on the fabric, pressed into flesh in the women I would later wear. Signora Caldaro, for example, who was the wife of a lawyer. To try on her future dress, she took off her clothes, leaving in our house a sad odor of illness. She put on the unfinished dress, its pieces just held together by pins and the white basting thread. Meanwhile she talked about her troubles and wept. My mother listened, as did I, and those stories of Signora Caldaro's disturbed me, I would have liked to offer consoling words. In general my mother did, she would intervene with a comforting tale, one similar to Signora Caldaro's that she had heard and that had a happy ending. The signora listened but couldn't believe it, she doubted that her affair would end well, felt sorry for herself and wept. When she left and the dress was lying on the dining room table I stroked it—scarred, pricked by the pins, because of the words of suffering, because of their malevolent touch—the body of a woman worn out by her troubles, without a head, without legs, without arms and hands.

Signora Caldaro's dress was for parties and balls, my mother sewed it, unsewed it and resewed it, she stitched and stitched. I was afraid of the needle, but I also liked the harmony of the sewing that it left behind, like a wake. My mother pricked the fabric with a swift, skillful movement. She sat concentrated on the chair, bent, the dress on her knees. Sometimes she let me thread the needle, if I insisted. I had to wet one end of the thread, sticking it in my mouth, then I had to squeeze and twist the part that was bathed in saliva between tongue and lips, finally I had to pass the prepared thread through the eye of the needle. Succeeding on the first try, while my mother praised me, was good, but it was just as good if I didn't succeed. She took the thread, passed the end between her lips,

and gave it back to me to try again. Sometimes I twisted the
wet thread between my thumb and index finger so that it
became taut and pointed like a pin.

But most important for me is the memory of the casual way
that my mother's hand and fingers pushed the needle and
thread through the fabric, lightly pulled it, stuck the point of
the needle back in. That pricking, pushing, pulling was done
so rapidly and expertly, moved straight forward with such precision, that today any well-performed operation makes me
think of it, and it vexes me that I no longer remember the
vocabulary she used. She spoke of running stitches, backstitch,
certainly of a chain stitch, of buttonhole stitches, but the rest
of the words have faded; she didn't want me to keep them, she
wanted me to learn other things. So it's her hand that remains,
with the nails that never grew, it was as if they curved forward,
and the swollen blue veins on the back and the rough fingertips, pricked and pricked again, almost never protected by the
thimble.

It was the sewing that cast a spell, much more than cutting.
The mobile skill of that hand put together the pieces of material, made the seams invisible, the pieces of fabric regained a
soft continuity, a new compactness, became a dress, the shape
of a female body, skin clinging to skin, an organism that lay in
her lap and sometimes slid down to her feet, which were in
motion like her hands, ready to go to the pedal of the sewing
machine. It was a back and forth that seemed like a dance to
me, the hand moved the needle, the mouth bit the thread, the
chest often rotated on the chair, turned to the machine to sew,
the feet, wide, with a powerful structure, rested on the pedal
and started the movement of the machine's needle, an
extremely rapid movement associated with a noise like rolling
metal.

The machine appeared to be racing and was still. The big
wheel below made the small one on top turn. It spun the bob-

bin on the pin, bobbins with different-colored thread, I saw the swirl of the blue, the green, the red, the brown, the black, pirouettes stamped by my mother's feet. The thread stretched to the head of the machine, hurtled down toward the needle, which moved rapidly up and down like an athlete jumping rope, and disappeared into the material, leaving behind a dense stitching escorted by the fingers.

I watched, there was a moment I didn't want to miss. It was when the thread was running out around the bobbin, and kept dwindling, became a thin covering, and finally unrolled completely. The tail end flew away, too, leaving the bobbin bare to rotate a few more times on the pin, until it stopped, revealing its true color, which had no attraction. It was a moment that made me sad. I took the bobbin off the pin like a corpse, its life was over, I felt, it had given all it had to give, no more joyous swirls of color. The thread was all in Signora Caldaro's dress, a transmigration of energy, and the dress was ready for the hot iron that would prepare the seams for felling, strokes of warmth, feverish caresses before the garment went to lie in the bedroom and become one with the body of the signora, the lawyer's wife, and take on the odor of her illness, perhaps of her despair.

My mother soon stopped making dresses for other women, and began to make them for us, her daughters, for relatives, for some neighbors, and mainly for herself. As a child I liked it when she made me a dress. I liked when she took my measurements, because she came very close, I smelled her smell, felt her breath on my face. The clothes she made for me were always clothes that seemed for playing; the ones she made for herself also had a playful aura. I remember when she took off her worn housedress and tried on the dress she was working on in front of the mirror or had a neighbor put it on so that she could see its flaws better. How I liked her dresses, the fragrance they had of creams, of lipstick, a smell of sugared almonds. I tried them on secretly, I put on her coats, her shoes, and if she discovered me she wasn't angry, she let me. Rather, she looked at me with her melancholy smile, her body concentrated on her sewing, her appearance uncared for.

But even then, around the time of the storeroom I told you about, those dresses communicated an anxiety, too; they contained a poison like the shirt of Nessus. Over the years her capacity for sewing began to weigh on me. By early adolescence I hated that skill, I was ashamed of going around in dresses she had made for me. I would have liked normal dresses, which would make me like other girls. In those dresses of hers, instead, there was something excessive, something eccentric, that was displayed especially in the dresses she made for herself.

She copied them from dresses worn by movie stars, princesses, from the models of fashion designers. But she had the gift of remaking them so that on her they seemed more charged with energy. My mother never sewed a dress for herself that didn't make her appear an extraordinary woman. Whereas at home she was diminished to a bundle of rags sitting on a chair, when she went out she endowed her body with the pride of the stunning appearance, the silver-screen splendor of the open-air cinemas on summer nights at the sea. She was a timid woman, yet in the way she dressed she demonstrated a boldness, an imagination that frightened and humiliated me. The more I hated her dressing up, the more, once outside, I felt around her my father's alarm, the admiration of other men, their overexcited talk, the effort at gaiety intended to please her, the envy and the insult for the way she could make herself beautiful. The effect my mother had in a tram, in the funicular, on the street, in the stores, at the movies embarrassed me. The fact that she dressed with such care to go out, with her husband or alone, gave me the impression that she concealed a desperate disgrace, and I felt shame and pity for her. When, in the clothes she made for herself, she radiated all the light she could, that exposure made me suffer: seeing her decked out, I found her a badly reared child, an adult woman humiliated by ridicule. In those striking outfits I felt alternately seduction, mockery, and death. So a mute fury gripped me, a wish to ruin her with my own hands and ruin myself, and then to erase the false look of a diva's daughter, the descendant of a queen, that she sought to give me by sewing night and day. I wanted her in her house clothes, that was my mother, even though I was pleased with her novel-like beauty. I wanted her without her flair for sewing. When I could avoid the clothes she made for me, I reacted with the desire to be sloppy: not to look like a pretty little daughter on special offer.

As a girl I was hostile to feminine traits. Putting on makeup, the wish to do so, the desire to wear a flattering dress, the very idea of the *flattering* dress irritated me, humiliated me. I was afraid that someone would think I was dressing like that to impress him and would laugh behind my back at the effort I had subjected myself to, the time I had devoted to that goal, would go around boasting: she did it for me. So I hid in big shirts, sweaters two sizes too large, baggy jeans. I wanted to eliminate the idea of being well dressed inherited from my mother; I would wear everyday clothes, not like her, who always wore nice dresses in spite of the wretchedness of her life as a woman. I wanted to be dressed *alla sanfrasò*—she used that expression when she saw me go out. It was a Gallicism of the dialect (*sanfasò, sans façon*, unfashionable) that she uttered with disgust, the term she used to say: one mustn't be like that, one doesn't live like that.

Sometimes I really felt slovenly, as if I were completely *alla sanfrasò*, and I suffered for it. But often I was sought after in spite of the dull tones, and then I felt I had on a sort of outfit that had never been worn, a beautiful garment that was clearly visible beyond the jeans and shapeless t-shirts. I think that the intense game of clothes in *Troubling Love* comes from that sensation. Delia, a liberated adult woman, in the tight-fitting clothes that are a carapace for her choked body, is as if assaulted by the clothes that her mother intended to give her; she is obsessed by their murky origin and will have to descend to the depths to find Amalia's blue dress and have the courage to put it on. I think that Olga's reaction to her daughter Ilaria's dressing up is fed by the same emotions. But it's hard to say what really ends up in books. Or sometimes it's too easy. I had given Delia a dream that consciously summed up many of the anxieties tied to clothes, to the dressmaking work that my mother did. This passage, too, is unpublished; I'll transcribe it for you.

As an adolescent I had a dream that I still have. It's pointless to give the details, the details always change.

In the dream the most varied things happened to me in the most diverse situations, but the moment always arrived when I was in front of a man and had to undress. I didn't want to, but he was there, he wouldn't go away, he looked at me with amusement, he waited. Then I tried cautiously to take off my clothes, but they wouldn't come off, it was as if they had been drawn on my skin. The man began to laugh, he laughed so hard he was bent over double; I became furious, I felt a violent wave of jealousy, I was jealous of him, surely he had another woman.

In the effort to keep him by pleasing him, I grabbed my chest with both hands and opened it, I opened up my own body as if it were a bathrobe. I didn't feel any pain, I saw only that inside me there was a live woman, and I suddenly understood that I was only someone else's dress, a stranger's.

I couldn't bear it, my jealousy increased. I was jealous now of that woman I had discovered inside, I tried to hit her in every possible way, grab her, I wanted to kill her. But between her and me was an impassable distance, I couldn't even touch her, and the laughter continued, uncontainable. In front of me, watching, however, was not the man but my mother, and I wasn't surprised, it seemed, rather, that she had always been there.

When I woke up, even though I knew the dream well, I was angry, I felt disgust and the wish to do harm.

Delia's dream was partly invented, and you can feel it, yet it came from that real adolescent anxiety. What was the secret dress that men saw on me? How had I put it on? If I had been able to take it off would I become someone other? What other?

Unfortunately dreams are difficult to relate; as soon as you write them they force you to invent, to put in order, and they become false. In novels especially they are so shamelessly functional to the requirements of the psychological construction of the character that their artificiality becomes intolerable. Sometimes, however, nightmares take the right form in a few lines. Of all the literary clothes I know, the one that best describes the emotional state I felt as a child is the dress worn by the very feminine Harey, the heroine of *Solaris*, by Stanislaw Lem, the ghost of a woman who has killed herself for love, a masculine word made woman. I'll cite a passage; the narrator is the protagonist, Chris.

"Harey, I have to go," I said. "If you really want to, come with me."

"O.K."

She got up suddenly.

"Why are you barefoot?" I asked, going to the closet and choosing two bright-colored overalls, one for me and one for her.

"I don't know . . . I must have lost my shoes some-whe..." she said uncertainly.

I pretended not to have heard. "You won't be able to put this on over your dress. You have to take it off."

"The overall . . . ? But why?" she asked, trying to take off her dress. But a strange thing happened: it was impossible to get it off, it didn't have buttons. The red buttons, on the front, were only decorative. It lacked any type of opening, a zipper or anything else. Harey smiled, embarrassed.

I find that smile of Harey's moving, as I do every one of Harey's actions in the book. That dress that you can't take off and therefore don't know how it got on terrifies me and attracts me. A few lines later, Chris, the novel's hero, takes a sort of chisel and cuts the dress off, starting at the neckline, so she can finally take it off and put on the overall "that's a little too big for her." But it's the classic brisk male move: I was never enthusiastic about that decisive surgical intervention. For me Harey's dress hides another one underneath, and then another and another, and no external intervention can resolve the problem. Besides, Lem makes Harey a ghost who returns, returns always with an invincible energy. And she always wears the same dress. And to undress her Chris needs to cut it again and again. If the ghost of Harey returned a thousand times, she would always wear the same dress, and Chris, by dint of cutting, would find in the room in the station of Solaris a thousand dresses all alike—that is, a single female dress that has a thousand reflections. What to do with a dress like that? Must one learn to take it off in order not to die? Must we resign ourselves to the idea that it is the dress of our death as women, and every attempt at resurrection only offers it to us again as a symbol of our humiliation? The passages in the books that influence us we rewrite according to our needs.

For example, also on the subject of clothes, I certainly put my own interpretation, as a girl, on *The Best of Husbands,* by Alba de Céspedes. I'm talking mainly about the first hundred and fifty pages, which is the story of a mother-daughter relationship and, more generally, a memorable catalogue of relations between women. When I read those pages for the first time, I was sixteen. I liked many things about them, others I didn't understand, still others annoyed me. But the point is the conflicted reading that developed, the fact that I couldn't seriously identify with the young Alessandra, the first-person narrator. Certainly I found the relationship between her and her mother, Eleonora, a pianist who is held back by a vulgar husband, very moving. Certainly, in the passages where Alessandra describes her deep bond with her mother, I recognized myself. But her absolute approval of the passion that Eleonora feels for the musician Hervey disturbed me: I mean, rather, that Alessandra's acceptance of it seemed to me sentimental and improbable, it made me angry. I would have fought a hypothetical extramarital love of my mother with all my strength, the mere suspicion kindled my rage, incited my jealousy much more than her definite love for my father. In short I didn't understand, I had the impression of knowing more about Eleonora than her daughter could perceive. And it was precisely the pages about the dress made for the concert with Hervey that marked the difference between me the reader and the narrator. They seemed to me brilliant, and I still love them today, as an important part of a book that now seems to me to have a great literary intelligence.

Let's look, then, if you don't mind, at the story of that dress, whose development is complex. Eleonora has talent as an artist, but, dulled by her role as the wife of a vulgar man, she is diminished, and has the faded appearance of a sensitive woman without love. Her mother, Alessandra's grandmother, also wasted her life: she was Austrian, and a talented actress, but she married an Italian artilleryman and had to pack up in a box the veils and feathers of her costumes for Juliet, for Ophelia: she, too, was fated to give up her talent. But now Eleonora, nearly forty, going from house to house giving piano lessons, ends up at a wealthy villa as the teacher of a girl named Arletta. She meets her brother, the mysterious musician Hervey, and falls in love. Love restores her talent, her desire to live, her artistic ambition, and she decides to give a concert with Hervey. It's at this point that the problem of the dress arises. What will Eleonora wear for her concert of liberation, in the luxurious house of Arletta and Hervey?

As an adolescent reader, I trembled at every line. I liked the fact that love counted so much in that book. I felt that it was true, that one can't live without love. But at the same time I perceived that something wasn't right. The clothes in Eleonora's closet distressed me, I recognized something I knew. "They were all of a neutral color," de Céspedes writes, giving voice to Alessandra: "brown, gray, two or three were of raw silk, with melancholy collars of white lace: clothes suitable for an old person . . . The dresses hung limply from the hangers. I said, softly, 'They seem like so many dead women, Mamma.' " There: the image of the clothes as dead women hanging on the hangers must have fit well with my secret feeling about clothes: I have often used it, I do still. And there is another image, a few pages earlier, which I immediately inserted in my vocabulary, which refers to the vanishing body of Eleonora in love: "She was so thin it was as if the dress held only a faint breath." The dress animated only by a warm breath seemed so true. I read. I read avidly to see how it was going to end. What dress would Eleonora wear? She jumps up, she goes to the dresser, she takes out a large box. The daughter, Alessandra, doesn't take her eyes off her mother: "The box was tied with old string: Mamma cut them with one snip. She took off the lid, and inside were pink and blue veils, feathers, satin ribbons. I didn't suppose she possessed such a treasure: so I watched, amazed, and she turned her eyes to the portrait of her mother. I understood that these were the silks of Juliet and Ophelia and I touched the material with reverence. 'How could we alter them?' she asked me uncertainly." I trembled. The dress of liberation would arrive through the maternal line; the costumes of Eleonora's actress mother, thanks to the dressmaker's wisdom of a noisy neighbor, Fulvia, become clothes for a concert performer, a garment enabling her to appear beautiful to Hervey. Eleonora puts aside the neutral clothes of her role as wife and uses pastel veils to make a dress that is the color of a woman in love, a lover. I was nervous. I didn't understand the joyful attitude of the daughter, Alessandra. Reading, I felt that things would not turn out well, and I was surprised that that sixteen-year-old girl—a girl the same age as me—didn't even suspect it. No, I wasn't blithely blind, like her. I perceived the tragedy of Eleonora. I felt that the passage from dull clothes to bright-colored clothes would not improve her situation. Rather, when Alessandra exclaims to Fulvia, the neighbor-dressmaker "We have to make a dress for Mamma out of Ophelia's robes!" I was sure of it, the tragedy was near. The new dress made from the old theatrical fabrics wouldn't save Eleonora. Alessandra's mother—it was clear—would kill herself, would surely drown.

In fact that's what happens. Alessandra doesn't understand, I did. The need to offer her beauty to the loved man seemed to me not liberating but sinister. Eleonora says, showing off her half-naked body to her daughter and the neighbor: "Every time I arrive and he looks at me, I have a desire to be as beautiful as a woman in a painting." The passage continues like that, in the voice of Alessandra: "She got up, she rushed to embrace Lydia and then Fulvia, and then me, she flew to the mirror and stopped there, observing herself. 'Make me beautiful,' she said, clasping her hands to her heart. 'Make me beautiful.' "

Make me beautiful. How I wept at those words. The

phrase remained in my memory not as a cry for life but as something deathly. A lot of time has passed and many things have changed, but the need that de Céspedes's Eleonora expresses still seems desperate, and therefore meaningful. Let's return to those passages as I felt them at my first, long-ago reading, and still feel them now. Eleonora, impelled by love, decides to take off the clothes of punishment, of suffering. But the only alternative she comes up with is the costume inherited from her mother, the dress worn by the female body exploited and put on display. Fulvia, the dressmaker, sews the dress, and Eleonora adorns herself as an offering to a distracted him: a Juliet dress, an Ophelia dress, a dress that is no less humiliating than the neutral dresses, the self-annihilating dresses of the roles of wife and mother. This I knew, this it seemed to me I had known forever. I knew that not only the demure clothes of Eleonora's domestic closet but also those meant for display are clothes that hang in the closet like dead women. It would take Alessandra the whole book to understand this. Too late: like her grandmother, like her mother, she, too, emerges into death. I had perceived it, I don't know how, in my mother's clothes, in her passion to make herself beautiful, and that perception tormented me. I didn't want to be like that.

But how did I want to be? When I thought of her, once I was an adult, once I was far away, I sought a means of understanding what type of woman I could become. I wanted to be beautiful, but how? Was it possible that you necessarily had to choose between dullness and ostentation? Don't both paths lead back to the same subservient dress, Harey's terrible dress, the one that is on you forever, anyway, and there's no way to get it off? I was anxiously searching for my path of rebellion, of freedom. Was the way, as Alba de Céspedes has Alessandra say, using a metaphor perhaps of religious origin, to learn to wear not clothes—those will come later, as a consequence—

but the body? And how does one arrive at the body beyond the clothes, the makeup, the customs imposed by the everyday job of making oneself beautiful?

I've never found a definite answer. But today I know that my mother, both in the dullness of domestic tasks and in the exhibition of her beauty, expressed an unbearable anguish. There was only one moment when she seemed to me a woman in tranquil expansion. It was when, sitting bent in her old chair, her legs drawn up and joined, her feet on the foot rest, around her the discarded scraps of material, she dreamed of salvific clothes, and drawing needle and thread straight she sewed together again and again the pieces of her fabrics. That was the time of her true beauty.

NOTE
The letter to Sandra Ozzola is from June, 2003. The letter from April 11, 2003, with the questions from Giuliana Olivero and Camilla Valletti that inspired Ferrante's text, follows.

Dear Elena Ferrante,

It would give us great pleasure to have an interview with you in the pages of *Indice*[7] (under the rubric devoted to contemporary fiction and provocatively titled "Unsuccessful Writing"). Our journal has closely followed your literary output, with reviews and comments. In particular, we have read your novels passionately, and we think your writing interprets the universe and the feelings of women by making them the center of a poetics, beyond and above literary conventions.

We would therefore be truly grateful if you would answer the questions that follow, sending us your answers by e-mail through Sandra Ozzola.

With affection,
Giuliana Olivero and Camilla Valletti

---

[7] *L'indice dei libri del mese*, Italian monthly magazine founded in 1984.

Questions

1. In very different ways, the protagonists of your novels come from archaic female models, myths of the Mediterranean matrix, from which they free themselves only in part. Is suffering the result of this intermittent relationship with one's own origins, of this difficult and unresolved detachment from traditional roles?

2. Guilt and innocence. None of your characters can call themselves innocent but neither are they entirely guilty. How does one analyze guilt for a female? For a male?

3. How is the original betrayal of the father/mother tied to the chain of successive betrayals? What importance does reading the relationships in your novels in an anthropological-psychoanalytic key have?

4. Naples and Turin: why do you attribute to places, to cities, an almost physical, almost repellent density, as if they had a body that breathes, that sickens along with your women?

5. What relationship do your protagonists have with the rituals of clothes and makeup?

17.
An Afterword

July 3, 2003

Dearest Elena,

Yesterday, here at the beach, I got your e-mail with the long answer to the questions from the editors of *Indice* attached. I found it extraordinarily interesting, and it gave me an idea: couldn't we make a book out of it? Not a ponderous essay, but reflections on subjects we've often discussed over the years, and certainly of interest not only to you and me but also to many other people (not just women) who are fans of your books and would like to follow you a bit more closely in your journey.

Your wish not to appear, which is absolutely legitimate, perhaps deserves a more general response, beyond the newspaper interviews, not only to placate those who get lost in the most far-fetched hypotheses on your real identity but also out of a healthy desire on the part of your readers (and I assure you that they are very many by now) to know you better.

We could publish a volume that contained, besides this most recent text, other materials that we have in our files. I don't know—I'm thinking of, for example, the correspondence with Martone when he was working on the film made from *Troubling Love*, or the answers to that interview with Fofi that never reached their addressee (I think he had pulled one of his usual stunts). Or the short piece on the story of a caper plant that you wrote on the occasion of the fifteenth anniversary of the publishing house: there was an interesting letter along with it, like most of the letters you've sent us. The piece about the caper tree was really sweet. Would publishing it seem too self-laudatory? What do you think?

In other words, think about it with your usual tranquility, but I think it could be a good idea to bring out for Christmas a "book of reflections" by Elena Ferrante or something like that. If it helps, don't think of a real book, think of a kind of *cahier* or of something like *Linea d'ombra's* publication of the correspondence between you and Martone. Nothing, in other words, that would be especially burdensome.

Let me know what you think as soon as you can, possibly before your departure. If you agree, we would have to start getting ready.

Fondly,
Sandra

Dear Sandra,

I've thought a lot about your proposal, it shows a lot of confidence in the good will of readers. I've taken it seriously, I've looked at all the old papers you've sent, and it's true, there is enough material to make a book. But what sort of book would it be? A collection of letters? And why should we publish my letters? And why only the letters I've sent you for editorial or other reasons and not those to friends and relatives or love letters or letters expressing political or cultural indignation, so as to truly touch the depths of fatuousness? Why, above all, add so much of my chatter to the two novels?

On the other hand I have to admit that I'm quite tired of always saying no to you—you've really been very patient over these twelve years. Especially since many of my nos, I know very well, were yeses, an inclination transformed into a rejection only out of timidity, out of anxiety. In this case, too, I think, it would be so.

In other words, I'm uncertain. I think a book like that might perhaps possess a cohesiveness but not autonomy. I think, that is, that by its nature it can't be a book in itself. You're very right to call it a book for readers of *Troubling Love* and *The Days of Abandonment*. With all consequences, however. Which is to say that, if you decide to publish it, you have to do so feeling that it is editorially, as an appendix to those two books, a sort of slightly dense afterword, as you used to do once at the end of your elegant volumes, an afterword that because of its excessive mass became a volume on its own. That's how I see it. Only then would I feel at ease, as much as I can feel at ease.

You will note that I moved from "I" to "you": you the publishing house, I mean. It's not a ruse, it's the result of reasoning. If this book that you have in mind isn't my third book, or, to put it clearly, isn't my new book, but an appendix to the first two, I can say to myself, to appease myself, that the decision to publish it belongs to you, you already have the material, I have only to be your ally in helping to clarify confusing formulations, eliminating an adjective or a line that is too much, giving a progressive order to material originating by chance.

Let me know,

Elena

II

Tesserae: 2003-2007

1.
AFTER *LA FRANTUMAGLIA*

Dear Elena,

Here are two new items that we'd like your opinion on. The first: Silvia Querini, the Spanish publisher, wants to publish all three of your books together, calling them *trilogía del desamor*, "the trilogy of unlove": what do you think?

The second: we'd like to put *La Frantumaglia* into our pocket editions, but with an appendix that updates the book through *The Lost Daughter:* do you agree? I looked in the files: there's the interview with the *Repubblica* for the publication of the *Frantumaglia*, something on Roberto Faenza's film, the questions from readers at Fahrenheit, and, finally, the in-depth conversation with Luisa Muraro and Marina Terragni. I also found a couple of pieces of yours that aren't precisely apposite. One is the piece on Patrice Chéreau's film *Gabrielle,* which I kept you from sending to the *Repubblica* because it was too "hard" for a daily paper. The other is the piece on *Madame Bovary*, which I think did come out in that paper, or am I wrong?

That's all for now. I'll send you the material, let me know quickly.

Fondly,
Sandra

Dear Sandra,

I looked at the texts, and they're all right, but you have to take care of the titles and the notes, I don't have time right now. I'd like it to be very obvious that this is an appendix. Over time I've become very attached to *La Frantumaglia*; today I feel it as a complete book, with a coherence that wasn't clear to me when you put it together.

As for the Spanish proposal, the books would come out in a single volume, if I understand correctly, and that would please me. I'm more hesitant about "*desamor*," I have to think about it. How does the word sound in Spanish? My characters are not at all without love, not in the sense that we give the word. The love that Delia, Olga, Leda have experienced in different forms has, in their confrontation with life, certainly been disfigured, as after a disaster, but it preserves a powerful energy, it's love put to the test, eviscerated, and yet alive. Or at least so it seems to me. Yes, give me some time to think about it. Meanwhile, work well, and thank you for your attention, care, everything.

Elena

2.

LIFE ON THE PAGE
Answers to questions from Francesco Erbani

E*rbani: Did you study literature? And, if not literature, what?*

Ferrante: I have a degree in classical literature. But degrees say little or nothing about what we've truly learned—out of necessity, out of passion. So it is that what has really formed us cannot, paradoxically, be catalogued.

Erbani: Do you have a job, besides writing? And what is it?

Ferrante: I study, I translate, I teach. But—like writing—studying, translating, and teaching don't seem like jobs to me. They are, rather, ways of being active.

Erbani: Who close to you knows about Elena Ferrante?

Ferrante: When one writes truthfully, the ties most at risk are precisely the close ones, of blood, of love, of friendship. The people who stay near us in writing, to the point of accepting even the most cruel and devastating effects, can be counted on the tips of one's fingers.

Erbani: Why did you leave Naples? Did you flee the city?

Ferrante: I needed a job and I found one outside Naples. It was a good opportunity to leave; my native city seemed to me without any possibility of redemption. Over time, this idea was reinforced. But one does not free oneself of Naples so easily. It remains in my gestures, my words, my voice, even when I put an ocean between us.

Erbani: It is said that you lived in Greece, and that now you are in Italy again. Is there any truth to this?

Ferrante: Yes, but Greece for me is also a condensed way of saying that over the years I've moved often, in general unwillingly, out of necessity. Now, however, I intend to become sedentary. Recently, there have been a lot of changes in my life: I'm no longer dependent on the movements of others, only on my own.

Erbani: Do you adopt any particular measures for keeping your activity as a writer hidden?

Ferrante: It's not I who keep my activity hidden, it's my activity that hides me. I read, reflect, take notes, ponder the writing of others, produce my own, and all this for a period that's always longer than my day. Reading and writing are closed-room activities, which literally take you away from the gaze of others. The greater risk is that they also remove others from your gaze.

Erbani: Does writing in secret condition your work? Does it influence aspects of the writing?

Ferrante: As long as one writes only for oneself, writing is a free act by means of which, to use an oxymoron, one secretly opens oneself. The problems begin when this secret act, this revealing oneself furtively to oneself, like an adolescent writing her diary, feels the need to become a public action. The question then is: what of what I write for myself can be offered to the gaze of another? Starting at that point, it's not the secrecy that conditions or influences the writing but the possibility of its being public.

Erbani: You say that you would not welcome "the idea of life where the success of oneself is measured by the success of the written page." But how is it possible to make a clear separation between life and the written page?

Ferrante: In fact, it's impossible, especially since, by vocation, I tend to throw into words—for the most part vainly—my
entire body. With the sentence you quoted I meant something
different. I meant that, ever since a bad period when I was very
young, and consumed by a frenzy of writing, I've tried to consider writing not as the only way of acting in the world but as
one of the three or four actions that give weight to my life.

*Erbani: Why do you maintain that nothing in an author's
personal history is useful in reading him better?*
Ferrante: I'm not a supporter of the idea that the author is
inessential. I would like only to decide myself what part of me
should be made public and what instead should remain private. I think that, in art, the life that counts is the life that
remains miraculously alive in the works. So I am very much in
agreement with Proust's stand against positivist biography and
against anecdotalism in the style of Sainte-Beuve. Neither the
color of Leopardi's socks nor even his conflict with the father
figure helps us understand the power of his poems.
The biographical path does not lead to the genius of a
work; it's only a micro-story on the side. Or, as Northrup Frye
would put it, the disruptive imaginative energy of *King Lear* is
not in the least affected by the fact that what remains of
Shakespeare is only a couple of signatures, a will, a baptismal
certificate, and the portrait of a fellow who looks like an imbe-
cile. The living body of Shakespeare (imagination, creativity,
drives, anxieties, but I would also say sounds of speech,
moods, nervous responses) will act forever from within *King
Lear*. The rest is curiosity, academic publications, wars and
skirmishes for visibility in the marketplace of culture.

*Erbani: You wanted to avoid the publishing circuit, not take
part in its mechanisms. But it is also said that among the reasons
for your reserve are coincidences between certain passages in*

Troubling Love *and your personal experience. Which of the two reasons is truer?*

Ferrante: Both are valid. They aren't the only ones, however; I've tried to list other, more complex ones. But even if you add up all the reasons, my books—I hope that you would agree—are not better or worse. Like all books, good or bad, great or mediocre, they remain what they are.

Erbani: Are you not afraid, in particular, that the secrecy of your life might distort the perception of your novels? Might it, for example, induce in those who read them an abnormal curiosity, pushing them to search artificially, even obsessively, in the novel, in the narrated material, for the reasons for your absence?

Ferrante: It's possible. When I published my first book, I hadn't thought of the effect that the physical absence of the author would have, if cast into the middle of the widespread war to gain a recognizable physical image, a following. On the other hand, I believe that the true reader shouldn't be confused with the fan. The true reader, I think, searches not for the brittle face of the author in flesh and blood, who makes herself beautiful for the occasion, but for the naked physiognomy that remains in every effective word.

Erbani: You recently described, in a kind of moral fable, the arrogance and insolence of a character and compared it to the figure of Silvio Berlusconi. Now you propose to write something on the transformation of Italians in public life. Does this signify a change of direction in your fiction?

Ferrante: I don't know, I hope not. Let's say that I'm interested in understanding the fact that everything in life is turning into a show, draining the very concept of citizenship. I'm also struck by how the person is more and more unhappily dedicated to becoming a personage. And it frightens me that a classical effect of fiction—the suspension of disbelief—is becoming an instrument of political domination in the very heart of democracies. It seems to me that for now Berlusconi embodies, more completely than Reagan or Schwarzenegger, the change taking place in the democratic election of representatives. But if I had to work in fiction on a subject like that (and it's only a remote hypothesis, inspired by indignation), I would turn to the expressive means that I've tried to develop over the years.

NOTE
The interview with Francesco Erbani appeared in *la Repubblica*, October 26, 2003, under the title "La scrittrice senza volto. Il caso di Elena Ferrante" ("The Writer Without a Face: The Case of Elena Ferrante").

3.

THE DAYS OF ABANDONMENT AT A CROSSROADS
Letter to Roberto Faenza

Dear Faenza,
Thank you for sending me your screenplay to read. I recognized events and characters of my book, reused more or less faithfully, and that gave me pleasure. I must confess, however, that I had a hard time imagining the film: I don't know how to read this type of writing, which tears off the literary covering and reduces events and characters to naked movements of bodies. As in the case of *Troubling Love,* I first had to find some reassurance. I said to myself that the stage directions will disappear, the dialogue will have the warmth of words thought and said, and the story will exist in the actions of living bodies, in real voices, in the strong sense of involvement produced by the setting. But I didn't really feel satisfied until I got over the impact of the reduction to scenes.

That doesn't mean that I don't have some questions, and I'll list them here.

1. The first scene seems to me very effective. Among other merits, it keeps Olga from returning in her thoughts to the first marital crisis, to her jealousy of Gina, to the discovery of the attraction between Mario and Carla. That creates a problem, however. We no longer know that Olga is a woman who is able to manage calmly, with equilibrium, with discipline, her marital relationship. And this weakens the impression that she is able to control the effects of abandonment, like a cultivated woman of today, and unlike the broken women of yesterday.

Thus that first scene and the ones that immediately follow are fine, but they risk losing an essential passage. Maybe it should be said in some other way that Olga isn't inexperienced, she doesn't easily lose her head, she knows how to confront the risks of a sentimental breakup. Because if that isn't communicated, the character is impoverished, the story is in danger of recounting yet again, and ineffectually, what Virgil already described in Dido. What *The Days of Abandonment* narrates, on the other hand, is how a woman who has an array of defenses is struck by one of the most unendurable experiences of disintegration, is overwhelmed by it, and yet she resists and, although disillusioned, saves herself and her children from death.

2. It seems to me that the "absence of sense" is cited too many times and in ironic contexts that diminish the value of the expression. Perhaps it's better not to wear out a statement that has a central role in the book and in the screenplay. Olga, abandoned, traverses precisely the absence of sense that for her husband is only a wretched self-justification. We have to feel its full weight when she emerges from her crisis and discovers that her love for Mario is finished.

3. It's true that the character of the *poverella* should have an important role from the start. But it seems to me that the hallucination of the tunnel arrives too soon, when Olga hasn't even begun her true descent to the depths. It contributes to making her seem fragile from the start and reduces the possibility of narrating her crisis as something that intensifies. Olga's initial solidity instead reinforces the dramatic effect of the collapse. So the memory of the dead woman should make slow progress in her, until it "emerges" and acts as a double.

4. I said that the screenplay used a great deal of the book. But something essential has been left out: the moment when the woman gives the paper cutter to her daughter and tells her to prick her whenever she might appear absent. The request

conveys two important things: that Olga intends to resist in every way possible the looming loss of herself; and that, to react, all she can count on is that small female creature who follows her around the house wavering between devotion and hostility. I don't really understand why that passage was taken out. In my book the mother-daughter relationship is very important.

5. The dog: maybe his intense bond with Mario, with Mario's things, should be emphasized. Neglecting it or making it inactive risks simplifying Olga's relationship with Otto and weakening the drama of the animal's death.

6. Carrano: His figure should perhaps be more disquieting at first (not aggressive: disquieting, as disquieting as it is seductive) and less sweet at the end. His role as savior and the symbolism of the metronome aren't convincing to me. I would prefer the character to preserve its ambiguity. I admit that there are reasons having to do with representation, but still I would trust more decisively in a figure at first irritating, then reassuring, then engaging and yet not decisive. Not coincidentally does the story end on that "I pretended to believe him," the point of arrival of Olga's journey to hell.

As you see, a great many of my fears are centered on the crescendo of Olga's days in hell. That doesn't mean that the text as it is doesn't already contain that journey. You have only to decide whether to make it more intensely marked, so as to reach a conclusion that sounds like a clear, disillusioned liberation.

Thank you for your good work.

NOTE
The screenplay referred to is taken from *The Days of Abandonment*, and the letter, unpublished, is dated June 3, 2003.

4.

The Unexpected Olga of Margherita Buy
Answers to questions from Angiola Codacci-Pisanelli

C odacci-Pisanelli: *Another book of yours has become a film. What impression do you have on "seeing" your stories?*

Ferrante: It's hard to say. When you write stories you daydream about them. When they become a film, you've already, in fact, "seen" them. The result is that for you the film inspired by your book is never a first viewing. Like it or not, you have to reckon a second time with the emotional complexity and imaginative density of what you did the first time, which is what really belongs to you. So I try to be sensible, and I go to the movies not to see my book but to see what someone else has seen in it.

Codacci-Pisanelli: Have you seen Faenza's film? What do you think of it?

Ferrante: I saw a videocassette, without music, when it was still being worked on, and I would be unjust to Faenza if I expressed a judgment on a work not yet completed. I prefer to form an opinion based on seeing it in the theater. Still, even though I saw it in those conditions, certain parts made a very favorable impression. Olga's violent or humiliating moments are powerful, they draw you in, and the actors are so good that they leave you speechless. I must confess that for Olga I would never have thought of Margherita Buy and just for that reason, perhaps, her brilliance struck me particularly. Words have a concreteness different from images, the worlds and figures they evoke seem to us precise and instead are malleable. Margherita Buy became an unexpected Olga, but one that I like.

Codacci-Pisanelli: Did you work on the screenplay of Faenza's film? Did you ask to see it?

Ferrante: He sent me the screenplay, I read it, I wrote down a few notes that I sent the director. No more than that.

Codacci-Pisanelli: In an interview Faenza said that he had "humanized" the character of the husband. But in the novel what drags Olga into tragedy is precisely his utter coldness.

Ferrante: Zingaretti is good. His portrayal of the character of a man who no longer feels love for the woman he lives with is effective. He is in love with someone else and doesn't have the strength or the courage or the cruelty to tell his wife that love is gone. Mario, in the book, is that, and it seems to me that he is on the screen as well. The problem is that Olga's story is a first-person story and films always have trouble with the first person. The story of Olga is the story of an intensifying disintegration that reaches the threshold of infanticide and madness, then abruptly stops. In the vortex of her monologue the "I" pulverizes everything and everyone, especially the husband. Probably what Faenza calls the humanization of Mario indicates only the difficulty of keeping together, on the screen, the bourgeois realism of a common marital crisis and a first-person woman's journey that is tense, anguished, borderline.

Codacci-Pisanelli: What relation did you have with the previous film, made from Troubling Love?

Ferrante: Martone sent me several drafts of the screenplay, we had a good correspondence. He invited me to see the film, but after much hesitation I decided not to. I saw it in the theater, some time after it came out, and it made a deep impression. It wasn't, naturally, what I had "seen" when I was writing. But at times I felt that it had expanded the book by other means, approaching in an extraordinary way the reality that I had disguised or hidden in telling the story. Maybe, when one chooses a book to make a film out of, the problem isn't to respect the structure faithfully or to violate it capriciously. The real problem, for a director, is to find solutions, the language with which to get the truth of his film from that of the book, to put them together without one ruining the other and dissipating its force.

Codacci-Pisanelli: A "hidden" author like you has of necessity to use others to get your stories to the screen. Have you ever thought of directing?

Ferrante: For a lifetime I've been trying to learn to tell a story with written words. It would take another to learn to do it with images.

Codacci-Pisanelli: In a recent article in la Repubblica *you spoke about* Madame Bovary. *How much of Madame Bovary is there in Olga, the protagonist of* The Days of Abandonment?

Ferrante: Bovary and Karenina are, in some way, descendants of Dido and Medea, but they have lost the obscure force that pushed those heroines of the ancient world to use infanticide or suicide as rebellion or revenge or curse. Rather, they experience the time of abandonment as a punishment for their sins. Olga, on the other hand, is an educated woman of today, influenced by the battle against the patriarchy. She knows what can happen to her and tries not to be destroyed by abandonment. Hers is the story of how she resists, of how she touches bottom and returns, of how abandonment changes her without annihilating her.

Codacci-Pisanelli: Are you working on a new novel?

Ferrante: No. I'm only putting in order an old story about children, dolls, beach, and sea.

Codacci-Pisanelli: A few months ago the fires of the search for your true identity were rekindled. An analysis of the text—the same weapon that led, in Holland, to "unmasking" Marrek van der Jagt, a pseudonym of Arnon Grunberg—led a philologist to name the novelist Domenico Starnone. What effect did that have on you? Will you ever come out into the open? (I myself remain faithful to one of the final dialogues in To Kill a Mockingbird: *"I think I'm beginning to understand why Boo Radley's stayed shut up [in the house all the time] . . . it's because he wants to stay inside."*

Ferrante: I come out into the open every time I publish something, even just the answers in this interview of yours. It seems to me sufficient. Otherwise I don't know what there is to discover. Words that become public belong to everyone. That one attributes them to this person or that is their fate. On the other hand, doesn't someone who reads one of my books make space in his own vocabulary for my words, doesn't he appropriate them, if necessary doesn't he reuse them? Books belong to those who have written them only when their cycle is complete and no one reads them anymore.

NOTE
The interview, with Angiola Codacci-Pisanelli, appeared in *Espresso*, September 1, 2005, under the title "Olga, la mia felice Madame Bovary" ("Olga, My Happy Madame Bovary"), on the occasion of the presentation, at the Venice Film Festival, of Roberto Faenza's film *The Days of Abandonment*.

5.
THE BOOK OF NO ONE

I saw Patrice Chéreau's *Gabrielle* and I read Conrad's *The Return*, the story that *Gabrielle* is taken from. I wondered what "taken from" means, but I found no comprehensive answers. Even to say that a film "is inspired" by a book wasn't convincing to me, and when I was informed that there exists an unpronounceable word, "transduction," which expresses with greater precision the passage from book to film, it didn't seem to me that the word helped; it merely indicated an operation of transferral. I said to myself: better to return to "taken from," "inspired." If the film *Gabrielle* is taken from the story *The Return*, does it mean that the story is a larger container than the film? Or: if a film is inspired by a book does it mean that the written page speaks through the film, like Apollo through the breast of the Pythia?

I don't know. The viewer who sees *Gabrielle* and has read *The Return* recognizes from the first scenes the literary source. But from the first scenes he is also aware that there are many differences between the film and the story. For example, we are not in London but in Paris. The male character is no longer named Alvan but Jean. And it doesn't take long to see that an Alvan, a wealthy Englishman in London at the end of the nineteenth century, is not identical to a Jean, a wealthy Frenchman in Paris in the early twentieth century. But above all it is not irrelevant that, in the transfer from the page to the film, a story in which there is a wife who returns after having left and a husband who never returns after trying desperately to stay ceases to be called *The Return* and is called instead *Gabrielle*.

Who is Gabrielle? In the story there is no Gabrielle. The wife, who, after leaving her husband a letter in which she says that she is abandoning him for another man, has second thoughts and, in the space of a few hours, returns to the conjugal roof, has no name in Conrad's pages, and it's significant that she doesn't; a reader of the story knows that that choice of anonymity is important. Why, then, is the nameless wife of Alvan, in becoming the wife of Jean, christened Gabrielle? Why does a story of male fear and trembling promise in the title the centrality of the female character? What pushes Chéreau to choose a name for the wife of Alvan-Jean, and even to title the film after her?

Those questions, in my opinion, have little to do with film and much with literature. I don't know how to say anything about the psychology of reading or the psychology of the spectator. But I've never believed that the thread of literary writing is an Ariadne's thread to be obediently unrolled. Of course, the reader holds that thread and is guided by it. Of course, the combination of words and phrases is, for the reader, as constricting as that which opens a safe. But there is no correct way to activate the power of a written story, and instructions for use are not worth much. The "right reading" is an invention of academics and critics. Every reader gets from the book he is reading nothing else but *his* book. The shelves where we line up the volumes we've read are deceptive. We have available there only titles, covers, pages. But the books we've *truly* read are phantoms conjured up by reading with no rules. Once, that lack of regulation was a purely private fact, at most leaving some public traces in the pages of professional readers. Things aren't like that anymore. The Internet is crowded with readers who write about *their* book. And screenwriters and directors more and more use literary texts as a runway for their imagination to take off from. This material testifies in a compact way to a single thing: that narrative writing remains today the most welcoming dwelling place for the turbulent or mute world of those in need of stories, both those who have only the capacity to read, and those who work as transductors from word to image. The as yet unsurpassed force of literature lies in its capacity to construct vibrating bodies from whose veins anyone can drink, as from those of the mythical Asclepius, gaining from them life or death, other works that have great power or are thin and pallid.

The director and the screenwriter of *Gabrielle* were nourished by Conrad's *The Return*. But, as is natural, their reading generated *another story*, different from the original, even though it respects all its points and even its literary quality. Is that story still Conrad's story or is it mainly Chéreau's story? Neither. I think it's *a story by no one*, even though it has its origins in the generous hospitality of Conrad's text. Chéreau entered and found in the silences of the wife's character, in the few sentences she utters, sufficient stimulus to imagine that he was reading the story of a rebellious and overwrought woman, desperate and ruthless, disgusted by her husband and her possible lover, a woman without love, suffocated by her role as wife. He *derived*, that is, from Conrad's story, even more than his film, *a story* that isn't written, isn't printed, isn't readable anywhere.

All of us, like Chéreau, read books by no one. I, for example, long ago read a *Return* that was like a stutter. The characters spoke only in cut-off sentences: the nameless wife broke off in mid-sentence, as did the husband, Alvan, and so they misunderstood each other, they didn't comprehend each other. Their attempt to stay together made use of the disconnected, reticent sentence, precisely because if the sentences had been spoken in their entirety the break would inevitably have taken place. And then there were the distorted sensations, each of which was a sign of dissolution. What really *made* that story, in my view, was the disconnected sentences and the warped senses. A groan emitted by the wife seems to Alvan to come from his own body. When he is about to place a glass on the table, he no longer perceives the dimensions of the piece of furniture, he has the impression that the glass goes past the wood, falls into emptiness. If he tries to open the door, he can't, he persists, he no longer remembers having locked it. The story for me was that. When, after seeing the film, I reread it, I found not only that what had seemed to me the heart of the story occupied just a few lines but that in fact I attributed to Conrad pages I had never read, that he had never written, and that there was naturally no trace of in Chéreau's film.

The *Return* that I draw on is therefore a very different story from the one that Chéreau draws on. In his, a wife of the late nineteenth century has an explicit, lashing, and bold language. While the husband remains a bourgeois man of a hundred years ago, Gabrielle has the exceptional nature of a woman of today. If Conrad sets most of the story in a room full of mirrors that multiplies the couple into a crowd of people like them, Chéreau keeps only his Alvan-Jean in the reflections, while he removes from Gabrielle every symbol of averageness. The Alvan of the writing feels so threatened by the shadowy enigma of women that he goes so far as to plan the firing of the silent maids in order to hire only males, a gender more reassuring to him. In Chéreau's film, on the other hand, there is an especially bold, especially talkative maid whose presence is important to the story. In other words, the film is the visible trace of *another text*, neither written by Conrad nor findable in the pages we have before our eyes as readers nor present in those which we think we read in the past. It is from *this other text*, created by Chéreau's world, by his sensibility, by the requirements of his job, by the needs of the film industry, that the film was truly "derived."

Is the right text the wrong one? I think a value judgment is legitimate but not conclusive. The force of literature lies precisely in this permanent possibility of a dream reading, of a fantastic stimulus, of a starting point for other works. I imagine that there are an infinite number of other "places" for Conrad's text, all inhabitable, all generators of stories, which on every rereading I don't see, I will never see, owing to the simple fact that I immediately rush to occupy the places that are more congenial to me. That's what reading is like for me.

Therefore I always listen with great curiosity to people who talk about books I love. I hear them discussing, precisely, *books by no one*. Between the book that is published and the book that readers buy there is always *a third book*, a book where beside the written sentences are those which we imagined writing, beside the sentences that readers read are the sentences they have imagined reading. This third book, elusive, changing, is nevertheless a real book. I didn't actually write it, my readers haven't actually read it, but it's there. It's the book that *is created* in the relationship between life, writing, and reading. Traces of such an object are found in the words of writers who reflect on their own works, or in the discussions of passionate readers. But it becomes evident above all when the reader is a privileged reader, one who isn't limited to reading but who gives a form to his reading, for example with a review, an essay, a screenplay, a film. It is, in particular, films inspired by literature that, precisely because they produce in a different language another, perfectly autonomous narrative organism, testify to the existence of that third book, not sold at booksellers, not to be found in libraries, and yet alive and active. It is from that book that the film derives, together with everything else generated by a text.

Naturally not all those intermediate books give good results. Among the many ways of reading, I disapprove of the one that smooths, normalizes stories. Movie readings often run that risk. Film increasingly digs into literature absent-mindedly, in search only of a starting point, raw material. What in a text is anomalous or disquieting the film often considers a negative and eliminates or doesn't even notice. It prefers to take from the book what is proved and what is assumed the audience will want to see and see again. It is therefore not the anarchic ransacking of a literary work that should worry the writer: a novel is written precisely so that its readers can appropriate it. Nor is there any need, on the part of directors with a strong authorial sense, to hide or deny by every means the literary origin of their own work: not to recognize their debts is a widespread vice and doesn't in the least damage the work they are indebted to, at most it wounds the vanity of the writer. It is, rather, the cinematographic normalization of the literary text that is disturbing. To return to *Gabrielle*, although Isabelle Huppert gives the best of herself and Chéreau's film engages us through the figure of the woman she depicts, we feel that the hospitality of Conrad's words has been abused, that the woman on the screen is less disturbing than the anonymous wife of the page, that the shadowy house that the writer has built for us has been exchanged for a habitation that is easily habitable. This, and only this, should grieve those who love literature.

NOTE
Unpublished, dated October 10, 2005.

6.
WHAT AN UGLY CHILD SHE IS

France for me—long, long before Paris—was Yonville-l'Abbaye, eight leagues from Rouen. I remember crouching inside that place-name one afternoon, when I was barely fourteen, traveling through the pages of *Madame Bovary*. Slowly, over the years, thousands of other names of cities and towns followed, some near Yonville, others far away. But France remained essentially Yonville, as I discovered it one afternoon decades ago, and it seemed to me that at the same time I came upon the craft of making metaphors and upon myself.

I certainly saw myself in Berthe Bovary, Emma and Charles's daughter, and felt a jolt. I knew that I had my eyes on a page, I could see the words clearly, yet it seemed to me that I had approached my mother just as Berthe tried to approach Emma, catching hold of her *par le bout, les rubans de son tablier* ("the ends of her apron strings"). I heard clearly the voice of Madame Bovary saying, with increasing annoyance, "*Laisse-moi! Laisse-moi! Eh! Laisse-moi donc!*" ("Leave me alone! Leave me alone! Won't you leave me alone!"), and it was like the voice of my mother when she was lost in her tasks or her thoughts, and I didn't want to leave her, I didn't want her to leave me. That cry of irritation of a woman dragged away from her own *bouleversements,* like a leaf on a rainy day toward the black mouth of a manhole, made a deep impression on me. The blow arrived right afterward, with her elbow. Berthe—I—*alla tomber au pied de la comode, contre la patère de cuivre; elle s'y coupa la joue, le sang sortit* ("fell at the foot of the chest of drawers, against the brass fittings; she cut her cheek, it began to bleed").

I read *Madame Bovary* in the city of my birth, Naples. I read it laboriously, in the original, on the orders of a cold, brilliant teacher. My native language, Neapolitan, has layers of Greek, Latin, Arabic, German, Spanish, English, and French—a lot of French. *Laisse-moi* ("leave me alone") in Neapolitan is *làssame* and *sang* ("blood") is *'o sanghe*. It's not so surprising if the language of *Madame Bovary* seemed to me, at times, my own language, the language in which my mother appeared to be Emma and said *laisse-moi*. She also said *le sparadrap* (but she pronounced it *'o sparatràp*), the adhesive plaster that had to be put on the cut I'd gotten—while I read and was Berthe—when I fell *contre la patère de cuivre*.

I understood then, for the first time, that geography, language, society, politics, the whole history of a people were for me in the books that I loved and which I could enter as if I were writing them. France was near, Yonville not that far from Naples, the wound dripped blood, the *sparatràp*, stuck to my cheek, pulled the stretched skin to one side. *Madame Bovary* struck with swift punches, leaving bruises that haven't faded. All my life since then, I've wondered whether my mother, at least once, with Emma's words precisely—the same terrible words—thought, looking at me, as Emma does with Berthe: *C'est une chose étrange comme cette enfant est laide!* ("It's strange how ugly this child is!") Ugly: to appear ugly to one's own mother. I have rarely read-heard a better conceived, better written, more unbearable sentence. The sentence arrived from France and hit me right in the chest, it's still hitting me, harder than the shove with which Emma sent—sends—little Berthe against the chest of drawers, against the brass fittings.

The words entered and emerged from me: when I read a book I never think of who has written it, it's as if I were doing it myself. So as a child I didn't know the names of authors;

every book was written by itself, it began and ended, it excited
me or not, made me cry or made me laugh. The Frenchman
named Gustave Flaubert came later, and by then I knew quite
a lot about France: I had been there not only thanks to books
and not happily, as in books; I could measure the true distance
between Naples and Rouen, between the Italian novel and the
French. Now I read Flaubert's letters, his other books. Every
sentence was well shaped, some more than others, but not
one—not one ever had for me the devastating force of that
mother's thought: *C'est une chose étrange comme cette enfant est
laide!* In certain phases of my life I've imagined that only a man
could conceive it, and only a man without children, a peevish
Frenchman, a bear shut up in his house honing his complaints,
a misogynist who thought of himself as both father and mother
just because he had a niece. In other periods I've believed,
angrily, bitterly, that men who are masters of writing are able
to have their female characters say what women truly think and
say and live but do not dare write. Today, instead, I've returned
to the beliefs of early adolescence. I think that authors are
devoted, diligent scribes, who draw in black and white following a more or less rigorous order of their own, but that the true
writing, what counts, is the work of readers. Although the page
of Flaubert is in French, Emma's *laisse-moi*, read in Naples,
has Neapolitan cadences, the brass fittings make *'o sanghe*
gush from Berthe's cheek, and Charles Bovary stretches the
child's skin by sticking *'o sparatràp* on it. It's my mother who
thought, but in her language, *comm'è brutta chesta bambina*
("How ugly this child is"). And I believe that she thought it for
the same reason Emma thinks it of Berthe. So I've tried, over
the years, to take that sentence out of French and place it
somewhere on a page of my own, write it myself to feel its
weight, transport it into the language of my mother, attribute it
to her, hear it in her mouth and see if it's a woman's phrase, if a
female really could say it, if I've ever thought it of my daughters,

if, in other words, it should be rejected and erased or accepted and elaborated, removed from the page of masculine French and transported into the language of female-daughter-mother. That is the work that truly leads to France, juxtaposing sexes, languages, peoples, eras, geography.

NOTE

The central passages of this essay were conceived as a response to the Swedish publisher Bromberg, who, after acquiring the rights to *The Days of Abandonment* and reading the translation, decided not to publish it, considering the behavior of Olga, the novel's protagonist, toward her children morally reprehensible. The essay was later published, with some modifications, by Uitgeverij Wereldbibliotheek, of Amsterdam, for the 2004 Paris Book Fair, in the anthology *Frankrijk, dat ben ik (Wereldbibliotheek*; 2004), under the title "Het gewicht van de taal" ("The Weight of Language"). It also appeared in *la Repubblica* of June 28, 2005.

7.
STAGES IN A UNIQUE QUEST
Answers to questions from Francesco Erbani

Erbani: *How are you?*

Ferrante: An interview that begins with "How are you" is a little frightening. What do you want me to say? If I start digging into the "how," I'll never stop.

So I will say: fine, I think, and I hope that you are, too.

Erbani: *After so many years, are you still convinced by your decision to remain in the shadows?*

Ferrante: "Remain in the shadows" is not an expression I like. It hints of plots, assassins. Let's say that, fifteen years ago, I chose to publish books without having to feel obliged to make a career of being a writer. So far, I haven't regretted it. I write and I publish only when the text seems of some value to me and to my publishers. Then the book makes its way, and I go on to occupy myself with something else. That's it, and I don't see why I should change my behavior.

Erbani: *How do you feel about the questions that are raised about your identity—are you amused, irritated, or something else?*

Ferrante: They are legitimate, but reductive. For those who love reading, the author is purely a name. We know nothing about Shakespeare. We continue to love the Homeric poems even though we know nothing about Homer. And Flaubert, Tolstoy, and Joyce matter only if a talented person changes them into the subject of an opera, a biography, a brilliant essay, a film, a musical. Otherwise they are names, that is to say labels.

Why would anyone be interested in my little personal story if we can do without Homer's or Shakespeare's? Someone who truly loves literature is like a person of faith. The believer knows very well that there is nothing at all at the bureau of vital statistics about the Jesus that truly counts for him.

Erbani: Among the identities that have been proposed for you—the novelist Domenico Starnone, the critic Goffredo Fofi, the writer Fabrizia Ramondino—which one intrigues you most?

Ferrante: None: it seems to me a banal media game. An insignificant name, mine, is associated with names of greater substance. The opposite never happens. It would not occur to any newspaper to fill a page with the hypothesis that my books were written by an old retired archivist or by a young, newly hired bank clerk. What can I tell you? I'm sorry that people I respect should be annoyed by this.

Erbani: When people speak of your novels, the problem of your identity often overshadows the literary questions. Does this disturb you? How do you think it can be avoided?

Ferrante: Yes, it disturbs me. But it also seems to me the proof that the media care little or nothing about literature in itself. Let's take these questions of yours: I've published a book, but, despite knowing that I would answer in very general terms, you have focused the whole interview on the theme of my identity. Up to now, if you will allow me to say so, there's been nothing that touched on *The Lost Daughter*, its subject, or its writing. You ask me how to keep people from talking only about who I am, and neglecting the books. I don't know. Certainly you—forgive me—aren't doing anything to reverse the situation and confront what you call the literary questions.

Erbani: Is one of the other reasons for your insistence on privacy still valid, that is to say the presence in your novels of auto-

biographical roles variously combined and disguised but still recognizable?

Ferrante: Yes. Like anyone who writes, I work with events, feelings, emotions that belong to me very intimately. But over time the problem has changed. Today it's important to me above all to preserve the freedom to dig deeply, without self-censorship, into my stories . . .

Erbani: What do you think of the attention that has been focused on Naples recently? In your view is it a media exaggeration or has the pressure of crime in fact become more acute?

Ferrante: It's a media exaggeration. Naples should always be in the spotlight. It has a long history of decline; it's a metropolis that has anticipated and anticipates the troubles of Italy, perhaps of Europe. So we should never lose sight of it. But the media makes its living on the exceptional: murders, garbage piling up, the wonderful book *Gomorrah*, by Roberto Saviano. The daily standard of unlivability isn't news. So when the exceptional passes, everything is silent and everything continues to rot.

Erbani: Naples, you said once, makes you extremely uneasy: a violent city, of sudden quarrels, beatings, a vulgar city, where people are rowdy, self-aggrandizing, quick with small cruelties. Does it still give you that feeling?

Ferrante: Yes, nothing has changed, except the fact that what seemed to me particular to my city, to my region, because of its history, now seems to be spreading into the rest of Italy.

Erbani: You escaped from this Naples as soon as you could, and yet you have carried it with you as "a surrogate for always keeping in mind that the power of life is damaged, humiliated by unjust modes of existence." Have you ever gone back? Would you ever live there again?

Ferrante: I return from time to time. As for living there, I don't know. I would if I were convinced that the change is not a rhetorical trick but a true political and cultural revolution.

NOTE
From an interview with Francesco Erbani that appeared in *la Repubblica*, December 4, 2006 entitled "Io, scrittrice senza volto" ("I, a Writer Without a Face"). Erbani noted in the introduction: "Elena Ferrante didn't like some of the questions, but she didn't avoid them. Owing to the way the interview was conducted, her answers are given without the interviewer having had the opportunity to reply."

8.
THE TEMPERATURE THAT CAN IGNITE THE READER
A Conversation with the Listeners of Fahrenheit

Why are your characters women who are suffering?
Eva

The suffering of Delia, Olga, Leda is the result of disappointment. What they expected from life—they are women who sought to break with the tradition of their mothers and their grandmothers—does not arrive. Old ghosts arrive instead, the same ones with whom the women of the past had to reckon. The difference is that these women don't submit to them passively. Instead, they fight, and they cope. They don't win, but they simply come to an agreement with their own expectations and find new equilibriums. I feel them not as women who are suffering but as women who are struggling.

I am simply in love with your writing. I am not at all curious about you as a person, because I know about you the only thing that interests me: what resonates within us through the words in your stories.

I know that you're a woman because in your pages a woman feels, suffers, and is tormented. A man would be able at most to understand those pages, but not to write them: not even that chameleon Tolstoy, who, in fact, didn't do a bad job with Anna Karenina. I would like to know: what do you read, what do you like to read?

Do you know Paula Fox, the author of Desperate Characters? *She is a writer I like as much as I like you. In her stories there is an analogous, terrible, pleasurable suspense. She has been translated into Italian, very well, by a man. So, at most, you could be a man of that type, trapped in the atmosphere of a book by a woman that he has translated, somewhat Zelig-like.*

Gratefully yours,
Cristina

Thank you for your encouraging words. Above all I was struck by your phrase "what resonates within us." I also like books for what resonates within us. While I was writing *The Lost Daughter*, I was reading a novel entitled *Olivia*, published by Einaudi in 1959 and translated by Carlo Fruttero. The book was published anonymously in 1949, by the Hogarth Press, in London. I think its pages have a fine resonance and I recommend it to you. As for Paula Fox's *Desperate Characters*, although I'm grateful for the comparison, you are too generous. *Desperate Characters* is a book that I love for its narrative intensity, but it has a richness of meaning that I feel unfortunately far from achieving myself.

I read The Days of Abandonment, *and I want to say that you are a woman, because one feels exactly like that when one is abandoned by those heartless beings, men. On the other hand, you could be a man, because you must also be someone who is aware of the harm you do (I'm thinking of the great Tolstoy of* The Kreutzer Sonata). *Congratulations, in any case. Reveal, if you will, the mystery of your identity, or, if not, well, art is superior in any case.*

Yours,
Mariateresa G.

Thank you for reading *The Days of Abandonment*. I don't think that art, as you say, can disregard artifice.

I think, rather, that one who writes ends up, whether he wants to or not, entirely in his writing. The author is always there, in the text, which therefore contains everything needed to solve the mysteries that matter. It's pointless to consider the ones that don't.

Dear Friends of Fahrenheit,

I'm writing to point out something rather unusual concerning the main character, Leda, in Elena Ferrante's latest book, The Lost Daughter *(which I haven't read yet, but which will soon be given to me as a gift). So, I live in Naples, my name is Leda, I have a degree in English (I teach and translate), I've been divorced for several years, and I have two teenage children. I'm curious: is the mysterious Elena (who, according to myth, is Leda's daughter) possibly someone who knows me?*

With best wishes and admiration,

Leda

Dear Leda, what can I tell you? Those who write stories hope that readers will find reason to identify with their characters, and not only with their vital statistics. When you've read the book, write and tell me if your affinities with my Leda extend beyond her name. I count on it, given that you are a reader who promises to give a certain gratification. In a few words in parenthesis, you made an observation that is important for me concerning the Leda-Elena link.

I did not choose the name Leda randomly. Leda—as high-school students and painters know better than anyone—is the girl with whom Zeus unites in the form of a swan. But if interested readers of *Fahrenheit* check, just to entertain themselves, in the third book of the *Library*, by Apollodorus, they will discover that, in a version of the myth that is less well known, Leda is in the middle of a complicated, modern question of maternity.

This is the story: Zeus, having taken the form of a swan, united not with Leda but with Nemesis, who, in order to escape from him, changed herself into a goose. "As a result of the union," Apollodorus summarizes, "Nemesis laid an egg that a shepherd found in the woods and brought to Leda as a gift. Leda placed it in an urn and, in due time, Elena was born and Leda reared her as her daughter." This Leda and this Elena, her daughter-non-daughter, gave me the names for the two characters in *The Lost Daughter*. If you read it, you'll see.

Dear author,

The mystery that surrounds you doesn't help me get a sense of you. I need the visual.

I would need to see you. Be sure whether you are a man or a woman. Establish an idea of your age. Deduce from your gaze what might have been your life style, in what social class to put you. I know that Carlo Emilio Gadda comes from a bourgeois family, that he was dominated by his mother and oppressed by the authoritarian character of his father. It's very important to have an overall sense of the personality of a writer. When I read something that fascinates me, I am immediately interested in the substance of the personality that has attracted my attention. The virtual disturbs me. I appreciate your writing but not the darkness that surrounds you. Darkness is always darkness.

Respectfully yours.

I thank you for your appreciation. I have to say, however, that, from my point of view, each reader, if he or she loves to read, must also love the virtual. What does writing describe, if not the outline of a virtual world? As for the question of darkness, what is better than reading in a room that is dark except for the light of a single reading lamp? Or what is better than the darkness of a theater or a cinema? The personality of a novelist exists utterly in the virtual realm of his or her books. Look there and you will find eyes, sex, lifestyle, social class, and the id.

Of Elena Ferrante's books I have read Troubling Love, The Days of Abandonment, *and some essays and interviews. Of the two novels, which are different in ideational structure and technical composition, I really loved* The Days of Abandonment, *for its angular, sharp writing.*

To strip down language means, for Ferrante, to strip down concepts. In her books, however, "pared to the bone" is equivalent not to a simplification but to what results from a thorough introspective analysis, which leads one to reflect on the basic questions: solitude, the elucidation of suffering, love. In the process of this fierce, inexhaustible search for meaning, the writing carves states of mind and feelings, displaying their contradictions and ambiguities.

Some questions: What does Elena Ferrante read? What is her relationship with the classics, Greek tragedy in particular? What does she think of the relationship between reading and school?

Thanks,
Roberta C.

I am grateful for your kind words. I was a passionate reader, and as a girl I wrote a lot about the classical world, for my own pleasure and also for school. In the tragedians, especially Sophocles, I always find something, even a few words that kindle my imagination. As for the relation of school with reading, I know little or nothing. From my observation post as a mother, I can say that the sensibility of the teacher is very important. A teacher who doesn't love reading communicates this deficiency even if he presents himself to his students as a passionate reader.

Dear Elena Ferrante, I'm a passionate reader of your stories, which I find to be extraordinary explorations of our inner complexity. I'm curious about one small thing: is the name you chose to sign your books an homage to Elsa Morante? I confess that even if you reject this hypothesis, I'd like to go on believing it.
Warm regards and best wishes for the future,
Carla A.

I love Elsa Morante's books very much, and, if it pleases you, by all means hold on to your hypothesis. Names and surnames are labels. My great-grandmother, whose name I bear and who has been dead so long that she is now a fictional character, will not be offended.

Dear author, Elena Ferrante,
I haven't read your books. From the films, which I've seen and liked not only for their power but also for the problems they raise, I imagined that your writing is important, readable, and powerful. Rarely have I seen such profound analyses of the feelings and the inner life of women. Our inner suffering is usually dismissed with an offensive phrase: hysteria. On what provokes the hysteria, absolute silence. Thank you for illuminating our subsoil. I'm sure you will help us to grow and to be respected. I recognize myself in what you bring to the surface. I, too, when my children (a male of forty-eight, a female of forty-two) left to follow their own paths, began to live and to appreciate the blue of the sky. The same thing happened when I realized that my love for my husband had no reason to exist. Like Olga, I, too,

after suffering and plunging into the abyss of despair, took the first steps toward self-esteem. I'm a little sorry that you have decided not to reveal who you are. Someone has suggested that behind your anonymity there is a man, Goffredo Fofi. I'm firmly convinced that when people can look each other in the eye everything becomes more tangible. However, my admiration for the subjects that you deal with will not diminish, whatever your physical form. Now that Fahrenheit *has drawn my attention to you, I will read your books. Ultimately, that's what counts.*

The body is all we have and it shouldn't be underestimated. The films you've seen are, precisely, literally, a "giving body" to what is in the writing of the books. I'm convinced, however, that potentially a page has more body than a film. We have to activate all our physical resources as writers and readers to make it function. Writing and reading are great investments of physicality. In writing and reading, in composing signs and deciphering them, there is an involvement of the body that compares only with writing, performing, and listening to music.

Dear Fahrenheit,
I was blown away by the novel Troubling Love *when it came out. On the contrary, I was bitterly disappointed by* The Days of Abandonment, *so much so that I suspected, given the mystery surrounding the author, that behind the same pseudonym there was another, less brilliant and less original mind. A negligible book with a predictable story, linguistically flat, stylistically unoriginal. I didn't want to buy the new book that has just come out under the name Elena Ferrante. But I was curious. I also saw the film* Troubling Love, *directed by Mario Martone, and rarely have I seen such stylistic consonance in a*

film adaptation of a novel, a sensibility so closely shared by two different artists. Might it be that the original Elena Ferrante is in reality Martone?
    Best wishes,
    Stella

Dear Stella, it is the sensibility of readers, tastes, and an occasional common place that establish difference, distance, and dissimilarity between the various books that one writes in the course of a lifetime. Without wanting to confuse wool with silk, I put it to you: why not ask if the original Verga is the same who wrote *The House by the Medlar-Tree*, if the author of *The House by the Medlar-Tree* is the same who wrote *Mastro Don Gesualdo*? The minute you remove the label "Verga" from those books, you will see how confusing it gets. To satisfy your curiosity, I can only assure you of one thing: judge the three books as you wish, but, for better or worse, all three are mine.

Questions for Ferrante: What books about abandonment did you read before writing The Days of*? Why do you hide?*
    Thanks,
    Carlotta

Dear Carlotta, none, if you mean works of nonfiction. But over the years I've read works of literature about many abandoned women, from Ariadne to Medea, from Dido to de Beauvoir's *Woman Destroyed*. Only after the publication of my book, very late, did I find in my hands a difficult but interesting text by the philosopher Jean-Luc Nancy. But right now I can't remember the exact title or the publisher.

Thank you, Elena. With your books, especially the latest, you have been able, in these thankless times, to clarify, to fill, the empty spaces in the lives of us women, mothers, daughters, workers, even if only for a moment, making us feel less alone. My partner, a man, deeply loved your book as well; it gave us pause for reflection, once again, on aspects of existence that are confusing or, at times, unspeakable.

Elisabetta

Dear Elisabetta, thank you for the verb "to fill"; it's a beautiful word when it's used to describe an effect of reading. A book for me must attempt to channel living, magmatic material that cannot easily be reduced to words or to the confessional genre, which is essential for our existence.

Dear Elena Ferrante,

I just read in la Repubblica *that the media attention concerning your identity disturbs you in that it distracts from your books. But don't you think that it is precisely this mystery that aids their success? Don't you think that if you (like everyone else) were available to talk about them, to show yourself, the "Ferrante phenomenon" would be deflated?*

Cristiano A.

Dear Cristiano, this is how I see it: I fear that this annoying insistence on "the mystery" has little, if any, effect on the books, and contributes nothing at all to their success. At most, it gives notoriety to the name of the person who wrote them. A reader, in order to enter a book, must establish a trusting relationship with the text. Media attention, which is based completely on giving voice and body to the star of the moment, has accustomed readers to the idea that the producer of the work counts more than the work. As if to say: I will read you because

I like you, I have faith in you, you are my small god. Avoiding this mechanism means, in fact, refusing the current ways of creating trust and trying to reestablish a relationship between the reader and the text alone. These matters aside, I don't feel that I need to communicate in any way other than through my writing. Not appearing is useful not for gaining readers, as you say, but for writing freely.

What does Elena Ferrante think about social questions like euthanasia? And, more generally, doesn't she think that for an intellectual (hence also for a writer) it's important (if not in fact a duty) to participate in the public debate on the great subjects of civic life?
Roberta

Dear Roberta, in my opinion, when life becomes pure suffering or, still worse, the negation of all that we consider to be human life, choosing to end life—a powerful expression of generosity, if taken literally—is a fundamental right. I should say, however, that to express myself like that, in a few conventional words on a very delicate issue, seems to me frivolous.

I have done so on this occasion but will not do so again. It is surely necessary to participate in public life, but not by resorting to pat phrases, today on one subject, tomorrow on another.

All your books, including the last, are characterized by the theme of abandonment, detachment, separation. Is it a personal wound? Or do you think that the incapacity to stay together, to live a shared life, is a compelling theme, representative of our time?
Dario M.

Dear Dario, I cling to the idea that we have to write about what has marked us deeply, but that we have to seek in our stories the temperature capable of igniting the reader. A book succeeds and endures if the story of our most incurable wounds captures a little of what used to be called, bombastically, the spirit of the time.

Dear Elena Ferrante, we were encouraged to avoid asking questions about your identity, but the temptation to do just that is strong. I will work around the problem by asking which of your three books is the most autobiographical. In which of your characters (perhaps Leda, from your most recent, beautiful book?) do you see yourself most?
Alberta

Dear Alberta, I feel that Delia, Olga, Leda, who are fictional characters, are very different women. But I am close to all three, in the sense that I share with them an intense relationship that is real. I believe that in fiction one pretends much less than one does in reality. In fiction we say and recognize things about ourselves, which, for the sake of propriety, we ignore or don't talk about in reality.

Elena Ferrante, I don't know how old you are, or where you live. But may I ask you, in your experience, what is happening to my (our?) city, Naples? What is the source of this explosion of violence? And how can one stop this decline?
Alice S.

In Naples nothing more and nothing less is happening than what has happened for decades: an increasingly vast and well articulated intertwining of the illegal and the legal. The new fact isn't the explosion of violence but how the city, with its ancient problems, is being traversed by the world and is spreading through the world.

Dear Elena Ferrante, what a great opportunity—to write to you and listen to your answers on the radio—is being offered to us by your publisher. I will take advantage of it immediately, because there is an invisible thread that connects us through a shared narrative project that you address with words and I with images. The suspended molecules, which give artists the possibility of perception, must have alighted on us, at least as far as certain themes are concerned, in the same way.

Some time ago, when my experience as a substitute mother expanded entirely, becoming responsibility and transforming my solidarity to emotional commitment, I felt the need to express myself. Mothering without being a mother, feeling divided between willingness and fear, alone and with no category to which I belonged, I looked around and fished out of my memory recollections of childhood and my relationship with my mother. I sought images that would give a narrative structure—which only now, after The Lost Daughter, *seems clear to me—to the scenographic logic that day by day was being composed on paper. It all started with photos, with black-and-white photos that were taken at the seaside. I arranged the scenes on the sand. Little girls sitting in fifties poses, Barbies buried amid pails and shovels, mother Barbies, big and bright-colored, like plastic totems, little girls walking along or playing pianos made of sand. Closeups, action plans.*

For an entire year I did nothing else: many drawings, employing all techniques, illustrations that were technically passable but artistically embarrassing, because they recounted my anxiety. Producing images as therapy in an attempt to grow. Lost daughters without mothers and mother dolls hidden in the sand. The other day I reopened the folder and I understood that those works were my way of dealing with the question of maternity, and that those dolls of mine (buried in the sand, mothers and friends, sisters) are like the characters in your book. The doll, Leda, Elena, Nina, Marta, Bianca . . .

With infinite admiration,
Miriam

Dear Miriam, I don't think that on the artistic level there is ever anything to be embarrassed about. It is you, a private individual, who, following that phase of artistic expression, find that you have returned to yourself, to normality, and, standing before your work, feel that there's something indecent about it. I understand this and I feel close to you. I'm curious about your manipulation of dolls and sand. If you want, you can send me a few photos. I know little about the symbolism of dolls, but I'm convinced that they are not merely a miniaturization of the daughter. Dolls can be stand-ins for women, in all the roles that patriarchy has assigned us. Do you remember the doll-sister of the future Nun of Monza? I was interested in recounting how an educated woman of today, a "new" woman, reacts to the age-old symbolic stratification.

Dear Signora Ferrante,

I am writing to you after having read the interview that you gave to la Repubblica. Of your books, I have read only The Days of Abandonment, *and later I saw the film. As often happens, the passage from one art form to another left me unsatisfied. Despite the success of the film, I felt that your writing had abandoned me.*

Like everyone else, I don't know your real name or even your gender, which, I admit, makes me happy. It's not simply that in this way, as you explain, you have assured yourself the freedom to manage your personal life, thus allowing yourself even greater ability to dig into your stories. Your choice is also a guarantee for us readers, to whom you speak as an "absolute author," in much the same way that Battisti and Mina did, with obvious differences, did before you. Free from the onus of your image, you remain "only" what you write. We must concentrate "only" on that. And in a world in which image and notoriety crush content and identity, that is a lot. As I read The Days of Abandonment *(a book I found myself discussing a couple of months back with a colleague, who had just emerged from a marriage that was destroyed owing to adultery—his, with a younger woman, obviously), even your writing felt "absolute." At times difficult and harsh, with your tense and analytical approach, but always and only "absolute."*

If you are a woman, emotion in you is not transformed into sentimental whimpering. If you are a man, you have been able to understand and describe without distracting sexist pieties. For me, the mother of a three-year-old daughter, a wife who is at times crushed by a stressful routine, a misunderstood daughter-Cassandra, a journalist with no career, a woman over forty but perennially in search of balance and identity, your reflections on the period in which the main character weaned her children, on the smell of formula and milk that sticks to the flesh, becoming an oppressive emanation of it, were especially important. I'm grateful to you for what you've written, for many reasons that are too long and boring to explain. And in reality I don't think there is any need, whether you are a woman or a man, a daughter, son, father, or mother.

Mafalda C.

Dear Mafalda, thank you so much for your letter. I like your way of reasoning with "if" and with double genders. I believe that we need to consider all authors in the same way. I don't think, however, that it is possible to be an "absolute" author. There is nothing absolute in this world, not even in the deepest depths of our biology. Naturally, gender is decisive, I know that my books can only be female. But I also know that female (or male) absoluteness is inconceivable. We are tornadoes that pick up fragments with the most varied historical and biological origins. This makes of us—thankfully—fickle agglomerations that maintain a fragile equilibrium, that are inconsistent and complex, that can't be reduced to any fixed framework that does not inevitably leave out a great deal. Which is why the more effective stories resemble ramparts from which one can gaze out at everything that has been excluded.

NOTE

The letters published here were sent to Elena Ferrante by listeners of *Fahrenheit*, a radio program devoted to books and broadcast by Radio 3, Italy. The occasion was the Rome book fair for small and mid-sized publishers, Più libri, più liberi (More Books, More Freedom), in December, 2006. Elena Ferrante's answers were read by the journalist and writer Concita De Gregorio, during the broadcast of December 7, hosted by Marino Sinibaldi.

The work of the French philosopher Jean-Luc Nancy that Ferrante refers to is entitled *L'essere abbandonato* (*The Abandoned Being*), a collection of three essays published in Italy by Quodlibet.

9.

THE EROTIC VAPOR OF THE MOTHER'S BODY
Answers to questions from Marina Terragni and Luisa Muraro

erragni and Muraro: Nina's child is named Elena, like you: is it a coincidence? You describe her as "off," dirty, homely. In your novels this pairing recurs, a beautiful, sensual mother, who emanates a magic vapor, and a dull, cold daughter, "with veins of metal," from whom the mother tries to flee. As if in the reproduction the power of the mother had weakened, become inferior.

Ferrante: In my experience the dominance of the mother is absolute, with no terms of comparison. Either one learns to accept her or one sickens. I have to admit that I never stopped feeling like a dull daughter, even when I became a mother. Rather, the tangle of the double function—the daughter with no weight who assumes the dominance of the mother—became even more snarled. There was a phase in which I planned to tell the story of the future very beautiful Helen of Troy as an unattractive child, full of animal fears and crushed by the splendor of her mother, Leda, loved by Zeus in the form of a swan. But the myth is very complex, with variants each more complicated than the next, and I did nothing. In *The Lost Daughter* the names remained: Elena, Leda come from that.

Terragni and Muraro: You say that in your writing you try "to seize what lies silent in my depths, that living thing which, if captured, spreads through all the pages and gives them life": for you, is it the relationship with the mother that asks insistently to be narrated?

Ferrante: I think so. I've written a lot of stories, over the years, but in the end none of them seemed to have any necessity. It was only with *Troubling Love* that I had, for the first time, the impression that I had touched on something compelling.

Terragni and Muraro: You quote Morante: "No one, starting with the mother's dressmaker, thinks that a mother has a woman's body." What does one discover, in freeing the body of the mother from shapelessness?

Ferrante: A desire for redemption. And everything that we are unable to see and are unable to understand. But my books don't focus on that. I've tried to describe the painful, more or less unhappy journey of the fabric—let's say—with which even we ourselves, the daughter-dressmakers, make the mother's body shapeless.

Terragni and Muraro: This unhappiness between mother and daughter, which lies at the heart of the relationship between women, through the thought of the difference becomes a point of leverage, a potentiality. Does it also constitute an opportunity for you? In Neapolitan civilization, for the women of that city, it seems instead to remain only unhappiness, a mortal illness that men take advantage of.

Ferrante: I don't know what the Neapolitan mother is like. I know what some mothers I've known are like, who were born and grew up in that city. They are cheerful and foul-mouthed women, silent victims, desperately in love with males and male children, ready to defend and serve them even though the men crush and torture them; prepared to claim that men have to be men; and incapable of admitting, even to themselves, that, with that, they drive them to become even more brutish. To be female children of these mothers wasn't and isn't easy. Their vital, obscene, suffering subjugation, full of plans for insurrection that end in nothing, makes both empathy and disaffected rejection difficult. We have to escape from Naples to escape from them as well. Only later is it possible to see the torture of women, to feel the weight of the male city on their existence, feel remorse at having abandoned them, and learn to love them, to make them, as you say, a point of leverage in order to redeem their hidden sexuality, and start again from there.

Terragni and Muraro: Leda's mother continually threatens to leave. Leda actually leaves, realizing her mother's dream. But then she returns home, says that she was fortunate to have taken only three years to understand, and that the risk was that she would never understand. Do women run that risk today?

Ferrante: Returning home, to her daughters, for Leda means putting at the center of her search not the pure and simple fact of having given birth to them but the totality of maternity. First, by fleeing, she has sought an emancipation and a confrontation on equal terms with the male world. Afterward, on her return, her public life, work, thoughts, loves center on what I would define as the dominance of the maternal function. The risk that Leda runs seems to me all in that question: can I, a woman of today, succeed in being loved by my daughters, in loving them, without having of necessity to sacrifice myself and therefore hate myself?

Terragni and Muraro: You say that there is more erotic power in the relationship of Elena with the doll and with her mother than in what she would ever feel in life: do you mean that women are wrong in wishing to escape from that relationship, in thinking that they are losing who knows what, in not enjoying that eroticism?

Ferrante: I mean that for our whole life, in the most varied circumstances, the erotic vapor that the maternal body gives off for us alone will be at the same time a cause for regret and a goal. Leda has the impression that she sees in the relationship between the child Elena and her doll a kind of happy miniature of the mother-daughter relationship. But a miniature is still always a simplification. And simplifications are blinding.

Terragni and Muraro: The doll that Leda steals seems the guardian of an apparently perfect maternity. But in her stomach there is a putrid liquid, a worm: is it the maternal ambivalence that we have to be able to accept?

Ferrante: I don't know. In an early version the story placed a strong emphasis on the crude concreteness of pregnancy, of birth. There were very harsh passages on the body that rebels, on the nausea, on the morning sickness, on the swelling of the belly, the breasts, on the initial pain of breast-feeding. I reduced that. But I remain convinced that it's also essential to describe the dark side of the pregnant body, which is omitted in order to bring out the luminous side, the Mother of God. In the story of Leda there is a pregnant woman, Rosaria. She's a Camorrist, without physical refinement or refinement of thought. For Leda, a cultivated woman, her pregnancy is coarse, uninteresting. But readers of the book will discover, page by page, that a thread of fury unwinds precisely from Rosaria's world. We tend to keep distant from us everything that hinders consistency, but a story shouldn't be consistent, in fact it's in inconsistency that we should find nourishment.

Terragni and Muraro: A word that recurs in The Lost Daughter *is "revulsion." There are the insects, the cicada, the lizards, the flies, the worm, which accentuate the basic nausea. What is it, this repellent?*

Ferrante: For Leda everything that refers to our animal nature is repellent. The relationship we have with insects, with creeping creatures, with all non-human living material, is contradictory. Animals frighten us, repulse us, remind us—like pregnancy when suddenly it changes us, bringing us much closer to our animal nature—of the instability of the forms assumed by life. But later—much more than men—we admit them among our words, we take care of them as of children, cancelling out fear and disgust with love. Recently, I've been trying to write a short story at whose center is the female attraction-repulsion toward the animal world and hence toward the animal nature of our bodies. I would like to narrate in a meaningful way how a woman approaches, through the requirements of caring for someone, through love, the repulsiveness of the flesh, those areas where the mediation of the word becomes weak. We are disgusted, of course; it's the disgust induced by taboos. But we also have the capacity to push ourselves along, in contact with the living material, to where language becomes reticent and leaves a space, enclosed between obscenity and scientific terminology, where everything can happen.

Terragni and Muraro: Leda says that since the time of her youth "the world . . . had not improved; in fact it had become crueler for women." What does she mean?

Ferrante: I think that the drive toward equality has put us in a competition with men but also with each other, multiplying the ferocity of the relations between woman and man and woman and woman. The sexual difference, repressed in the name of a disguised egalitarianism, is in danger of being pushed back into old roles that we ourselves have slightly touched up or eliminated out of opportunism. The patriarchy, in short—I say this in anger—seems to me more alive than ever. It holds the planet firmly in its hands and whenever it can it insists even more than before on making women cannon fodder. That doesn't mean that the truths we've brought to light haven't produced change. But I write stories, and whenever the words arrange things with beautiful consistency I become suspicious and I keep an eye on the things that ignore the truth of words and mind their own business. It seems to me that we are in the midst of a very hard battle and every day we are at risk of losing everything, even the syntax of truth.

Terragni and Muraro: "I'm dead but I'm fine," the novel concludes. Does it mean: I'm dead but I'm reborn, I've made my journey of passion, I've been through all the stations, all the reckoning I had to do?

Ferrante: I don't think that all the stations and all the reckoning are ever done. As for that final remark, I use "die" in the sense of eliminating something from oneself forever. An action that can have at least two results: mutilation, irreparable disfigurement; or removal of a living but sick part, with right afterward a sense of well-being. All three of the women in my books know, in a different way, both things.

Terragni and Muraro: Your protagonists move on dangerous ridges, they live on borderlines, they shatter, they are in danger of dissolution—we're thinking especially of Olga—and then find a more coherent unity, more compatible with life, in which they learn to live with their ghosts: it seems like the journey of a successful analysis.

Ferrante: I've never been in analysis. But I know what it means to break apart. I observed it in my mother, in myself, in many women. The process of fragmentation in a woman's body interests me very much from the narrative point of view. It means telling the story of a present-day female I that suddenly perceives itself disintegrating, it loses the sense of time, it's no longer in order, it feels like a vortex of debris, a whirlwind of thoughts-words. It stops abruptly and starts again from a new equilibrium, which—note—isn't necessarily more advanced than the preceding or even more stable. It serves only to say: now I'm here and I feel like this.

Terragni and Muraro: Do you think that this emotional jour-

ney, this coming apart into a jumble of fragments and then put-
ting oneself back together, is an inevitable passage in the lives of
women, with or without analysis?

Ferrante: In the women I feel close to it was. In some cases
it seemed to me that feeling literally in pieces could be traced
back to that sort of original fragmentation that is bringing into
the world-coming into the world. I mean feeling oneself a
mother at the price of getting rid of a living fragment of one's
own body; I mean feeling oneself a daughter as a fragment of
a whole and incomparable body. Leda is the explicit product
of that suggestion.

Terragni and Muraro: In your writing it's as if the phantoms
and the flesh, as if what happens, what could happen, and mem-
ory stood on the same plane, had the same density as reality. Is
that space which lacks distinction a female space? Is that female
writing?

Ferrante: I don't know if it's female writing. Certainly in my
experience the word is always flesh. I write with greatest pleasure when I feel that the story has no need of preamble or even
of a perspective. There it is, it's there, I see it and feel it, it's a
world made up entirely of living material, of breath, of heat
and cold. I who am writing sit with fingers on the keys of the
computer and, at the same time, in the middle of that world,
and I let myself be carried along by its vortex, which drags in
everything, without before or after. Over the years, I have to
admit, I've come closer and closer to the idea that real writing
is what emerges by itself, from an ecstatic condition. But often
I discover that ecstasy is imagined as a disembodiment. The
ecstasy of writing is feeling not the breath of the word that is
liberated from the flesh but the flesh that becomes one with
the breath of the words.

Terragni and Muraro: Among the many identities the media

attribute to you a good majority are of the male sex: do you recognize something non-female in your writing?

Ferrante: I'm afraid I learned to write by reading mainly works by men and constantly redoing them. It took time for me to learn to love women writers. The female of men, I must admit, attracted me more than the female of women. Emma Bovary, Anna Karenina, even Chekhov's ladies with the little dog—those, yes, they seemed like real women. It's likely, of course, that my reading of literature as a young woman endures in aspects of my current writing, but I don't think that's the problem. At some point, it will be necessary to describe what it means to write like a woman, what it means to seriously reckon not only with the male but with that female of males which belongs to us and inhabits us. It's not our relationship with the masculine that is primary today but the much more complex relationship with the masculine feminine or the feminine masculine.

Terragni and Muraro: You have said that you don't value a life in which literature counts more than every other thing, and that your desire to write was also fed by certain low sources, like photo-romances. What did you find, in those depths?

Ferrante: The taste for engaging readers. The photo-romance was one of my early pleasures as a fledgling reader. I'm afraid that the obsession with achieving a very tense narrative, even when I'm telling a short story, comes to me from there. I feel no pleasure in writing if I don't feel that the page is exciting. Once I had very grand literary ambitions and I was ashamed of that impulse toward the techniques of popular novels. Today I'm pleased if someone says to me that I've written an absorbing story—for example, like those of Delly.[8]

---

[8] M. Delly was the pseudonym of the siblings Jeanne-Marie Petitjean de La Rosière (1875-1947) and Frédéric Petitjean de La Rosière (1876-1949), authors of popular romance novels.

Terragni and Muraro: Women who read you often say that your writing is irresistible but "disturbing": what do you think it is that is disturbing?

Ferrante: I've received letters that speak of this double effect. I think it depends on the fact that, when I write, it's as if I were butchering eels. I pay little attention to the unpleasantness of the operation and use the plot, the characters, as a tight net to pull up from the depths of my experience everything that is alive and writhing, including what I myself have driven away as far as possible because it seemed unbearable. In the first drafts, I must admit, there is always much more than what I later decide to publish. It's my own fastidiousness that censors me. I feel, nevertheless, that this is not always the right thing to do, and often I reintegrate what I've eliminated. Or I wait for an occasion to use elsewhere the passages that were taken out.

NOTE
The interview with Marina Terragni and Luisa Muraro appeared in *Io Donna*, January 27, 2007, under the title "Elena Ferrante Speaks: The Writer Without a Face. 'Thus I describe the obscure love of the mother.'"

III

LETTERS: 2011-2016

A Companion Book

Dear Sandra,

Maybe we ought to tell readers why we've decided to collect some of these interviews. It's something I've felt we should do since September 23, 2015, when your cryptic email arrived, with a file of interviews attached and, as the only text, the subject line, which said: "Interviews. Will you let me know if you can open them and understand anything?" When did it begin to seem to you and Elena that it made sense to collect them?

In the interviews Elena speaks of the importance that the point of view of others, the written dialogue with journalists from so many countries, has had in nurturing her own reflections on writing, and that much is clear to me. But when did you two look each other in the eye and think: it would be nice to collect them, so that readers, too, can find them all in one place? You didn't at first have the idea of a whole section, right, and wanted to publish just a few? Or maybe you didn't look each other in the eye?

Ciao, Simona

Dear Simona,

I'm going to answer—Elena wanted to but says she would drag it out and bore you.

So, as to your little question, we didn't look each other in the eye because we were on the telephone. I told the author that we were going to reprint *Frantumaglia* in Italy and suggested that it might be a good idea to publish the text in English as well, because in English we had brought out only a few excerpts, and they had appeared only in digital form.

As you know, I am extremely fond of this book, which to me reads almost like a story, with its variety of themes and characters. So I thought it could be enhanced with a collection of the interviews that Elena has done since the publication of the four installments of *My Brilliant Friend*, or the Neapolitan Quartet, as it's called in English.

The little problem was that, having promised the first publishers to whom we sold the rights that Elena would do an interview for each of those countries, the author suddenly found herself having to respond to some forty interviews, from all over the world. Certainly too many for an appendix. We thought it would be helpful to bring you into the discussion as we tried to figure out what to do and how to organize the section.

Anyway, looking through the interviews we realized that the material is consistent with the structure of *Frantumaglia*, which over all contains the now twenty-five-year history of an attempt to show that the function of an author is all in the writing: "It originates in it, is invented in it, and ends in it," as Elena says. And I think that readers would be interested in the growing number of questions in recent years about the literary and cultural tradition that the novels draw on, about the role of female thought in the construction of figures like Lena and Lila, about the reasons that the two girls have broken through into contexts and cultures far from Naples and from Italy.

Michael's observations also seemed important to the author, helping to clarify the point of this last part of the book. Michael says that with this section we'll give readers a sort of internal history of Elena's motivations, of the struggle to give them shape, and of how they changed over time. Which is true.

In her answers one feels the effort involved in finding the words, in explaining herself; I like this, and I know she does, too. After all, the *Frantumaglia* project has always been to give her readers, from *Troubling Love* up to now, work that, without too many veils, and by making use of various fragments, notes, explanations, even contradictions, accompanies the works of fiction like a companion book.

Ciao, Sandra

NOTE
In this e-mail exchange, the editors referred to are Simona Olivito, of Edizioni E/O, and Michael Reynolds, of Europa Editions.

1.

THE BRILLIANT SUBORDINATE
Answers to questions from Paolo di Stefano

Di Stefano: *Elena Ferrante, how did you make the tran-sition from one type of psychological-family novel* (Troubling Love *and* The Days of Abandonment) *to a novel that, like this, promises to be the first of a trilogy or a tetralogy, and which is in plot and in style so centrifugal and, at the same time, so centripetal?*

Ferrante: I don't feel that this novel is so different from the preceding ones. Many years ago I had the idea of telling the story of an old person who intends to disappear—which doesn't mean die—without leaving any trace of her existence. I was fascinated by the idea of a story that demonstrated how difficult it is to erase yourself, literally, from the face of the earth. Then the story became complicated. I introduced a childhood friend who served as an inflexible witness of every event, small or large, in the life of the other. Finally, I realized that what interested me was to dig into two female lives that had many affinities and yet were divergent. That's what I did. Of course, it's a complex proj-ect, as the story covers some sixty years. But Lila and Elena are made of the same material that fed the other novels.

Di Stefano: The two friends whose childhood story is told, Elena Greco, the first-person narrator, and her friend-enemy Lila Cerullo, are similar yet different. They continuously overlap just when they seem to be growing apart. Is it a novel about friend-ship and how an encounter can determine a life? But also about how attraction to the bad example helps develop an identity?

Ferrante: Generally, someone who asserts his personality, in doing so, makes the other opaque. The stronger, richer personality obscures the weaker, in life and perhaps even more in novels. But, in the relationship between Elena and Lila, Elena, the subordinate, gets from her subordination a sort of brilliance that disorients, that dazzles Lila. It's a movement that's hard to describe, but for that reason it interested me. Let me put it like this: the many events in the lives of Lila and Elena will show how one draws strength from the other. But beware: not only in the sense that they help each other but also in the sense that they ransack each other, stealing feeling and intelligence, depriving each other of energy.

Di Stefano: How did memory and the passage of time, distance (temporal and perhaps spatial), influence the development of the book?

Ferrante: I think that "putting distance" between experience and story is something of a cliché. The problem, for the writer, is often the opposite: to bridge the distance, to feel physically the impact of the material to be narrated, to approach the past of people we've loved, lives as we've observed them, as they've been told to us. A story, to take shape, needs to pass through many filters. Often we begin to write too soon and the pages are cold. Only when we feel the story in each of its moments, in every nook and cranny (and sometimes it takes years), can it be written well.

Di Stefano: My Brilliant Friend *is also a novel about violence in the family and in society. Does the novel describe how a person manages (or managed) to grow up in violence and/or in spite of violence?*

Ferrante: In general, one grows up warding off blows, returning them, even agreeing to receive them with stoic generosity. In the case of *My Brilliant Friend*, the world in which the girls grow up has some obviously violent features and others that are covertly violent. It's the latter that interest me most, even though there are plenty of the first.

Di Stefano: On page 130 there's a wonderful sentence, about Lila: "She took the facts and in a natural way charged them with tension; she intensified reality as she reduced it to words." And then on page 227: "The voice set in the writing overwhelmed me . . . It was completely cleansed of the dross of speech." Is that a statement of style?

Ferrante: Let's say that, among the many methods we employ to give a narrative order to the world, I prefer one in which the writing is clear and honest, and in which when you read about the events—the events of everyday life—they are extraordinarily compelling.

Di Stefano: There is a more sociological thread: Italy in the years of the boom, the dream of prosperity that reckons with ancient hostilities.

Ferrante: Yes, and that thread runs through to the present. But I reduced the historical background to a minimum. I prefer everything to be inscribed in the actions of the characters, both external and internal. Lila, for example, already at the age of seven or eight, wants to become rich, and drags Elena along, convinces her that wealth is an urgent goal. How this intention works inside the two friends; how it's modified, how it guides or confuses them, interests me more than standard sociology.

Di Stefano: You seldom yield to dialectal color: you use a few words, but usually you prefer the formula "he/she said in dialect." Were you never tempted by a more expressionistic coloring?

Ferrante: As a child, as an adolescent, the dialect of my city frightened me. I prefer to let it echo for a moment in the Italian, as if threatening it.

Di Stefano: Are the next installments finished?
Ferrante: Yes, in a very provisional state.

Di Stefano: An obvious but necessary question: how autobiographical is the story of Elena? And how much of your literary passions are in Elena's readings?
Ferrante: If by autobiography you mean drawing on one's own experience to feed an invented story, almost entirely. If instead you're asking whether I'm telling my own personal story, not at all. As for the books, yes, I always cite texts I love, characters who molded me. For example, Dido, the Queen of Carthage, was a crucial female figure of my adolescence.

Di Stefano: Is the game of alliteration "Elena Ferrante—Elsa Morante" (a passion of yours) suggestive? Is any relationship of Ferrante to Ferri (your publishers) only imaginary?
Ferrante: Yes, absolutely.

Di Stefano: Have you never regretted choosing anonymity? Reviews tend to linger more on the mystery of Ferrante than on the qualities of the books. In other words, have the results been the opposite of what you were hoping for, in emphasizing your hypothetical personality?
Ferrante: No, I have no regrets. As I see it, extracting the personality of the writer from the story he offers, from the characters he puts onstage, from the landscapes, from the objects, from interviews like this—in short, from the tonality of his writing entirely—is simply a good way of reading. What you call emphasizing, if it's based on the works, on the energy of the words, is an honest emphasis. What's very different is the media's emphasis, the predominance of the author's image over his work. In that case the book functions like a pop star's sweaty T-shirt, a garment that without the aura of the star is

completely meaningless. It's this last type of emphasis that I don't like.

Di Stefano: Does the suspicion that your work is the product of several hands bother you?

Ferrante: It seems a useful example for the conversation we're having. We are accustomed to deriving a body of work's coherence from the author, not the author's coherence from the work. That particular woman or that particular man has written the books and that is enough for us to consider them elements of a journey. We'll speak with assurance of the author's beginnings, of successful books and others that are less successful. We'll say that he immediately found his way, that he has experimented with different genres and styles, we'll trace recurring themes, circumstances, an evolution or an involution. Let's say instead that we have available *House of Liars* and *Aracoeli*, but not a writer named Elsa Morante. We are so unused to starting from the works, to seeking in them coherence or difference, that we're immediately confused. Accustomed to the supremacy of the author, we end up, when the author isn't there, or is removed, seeing different hands not only in the development from one book to the next but even from one page to the next.

Di Stefano: So will you tell us who you are?

Ferrante: Elena Ferrante. I've published six books in twenty years. Isn't that sufficient?

NOTE
The interview with Paolo Di Stefano appeared in the *Corriere della Sera* (Italy) November 20, 2011, under the title "Ferrante: Felice di non esserci" ("Ferrante: Happy Not to Be There") and with the following introduction:

My Brilliant Friend is very different from Elena Ferrante's earlier novels. It's a wonderful Bildungsroman, or, rather, two, or more than two—it's the story of a generation of friends-enemies. An interview with Ferrante requires the mediation of her publishers, Sandro Ferri and Sandra Ozzola. The questions are asked by e-mail and answered by e-mail.

2.

V*alby: What is your writing routine and how do you recover, particularly after writing some of the more furious interactions between the women?*

Ferrante: I don't have a routine. I write when I want to. Telling stories requires a lot of effort—what happens to the characters also happens to me, their good and their evil feelings belong to me. This is how it has to be, or else I don't write. When I feel exhausted, I do the most obvious thing: I stop writing and busy myself with the thousands of urgent matters that I've ignored and without which life no longer functions.

Valby: Elena and Lila's friendship is so messy and true, a great portrait of female friendship (of which there are too few in literature). What was your inspiration for these women?

Ferrante: I had a friend whom I cared for very much, and I began from that experience. But real events don't count much when one writes; at most they are like getting shoved while out on the street. Rather, a story is a deep chasm of very different experiences that have accumulated in the course of a lifetime, and that miraculously nourish events and characters in the story. There are some experiences that are difficult to use, that are elusive, embarrassing, at times unsayable, because they belong to us so intimately. I am in favor of stories that are fed by these kinds of experience.

Valby: Between Elena and Lila, whom do you relate to more, and who causes you the most suffering?

Ferrante: Neither one of them came easily to me. I love Lila more, but only because she forced me to work very hard.

Valby: Has there been interest in adapting the series for movies or TV, and can you bear such an idea?

Ferrante: Two movies have been made from my books, a fact that makes me curious. There is talk of a TV series for the Neapolitan novels. I don't care for directors and screenwriters who approach a book with arrogance, as if it were a mere catalyst for their own work. I prefer those who dive into the literary work, taking inspiration from it for new ways of telling a story with images.

Karen Valby: Why did you decide to write under a pseudonym? Why did you choose to use the name Elena? Have you ever regretted not revealing your identity? Felt a surge of ego that made you want to throw open your window and cry "It's I who have created this world!"? What would you lose by living a public life?

Ferrante: Anyone who writes knows that the most complicated thing is the rendering of events and characters in such a way that they are not realistic but real. In order for this to happen it's necessary to believe in the story one is working on. I gave my name to the narrator to make my job easier. Elena is, in fact, the name that I feel is most mine. Without reserve, I can say that my entire identity is in the books I write. Your image of the window is amusing. My home is on the upper floors, I'm afraid of heights, and my ego gladly avoids leaning out the window.

NOTE
The interview with Karen Valby, translated by Michael Reynolds, appeared in *Entertainment Weekly* (U.S.A.), under the title "Elena Ferrante: The Writer Without a Face," on September 5, 2014, online and in the print issue of September 12th.

3.

EVERY INDIVIDUAL IS A BATTLEFIELD
Answers to questions from Giulia Calligaro

Calligaro: How do you produce a story like this? And what did you know about it when you started?

Ferrante: I had thought for years about certain events that were important to me and that I wanted to write about: the business of the lost child, for example. But the story as a whole emerged as I wrote, and I never imagined that it would be so long. It's the writing that brings a story to light, that breathes life into the inert material preserved by memory and draws it out of oblivion. If one hasn't perfected, over the years, an adequate expressive tool, through trial and error, the story doesn't emerge, or emerges without truth.

Calligaro: The obsessive comparison between Lila and Elena teaches us that friendship between women, even if it's affectionate, is always antagonistic. Why this fear of coming in second?

Ferrante: Friendship between women has been left without rules. Male rules haven't been imposed on it, and it's still a territory with fragile codes where love (in our language the word "friendship"—*amicizia*—has to do with love, *amare*), by its nature, carries with it everything, lofty sentiments and base impulses. As a result I described a very strong bond that lasts a lifetime, and that is made up of affection but also of disorder, instability, incoherence, feelings of inferiority, bullying, bad moods.

Calligaro: Love is the engine of the story. But the happy parts are those which the reader experiences with the most suspicion:

one knows that sooner or later there will be a hitch. What stands in the way of a happy ending?

Ferrante: The Neapolitan Quartet is a story conceived in such a way that the most intense, most lasting, happiest, and most devastating relationship turns out to be the one between Lila and Lena. That relationship endures, while relations with men begin, develop, and die. Neither of the two devotes herself to a man to the point of conclusively leaving the emotional field of the other. In such a long story, there are moments when the relations between woman and man are happy; you'd just have to break off the story there and you'd have a happy ending. But the happy ending has to do with the tricks of the narrative, not with life, or even with love, which is an uncontrollable, changeable feeling, with nasty surprises that are alien to the happy ending.

Calligaro: Men are inadequate. What gets in the way of the encounter between the sexes? Have the struggles for equality increased the distance?

Ferrante: Female expectations became very high. The behavioral models that made the sexes mutually recognizable, unfortunately, were torn apart and couldn't be mended, nor has a radical redefinition of mutual satisfaction been possible so far. The greatest risk now is female regret for the "real men" of bygone days. Every form of male violence should be fought against, but the female desire to regress should not be neglected. The crowd of women who adore the sensibility and sexual energy of the worst male characters in *My Brilliant Friend* illustrate this temptation.

Calligaro: Lila and Elena "dramatize" the duel between Nature and History. Elena seems to "make it," but in reality everyone becomes what he or she has always been. Can nothing change? And is the mixing of social classes an arduous undertaking?

Ferrante: The drive to change one's state must face countless obstacles. One can act on genetic conditioning but not ignore it. Belonging to one class or another can be camouflaged but not canceled out. The individual is in the end only a battlefield, in which privileges and disadvantages war fiercely. What counts in the end is the collective flow of generations. Even when there is both merit and luck, the efforts of a single individual are unsatisfying.

Calligaro: The neighborhood is the laboratory where the fragility of History is revealed. About progress you write: "The dream of unlimited progress is in reality a nightmare of savagery and death." What is the alternative? Is Naples a testing ground for national events?

Ferrante: For Lila and Lena, Naples is the city where beauty spills over into horror, where good manners can be instantly transformed into violence, where every Reclamation covers a Demolition. In Naples one learns immediately to distrust, laughing all the while, both Nature and History. In Naples progress is always the progress of the few to the detriment of the many. But, as you see, we are speaking no longer of Naples but of the world. What we call unlimited progress, for example, is the great cruel squandering of the wealthy classes of the West. Things may go a bit better when we prefer to take care of the entire planet and each of its inhabitants.

Calligaro: About Nino, loved by Lila and then by Lena, you say: "One who seeks more to be likable to the powerful than to defend an idea at all costs." Later: "He has the worst kind of meanness, superficiality." About Lila: "She stood out among so many because she, naturally, did not submit to any training, to any use, or to any purpose." Two opposing versions of humanity. Will you comment on them?

Ferrante: Nino's traits are more widespread today. Wanting to please those who exercise any sort of power is a characteristic of the subordinate who wants to emerge from his subordinate position. But it's also a feature of the permanent spectacle in which we are immersed, which by its nature goes hand in hand with superficiality. Superficiality is a synonym not for stupidity but for the display of one's own body, pleasure in appearances, imperviousness in the face of the spoilsport par excellence, the suffering of others. Lila's traits instead seem to me the only possible pathway for those who want to be an active part of this world without submitting to it.

Calligaro: You're an international success, among both general readers and intellectuals. Now in the United States you're being compared to Elsa Morante. What is the target you've hit that is common to so many readers?

Ferrante: I don't know if I've hit a target. I'm interested in stories that are hard for me to tell. The criterion has always been this: the more uneasy a story makes me, the more stubbornly I persist in telling it.

Calligaro: This might also be the story of Lila's erasure. What does erasure mean to you?

Ferrante: To remove oneself systematically from the cravings of one's own ego, to the point of making it a way of life.

Calligaro: We readers don't know how we'll manage: how will you manage without Lila and Lenù?

Ferrante: It was wonderful and demanding to live with them for years. Now I feel the need to move on to something else, as happens when a relationship is over. But with writing the rule is simple: if you have nothing worth writing, don't write anymore.

NOTE
The interview with Giulia Calligaro appeared in *Io donna* (Italy) November 8, 2014, under the title "È ora di dire addio a Elena e Lila" ("It's Time to Say Goodbye to Elena and Lila").

4.

COMPLICIT EVEN THOUGH ABSENT
Answers to questions from Simonetta Fiori

Fiori: *The American magazine* Foreign Policy *included you in the hundred most influential people in the world, for your capacity "to write honest, anonymous fiction." How do you explain "Ferrante fever"?*

Ferrante: I'm especially pleased that *Foreign Policy* generously gives me credit for having demonstrated that the power of literature is autonomous. As for the success of my books, I don't know the reasons for it, but I have no doubt that they should be sought in the story the books tell and how they tell it.

Fiori: More than twenty years ago, you wrote: "I believe that books, once they are written, have no need of their authors. If they have something to say, they will sooner or later find readers; if not, they won't." Don't you think that that bet has been won, and that your books therefore no longer have any need for anonymity?

Ferrante: My books aren't written anonymously; they have a name on the cover, and have never needed anonymity. It happened simply that I wrote them, and then, avoiding common editorial practice, I put them to the test without any protection. If there is a winner, they are the winners. It's a victory that testifies to their autonomy. They have won the right to be appreciated by readers just as books.

Fiori: Hasn't the decision to remove yourself been transformed into its opposite? The mystery rouses curiosity, the author thus becomes a Personality.

Ferrante: I fear that such considerations concern only the narrow circle of those who work in the media, and, with the usual exceptions, have too much on their plate and either are not readers or are hasty readers. There is a much wider world outside the media circuit, with different expectations. That is, like it or not, you, because of your job and apart from your sensibility as a cultured person, feel called on to fill in the space that I purposely left empty with a face, while readers fill it in by reading.

Fiori: Are you really convinced that the life of an author doesn't add anything? Italo Calvino avoided personal questions, but we know a lot about him and his editorial work.

Ferrante: There's a statement of Calvino's that made a great impression on me as a girl. He said, more or less: Go ahead and ask me about my private life; I won't answer you or I'll always lie. Northrup Frye, later, seemed to me even more radical, saying: writers are rather simple people, at most neither wiser nor better than anyone else. And he continues: what matters about them is what they can do well—string together words. *King Lear* is marvelous even if all that remains of Shakespeare is a couple of signatures, some addresses, a will, a certificate of baptism, and a portrait that shows a man with the face of an idiot. Well, I see it exactly like that. Our faces, all of them, do not do us any favors, and our lives add nothing to the work.

Fiori: If you revealed your identity, the curiosity would decrease. Don't you think that insisting on the mystery risks making you complicit?

Ferrante: May I answer you with another question? Don't you think that if I did as you say I would betray myself, my writing, the pact I've made with my readers, my motivations, which they have in essence sustained, even with the new way they've ended up reading? As for my complicity, look around.

Don't you see the crush there is around Christmastime to appear on TV? Would you still talk about complicity if at this moment I were in front of a camera, or would you simply find it normal? No, to say that absence is complicity is an old, predictable game. As for morbid curiosity, it, too, seems to me only pressure from the media machine, intended to make me not only complicit but inconsistent.

Fiori: Is it onerous to have to dissemble?
Ferrante: I don't dissemble. I live my life, and those who are part of it know everything about me.

Fiori: But how does one live in the lie? You insist on anonymity in part to protect your life. But what can have a greater effect—on a person's life—than secrecy surrounding his or her job?
Ferrante: Writing for me is not a job. As for the lie, well, technically literature is one, it's an extraordinary product of the mind, a self-contained world made up of words that are directed toward telling the truth of the writer. To sink into this particular type of lie is a great pleasure and a difficult responsibility. As for petty lies, well, in general I don't tell them to anyone, except to avoid danger, to protect myself.

Fiori: My Brilliant Friend *is being made into a TV series, and the writing has been entrusted to Francesco Piccolo. What do you expect?*
Ferrante: I expect that the characters won't be simplified and that the story won't be impoverished or distorted. If I make any contributions to the screenplay, I'll do it by e-mail.

Fiori: Anonymity in a time of total exposure has something heroic about it, but doesn't success now oblige you to "show your face"?
Ferrante: Our prime minister often uses that expression, but

I'm afraid that it serves to conceal rather than to reveal. The limelight does that: it conceals, it doesn't reveal, it disguises democratic practice. It would be nice if, instead—not in a few months or years but now—we could evaluate clearly what is coming and avoid disasters. Yet we have not works to examine but faces, which beyond the clamor of television are all by their nature like that of Frye's Shakespeare, whether they've written *King Lear* or are touting the Jobs Act. I, success or not, know enough about mine to choose to keep it for myself.

Fiori: Your friend the editor Sandra Ferri is convinced that if your identity were discovered you would be unable to write anymore.

Ferrante: I say a lot of things to my friend Sandra, all of them true. But I have to explain that I was talking about publishing, not writing. And then I want to add that something has changed. At first, anxiety about the story I was telling weighed on me. Then the small polemic against every form of publicity was added to it. Today what I fear most is the loss of the completely anomalous creative space I seem to have discovered. It's not a small thing to write knowing that you can orchestrate for readers not only a story, characters, feelings, landscapes but the very figure of the author, the most genuine figure, because it's created from writing alone, from the pure technical exploration of a possibility. That's why either I remain Ferrante or I no longer publish.

NOTE

The interview with Simonetta Fiori appeared in *La Repubblica* (Italy) on December 5, 2014, under the title *Elena Ferrante* "Se scoprite chi sono mollo tutto" ("If You Discover Who I Am I'll Give It All Up") and with the following text.

To the editors: There must have been a misunderstanding. "Metterci la faccia" ("Show Your Face") was, in a word, supposed to be an article on the prime minister. Politics, in other words: it had almost nothing to do with my decision to be an absent author. But never mind, I must tell you that in the end I was just as glad to answer your questions.

Thank you.

Elena Ferrante

From misunderstandings many things can arise, including an unusual interview. At first, there was to be an article written by Ferrante on the subject that she suggested: "Show Your Face." Given the mystery of her identity, magnified by her global success, the idea seemed to us timely and unambiguous. Then, however, Ferrante couldn't write her article, and it was replaced by the format of an interview, which inherited its perspective: the presence/absence of an author in today's celebrity society, the reasons for a withdrawal that has been stubbornly defended for twenty years. Written questions and answers, without the possibility of a dialogue. An agreement happily made, which today we discover was based on a misunderstanding. Let misunderstandings flourish. There exist only a few doubts about the author's convictions. Is it really true that readers don't care about her identity? Is the biography of a writer really so irrelevant? Is the media world merely a horde of obsessed illiterates? Maybe things are a bit more complicated, but a great writer is allowed anything, even caustic answers.

Simonetta Fiori

5.

NEVER LOWER YOUR GUARD
Answers to questions from Rachel Donadio

D onadio: *You insist on anonymity and yet are developing a cult following, especially among women, first in Italy and now in the United States and beyond. How do you feel about the reception of your books in the United States in recent years, and your growing readership, especially after James Wood's review in* The New Yorker, *in January, 2013?*

Ferrante: I appreciated James Wood's review very much. The critical attention that he dedicated to my books not only helped them find readers but in a way also helped me to read them. Writers, because they write, are condemned never to be readers of their own stories. What happens to the reader when he reads a story for the first time is effectively what the narrator experiences while he writes. The memory of first putting a story into words will always prevent writers from reading their work as an ordinary reader would. Critics like Wood not only help readers to read but especially, perhaps, help the author as well. Their function also becomes fundamental in helping faraway literary worlds to migrate. I never asked myself how the women in my stories would be received outside Italy. I wrote first and foremost for myself, and if I published I did so leaving the task of finding readers to the book itself. Now I know that thanks to Europa Editions, to Ann Goldstein, and to Wood and so many other reviewers and writers and readers, the heart of these stories has burst forth, and it is not only Italian. I'm both surprised and happy.

Donadio: Do you feel your books have found the following they deserve in Italy?

Ferrante: I don't do promotional tours in my own country or anywhere. In Italy my first book, *Troubling Love*, sold immediately, thanks to the word of mouth of readers who discovered it and appreciated the writing, and to reviewers who wrote about it positively. Then the director Mario Martone read it and turned it into a memorable film. This helped the book, but it also shifted the media attention onto me personally. Partly for that reason, I didn't publish anything else for ten years, at which point, with tremendous anxiety, I decided to publish *The Days of Abandonment*. The book was a success and had a wide readership, even if there was also a lot of resistance to Olga's reaction to being abandoned—the same kind of resistance faced by Delia in "Troubling Love." The success of the book and of the film that was made from it focused even more attention onto the absence of the author. It was then that I decided, definitively, to separate my private life from the public life of my books, which overcame countless difficulties and have endured. I can say with a certain pride that in my country, the titles of my novels are better known than my name. I think this is a good outcome.

Donadio: Where do you see yourself in the Italian literary tradition?

Ferrante: I'm a storyteller. I've always been more interested in storytelling than in writing. Even today, Italy has a weak narrative tradition. Beautiful, magnificent, very carefully crafted pages abound, but not the flow of storytelling that despite its density manages to sweep you away. A bewitching example is Elsa Morante. I try to learn from her books, but I find them unsurpassable.

*Donadio: The opening scene of the fourth and final install-
ment in your Naples series,* The Story of the Lost Child, *echoes
some scenes in* The Lost Daughter, *a book in which the protagonist, Leda, also writes that she likes the echoes of names: Nani,
Nina, Nennella, Elena, Lenù, etc. Why these echoes? Do you see
your protagonists as some variation on the same woman or
women?*

Ferrante: The women in my stories are all echoes of real
women who, because of their suffering or their combativeness,
have very much influenced my imagination: my mother, a
childhood girlfriend, acquaintances whose stories I know. In
general I combine their experiences with my own and Delia,
Amalia, Olga, Leda, Nina, Elena, Lenù are born out of that
mix. But the echo that you noticed maybe derives from an
oscillation inside the characters that I've always worked on. My
women are strong, educated, self-aware and aware of their
rights, just, but at the same time subject to unexpected breakdowns, to subservience of every kind, to mean feelings. I've
also experienced this oscillation. I know it well, and that also
affects the way I write.

*Donadio: It seems fair to surmise from your books that you
are a mother. Even if that's not the case, how has the experience
of motherhood—lived or observed—affected your writing?*

Ferrante: The roles of daughters and mothers are central to
my books; sometimes I think I haven't written about anything
else. Every single one of my anxieties has ended up there. To
conceive, to change shape, to feel inhabited by something
increasingly alive that makes you feel ill and gives you a sense
of well-being is both thrilling and threatening. It's an experience akin to awe, that ancient feeling that mortals had when
they found themselves facing a god, the same feeling that Mary
must have felt, immersed in her reading, when the angel
appeared. As for my writing, it began before the children came

along, it was already a very strong passion, and it often came into conflict with my love for them, especially with the obligations and pleasures of taking care of them. Writing is also a kind of reproduction of life, one marked by contradictory and overwhelming emotions. But the continuum of writing—even with the anguish that you might not always know how to revive it and that no life might ever pass through it again—can be severed, if you need to, out of necessity or other pressing matters. In the end, you have to separate yourself from your books. But you never really cut the umbilical cord. Children always remain an inescapable knot of love, of terrors, of satisfactions and anxieties.

Donadio: There are many, many classical references in your work, not least the names Elena, or Helen, and Leda. Why the interest in the classical world? What about it speaks to you?

Ferrante: I studied classics. You've recognized the traces of it in my works and I'm pleased by that, but I hardly notice it myself. I recognize my education more in stories that I wrote as exercises and that fortunately have never seen the light of day. I have to say that I've never seen the classical world as an ancient world. Instead I feel its closeness, and I think I've learned many things from the Greek and Latin classics about how to put words together. As a girl I wanted to make that world my own, and I practiced with translations that tried to remove the lofty tones that I had been taught to use in school. But at the same time I imagined the Bay of Naples filled with Sirens who spoke in Greek, as in a lovely story by Giuseppe Tomasi di Lampedusa. Naples is a city in which many worlds coexist. The Greek, Latin, and Eastern worlds; medieval, modern, and contemporary Europe; even the United States, are all side by side, neighbors, especially in the dialect and also in the historical stratification of the city.

Donadio: How did the Naples tetralogy come into being? Did you envision the books as four distinct novels from the start or did you start writing My Brilliant Friend *without knowing where the story would end?*

Ferrante: Almost six years ago I started writing a story of a difficult female friendship that came directly from inside a book that I'm very attached to, *The Lost Daughter.* I thought I could manage it in a hundred, a hundred and fifty pages. Instead, the writing, I would say extremely naturally, unearthed memories of people and places from my childhood—stories, experiences, fantasies—so much so that the story went on for many years. The story was conceived and written as a single narrative. Its division into four hefty volumes was decided when I realized that the story of Lila and Lenù couldn't easily be contained in one book. I always knew the end of the story, and I knew some central episodes very well—Lila's wedding, the adultery on Ischia, the work in the factory, the lost daughter—but the rest was a surprising and demanding gift that came from the pure storytelling pleasure.

Donadio: The third installment in the Naples books is more cinematic. Have you also worked in cinema?

Ferrante: Absolutely not. But I adore the cinema and have since I was a child.

Donadio: How did you start writing novels? What book of yours do you consider a breakthrough in your own writing and why?

Ferrante: I discovered as a girl that I liked telling stories. I did it orally and with some success. Around age thirteen I started to write stories, but writing didn't become a permanent habit until I was in my twenties. *Troubling Love* was important. I felt that I'd found the right tone. *The Days of Abandonment* confirmed that for me, after much struggle, and gave me confidence. Today I think *My Brilliant Friend* was my most arduous yet most successful book. Writing it was like having the chance to live my life over again. But I still think that the most daring, the most risk-taking book is *The Lost Daughter*. If I hadn't gone through that, with great anxiety, I wouldn't have written *My Brilliant Friend*.

Donadio: In which order did you write your seven novels compared with their publication dates?

Ferrante: As I said, I consider the four installments of *My Brilliant Friend* to be a single story, so I've published four novels, the last one in four volumes, and all of them pubblished in the order in which they were written. But they ripened during the years when I wrote privately. It's as if I found them by painstakingly organizing countless narrative fragments.

Donadio: Can you describe your writing process? You told the Financial Times *that you made a living doing what you've always done, "which is not writing." How much of your time are you able to devote to your writing compared with your other job? Can you tell us what that other job is?*

Ferrante: I don't consider writing a job. A job has fixed hours—you start, you finish. I write continuously and everywhere and at every hour of the day and night. What I call my job is orderly and quiet, and when necessary it retreats and leaves me time. Writing has always been a great struggle for me. I would polish it line by line and I wouldn't move forward if I didn't think that what I had already written was perfect, and since the work never seemed perfect I didn't even try to find a publisher. The books that I ultimately published all came with surprising ease, even *My Brilliant Friend*, although it took me years.

Donadio: What about the editing process? You send your work to Edizioni E/O and do they do much editing?

Ferrante: The editing is extremely attentive, but delicate and done with great courtesy. I'm the one who welcomes doubts. I add them to my own questions and write, rewrite, erase, add until the day before the book goes to press.

Donadio: I fully respect your choice, and I'm sure you are tired of this question, but I have to ask it: At what stage in your writing life, and in what spirit, did you choose anonymity? Was it meant, as in the ancient epics, to give the story precedence over the storyteller? To protect your family and loved ones? Or simply to avoid the media, as you've said in the past?

Ferrante: If I may, I didn't choose anonymity; the books are signed. Instead, I chose absence. More than twenty years ago I felt the burden of exposing myself in public. I wanted to detach myself from the finished story. I wanted the books to assert themselves without my patronage. This choice created a small polemic in the media, whose logic is aimed at inventing protagonists while ignoring the quality of the work, so that it seems natural that bad or mediocre books by someone who has a reputation in the media deserve more attention than books that might be of higher quality but were written by someone who is no one. But today what counts most for me is to preserve a creative space that seems full of possibilities, including technical ones. The structural absence of the author affects the writing in a way that I'd like to continue to explore.

Donadio: At this point, now that you've had a certain success, would you ever reconsider the anonymity and reveal who you are? For Hollywood stars, they say that fame can be lonely. But anonymous literary success must also be a bit lonely, no?

Ferrante: I don't feel at all lonely. I'm happy that my stories have migrated and found readers in Italy and in other parts of the world. I follow their journeys with affection, but from afar.

They are books that I have written to put my writing on display, not me. I have my life, which for now is quite full.

Donadio: In Italy in particular, people often say that your anonymity must mean that you're a man. What do you make of that assumption? The Neapolitan novelist Domenico Starnone has given interviews saying that he is very tired of everyone asking if he's you. What would you say to him?

Ferrante: That he's right and I feel guilty. But I hold him in great esteem and I'm certain that he understands my motivations. My identity, my sex can be found in my writing. Everything that has sprouted up around that is yet more evidence of the character of Italians in the first years of the twenty-first century.

Donadio: Any comments you'd like to make about the current state of Italy?

Ferrante: Italy is an extraordinary country, but it has been made completely ordinary by the permanent confusion between legality and illegality, between the common good and private interest. This confusion, concealed behind verbose self-promotion of all kinds, runs through criminal organizations as well as political parties, government bureaucracies, and all social classes. That makes it very difficult to be a truly good Italian, different from the models constructed by newspapers and television. And yet good, excellent Italians exist in every corner of civic life, even if you don't see them on television. They are evidence of the fact that Italy, if it still manages, in spite of everything, to have excellent citizens, is truly an extraordinary country.

Donadio: Besides wonderful material, what else has Naples given you? What for you sets that city apart?

Ferrante: Naples is my city, the city where I learned quickly, before I was twenty, the best and worst of Italy and the world. I advise everyone to come and live here even just for a few weeks. It's an apprenticeship, in all the most stupefying ways.

Donadio: Flaubert famously said, "Madame Bovary, c'est moi." Which of your books—and which of your protagonists—would you say is closest to your own experience or your own heart, and why?

Ferrante: All my books derive their truth from my own experience. But together Lenù and Lila are the ones that best capture me. Not in the specific events of their lives, or in their concreteness as people with a destiny, but in the movement that characterizes their relationship, in the self-discipline of the one that continuously and brusquely shatters when it runs up against the unruly imagination of the other.

Donadio: What is the best thing that you hope readers could take away from your work?

Ferrante: That even if we're constantly tempted to lower our guard—out of love, or weariness, or sympathy, or kindness—we women shouldn't do it. We can lose from one moment to the next everything that we have achieved.

Donadio: Is there anything else you'd like to add?
Ferrante: No.

NOTE
The interview with Rachel Donadio, translated by Donadio, appeared online in *The New York Times* (U.S.A.) December 9, 2014, under the title "Writing Has Always Been a Great Struggle for Me: Q. & A.: Elena Ferrante."

WOMEN WHO WRITE
Answers to questions from Sandra, Sandro, and Eva

Sandra: What happens to reality as it enters a novel? How do you begin a new work?

Ferrante: I can't say precisely. I don't think anyone really knows how a story takes shape. When it's done you try to explain how it happened, but every effort, at least as far as I'm concerned, is insufficient. In my experience there is a *before*, made up of fragments of memory, and an *after*, when the story begins. But *before* and *after*, I have to admit, are useful only for answering your question in a sensible way.

Sandro: What do you mean by fragments of memory?

Ferrante: A heterogeneous mass of material that's hard to define. You know how when you have in your head a few notes of a tune but you don't know what it is, and if you hum it, it ends up becoming a different song from the one that's nagging at you? Or when you remember a street corner but you can't remember where it is? To give a label to those fragments I use a word that my mother used: *frantumaglia*. Bits and pieces whose origin is difficult to pinpoint, and which make a noise in your head, sometimes causing discomfort.

Eva: And any one of them could be the origin of a story?

Ferrante: Yes and no. They might be separate and identifiable: childhood places, family members, schoolmates, insulting or tender voices, moments of great tension. And once you've found some sort of order you start to narrate. But there's almost always something that doesn't work. It's as if from those splinters of a possible narrative come equal and opposite forces: the need to emerge clearly, on the one hand, and to sink farther into the depths on the other. Take *Troubling Love:* for years I had in my mind many stories about the outlying neighborhood of Naples where I was born and grew up; I had in my mind cries, crude family acts of violence I had witnessed as a child, domestic objects, streets. I nourished Delia, the protagonist, on those memories. The figure of the mother, Amalia, on the other hand, appeared and immediately withdrew—she almost wasn't there. If I imagined Delia's body merely touching her mother's I was ashamed of myself and I went on. Using that scattered material I wrote many stories over the years—short, long, and very long, all in my eyes unsatisfying, and none having to do with the figure of the mother. Then suddenly many of the fragments vanished, while others came together, before the dark background of the mother-daughter relationship. In this way, over a couple of months, *Troubling Love* emerged.

Sandro: And The Days of Abandonment?

Ferrante: Its birth certificate is even more vague. For years I had in mind a woman who closes the door of her house one night, and in the morning when she goes to open it she realizes she's no longer able to. Sometimes sick children came into it, sometimes a poisoned dog. Then in a natural way everything settled around an experience of mine that had seemed to me indescribable: the humiliation of abandonment. But how I moved from the *frantumaglia* that I'd had in my mind for years to a sudden selection of fragments, combining to make a story that seemed convincing—that escapes me, I can't give an honest account. I'm afraid that it's the same as with dreams. Even as you're recounting them, you know that you're betraying them.

Eva: Do you write down your dreams?

Ferrante: The rare times that I seem to remember them, yes. I've done so since I was a girl. It's an exercise that I would recommend to everyone. To subject a dream experience to the logic of the waking state is an extreme test of writing. A dream has the virtue of showing us clearly that reproducing something exactly is always a losing battle. But putting into words the truth of a gesture, a feeling, a flow of events, without domesticating it, is also an operation that's not so simple as you might think.

Sandra: What do you mean by domesticating the truth?
Ferrante: Taking overused expressive paths.

Sandra: In what sense?
Ferrante: Betraying the story out of laziness, out of compliance, out of convenience, out of fear. It's easy to reduce a story to well-tested representations that are fit for mass consumption and are therefore effective.

Sandro: This seems to me a subject we should look at more closely. James Wood and other critics have admired the authenticity, even the brutality, of your writing. How do you define sincerity in literature?
Ferrante: As far as I'm concerned it's the torment and, at the same time, the engine of every literary endeavor. You work for your whole life trying to gain adequate expressive tools for yourself. In general the most urgent question for a writer may seem to be: what experiences do I know I can be the voice of, what do I feel able to narrate? But it's not so. The more pressing questions are: what is the word, what is the rhythm of the sentence, what is the suitable tone for the things I know? These seem like questions of form, of style, all in all secondary. But I am convinced that without the right words, without long practice in putting them together, nothing alive and true

emerges. It's not enough to say, as we are increasingly accustomed to do nowadays: these are events that truly happened, it's my real life, the names and last names are real, I'm describing the real places where the events occurred. Writing that is inadequate can falsify the most honest biographical truths. Literary truth isn't founded on any autobiographical or journalistic or legal agreement. It's not the truth of the biographer or the reporter or a police report or a sentence handed down by a court; it's not even the plausibility of a narrative constructed with professional skill. Literary truth is the truth released exclusively by words used well, and it is realized entirely in the words that formulate it. It is directly proportional to the energy that one is able to impress on the sentence. And when it works, there is no stereotype, cliché, worn baggage of popular literature that resists it. It reanimates, revives, subjects everything to its needs.

Sandra: How does one obtain this truth?
Ferrante: It's certainly the product of skill, and that can always be improved. But in large part that energy simply *appears, happens*, and you can't say how, you can't say how long it will last, you tremble at the idea that it might suddenly stop and leave you midstream. If the writer is frank with himself, he has to admit that he never knows if he has found the right kind of writing and has been able to get the most out of it. To be clear, anyone who puts writing at the center of his life ends up in the situation of Dencombe, in Henry James's *The Middle Years*, who, at the peak of his success, as death approaches, hopes to have another opportunity to test himself and discover if he can do better than what he's already done. The writer always has on the tip of his tongue the desperate exclamation of Proust's Bergotte before Vermeer's little patch of yellow wall: "I should have written like that."

Eva: When was the first time you thought you had written with that truth?

Ferrante: Late, with *Troubling Love*. If that impression hadn't persisted, I wouldn't have published it.

Eva: You said that you worked on that material for a long time unsuccessfully.

Ferrante: Yes, but that doesn't mean that *Troubling Love* was the product of a long effort. It's exactly the opposite. The effort was all spent on the unsatisfying stories that had preceded it over the years. They consisted of obsessively worked-over pages, certainly truthful—or rather they possessed a truth that was packaged according to the standards of more or less well made stories about Naples, the periphery, poverty, jealous males, and so on. Then all of a sudden the writing assumed the right tone, or at least it seemed that way to me. I realized it from the first paragraph: that *that writing* told a story that until that moment I had never attempted, or, rather, I hadn't even tried to conceive it—a story of love for the mother, an intimate, carnal love mixed with an equally carnal repulsion. Then suddenly it filtered out of the depths of memory, and I didn't have to look for words; instead, it was the words that seemed to dislodge my most secret feelings. I decided to publish *Troubling Love* not so much because of the story it told, which continued to embarrass me and frighten me, but because for the first time it seemed to me that I could say: here's how I have to write.

Sandra: Let's pause on the writing of Troubling Love. *You're talking about it as of a surprising achievement, and you perceive a disconnection between what you were writing before, for yourself, and which didn't seem to you worthy of publication, and this book, which, instead, was born over a couple of months and without the effort of the preceding texts. Does an author therefore have several kinds of writing? I ask because quite a few Italian reviewers and writers, either truly disoriented or provoked by baser sentiments, attribute your books to different authors.*

Ferrante: Evidently, in a world where philological education has almost completely disappeared, where critics of style no longer exist, the decision not to be present as an author generates ill humor and this type of fantasy. The experts stare at the empty frame where the image of the author should be and they don't have the technical tools, or, more simply, true passion and sensitivity as readers, to fill that space with the works. So they forget an obvious fact: that every instance of writing has its own individual story, and the disconnections between these stories are very often conspicuous—so conspicuous that they can make the common features difficult to see. To be clear, only the label of the author's name or a rigorous philological examination allows us to accept that the author of *Dubliners* is the same who wrote *Ulysses* or *Finnegans Wake*. And I could continue to list apparent disparities between works that are unequivocally by the same hand. In other words, the cultural education of any high-school student should include an introduction to the idea that a writer adapts his writing to ever-changing expressive needs and that a higher or lower note doesn't mean that the singer has changed. But evidently it's not like that. For a long time, the prevailing belief has been that to write a story all you need is to be somewhat literate, and few by now recall that wanting to write means above all working hard to learn a flexible skill, ready for the most disparate trials, the outcome of which, naturally, is uncertain.

Sandra: So not several kinds of writing but a single hand that laboriously fashions a tool and each time probes its possibilities?

Ferrante: I would say yes. The writing of *Troubling Love* was for me a small miracle that arrived after years of practice. With that book, for example, it seemed to me I had achieved writing that was firm, lucid, controlled, and yet open to sudden breakdowns. The satisfaction didn't last, however; it diminished and soon vanished. That result seemed fortuitous, and it took me ten years to separate the writing from that specific book and make an autonomous tool that could also be used elsewhere, like a good solid chain that can pull up the full bucket from the very bottom of the well. I worked a lot, but only with *The Days of Abandonment* did I feel that I again had a text that could be published.

Sandro: When does a book seem to you publishable?

Ferrante: When it tells a story that for a long time, unintentionally, I had pushed away, because I didn't think I was capable of telling it, because telling it seemed to me uncomfortable. Also in the case of *The Days of Abandonment,* the writing both outlined and freed the story in a short time, during a summer. Or, rather, it was like that for the first two parts. Then suddenly I began to make mistakes. I lost the tone that had seemed right, I wrote and rewrote the last part all that fall. It was a time of great anxiety. It doesn't take much to convince yourself that you no longer know how to tell a story. You feel a strong sense of regression, you're sure you've lost the story forever. It was like that with the last part of *The Days of Abandonment*. I didn't know how to get Olga out of her crisis with the same truth with which I'd narrated her falling into it. The hand was the same, the writing was the same, the same choice of vocabulary, same syntax, same punctuation, and yet the tone had become false. I feel a similar thing when the authority of someone else, male or female, seems so strong that I lose faith in myself, my head is emptied out, I no longer know how to be me. For months I felt that the preceding pages had emerged as pages that I would never have thought myself capable of writing, and now I no longer felt equal to my own work. You prefer losing yourself rather than finding yourself, I said to myself bitterly. Then everything started up again. But even today I don't dare reread the book, I'm afraid that the last part has only the features of good writing.

Eva: Does the anxiety associated with publishing nothing less than the best book you're capable of seem to you to be a characteristic of female writers? Let me explain: have you published so little out of fear that you're not the equal of male writers? Or rather: does being a woman mean that you have to work harder to produce work that the male tradition can't dismiss as merely "women's fiction"? Put more simply, do you think there are fundamental differences between female and male writing?

Ferrante: I'll answer with a story. As a girl—twelve, thirteen years old—I was absolutely certain that a good book had to have a man as its protagonist, and that depressed me. That phase ended a couple of years later, and at fifteen I began to put brave girls who were in serious trouble at the center of the stories I was writing. But the idea remained—in fact, I would say, it became firmer—that the great, the greatest narrators were men and that one had to learn to narrate like them. I devoured books at that age, and—it's pointless to beat around the bush—my models were masculine. So even when I wrote stories about girls I tried to give the heroine a wealth of experiences, a freedom, a determination that I sought to imitate from the great novels written by men. To be clear, I didn't want to write like Madame de La Fayette or Jane Austen or the Brontës—at the time I knew very little about contemporary literature—but like Defoe or Fielding or Flaubert or Tolstoy or Dostoyevsky or even Hugo. While the models offered by women novelists were few and seemed to me for the most part thin, those provided by male novelists were numerous and almost always dazzling. That phase lasted a long time, till I was in my twenties, and left profound traces. To my eyes the male narrative tradition offered a richness of structure that didn't seem to exist in fiction written by women.

Eva: So you think that female fiction is constitutionally weak?
Ferrante: No, not at all, I'm talking about my adolescent anxieties. Many of the opinions I had then changed later. For obvious historical reasons, women's writing has a less dense and varied tradition than male writing, but it has extremely high points and also an extraordinary foundational value—the works of Jane Austen, for example. The twentieth century, besides, was a century of radical change for women. Feminist thought and feminist practices liberated energies, set in motion the most radical and profound transformation of the many that took place in the last century. I wouldn't recognize myself without women's struggles, women's nonfiction writing, women's literature: they made me adult. My experience as a novelist, both published and unpublished, culminated, after twenty years, in the attempt to relate, with writing that was appropriate, my sex and its difference. But for a long time I've thought that if we have to cultivate *our* narrative tradition, we should never renounce the entire stock of techniques that we have behind us. We have to demonstrate, precisely because we are women, that we can construct worlds as wide and powerful and rich as those designed by male writers, if not more. So we have to be well equipped, we have to dig deep into our difference, using advanced tools. Above all we mustn't give up our greatest freedom. Every woman novelist, as with women in many other fields, should aim at being not only the best woman novelist but the best of the most skilled practitioners of literature, whether male or female. To do so we have to avoid every ideological conformity, every false show of thought, every adherence to a party line or canon. Writers should be concerned only with narrating as well as possible what they know and feel, the beautiful and the ugly and the contradictory, without obeying any

prescription, not even a prescription that comes from the side you're on. Writing requires maximum ambition, maximum audacity, and programmatic disobedience.

Sandra: In which of your books do you feel that you were able to do this most thoroughly?

Ferrante: In the book that made me feel most guilty, *The Lost Daughter*. I pushed the protagonist much farther than I thought I myself, writing, could bear. Leda says: "The most difficult things to tell are those which we ourselves can't understand." It's the motto—can I call it that?—which is at the root of all my books. Writing should always take the most difficult path. The narrating "I" in my stories is never a voice giving a monologue; she is writing—that is, struggling to organize in a text what she knows but doesn't have clear in her mind. Delia, Olga, Leda, and Elena are all doing this. Delia, Olga, and Elena set off on their path and arrive at the end of the story bruised but safe. Leda on the other hand develops a text that leads her to tell things that are intolerable to her both as a daughter and as a mother, and as the friend of another woman. And mainly she has to account for a reckless gesture—the heart of the story—whose meaning not only escapes her but surely can't be deciphered if she remains inside her writing. There I demanded of myself more than I could easily give: a story that was compelling but, at the same time, whose meaning the writer, by the very nature of what she is narrating, is unable to understand; because, if she did, she might die of it. *The Lost Daughter* is, among the stories I've published, the one I'm most painfully bound to.

Eva: You insist on the centrality of the writing, you called it a chain that pulls up water from the bottom of a well. What are the features of your approach to writing?

Ferrante: The only thing I know for certain is this: it seems to me that I work well when I can start from a flat, dry tone, that of a strong, lucid, educated woman, like the middle-class women who are our contemporaries. At the beginning I need curtness, terse, clear formulas that are free of affectations and demonstrations of beautiful form. Only when the story begins to emerge with assurance, thanks to that initial tone, do I begin to wait with trepidation for the moment when I will be able to replace the series of well oiled, noiseless links with a rusty, rasping series of links and a pace that is disjointed, agitated, increasing the risk of absolute collapse. The moment I change register for the first time is both exciting and anguished. I very much enjoy breaking through my character's armor of good education and good manners, upsetting the image she has of herself, undermining her determination, and revealing another, rougher soul; I make her raucous, perhaps crude. I work hard to make the fracture between the two tonalities surprising and also to make the re-entry into the tranquil narration happen naturally. While the fracture comes easily—I wait for that moment, and slip inside it with satisfaction—I very much fear the moment when the narrative has to compose itself again. I'm afraid that the narrating "I" won't be able to calm down. But above all, now that readers know her calm is false, that it won't last, that the narrative orderliness will break up again, with ever greater decisiveness and pleasure, I need to take care to make that transitory calm believable.

Sandra: Your openings have often been praised, especially by English and American critics. Do they have to do with this alternation of smooth narration and sudden breaks?

Ferrante: I think so. Right from the first lines, I strive to establish a tone that is placid but with unexpected wrinkles. I've always done this, except where there is a sort of prologue—as in *The Lost Daughter* and *My Brilliant Friend*—that by its nature has a duller tone. But in every case when I get to the real start of the story I tend toward an expansive sentence that has a cold tone but at the same time exposes a magma of unbearable heat. I want readers to know from the first lines what they are dealing with.

Sandro: Are you concerned with your readers? Do you think it's important to excite them, challenge them, even trouble them?

Ferrante: I publish to be read: it's the only thing that interests me about publishing. So I employ all the strategies I know to capture the reader's attention, stimulate curiosity, make the page as dense as possible and as easy as possible to turn. But I don't think the reader should be indulged as a consumer, because he isn't. Literature that indulges the tastes of the reader is a degraded literature. My goal, paradoxically, is to disappoint the usual expectations and inspire new ones.

Sandro: The novel, since its beginnings, has aimed at keeping narrative tension high. Then, in the twentieth century, everything seemed to change. Which tradition is the literature of the twenty-first century following?

Ferrante: I think of literary tradition as a single large depository, where anyone who wants to write goes to choose what is useful to him, without excluding anything. And it seems to me that today we have a need for precisely this. An ambitious novelist has a duty, even more than in the past, to have a vast literary culture. We live in times of great change, and the outcomes are unpredictable; it's good to be prepared. We need to be like Diderot, the author of both *The Nun* and *Jacques the Fatalist and His Master*, capable, that is, of reusing both Fielding and Sterne. The great twentieth-century quest can and should be connected to the great foundational novels, the violations of their tenets, and even the most effective devices of genre literature. Without ever forgetting that a story is truly alive not because the author is photogenic or the reviewers say good things about it or the marketing makes it desirable but because in a certain number of dense pages it never forgets the reader—for it is the reader's job to light the fuse of the words. I renounce nothing that can give pleasure to the reader, not even what is considered old, trite, vulgar. As I was saying, what makes everything new and acceptable is literary truth; whether a text is short, long, or endless, what counts above all is richness, complexity, the fascination of the narrative texture. If a novel has these qualities—and no trick of marketing can truly provide them—it needs nothing else, it can continue on its way, drawing its readers along, even, if necessary, in the direction of the antinovel.

Sandro: Only the quality of the writing counts, and it redeems everything: this seems to be an important point and I'd like to return to it later. Many American reviews seem to make a direct connection between your writing—its sincerity, its honesty—and your keeping out of the public eye. As if to say, the less one appears, the better one writes.

Ferrante: Two decades are a long time, and the reasons for the decisions I made in 1990, when we first considered my need to avoid the rituals that accompany the publication of a book, have changed. Then I was frightened by the possibility of having to come out of my shell—timidity prevailed, the desire for intangibility. Later, it was hostility toward the media, which pays scant attention to the books themselves, and tends to assign importance to a work especially if the author already has a solid reputation. It's surprising, for example, how the most widely admired Italian writers and poets are also well-known academics or are employed in high-level editorial jobs or in other prestigious fields. It's as if literature were not capable of demonstrating its seriousness of intention simply through texts but needed to provide "external" credentials as proof of its quality. In a similar category—if we leave the university or the editorial office—are the literary contributions of politicians, journalists, singers, actors, directors, television producers, etc. Here, too, the works do not have intrinsic authorization for their existence but need an entry pass generated by work done in other fields. "I'm a success in this or that field, I've acquired an audience, and *therefore* I wrote and published a novel." The media place great importance on this nexus. It's not the book that counts but the aura of its author. If the aura is already there, and the media reinforce it, the editorial world is happy to open its doors and the market is very happy to welcome you. If it's not there but the book miraculously sells, the media *invent* the author, engaging a mechanism by which the writer sells not only his work but himself, his image.

Sandra: You were saying that the reasons for staying in the shadows have changed a bit.

Ferrante: I'm still very interested in testifying against the self-promotion obsessively imposed by the media. The demand for self-promotion not only diminishes the role of the works in every possible sector of human activity; it now rules everything. Nothing can function without the designated media protagonists. And yet there is no work that is not the fruit of tradition, of many skills, of a sort of collective intelligence. By insisting on a protagonist—a protagonist, note, not an individual, not a single person, whose function is fundamental—we wrongly diminish the role played by this collective intelligence. But, I must say, what has never lost importance for me, during what has been by now a long period of absence, is the creative space that it opens. Here I'd like to return to the writing itself. Knowing that the book, once completed, will make its journey without being accompanied by my physical person, knowing that nothing of the concrete, definite individual I am will ever appear beside the volume, printed as if it were a little dog whose master I am, showed me sides of the writing that were obvious, of course, but which I had never thought of. I had the impression of having released the words from myself.

Eva: You mean you felt you'd been censoring yourself?

Ferrante: No, self-censorship doesn't enter into it. I wrote for a long time without the intention of publishing or having others read what I was writing, and it was important training in not censoring myself. I mean, rather, a problem affecting the writing's potential. Keats said that for him the poet is everything and nothing, that it's not him, that he has no self, that he has no identity, that he is whatever there is that is most unpoetic. In general one reads that letter of his as an announcement of aesthetic chameleonism. I on the other hand see in it an untying in which the author boldly separates himself from his writing, as if he were saying: writing is everything and I am nothing, address it, not me. It's a disruptive position. Keats draws the poet away from his own art, calls him unpoetic, denies him an identity outside of writing. And today it seems important to remember this. Removing the author—as understood by the media—from the result of his writing highlights a sort of new creative space that requires expert attention. Starting with *The Days of Abandonment*, it seemed to me that what the media considered to be the empty space created by my absence was filled up by the writing.

Eva: Could you explain more clearly?

Ferrante: Let me try to explain it from the reader's point of view, which was summarized well by Meghan O'Rourke in *The Guardian*. O'Rourke emphasized that "our relationship to her," meaning the relationship that is established between the reader and the writer who chooses to separate herself in a radical way from her own book, "is like that which we have with a fictional character. We think we know her, but what we know are her sentences, the pattern of her mind, the path of her imagination." It may seem like a small distinction, but to me it's not. It has become natural to think of the author as a particular individual who exists, inevitably, outside the text, and if we want to know more about what we're reading we should address that individual—to understand the works better we should find out everything about his more or less banal life. Yet, if we simply remove that individuality from the public eye, it's evident that what O'Rourke points out is true: the text has more in it than we imagine. It has taken possession of the person who writes, and if we want to find that person, she, too, is there, revealing a self that she may not even truly know. When one offers oneself to the public as a pure and simple act of writing—the only thing that really counts in literature—that self becomes inextricably part of the story or the verse, part of the fiction. This is what I have been working on over the years with increasing awareness, especially in *My Brilliant Friend*. The truth of Elena Greco, who is very different from me, depends on the truth with which my writing creates her, and thus on the truth with which I can refine my writing.

Sandro: You mean that while the media rush to fill the empty space you have left by your absence with gossip, readers fill it, more appropriately, by reading, finding all that they need in the text?

Ferrante: Yes. But I also mean that, if this is true, the task of the writer is further enhanced. If there is a blank space, in terms of social or media rituals, which for the sake of convention I call Elena Ferrante, I, Elena Ferrante, can and should exert myself—am obliged by my curiosity as a novelist, by the craving to test myself—to fill that empty space in the text. How? By providing the reader with the elements that enable him to distinguish me from the narrating "I," whom I call Elena Greco, and to perceive me as true and present precisely in what I say about Elena and Lila, precisely in the ways in which I combine words in a vivid and authentic way. The author, who outside the text doesn't exist, inside the text offers herself, *consciously adds herself* to the story, exerting herself to be truer than she could be in the photos of a Sunday supplement, at a presentation in a bookstore, at a festival of literature, in some television broadcast, in the spectacle of a literary prize. The passionate reader deserves to be enabled to *also* extract the author's physiognomy from every word or grammatical violation or syntactical knot in the text, just as happens for characters, for a landscape, for a feeling, for a slow or agitated act. So the writing becomes even more crucial both for the one who produces it (who has to offer himself to the reader with the utmost honesty) and for the one who enjoys it. This seems to me much more than signing copies in a bookstore, defacing them with trite phrases.

Sandra: You were saying that the Neapolitan Quartet is the novel in which you worked most consciously on the possibilities offered by the creative space that you produced.

Ferrante: Yes. But first comes the experience of *The Lost Daughter*. If in the first two books I published I was almost frightened by recognizing myself in the writing—above all in the use of that double register I mentioned—in this third book I was afraid of having pushed myself too far, as if I could not control Leda's world by following the same procedure I had employed in the first two stories. I realized later that with the act of stealing the doll, and in Leda's fascination with the mother of the girl who's been robbed, there was technically no return. Those two elements—the dark background of the mother-daughter relationship and a budding friendship that's equally dark—carried me farther and farther into the complicated relationship that forms between women. The writing dragged in unspeakable things, so that I erased them myself, the next day, because they seemed important and yet had ended up in a verbal net that couldn't sustain them. If Leda couldn't get to the bottom of that act—something that she was more and more mired in: she, an adult, stealing a doll from a child—I was drowning with her as I wrote, and I couldn't get either of us out of the vortex as I had done with Delia and Olga. Eventually the story was finished, and feeling great anxiety I published it. But for several years I continued to circle around it, I felt I had to return to it. It's no coincidence that when I came to the Neapolitan Quartet I started off again with two dolls and an intense female friendship captured at its beginning. It seemed to me that there was something that needed to be articulated again.

Eva: Let's move on to the Neapolitan Quartet. The relationship between Lila and Elena doesn't seem to be invented, or even to be narrated by means of standard techniques; it seems to flow directly from the unconscious.

Ferrante: Let's say that The Neapolitan Quartet doesn't have to make its way like the other stories in the *frantumaglia*—that mass of incoherent material. From the start I had the sensation, completely new for me, that everything was already in place. Maybe that was the result of the connection with *The Lost Daughter*. There, for example, Nina, the young mother who clashes with the camorristic context she's inserted into, and who, for that very reason, fascinates Leda, already occupies a central position in the story. With the Neapolitan Quartet the first narrative blocks that I had in mind were certainly those concerning the loss of the two dolls and the loss of the child. But it seems pointless to make a list of the more or less conscious connections that I see between my books. I only mean to say that the impression of order, surely deriving from various pre-existing ideas for the story, was something new for me. I don't know, the very theme of female friendship is certainly connected, at least in some respects, to a friend of mine, whom I talked about some time ago in the *Corriere della Sera*, a few years after her death: that's the first written trace of the friendship between Lila and Lenù. And then I have a small private gallery—stories, fortunately unpublished—of uncontrollable girls and women, who in vain are repressed by their men, by their environment, they are bold and yet weary, always a step away from disappearing into their mental *frantumaglia*, and who converge in the figure of Amalia, the mother in *Troubling Love*. Amalia, yes, if I think about it, has many features of Lila, even her dissolving margins.

Eva: How do you explain the fact that readers find it easy to recognize themselves in both Elena and Lila, in spite of their profoundly different natures? They're both very complex, and yet while Elena tends to extreme verisimilitude, Lila has a sort of superior truth, she seems to be made of a more mysterious material, delineated with greater depth, and with a sometimes symbolic significance.

Ferrante: The difference between Elena and Lila influences quite a few narrative choices, but they can all be traced back to the changing condition of women that is at the center of the narrative. Think of the role of reading and studying. Elena is extremely disciplined; she diligently acquires, each time, the tools she needs, she recounts her journey as an intellectual with controlled pride, she demonstrates her intense engagement with the world and at the same time emphasizes how Lila has remained behind, in fact she repeatedly insists on how she has outdistanced her. But every so often her story breaks down and Lila appears much more active, above all more ferociously—I would say also: more basely, more viscerally—involved. But then she truly withdraws, leaves the field to her friend, remaining a victim of what most terrorizes her: dissolving margins, disappearing. What you called a difference is an oscillation innate in the relationship between the two characters and in the very structure of Lenù's story. It's this difference that allows female readers in particular—but I think also male readers—the possibility of feeling that they are both Elena and Lila. If the two friends had the same pace, they would be doubles of each other, by turns they would appear as a secret voice, a mirror image, or something else. But it's not like that. The pace is broken from the start, and it's not only Lila who produces the gap but also Lenù. When Lila's pace becomes unsustainable, the reader grabs onto Lenù. But if Lenù falls apart, then the reader relies on Lila.

Sandra: You've mentioned disappearance—it is one of your recurring themes.

Ferrante: Yes, I think so, in fact I'm certain it is. It has to do with being driven back, but also with driving oneself back. It's a feeling I know well, I think that all women know it. Whenever a part of you emerges that's not consistent with the canonic female, you feel that that part causes uneasiness in you and in others, and you'd better get rid of it in a hurry. Or if you have a combative nature, like Amalia, like Lila, if you're not someone who calms down, if you refuse to be subjugated, violence enters. Violence has, at least in Italian, a meaningful language of its own: smash your face, bash your face in. You see? These are expressions that refer to the forced manipulation of identity, to its cancellation. Either you'll be the way I say or I'll change you by beating you till I kill you.

Eva: But one cancels oneself, too. Amalia may have killed herself. And Lila can't be found. Why? Is it a surrender?

Ferrante: There are many reasons to disappear. The disappearance of Amalia, of Lila, yes, maybe it's a surrender. But it's also, I think, a sign of their irreducibility. I'm not sure. While I'm writing I think I know a lot about my characters, but then

I discover I know much less than my readers. The extraordinary thing about the written word is that by nature it can do without your presence and also, in many respects, without your intentions. The voice is part of your body, it needs your presence—you speak, you have a dialogue, you correct, you give further explanations. Writing, on the other hand, once it's fixed on a support structure, is autonomous, it needs a reader, not you. You, let's say, you leave your act of writing, and go away. The reader reckons, if he likes, with the way you've put together the words. Amalia, for example, is filtered through Delia's writing, and the reader has to unravel the knot of the daughter if he wants to try to unravel the knot of the mother. Even more complicated is the setting of Lila inside Lenù's story: the plot, the narrative fabric of their friendship, is very elaborated. Yes, maybe the Delia-Amalia relationship is at the origin of the Lenù-Lila relationship. The books slip inside one another without you the writer realizing it; one experience of writing feeds a new experience and gives it strength. For example, a figure from childhood, a woman who has gone off the rails, is central in *The Days of Abandonment*, and there she's called the *poverella*, the poor woman. Well, I realize only now that the *poverella* is reincarnated in Melina, a character in the Neapolitan Quartet. It's probably this essentially unconscious continuity among many experiences of writing, both published and unpublished, that with the Neapolitan Quartet gave me the impression of having in hand a simple story. Unlike the other books, which derived from an abrupt selection of many fragments that were in my mind, this book, it seemed to me, was all ready, and I knew just what to do.

Sandro: What is your relationship with plot, and how much, in the Neapolitan Quartet, did it change along the way?

Ferrante: Plot is what excites me and my readers. But for that very reason it is woven with the thread of the writing. It comes in large part while I'm writing, always. I know, for example, that Olga will remain locked in her house, without a telephone, with her sick son, her daughter, and the poisoned dog. But I don't know what will happen when these elements are set in motion. It's the writing that pulls me along—and it has to pull me seriously, in the sense that it has to involve me, agitate me—from the moment the door doesn't open to the moment it opens as if it had never been locked. Naturally I speculate about how things will develop, before and while I write, but I keep these speculations in my head, in a confused way, ready to vanish as the story advances. For example, a character may lose substance simply because I can't resist talking about him or her with a friend. The story told aloud instantly destroys everything. However remarkable the development I had in mind, from that moment on it doesn't seem worth the trouble of writing it. In the case of Lila and Lenù, however, the plot unfolded with naturalness, and I rarely changed course.

Sandra: Some of your stories have the pacing of thrillers, but then they become love stories, or something else again.

Ferrante: Naturally plot is equated with genre fiction, and here things get more complicated. I use plots, yes, but, I have to say, I can't respect the rules of genres—the reader who reads me convinced that I will give him a thriller or a love story or a Bildungsroman will surely be disappointed. Only the weave of events interests me and so I avoid cages with fixed rules. In the Neapolitan Quartet the plot crossed every area like that, without getting stuck, and in fact it progressed without faltering and without second thoughts on my part. Despite the fact that it developed not over months but, rather, over years, what emerged as I wrote generally stayed in the final, published version.

Sandro: And yet it is a very complex book, far from simple both in its conception and in its writing.

Ferrante: Maybe, but I would insist: at first I didn't feel that way about it. When, almost six years ago, I began to write, I knew clearly the story I would tell: a friendship that begins with the treacherous game of the dolls and ends with the loss of a daughter. I had in mind a story no longer than *Troubling Love* or *The Lost Daughter*. As a result there wasn't a phase of looking for the heart of the narrative. As soon as I began to write, it seemed to me that the writing went smoothly.

Eva: What distinguishes writing that goes smoothly from writing that doesn't?

Ferrante: The attention that I put into every word, every sentence. I have stories, unpublished, in which the attention to form was inordinate, I couldn't go on if every line didn't seem perfect. When that happens, the page is beautiful but the story false. I want to insist on this point, it's something I'm very familiar with: the story moves forward, I like it, in general I finish it. But in fact it's not a narrative that gives me pleasure. The pleasure—I soon discover—all came from my obsessive refinement of expression, from maniacally polishing the sentences. I would say, in fact, that, at least as far as I'm concerned, the greater the attention to the sentence, the more laboriously the story flows. A state of grace begins when the writing is concerned only with hanging on to the story. With the Neapolitan Quartet that happened immediately, and it lasted. Months passed, the story spun out rapidly, I didn't even try to reread what I had written. For the first time, in my experience, memory and imagination provided me with an increasingly substantial quantity of material that, instead of crowding the story and confusing me, arranged itself there in a sort of tranquil crush, useful for the increasing needs of the narrative.

Eva: In that state of grace the writing emerges without corrections and reworkings?

Ferrante: No, the writing no, but the story yes. And that happens when you have a clamor in your head and you continue to write as if taking dictation, even while you're doing the shopping, even when you eat, even in your sleep. Thus the story—as long as it keeps going—has no need of reorganization. For all sixteen hundred pages of the Neapolitan Quartet I never felt the need to restructure events, characters, feelings, turning points, reversals. And yet—I am amazed myself, since the story is so long, so rich in characters who develop over a long period of time—I never resorted to notes, chronologies, plans of any sort. I must say, however, that it's not unusual, I've always detested preparatory work. If I try to do it, the desire to write passes, I feel that I can no longer surprise or excite myself. Thus everything happens in my head and, in essence, while I'm actually writing. Then a moment arrives when I need to catch my breath. I stop, reread, and work with pleasure on the quality of the prose. But in the previous books that happened, I don't know, after two, three, four pages, at most ten—in *My Brilliant Friend* it happened after fifty or even a hundred pages that were written without rereading.

Eva: Attention to form seems to have an ambiguous value for you—it can be positive or negative for the story.

Ferrante: Yes. Beauty of form, at least in my experience, can become an obsession that hides more complex problems: the story isn't working, I can't find my way, I lose faith in my ability to tell a story. The opposite of this is those moments when the writing seems to be concerned only with getting the story out. Then the joy of writing is there. I'm sure that the narrative has gotten started, and now it's a matter of making it flow better.

Sandra: How do you proceed in the second case?

Ferrante: I reread from time to time, and I intervene mainly to take out or to add. However, that first reading is very far from a meticulous examination of the text, which comes only when the story is finished. At that point there will be various drafts and corrections, reworkings, inserts, until a few hours before the book goes to press. In that phase I become sensitive to every detail of daily life. I see an effect of light and make a note of it. I see a plant in a meadow and try not to forget it. I make lists of words, I write down phrases I hear on the street. I work a lot, on the proofs, too, and there is nothing that can't, at the last moment, end up in the story, become an element in a landscape, the second term of a simile, a metaphor, a new dialogue, the not trite and yet not outlandish adjective I was looking for. The first reading, on the other hand, is only a recognition. I take possession of what I've written, I get rid of redundancies, I fill in what seems barely sketched, and I explore paths that the text itself now suggests to me.

Sandra: Do you mean that there's a phase in which it's the existence of the text that further determines the story, that amplifies it?

Ferrante: In essence, yes. It's a relief to have some pages, when before there was nothing. In their pure and simple combination of signs, the words, the sentences are material, you can now act upon them with all the skill you have. The places are places, the people are people, what they do or don't do is there, it happens. And all this, as one looks it over, demands to be perfected, to be increasingly vivid and true. So I begin a reading by rewriting. And this reading by rewriting is great. I must say it always seems to me that skill truly plays a part during this first reading-writing. It's like a second wave, but one that is less laborious, less anxious, and yet—if the pages don't disappoint me—even more absorbing than the first.

Sandra: Let's go back to the Neapolitan Quartet. *What happened that was new, compared with your previous experiences?*

Ferrante: There were many new things. First, at no moment in my previous experience had I intended to write a story so long. Second, I didn't imagine that such an extensive historical period, so full of changes, could be important in the life of the characters in such a complex way. Third, I would never have dreamed of managing so many minor figures. Fourth, I had always rejected, out of a personal distaste, giving space to social ascent, to the acquisition of a cultural and political point of view, to the instability of the convictions acquired, to the weight of class origins, a weight that not only doesn't disappear but doesn't even really diminish. My themes and also my abilities seemed ill-suited to these questions. And yet in effect that story wouldn't end. The historical period slipped naturally into the characters' gestures, thoughts, and choices about life, although it never imposed itself, settling outside them as a detailed background. As for the minor characters, it seemed natural for each of them to have his good or bad moment in the life of the protagonists and then slip into the background, just as when we think back on our existence and, of the many people who entered the flow of our lives, remember almost nothing. As for my distaste for politics and sociology I discovered that it was a screen, behind which lurked the pleasure—yes, I mean it—the pleasure of narrating a sort of female alienation-inclusion.

Eva: Alienation and inclusion in relation to what?

Ferrante: I felt as if Elena and Lila were alienated from History, with all its political, social, economic, cultural apparatus, and yet included in it almost without knowing it, in every word or act. That alienation-inclusion seemed to me outside the frame, difficult for me to recount, and so, as usual, I decided to do it. I wanted the historical period to be a faintly defined background and also to emerge from the changes that had an impact on the characters' lives, from their uncertainties, decisions, actions, language. Naturally even the tiniest sense of a false tone would have been enough to stop me. But the writing continued to glide along, and I almost always felt certain—wrongly or rightly—that the tonality supported and gave to the small facts of the Neapolitan Quartet that truth which, if it succeeds, makes the larger facts less trite.

Sandra: And the novelty of female friendship as a theme? Everyone today is suggesting that there wasn't, before the Neapolitan Quartet, a literary tradition to draw on. You yourself, in your previous books, told stories of women alone, without friends to turn to. Although when Leda is at the beach—as you pointed out—she tries to establish a friendly relationship with Nina, she left for her vacation in absolute solitude, as if she had no friends.

Ferrante: You're right. Delia, Olga, and Leda confront their experiences without ever turning to other women for help or support. Only Leda in the end breaks out of her isolation and establishes a friendly relationship with another woman. But meanwhile she performs an act that in essence means that her need for friendship cannot be met. Elena, on the other hand, is never truly alone, her life is closely bound up with that of her childhood friend.

Sandra: However, if you think about it, Lila as a child does something equally serious and carries that childhood decision with her for her whole life.

Ferrante: It's true. But before considering the originality of the two protagonists and their friendship, let me emphasize a couple of features that remain identical from one book to the other. All four of the stories are told in the first person, but, as I've already noted, in none of the stories did I imagine the narrating "I" as a voice. Delia, Olga, Leda, Elena write, they have

written or they are writing. On this I would insist: the four protagonists are imagined not as first but as third persons who
have either left or are leaving a written testimony about their
experience. It very often happens that women, in moments of
crisis, try to calm ourselves by writing. It's private writing
intended to control unease—we write letters, diaries. I always
started from this assumption—women who write about themselves in order to understand themselves. The assumption
becomes explicit, however, in fact an essential part of the narrative development, only in the Neapolitan Quartet.

Sandro: Why are you eager to emphasize that point?
Ferrante: To indicate that my women figures have expressed
themselves in the way they write. Italo Svevo believed that, even
before the reader, the writer had to believe in the story he was
telling. More than in the story, I have to believe in how, I don't
know, Olga or Leda is writing her experience; it's principally
the truth of her writing that engages me. And here I come to
the second constant I mentioned: in all four novels the narrator preserves a basic characteristic that is entrusted completely
to the writing. Delia, Olga, Leda, Lenù seem to know thoroughly what they have to tell. But as the story advances, the
more uncertain, reticent, unreliable they appear, almost without realizing it. There, that's the trait I've worked on the hardest in these years: to achieve a feminine "I" who, in her vocabulary, in the structure of her sentences, in the oscillation of
expressive registers, would demonstrate solidity of intention,
sincere thinking and feeling, and at the same time would have
reprehensible thoughts, feelings, and actions. Naturally what
was most important to me was that there be no hypocrisy: my
narrator had to be honest with herself in both cases, she had to
consider herself honest when she is tranquil, and when she is
enraged, envious, and so on.

Sandra: Elena is the one who most explicitly has those characteristics.

Ferrante: Yes, and it couldn't be otherwise. Lenù intends, in the first pages, to prevent her friend Lila from disappearing. How? By writing. She wants to fix everything she knows about her in a minutely detailed story, as if to convince her that cancelling herself out is impossible. At first Elena seems to be in a position of strength; she expresses herself as if she were certainly capable of capturing her friend with her writing and bringing her home. In reality the more the story continues, the less successful she becomes at pinning Lila down.

Eva: Why? Does Lenù discover that she can't subdue her friend even with writing?

Ferrante: Here we come to the basic characteristic of Lenù's writing. It is imagined as dependent on Lila's. Of what Lila writes we know little, but we know a lot about how and the extent to which Lenù makes use of it. The pages of the Neapolitan Quartet are thought of as the point of arrival of Lila's long influence on Lenù in two different ways: first, through what she has written, which Lenù has been able to read; second, through the writing that Lenù on various occasions believes her to be capable of and which she tries to conform to, with a permanent sense of dissatisfaction. In every case Lenù as a writer is destined to constantly question herself. Her success proves that she is good, but she feels insufficient, since Lila is more and more elusive in a story that should capture her fully.

Sandra: But if Elena's writing is in fact yours, aren't you almost systematically displaying your insufficiency?

Ferrante: I don't know. Certainly, starting with *Troubling Love,* I have produced writing that is dissatisfied with itself, and Lenù's writing not only declares and recounts that dissat-

isfaction but speculates that there is a writing that is more powerful, more effective, which Lila has always known and practices, but that is barred to her. The mechanism is, I repeat, the
following: Lenù is a writer; the text we're reading is hers;
Lenù's writing originates, like many other things in her experience, in a sort of secret competition with Lila; Lila herself, in
effect, has always had a writing of her own, a writing that is not
imitated and perhaps not imitable, and which goads Lenù; no
doubt the text we're reading therefore shows traces of that
goad; Lila's writing, in other words, is inscribed in Elena's writing, whether or not she has intervened directly in the text.
That's it in a nutshell. But it's a fiction, naturally, which is part
of the many other fictions that make up the story. My act of
writing, which is the most impalpable, the least reducible to all
rules, is inventing everything.

*Eva: When you talk about Lila's elusive writing are you
alluding symbolically to an ideal writing, a writing that you
aspire to when you write?*

Ferrante: That's certainly the case for Lenù. It's always
struck me how writers circle around their writing and in the
end avoid it, they start talking about the rituals that help them
get to work, but not actually about writing. I am no different
and, even though I've always thought about writing and have
tried to focus on the self-sufficiency of the writing by exiling
myself from my books, I nevertheless haven't much to say. So
I'll try to return to my experience and to Keats, in his letter to
Woodhouse, cited above. He said that the poem is not in the
person of the poet but in the making of the lines, in the faculty of language that is made apparent in writing. I've already
mentioned, I think, the fact that for me the story truly functions when you have in your head the steady sound of the *frantumaglia* that has prevailed over everything and now is pressing steadily to become a story. You the individual, you the

person, in those moments aren't there, you're only that noise and that writing, and so you write, you continue to write even when you stop, even when you're busy with daily life, even in your sleep. The act of writing is the continuous conveyance of that *frantumaglia* of sounds, emotions, and things to the word and the sentence, to the story of Delia, Olga, Leda, Lenù. It's a choice and a need, a flow, like running water, and at the same time the result of study, the acquisition of techniques, skills, a pleasure and an unnatural effort of the brain and the whole body. In the end what is set on the page is a highly composite, immaterial organism, made up of me who writes and of Lenù, let's say, and of the many people and things she narrates and the way in which she narrates and in which I narrate her, not to mention the literary tradition I draw on, and learned from, and everything that makes the writer a component of a creative collective intelligence—the language as it's spoken where we were born and grew up, the stories that were told to us, the ethics we acquired, and so on—in other words the fragments of a very long history that drastically reduces our function as "authors," as we understand the word today. Is it possible to make of that immaterial organism a concretely narratable object, that is, to employ techniques capable of conveying that organism to the reader as one does with the wind, the heat, a feeling, the events that make up the plot? To control that noisy permanent fragmenting in your head, explore that transformation into words that lasts as long as the story lasts is, I think, the secret ambition of anyone who fully dedicates himself to writing. When Keats said the poet has no identity he meant, I think, that the only identity that counts is that of the immaterial organism that breathes in the work and that is released for the reader, not, certainly, that which you attribute to yourself afterward when you say: I'm an author, I wrote that book.

Sandra: A last question. Lila's writing is very present in the story and has an influence on Elena starting in childhood. What are the characteristics of Lila's writing?

Ferrante: We'll never know if Lila's rare writings really have the power that Elena attributes to them. What we know is, rather, how they end up producing a sort of model that Elena strives to adhere to all her life. She tells us something about that model, but that's not what counts. What counts is that without Lila Elena wouldn't exist as a writer. Any writer takes his texts from an ideal writing that is always before us, unreachable. It's a fantasy, which can't be grasped. As a result the only trace that remains of how Lila writes is Lenù's writing.

NOTE

The interview—a long conversation with Sandra Ozzola, Sandro Ferri, and Eva Ferri—appeared in an edited form in the spring of 2015 in *The Paris Review* (U.S.A.), under the title "The Art of Fiction No. 228: Elena Ferrante." The version published here is less structured and more wide-ranging. The interview in *The Paris Review* had the following introduction:

Our conversation with Ferrante began in Naples. Our original plan was to visit the neighborhood depicted in the Neapolitan Quartet, then walk along the seafront, but at the last moment Ferrante changed her mind about the neighborhood. Places of the imagination are visited in books, she said. Seen in reality they may be hard to recognize; they are disappointing, they might even seem fake. We tried the seafront, but in the end, because it was a rainy evening, we retreated to the lobby of the Hotel Royal Continental, just opposite the Castel dell'Ovo.

From here, out of the rain, we could every so often glimpse people passing along the street and imagine the characters who have for so long occupied our imaginations and our hearts. There was no particular need to meet in Naples, but Ferrante, who was in the city for family reasons, invited us and we took advantage of the occasion to celebrate the completion of *The Story of the Lost Child*. The conversation continued late into the night and resumed the next day over lunch (clams), then again in Rome, at our house (tea and tisane). At the end, each of us had a notebook full of notes. We compared them and reorganized the material according to Ferrante's directions.

7

EXTREME PEOPLE
Answers to questions from Gudmund Skjeldal

*S*kjeldal: I've been told that people take sick leave from work in order to read the novels. They're absent-minded, as if they were drugged; will I be able to read Ferrante while I'm standing in line over there? Or in the lavatory? They forget about their children, they forget about their spouse. Are you aware of what you're doing to your readers? Doesn't it make you want to meet them? Go on tour and visit literary festivals the way other authors do?

Ferrante: I'm happy when my books establish an intense and lasting relationship with readers. It seems to be proof that I've given the books what's necessary and that they truly have no more need of me. If now I were to accompany them throughout the world, I would feel like those mothers who follow their children around even when the children are adults, and who on every occasion speak in their place or embarrass them by singing their praises.

Skjeldal: The second volume of the series has just come out in Norwegian. And I feel torn between waiting for Kristin Sørsdal's excellent translation of the last two books, to be published in March next year, or buying them in English. Do you follow the work of your translators? Are they able to consult with you, as translators often do with writers?

Ferrante: The translators write and I respond. Their queries can take me a long time. I like helping them find solutions.

Skjeldal: When I told my nine-year-old son about the book I'm reading, he was bewildered by the fact that you don't want to be known: everybody wants to be famous, in his view. What do your daughters say? Do they understand your decision?

Ferrante: My daughters and I have a long-standing pact: I can do what I want, except things that could embarrass them. I don't know that I've always respected our agreement. Certainly they've appreciated and appreciate the fact that I've managed to resist the desire for self-promotion, the mania for success. For children parents are always a burden. But parents who draw too much attention to themselves are intolerable.

Skjeldal: The Neapolitan Quartet is about two girls—and then women—Lila and Elena. Would I be wrong to think that they would not have understood your choice of anonymity? Their dream is to get out of Naples, to become rich and famous— and then, they hope, free.

Ferrante: Elena would say that she envied my choice and then would have continued on her path. Lila would have found it insufficient and would ask me to give up writing even these answers. As for me, I long ago got rid of my desire for fame. But I'm very happy about the fame that Lila and Lenù are gaining in the minds of readers.

Skjeldal: The Neapolitan Quartet has a definite feminist vein: it can be seen in the two women's struggle against tradition, in how they feel persecuted by men. Yet your books made me reflect on my male friendships, on how involved I am, and on our competitiveness. I identify even more with the two girls than with the men portrayed in the books. Have there been major changes in the male culture of Naples in the decades of the nineteen-fifties and sixties, compared with today?

Ferrante: Males have changed a lot, in Naples and in the world, as, indeed, we women, too, have changed. But we'd have to discuss the depth of the changes. In not a few of the characters in my book, male and female, the changes are superficial and regression is always possible. The problem is that real change takes a long time, while life hits us right away, now, with all its contradictions.

Skjeldal: The dynamics between the two friends, Elena and Lila, are wonderfully portrayed: the close but competitive relationship, the impulse toward both mutual dependence and distance. I can't think of anything like it in what I've read. Do you have any thematic ideals, or did you set out to clear new literary terrain with this friendship?

Ferrante: I'm convinced that the reality of the facts, which we generally appeal to as if it were simple and linear, is an inextricable tangle, and that the task of literature is to enter that tangle without convenient or easy plans. Exploring the disorderliness of female friendship meant learning to set aside every literary idealization and every temptation to instruct.

Skjeldal: I read in an interview that the novel that is most important to you is Elsa Morante's House of Liars. *Could you describe why?*

Ferrante: It's the book through which I discovered that an entirely female story—entirely women's desires and ideas and feelings—could be compelling and, at the same time, have great literary value.

Skjeldal: It's tempting to interpret the importance given in your novels to friends and siblings in a person's development as a revolt against all the portraits of parents we find in novels (see, for example, the works of the Norwegian Karl Ove Knausgård). It's not clearly stated, but could it nevertheless be interpreted as a corrective to Freudian psychology?

Ferrante: I don't know. Parental figures can't be ignored,

and in my books they have an important role, especially mothers. But siblings and friends are no less critical. How do we fabricate their images? Hard to say. Siblings and friends seem extraordinarily like us and yet they remain the Other, never reducible to us, never completely reliable, and so at times dangerous, treacherous. They make up a small world where we can joust without the great risks we'll be exposed to when we cross over to find ourselves among the strangers of the big world. Sometimes we resort to siblings and friends to take a breath, to feel that we're understood. But more often it's to give vent without restraint to our frustrations and our rages, as if they were the primary cause of some infinite disappointment.

Skjeldal: Do you yourself understand Lila? She marries far too young, even though she doesn't really need to; she's good and bad at the same time; she absorbs the energy from everything; and yet, for Elena, she colors everything. Maybe with Lila you thought of a less ordinary, possibly Nietzschean, character, given the way she embodies the Dionysian force in the world, while with Elena you imagined a more rational woman?

Ferrante: I've always been fascinated by people who are extreme in their every manifestation. Lila has many features of a friend of mine who died some years ago. There was nothing Dionysian about her. She was, rather, one of those people who are curious about everything and who without apparent effort are good at everything, except then they get bored and enthusiastically move on to something else. I tried to describe the wake of sparkling incompleteness that trails behind these many-sided intelligences, who can never be defined.

Skjeldal: If I were a scriptwriter I think I'd be very happy to work on these four books. Films have been made from several of your earlier books. Do you think in scenes? Or do you concen-

trate, rather, on making good sentences? Is it possible to separate these two passions?

Ferrante: Shklovsky said that we don't know what art is but in exchange we regulate it punctiliously. Borders are fixed, rules are established. One of these is that the evil spells of cinema and television disturb the chiseled quality of the sentences, poison the literature. And yet the writer, precisely in the name of literature, has the duty to frequent all languages and violate them all, if it's useful. I've never worked in cinema or television, but I've been an assiduous spectator for a long time and when I write I have recourse to films but also to paintings, and to everything that lies in the great repositories of artistic tradition. Literature dries up if it erects dividing walls.

Skjeldal: If I may mention something that I find slightly irritating: the detailed description of the characters at the beginning of each book: they have a disorienting effect, as if these were characters or actors in a play. Does the reader really need that sort of help in an otherwise crystal-clear text?

Ferrante: The reason for the detailed list of characters is that although the four volumes make up a single story, they came out a year apart. The list was to function as a memory aid to the reader. But now that the entire story is available, from the first page to the last, there's no longer any need and in a likely definitive edition those lists will be eliminated.

Skjeldal: We are often, perhaps far too often, told that the novel is dead. Knausgård, for example, captivated the entire world by pulling the veil off reality. You, however, with your Bildungsroman in four volumes, have demonstrated that the novel is anything but dead. And your work is so convincing that I don't feel I'll need to read essays about Italy ever again. Is the novel the only literary genre that interests you?

Ferrante: I'm very interested in autobiographical writings,

private writings, diaries, chronicles. The Italian tradition is full of them. I'm interested mainly in writings in which educated modes of expression are not imitated, or, even more, those where the educated, in the grip of emotion, set aside elaborate formulas. I'm looking for a truth in the writing that can be studied, learned. I'm not interested, I have to say, in the fate of the novel. What interests me, I think, is a writing of truth. It's an arduous and increasingly rare thing, but also the only one that can demonstrate, as in my view Knausgård does, that the novel isn't dead.

Skjeldal: One thing that really made an impression on me, in the first volume, is that these Neapolitan kids don't get to see the ocean before they are teenagers. It reminded me of something Martin Scorsese said about Little Italy in Manhattan: that as a child he never once left the neighborhood. Was your childhood similarly confined to certain Neapolitan streets?

Ferrante: I was born in a city on the sea, but I discovered it late and it became part of me only as an adult. It's hard to explain, but often between the poor areas and the rich areas there are distances that can't be crossed. For my friends and me to leave the rough streets we had known since birth and go to unknown places, with handsome buildings and the avenue along the sea and a beautiful view over the bay, was a dangerous adventure. Somewhat the way it happens today on a vast scale: if the poor spill over, washing up against the borders of prosperity, the wealthy get frightened and turn violent.

Skjeldal: The childhood narrated in the first and also the second volume is seething with violence. Vesuvius is mentioned at one point. At another point Elena claims that violence is something that Neapolitans have in their blood. In a third place class conflict is offered as an explanation for the high level of violence in Naples. What do you think is the source of this violence, and how might Southern Italy emerge from it?

Ferrante: Violence is an essential trait of the human animal and it's always lying in wait, everywhere, even in your marvelous country. The perpetual problem is how to keep it under control. Naples is one of many places in the world where the factors that lead to violence are all present and all ungoverned: intolerable economic inequalities, poverty that provides manpower to powerful criminal organizations, institutional corruption, the extremely culpable lack of organization of civic life. But it's also a city of spectacular beauty, with great traditions belonging to both élite culture and popular culture. This means that the infected wounds in its body are more visible and more intolerable. What we could be, on this planet, and what, instead, unfortunately, we are, can be seen more clearly in Naples than elsewhere.

Skjeldal: The human heart never changes, according to several poets, at least here in Norway. But I wonder if my children, and perhaps yours, can ever really understand the upbringing that Elena and Lila had? They take freedom for granted, almost like the air they breathe. Or am I wrong?

Ferrante: It's likely that the human heart will never change, but I'm no longer so sure of it. Biotechnologies are always creating new, astonishing, anguishing miracles. Certainly, the circumstances in which our hearts beat are always changing. And it's this which in the end produces stories, always the same and always different. Like us, our children will reckon with the small and large shocks that overturn what today seems to them stable and conclusive. And, like us, they will learn to their cost that nothing, for good and for ill, is given to us forever, and that our fundamental rights have to be won over and over again.

Skjeldal: The Norwegian sculptor Gustav Vigeland has said

that the only thing he finds restful is to start a new project. Do you feel the same way, after the Neapolitan Quartet? Are you on to a new project?

Ferrante: I have many projects—it's always been that way. What I don't know is if one of them will succeed in asserting itself strongly enough to become a book.

NOTE
The interview with Gudmund Skjeldal appeared in *Bergens Tidende & Aftenposten* (Norway), under the title *Den briljante Ferrante*, online on May 1, 2015, and in print on May 2nd.

8.
THIRTEEN LETTERS
Answers to questions from Maurício Meireles

M eireles: *It's impossible not to construct stories around your biography. Whether you're a woman or not, Italian or not, a mother, et cetera. The novel you've constructed and are constructing about your life keeps pace with your novels, with the fictions you create. Many readers try to find signs of the writer, and it's as if there were two levels of reading, the one that comes from the fiction and the one that you suggest regarding the creator of that fiction. She remains a mystery, in spite of some details disclosed in the interviews you've given in recent years. I'd ask you to analyze this idea: the novelized biography and the Elena Ferrante who works on the fiction of herself.*

Ferrante: My experiment is intended to call attention to the original unity of author and text and to the self-sufficiency of the reader, who can get all he needs from that unity. I'm not inventing a biography, I'm not concealing myself, I'm not creating mysteries. I exist intentionally both in my novels and in these answers to your questions. The only space in which the reader should seek and find the author is his writing.

Meireles: In an interview about the reasons for your anonymity you said that "writing in the knowledge that I will not appear produces a space of absolute creative freedom." Do you think your writing would be different if you hadn't decided not to reveal who you are?

Ferrante: I'm sure of it. Sending one's person around, along

with the book, in accord with the rituals of the culture industry, is completely different from shutting oneself up in the text
and not coming out except in the imagination of the reader.

*Meireles: The name Elena Ferrante begins and ends in the
pages of each of your books. Your name came with your writing,
which gave you an identity. Much has been written about you.
I'd like you to describe yourself. Who is Elena Ferrante, writer?
How would you define her?*

Ferrante: Elena Ferrante? Thirteen letters, no more or less.
Her definition is all there.

*Meireles: In your case it's impossible not to make a distinc-
tion between author and work. You've always wanted the author
to remain discreet, almost invisible, while your work slowly
made its way, until it became impossible not to speak of the
author. What has watching this process been like? How have you
experienced it?*

Ferrante: The path of my works is my path. Readers are
content with that, and some have even written asking me not
to reveal other, more private and therefore less interesting
facts. It's the media which, by their nature, are not content
with the works but want faces, persons, fanciful protagonists.
But one can easily do without what the media want.

*Meireles: In the Neapolitan Quartet Lenù pursues an honest
form of writing. What does honesty in literature mean for you?*

Ferrante: To tell the truth as only literary fiction can dare to
tell it.

Meireles: How and when does writing impose itself?

Ferrante: How? Gently. And when? When you no longer
feel you're struggling to find the words.

Meireles: Where does everything begin? An idea, an image, a person, a place?

Ferrante: I don't know. In the beginning there may be flashes, collisions, words that emerge to form vaguely defined images. It's not much, but still it has to be tested. In general I don't go beyond half a page, a note. Sometimes I write a lot, but I'm not satisfied, the words remain crude and ordinary. Only when the writing extends like a fishing line and then begins to pay out rapidly—then I know that the hook was good and I start hoping to get something meaningful.

Meireles: In one interview you describe yourself as a story-teller, something that in a certain sense is contrary to the Italian way of writing.

Ferrante: When I say I'm a storyteller, I go back to a very Italian tradition in which writing is one with the story and is "good" because it has the energy to create a world, not because it strings together metaphors. Our literature is full of possibilities, some to be rediscovered; the would-be writer has only to read the texts and will surely find what he needs. The problem, if anything, is the cult of the beautifully wrought page, a recurring feature that I've long struggled with in myself. Today I throw out the pages that are too written—I prefer the rough draft to the final version.

Meireles: Geography is a defining feature in your stories, as if they could happen only in that place. How much does the space determine your writing?

Ferrante: A story has a time and that time has to have a precise space within which to flow in a linear manner or rise suddenly into the present from the past, bringing with it traditions, ways of using the language, gestures, feelings, the rational and the irrational. Without a space that is drawn precisely, yet with broad margins of indeterminacy offered to the

reader's imagination, the story is in danger of losing concreteness and not gaining purchase.

*Meireles: Naples is an emblematic place, almost one of the
main characters. What is your relation to the city, or how did it
happen that the city became so significant in your writing?*

Ferrante: Naples is my city, and I don't know how to break
away from it even when I hate it. I live elsewhere, but I have to
return often, because only there do I feel that I can redeem
myself and go back to writing with conviction.

*Meireles: Your female characters are almost always women in
extreme situations, who experience moments of passion or abandonment, who are disappointed, marked by a past from which
they can't free themselves. Where do those voices come from?*

Ferrante: From myself, from the experiences that were
important to me. And from what I've known and seen of the
lives of other women that has wounded, angered, depressed,
gladdened me.

*Meireles: It was those female characters who unveiled you, and
who lead us to think that you must be a woman. It's considered
impossible for a male writer to get so close to the female, to express
such apprehension about the condition of many women. Some critics have called you a feminist writer. What is your view of that?*

Ferrante: Feminism was very important to me. I learned to
dig inside myself thanks to the practice of consciousness raising, and it was women's thought that redeveloped my point of
view. It's in the confrontation between women, which can be
harsh, that I seemed to understand that to write you can't be
distant from the facts but, rather, need to reduce the distance
until it's unbearable. Anyway, I don't write to illustrate an ideology—I write to tell without distortions what I know.

Meireles: What are your habits when you write?

Ferrante: The only important thing is urgency. If I don't feel the urgency to write, there is no propitiatory rite that can help me. I prefer to do something else—there's always something better to do.

Meireles: You pay a lot of attention to surroundings. Can you describe for us the place where you usually write?

Ferrante: I don't have a specific place; I settle down anywhere. But in general I prefer small spaces, or a hidden corner in a big space.

Meireles: What authors have influenced and influence you?

Ferrante: Writers often give themselves grand literary forebears whose echo in their works is in fact tenuous. So it's better not to name famous names—they indicate only the degree of our pride. I would prefer instead to present a method: since we are influenced more by what the specialists say about great books than by reading them, it's better to read the texts, whether great or minor, in order to look for the pages that, now and here, help us to get away from the obvious.

Meireles: Do you read what is written about your books?

Ferrante: Yes, everything my publisher sends me. But I do it systematically, with some delay, when my books are sufficiently distant and I can accept that they are, for good or ill, in the words of others.

Meireles: You were a finalist for the Strega Prize, the most important Italian literary prize. What does this mean to you?
Ferrante: Nothing.

Meireles: Can you tell us a little who Elena Ferrante is when she's not writing, the person who has made her books possible?

Ferrante: Someone who always carries a book and a notebook in her purse as she goes about her daily life.

Meireles: You have written: "The point of every story is always this: is this the right story to seize what lies silent in my depths, that living thing which, if captured, spreads through all the pages and gives them life?" Does the story originate in a confrontation with the external world?

Ferrante: Perhaps "right story" is an expression that I was led into by laziness. In fact I never have in mind a story that is complete enough for me to evaluate whether it's right or not. I need to work on it for a long time and understand where it's taking me. The confrontation with the world, as you call it, happens in this phase, and in fact it's hand-to-hand combat with the words. I have to find an opening, to have the impression that daily life will allow me to give the sentences more meaning. If it doesn't happen, I retreat. I have drawers full of failed attempts.

NOTE
The interview with Maurício Meireles appeared on May 28, 2015, in *O Globo* (Brazil), under the title *Elena Ferrante, que esconde sua identidade há mais de 20 anos, tem livro lançado no Brasil.*

9.

NARRATING WHAT ESCAPES THE NARRATIVE
Answers to questions from Yasemin Çongar

C*ongar: The letter you sent to your publisher in 1991 explains the reasons for your decision to be "absent" from the life of your books from the moment of publication. Yet there are many articles about your work these days—my own recent essay on the Neapolitan novels included—and inevitably they deal with this "absence." The discussion of your identity may sometimes overshadow reflections on your books. Do you ever feel uneasy about the speculations concerning your identity? Do you think that your decision to be absent might have backfired, provoking an even stronger "presence," and that the subject of your identity is discussed at the expense of your writing?*

Ferrante: For almost twenty years, in Italy and abroad, my books had an audience and a good critical reception, despite my absence, which people became aware of slowly and without any special insistence from the media. It was the publication, both here and abroad, of the Neapolitan Quartet, and its success, that roused the interest of editorial offices, especially in Italy. And the media, addressing the audience of the tetralogy, put my identity at the center. In brief: one need only glance at the publication history of my books to realize that it's not the absence of the writer that has produced their success but their success that has made the subject of my absence central, and frankly this doesn't seem surprising to me. Rather, what has been surprising is the discovery that those who became aware of the books later, and at times as a result of the media atten-

306 · ELENA FERRANTE

tion, at least here in Italy, encounter them with an initial distrust, if not hostility, as if my absence were an offensive or culpable type of behavior.

Çongar: What do you think is the source of this "initial distrust"? How do you manage not to be affected by it?

Ferrante: This distrust is provoked by media gossip about the absence of the author. The only thing I can do is continue my small battle to put the work at the center. What is important about the writer is, I believe, there in its most complete form, and is one with the text.

Çongar: You have presented yourself in interviews and essays as a woman and a mother. One also senses a strong "female voice" in your novels, so strong I felt that only a woman and a mother could write so authentically about the ordeals of womanhood and motherhood, even though this goes against my own belief that a good novelist can identify with anyone—Madame Bovary, c'est moi! Am I mistaken? If you were a man, could you have written with such frankness about women? Can you name the male writers who you think have depicted female characters with the same authenticity as you have? Are there any such writers?

Ferrante: I agree with you. A good writer—male or female—can imitate the two sexes with equal effectiveness. But to reduce a story to pure mimesis, to the technical skill with which it represents the experience of the other sex, is wrong. The true heart of every story is its literary truth, and that is there or not there, and if it's not there, no technical skill can give it to you. You ask me about male writers who describe women with authenticity. I don't know whom to point you to. There are some who do it with verisimilitude, which is very different, however, from authenticity. So different that when verisimilitude is well orchestrated it risks asserting itself to the point of making the truth of female writing seem inauthentic.

And that is bad. And it's the reason that the pure and simple genuineness of women's writing is always inadequate: that I, a woman, write is not sufficient; my writing has to have adequate literary power.

Çongar: Would you elaborate on the difference between verisimilitude and authenticity in literature? When and why does "pure and simple genuineness" fall short?

Ferrante: To obtain an effect of resemblance to the true is a matter of technical skill. Authenticity in literature, on the other hand, sweeps away tricks and effects. The true sweeps away any false semblance of truth, and that is often disorienting. We prefer the impression of truth rather than the irruption of the authentic into the sphere of the symbolic.

Çongar: In the writings of which women authors do you find the kind of literary power that you mention in your answer?

Ferrante: Jane Austen. Virginia Woolf. Elsa Morante. Clarice Lispector. Alice Munro. I could continue; finally, it's a long list, and, finally, it includes an astonishing variety of female writing from the classics to today. But it's hard to acknowledge. For example, women writers are still compared only with one another. You can be better than other well-known women writers but not better than well-known male writers. Just as it's extremely rare for great male writers to say they've taken as a model great women writers.

Çongar: In your recent interview in The Paris Review *you talk about a conscious effort to resist "domesticating the truth" while writing, and you explain that as "taking overused expressive paths." In the Neapolitan novels your subject is—on one level—the most domestic and common there is. It's the story of a neighborhood, a family, a friendship, growing up, maturing, etc. Your style is also far from being overtly experimental. Given all that, how do you manage to avoid "reducing your story to clichés"; what is it in your writing that opens up an unused path of expression? What do you think makes your voice so new? What is the untamed truth of your novels?*

Ferrante: I don't know what results I've achieved as a writer, but I know what I aim for when I write. I don't care whether the story has been told before: the stories that are presented to readers as new can always be easily reduced to an ancient core. Nor am I interested in revitalizing some overused tale by injecting into it a beautiful style, as if writing were the continual embellishment of a story. Further, I tend not to deconstruct time, or space, when it would be more a proof of skill than a narrative necessity. I describe common experiences, common wounds, and my biggest worry—not the only one— is to find a tone in writing that can remove, layer by layer, the gauze that binds the wound and reach the true story of the wound. The more deeply hidden the wound seems—by stereotypes, by the fictions that the characters themselves have tacked on to protect themselves; in other words, the more resistant it seems to the story—the harder I insist. Beautiful writing doesn't interest me; writing interests me. And I resort to everything tradition offers, bending it to my purposes. What's important is not innovation but the truth that we ourselves, out of prudence, or conformity, conceal within shapely forms, or, why not, within experimental exercises.

Çongar: Naples, of course, is central to these four novels. Whether it is Elena and Lila's old neighborhood or the beach in Ischia or more affluent parts of Naples, there is always a very strong sense of place. However, you achieve this without writing lengthy descriptive passages about the scenery, without romanticizing the images of the city. How do you manage to achieve an almost cinematic vividness of place? What do you think is the reason that I—a reader from Turkey—feel not only that I really see those places where I have never been but also that I belong there, that I come from the same neighborhood. What enlivens the place? What makes it breathe in your pages?

Ferrante: If that happens, it happens thanks to the filters I use. The presence of the city is never given in itself; I don't think it would be possible except by producing labels, pure illustrations. My goal is, rather, to provide impressions perceived or imagined by Lenù and, through her story, by Lila. It's a double layer that makes the neighborhood not the background of the story, not a distant behind-the-scenes, but a world learned, a world perceived, a world imagined.

Çongar: In interviews, you have often paid homage to writing by women, and the struggles of women, for their part in your own development. And several critics, including James Wood, see your novels as écriture féminine *in the sense that Cixous, Irigaray, Kristeva, and others intended it. Do you want in your writing to contribute to the feminist struggle or feminist discourse? Do you think your novels have a feminist function or mission? Is it possible not to give in to political ideology or social conventions when writing about the inequalities and sufferings caused by the class-bound and patriarchal structure of society?*

Ferrante: The passage through feminist culture is an indispensable part of my experience, of my way of being in the world, but telling a story doesn't, for me, mean making it part of a political-cultural battle, even a just one. I fear the linearity of militant causes; in literature they have a terrible effect. I describe points of incoherence. The more intensely a moment of my experience struggles within the set of formulas that guide me even in daily life, the more right and urgent it seems to me to make a story out of it.

Çongar: For you the rhythm, the tone of every sentence are as important as—if not more important than—the story that is being told. Why is that so? Do you ever struggle with finding the right tone, the right language in which to tell your story? When do you know you have it? In what writers have you found the rhythm and the tone to be perfect?

Ferrante: The search for the right tone is for me the synthesis of every possible experiment. I think it's the impetus that drives all literary writing, but in the past century it's become an obsession. What is the magic spell that brings me close to the thing, to its truth? How must I act to decipher the world, make the illegible legible, what strategies should I follow not to find the right distance but to reduce it as much as possible? The "search for tone" is the formula I use to synthesize the long struggle in twentieth-century writing between decipherability and indecipherability of the other. In the Neapolitan Quartet the synthesis is represented by the collision between staying within the boundaries and dissolving the boundaries.

Çongar: Elena and Lila's friendship is extremely nuanced and feels amazingly real to the reader. Moreover, the conflict between the two women is perceived as an internal conflict present in each of them separately. In the differences between the two friends we can recognize the divergent impulses that we carry inside ourselves.

"You're my brilliant friend," the line in the first installment that provides the title, belongs to Lila. It's what she says to Elena to encourage her to continue her education. Yet the "I" in the book is Elena, and it is through her narration that we see Lila as her "brilliant friend."

Why did you place the friendship of these two very different but equally effective characters at the center of the four books? What is the function of the continuous differences between them?

Ferrante: I wanted to tell the story of a lifelong friendship and I wanted to tell the story in all its complexity. But, as I usually do, I also wanted to tell it in a way so that the narrative voice is openly silent about a part of the story, as if she couldn't complete it, or as if its pages were the rough draft of a story that will never achieve a finished version, because it's the other, she who doesn't describe but is described, who has the power to bring it fully to the end. When I write I have two objectives: to tell everything I know and at the same time to let into the story everything that I don't know, that I don't understand. In the Neapolitan Quartet this second objective is obsessively pursued. I think that the power of the story, if it exists, lies in what reaches the page not in spite of the writer but in spite of what is written.

Çongar: Italo Calvino famously asked: "How much of the I who shapes the characters is in fact an I who has been shaped by the characters?" How much of Elena Ferrante is shaped by Lila and Elena?

Ferrante: All. As long as you write you are only what you write; the nest is there, holding you, intertwined with you. The rest, what you are outside the writing, is an invisible gutter.

Çongar: The recurring themes in your novels, the common features of your characters, and the places you write about have convinced many people that your fiction is autobiographical. To what extent is your writing autobiographical?

Ferrante: I use my experience a lot but only if I can put it into a plot without losing its truth.

Çongar: Karl Ove Knausgård, the Norwegian writer whose six-volume My Struggle *has been very successful and has been compared to the Neapolitan Quartet, stated in the second volume that he decided to write an autobiographical novel at a time of crisis, when he felt that "the nucleus of all fiction, whether true or not, is verisimilitude and the distance it maintains from reality is constant." Do you ever feel troubled by the distance between narrative verisimilitude and reality when you are reading a literary work? How do you overcome that distance when you write?*

Ferrante: It happens to me only when the goal of the writer is pure verisimilitude. Verisimilitude is the real that has long since found a reassuring symbolism. The writer, on the other hand, has the job of describing what escapes the story, what escapes the narrative order. We have to get as far away as possible from verisimilitude and instead shrink the distance to the true heart of our experience.

Çongar: Roberto Saviano and others publicly nominated you for the Strega Prize, and now you're among the finalists. Your publisher Sandro Ferri has said that you would be happy if you won, but he adds that this prize is very much part of the establishment that you have chosen not to be part of. How do you think recognition—or the lack of it—by the establishment (prize juries, critics, literary theoreticians, the academy) influences the written word? Can being recognized and/or ignored by the establishment hamper the freedom that is essential to writing?

Ferrante: My books belong to those who read them. I have great respect for all readers, and it changes nothing if they are prize jurors, academics, journalists, radio or television hosts. A published book has its journey: what's essential is that it should make it without me, or rather without the part of me that has remained rigorously outside the pages.

Çongar: In your work, the interior life of your characters, especially the women, is very vivid. What is the relationship between the frantumaglia—*to use your mother's word—and that interiority?*

Ferrante: The *frantumaglia* is the part of us that escapes any reduction to words or other shapes, and that in moments of crisis dissolves the entire order within which it seemed to us we were stably inserted. Every interior state is, ultimately, a magma that clashes with self-control, and it's that magma we have to try to describe, if we want the page to have energy.

Çongar: Do you write in a state of frantumaglia? Or is it a more disciplined, planned, calculated process? Does it differ from book to book?

Ferrante: I have to start from an orderly place; I have to feel safe. But I also know that every book becomes in my eyes worth writing only when the order that has allowed me to begin shatters and the writing flows, and puts me, above all, at risk.

Çongar: What's next? Are you currently working on a new book? What will follow the Neapolitan novels?

Ferrante: I'm writing, but it will take some time before I'm persuaded to publish something else.

NOTE
The interview with the Turkish journalist Yasemin Çongar appeared on July 20, 2015, in the online journal *T24*, in the cultural section, K24, under the title *Yazarın görevi metinden kaçanı anlatabilmektir.*

10.
THE TRUTH OF NAPLES
Answers to questions from Árni Matthíasson

M*atthíasson: What led you to write? Was it a desire to emulate any favorite writer or writers, or did you feel a need to express yourself?*

Ferrante: I write out of a desire to tell a story. Writing, naturally, is nourished by the pleasure of reading and the wish to understand how that pleasure is achieved. Everything I've learned I've learned by reading and rereading books. I don't know how many times I've read *Les Misérables* without knowing absolutely anything about Victor Hugo.

Matthíasson: Your first novel, Troubling Love, *was published in 1992. Did you see that as a start of your writing career or were you not looking any further than getting that one story published?*

Ferrante: I never thought of any sort of career as a writer. I wrote, yes, but I had a different job. I didn't feel the publication of that first book as a beginning. I continued to write, but I didn't publish a new story until ten years later. The truth is that I'm never sure of having written something that's worth publishing.

Matthíasson: For a journalist, writing about a book in the absence of the author, without a photograph or a biography, can be problematic. I'm not complaining, but I think that when people talk about your books your absence too often becomes a prominent part of the discourse and can obscure the book itself. You've said that you prefer that the books speak for themselves: do you think that people put too much emphasis on your anonymity?

Ferrante: It's not my absence that generates interest in my books but the interest in my books that generates media interest in my absence. I'm afraid, in other words, that my decisions are more a problem for journalists—that said, it is their job—than for the public. In my view, what interests readers is the book and the energy it releases. If there's no photo on the cover, so what. If the author doesn't appear on television, so what. In fact, readers find my true image as an author in the writing. If the book doesn't work, why should the reader be concerned with the author? And if it does work, doesn't the author, too, emerge from it, like the genie from Aladdin's lamp? The book is everything and comes before everything, if we really love reading. Outside of my books what am I? A woman not unlike many others. Forget about authors, then; love—if it's worthwhile—what they write. This is the meaning of my little polemic.

Matthíasson: In a recent interview you said that the Naples described in your novels is a place of the imagination. Do you mean that the city of your youth has changed over time or that it is continually modified by a sort of reworking of the past?

Ferrante: The Naples I describe is part of me, I know it thoroughly. I know the names of the streets, the colors of the buildings, the shops, the dialectal voices. But whatever piece of reality enters a story has to reckon with literary truth, which is a truth different from that of Google maps.

Matthíasson: There has been a lot of discussion in the past few years about the situation of women in the arts: how they are often marginalized, and have to raise their voices to be heard. Take, for example, Björk, who said recently: "Everything that a guy says once, you have to say five times." It seems to me that this is even more true of the literary world, where it's easier to get published as a male writer and books by male writers are more likely to be reviewed and win awards. Yet women read far more than men. Did this influence you in any way when you started writing?

Further: researchers claim that men read books by men, whereas for women it doesn't matter if the work was written by a man or a woman. The idea of a female protagonist seems especially troubling for male readers, and your Neapolitan Quartet has women at the center. Was the decision to have women as the focus a choice, or was it implicit in the original idea?

Ferrante: What to say? I wanted to tell the story of a friendship between women; and so it was inevitable that two women should be at the center of the story. As for the fact that the audience is now substantially female, yes, it's very true, but that hasn't improved the situation of women writers. Although there has been a robust, distinguished female literary tradition for a long time, books written by women have a hard time getting attention. Or, rather: they are judged by the critics according to their merits only within the category of books by women and for women, that is, as texts that can't be compared with the powerful age-old male tradition. For most people—sometimes for women, too—great literature is generally felt to be literature made by men. Apart from a few fine souls, men don't read books by women, as if such reading would weaken their virile power. But it's a subject that concerns women's creations in every field. Educated, broad-minded men treat female thought with polite irony, as a by-product, good only as a pastime for women.

Matthíasson: The Neapolitan cycle is developed in four novels. Did you have in mind all four books or did the story develop gradually?

Ferrante: I thought for a long time that I could contain the story in a single volume. In general, when I start telling a story, I never know how many pages I'll need. I work and don't worry that the first draft comes out like a waterfall—in fact I'm glad. It means that the story is developing easily, and that's what counts. Afterward—I think—I'll throw away a good half of what I write, and never mind. It's something I'm used to, and I do it willingly when the story has assumed the right form and it's just a matter of working with the scalpel and the hatchet. But in the case of *My Brilliant Friend* cutting out the superfluous and the unsuccessful was of little use. At a certain point, and with regret, I had to give up the idea of the single volume and accept the idea that the story, in spite of its unity, had to be published in four heavy tomes.

Matthíasson: You have been called the most important Italian writer of your generation. Does that have any effect on your writing?

Ferrante: In general, in the game that the cultural pages play, a flattering judgment is flanked by a devastating criticism and vice versa. For more than twenty years I've let go of the anxiety of success and the anguish of lack of success. I write as I like and if I want to. And I publish only when it seems to me that the book can find its way on its own. Otherwise I leave it in the drawer.

Matthíasson: What other Italian writers do you read or would you recommend?

Ferrante: I'll purposely name only some women, who are very different from one another in their interests, thematic and expressive choices, cultural background: Simona Vinci, Michela Murgia, Silvia Avallone, Valeria Parrella, Viola Di Grado. I could continue, but making lists isn't that useful. You have to read the books.

NOTE
The interview with Árni Matthíasson: appeared on August 16, 2015, in the daily *Morgunblaðið* (Iceland) under the title *Skrifað af ástríðu*.

11.
THE WATCH
Answers to questions from the art magazine Frieze

Frieze: What images keep you company in the space where you work?

Ferrante: A reproduction of a Henri Matisse painting (an open window, a woman reading at a table with a child); a print by the illustrator Mara Cerri; a small, round pebble that perfectly recalls an owl; an early-nineteenth-century painted fan folded up in an antique case; a faded red metal bottle cap that I picked up off the street when I was twelve years old and that I have managed to hold on to for my whole life.

Frieze: What was the first piece of art that really mattered to you?

Ferrante: Certainly, in early adolescence, I was overwhelmed by Caravaggio's *The Seven Acts of Mercy*: my veneration for this artist started then and continues to this day. But the first piece of art that really mattered to me—I say this only half in jest—was the shape of a watch a childhood friend would make on my wrist by biting it. It was a game. Her teeth left a circle on my skin that I would look at, pretending to tell the time, until the circle faded away. Except I didn't pretend: I really thought it was a beautiful watch.

Frieze: If you could live with only one piece of art, what would it be?

Ferrante: I don't know. It's difficult to give a single answer that would be true. Maybe I'd choose the folder where I keep all the versions of the Annunciation I've been able to find. That's it: a single subject, rather than a single work of art. Ever since I was a young woman I've been interested in the way in which the moment Mary is forced to put aside the book she's reading has been imagined. When she opens it again, it will be her son who tells her how to read.

Frieze: What is your favorite title of an art work?
Ferrante: *Untitled.* I'd like to use it as a book title; I don't know if it's been done already. I also love *The Artist Is Present.* I admire the reversal that Marina Abramović imposed on a formula that I once detested. The artist is present, but as body/work.

Frieze: What subjects do you wish you knew?
Ferrante: Math, physics, astronomy—to understand what stage we're at in the universe and if we'll be able to clarify our ideas before the human race is extinguished.

Frieze: What would you like to change?
Ferrante: The amount of time I've dedicated to writing. I could have done with more.

Frieze: What would you like to keep the same?
Ferrante: The desire to tell stories.

Frieze: What could you imagine doing if you didn't do what you do?
Ferrante: Being a dressmaker.

Frieze: What music are you listening to?
Ferrante: I know an inordinate number of songs, but I don't have a proper musical education. At times, books have prompted me to listen to great music: for example, after read-

ing Tolstoy's *The Kreutzer Sonata*, I went on a Beethoven binge. Similarly, having recently read the letters that Arnold Schoenberg and Thomas Mann exchanged about *Doctor Faustus*, I have gone on to listen maniacally to anything by Schoenberg I can find. But it's an effort that requires willpower; musically I remain a novice.

Frieze: What are you reading?
Ferrante: *Stasis: Civil War as a Political Paradigm* by the Italian philosopher Giorgio Agamben. The book is based on two seminars led by Agamben at Princeton University in 2001. In the second, he works on the very famous etching on the frontispiece of Thomas Hobbes's *Leviathan*. I've always been fascinated by those who use images to make history, philosophy, literature. I've just finished reading *Triptych: Three Studies After Francis Bacon*, by Jonathan Littell.

Frieze: What do you like the look of?
Ferrante: I belong to the ranks of those who feel attracted to anything that is enclosed within a frame, partly because it helps me to imagine what has remained outside it.

NOTE
The interview with the magazine *Frieze* (U.K.), translated by Daniela Petracco, appeared in the August 16, 2015, issue under the title "Questionnaire: Elena Ferrante."

12.
THE GARDEN AND THE WORLD
Answers to questions from Ruth Joos

J oos: *What is the mystery of your opening lines? The first time I read the start of one of your books, it took my breath away. Is it a special element in your writing, something you pay particular attention to? Or do those first sentences write themselves?*

Ferrante: I generally need a beginning that gives me the impression of being on the right path. It rarely comes right away, but it happens. Mostly I work and rework for a long time. Sometimes, after several attempts, I may seem to have found the beginning that's useful to me, and I go on. But then I realize that it has led me astray, that I'm struggling. What decides if a beginning is good or not is the energy with which the story starts to flow.

Joos: The Irish writer Anne Enright once told me that the first page is of primary importance. "Read all the classics," she said, "it's all there, right from the start." Do you agree with her? In what sense (or not)? Can the importance of that first sentence be paralyzing for you?

Ferrante: I don't know if everything is in the beginning. Of course, I look for first words as a magic formula that can open the only true door to the story. Often first sentences are found at the end of a long journey of writing. Then I have to have the strength to throw away everything except those few words, and start again from there. Otherwise readers will have the impression that the truth and the power of the story are coming in too late.

Joos: Do you share our impression that your first novels were necessary in order for you to develop the broader perspective, the more detailed narrative of the Neapolitan Quartet? As if The Days of Abandonment *and* The Lost Daughter *had to be written before you could then write something with a slower pace? Something less immediate? More epic?*

Ferrante: Over the years I've written much more than I've published, and so it's hard to answer. I might think of everything I have in my drawer as part of a chain that leads necessarily to the four volumes of the Neapolitan Quartet, link after link. In reality the tetralogy was a surprise for me, too: I didn't think I was capable of completing such a long and wide-ranging story. That said, I don't think I've gone far from the tonality and the intentions of the earlier novels.

Joos: In the Neapolitan novels, can Elena and Lila be interpreted as a single character? As two sides of a single person? Does every writer consist of two halves?

Ferrante: If we were made only of two halves, individual life would be simple, but the "I" is a crowd, with a large quantity of heterogeneous fragments tossing about inside. And the female "I", in particular, with its long history of oppression and repression, tends to shatter as it's tossed around, and to reappear and shatter again, always in an unpredictable way. Stories feed on the fragments, which are concealed under an appearance of unity and constitute a sort of chaos to depart from, an obscurity to illuminate. Stories, characters come from there. Reading Dostoyevsky when I was young, I thought that all the characters, the pure and the abominable, were actually his secret voices, hidden, cunningly wrought fragments. Everything was poured, unfiltered, and with extreme audacity, into his works.

Joos: What do you think of the relationship between the particular and the universal? Are you surprised by the fact that the setting of your stories (Naples, the various social classes, the landscape, the language) doesn't get in the way of understanding, even far from Italy?

Ferrante: It's an old subject, and difficult to sort out. I think it has to do not with the technical skill of the writer but with the power of the authentic. If the representation goes beyond a skillful verisimilitude, carrying with it the pure and simple truth, maybe it can transform its own private little plot of land into a garden open to all. But nothing guarantees this outcome. The task of the writer is to give shape, without self-censorship, to the reality that he or she knows well, as if he or she were the only possible witness.

Joos: As a reader I've rarely had an experience as intimate as reading The Lost Daughter*: it's almost embarrassing to read—it touches something almost unspeakable. It's as if the beating heart of your work could be found precisely in that novel. What do you think?*

Ferrante: I'm very fond of *The Lost Daughter*. It cost me a lot to write. A story has to push beyond your very capacity to write it, you have to fear at every line that you won't make it. The books I've published all originated like that, but *The Lost Daughter* left me feeling the way you do when you swim until you're exhausted and then realize you've gone too far from the shore.

Joos: Have you ever been afraid of being unable to reach that degree of intensity again?

Ferrante: Yes, but I'm not distressed about it. Writing, trying and trying again, has always been part of my private life, and that's fine. No one obliges me to publish. If a book doesn't come out the way I want, I don't publish it. And if I never again write a book that comes out the way I want, I won't publish anymore.

Joos: It will soon be twenty-five years since your début: what do you feel about this? And about the fact of having been translated into so many languages?

Ferrante: I'm happy for my books. They're still in good health and they travel all over the world. They've been lucky.

Joos: When did you realize you were a writer? When did you begin to feel you were a writer?

Ferrante: I realized early, as a child, that I liked to tell stories. But I say to you in all frankness that, if by writer you mean someone who has a role that defines her socially and in the working world, I don't feel and have never felt myself a writer. I wrote and I write whenever I can, but for a long time I've done other work.

Joos: Do you think that writing about female characters from a female perspective requires courage? And, if not, why, in your view, has it been done so rarely and with so little care?

Ferrante: I don't know if it takes courage. Certainly you have to get beyond the female gender, beyond the image, that is, that men have sewed onto us and that women attribute to themselves as if it were their true nature. You have to project beyond the great male literary tradition, which is arduous but easier than it was a century ago: we have an outstanding female tradition, which by now has some real high points. But above all we have to look beyond the new image of woman that has been constructed in the daily struggle with the patriarchy; this image is essential on the social, cultural, political plane but dangerous for literature. The writer has to tell what she truly knows or thinks she knows, even if it contradicts the ideological structures that she subscribes to.

Joos: Are you aware that you often confront your readers with "an inconvenient truth"?

Ferrante: Inconvenient truths are the salt of literature. They don't guarantee that the results will be good, but it's where words derive their power and flavor.

Joos: Do you know that some readers feel an aversion for what you write about women, about mothers and daughters, and about their relationships, while others have the sensation that you know them profoundly?

Ferrante: A book should push the reader to confront himself and the world. Then it can end up on a shelf or in the trash.

Joos: Are you ever frightened by the fact that your readers feel so close to your work, as if you were saying for them what can't be said?

Ferrante: If it were true, I would feel happy about it and also distressed. To say what is unsayable is the task of literature and, at the same time, a grave responsibility. But it happens to very few and I don't think it's true in my case. I try only to be a truthful witness of what I've seen in myself and others.

Joos: Do you have an idea of what we lose by reading your novels in a language different from the original? Does it distress you to "abandon them" to another language?

Ferrante: At first I thought I could maintain control over the translations. But it's impossible. The books leave and one has to hope only that the other languages are, within the limits of possibility, sensitive and generous hosts.

Joos: What is the function of dialect in your novels? And of the different registers?

Ferrante: Dialect for me is the repository of primary experiences. Italian extracts them and arranges them on the page in a search for adequate expressive registers. But my characters always have the impression that Neapolitan is hostile and holds secrets that will never be able to enter completely into Italian.

Joos: What's special about the Neapolitan dialect? What can be said in that dialect that can't be said in Italian?

Ferrante: My conquest of Italian was arduous; I felt Neapolitan as a claw that was holding me down. Over time things changed, but in my mind they remain two enemy languages, and Neapolitan can say of me, of my women friends, of our doings, many things that I'm ashamed of, or that I love, but anyway more than can be transferred into Italian.

Joos: A recurring theme in your novels is that of borders and passing beyond them: inside and outside the city, inside and outside the I, inside and outside motherhood, marriage, borders that vanish . . .

Ferrante: Borders make us feel stable. At the first hint of conflict, at the least threat, we close them. The border serves to gather us into a unit, to diminish the hidden centrifugal thrusts that undermine our identity. But it's purely an appearance. A story begins when, one after another, our borders collapse.

Joos: What's the value of crossing borders?

Ferrante: The basic value that limits have. To calm us within a perimeter, so that we can look critically inside and outside. Until we try to stick our nose out to cross it.

Joos: Are women more conscious of that crossing?

Ferrante: The history of women in the past hundred years is based on the very dangerous "crossing of the boundary" imposed by patriarchal cultures. The results have been extraordinary in all fields. But the force with which they want to carry us back inside the old borders is no less extraordinary. It is manifested as pure crude, bloody violence. But also as the good-natured irony of educated men who belittle or demean our achievements.

Joos: A step beyond the borders can involve disappearance, another major theme in your work. What is the meaning, the value of disappearance? (It's one of the most interesting themes in the work of Siri Hustvedt, just to give an example: she, too, has mothers who disappear.)

Ferrante: My first book, *Troubling Love*, was the story of a disappearance. The disappearance of women should be interpreted not only as giving up the fight against the violence of the world but also as clear rejection. There is an expression in Italian whose double meaning is untranslatable: "*Io non ci sto.*" Literally it means: I'm not here, in this place, before what you're suggesting. In common usage, it means, instead: I don't agree, I don't want to. Rejection means shunning the games of those who crush the weak.

Joos: Do you find it natural that we as readers have the feeling that we know you? Do you feel comfortable in that situation?

Ferrante: Authors, as authors, live in their books. It's where they appear most truthfully. And good readers have always known it.

NOTE
The interview with Ruth Joos appeared in the daily *De Standaard* (Belgium) on August 21, 2015, under the title *Ongemakkelijke waarheden zijn het zout van de literatuur.*

13.

THE MAGMA BENEATH THE CONVENTIONS
Answers to questions from Elissa Schappell

S *chappell: You grew up in Naples. It's been the setting for a number of your books—what is it about the city that inspires you?*

Ferrante: Naples is a space containing all my primary, childhood, adolescent, and early adult experiences. Many of my stories about people I know and have loved come to me both from that city and in its language. I write what I know, but I nurse this material in a disorderly way—I can only extract the story, invent it, if it appears blurred. For that reason, almost all of my books, even if they unfold today or are set in different cities, have Neapolitan roots.

Schappell: Can we assume that the friendship between Lena and Lila is inspired by an actual friendship?

Ferrante: Let's say that it comes from what I know of a long, complicated, difficult friendship that began at the end of early childhood.

Schappell: The fact that Lena is telling the story, and that the narrative subverts stereotypical notions of female friendship— friendship is forever, steady and uncomplicated—feels radical. What made you want to mine this material in this way?

Ferrante: Lena is a complex character, obscure to herself. She takes on the task of keeping Lila in the net of the story even against her friend's will. These actions seem to be motivated by love, but are they really? It has always fascinated me how a story comes to us through the filter of a protagonist whose consciousness is limited, inadequate, shaped by the facts that she herself is recounting, though she doesn't feel that way at all. My books are like that: the narrator must continually deal with situations, people, and events she doesn't control, and which do not allow themselves to be told. I like stories in which the effort to reduce experience to story progressively undermines the confidence of she who is writing, her conviction that the means of expression at her disposal are adequate, and those very conventions that at the start made her feel safe.

Schappell: Friendship between women can be particularly fraught. Unlike men, women tell each other everything. Intimacy is our currency, and, as intimates, we are uniquely skilled in eviscerating each other.

Ferrante: Friendship is a crucible of positive and negative feelings that are in a permanent state of ebullition. There's an expression: With friends God is watching me, with enemies I watch myself. In the end, an enemy is the fruit of an oversimplification of human complexity: the hostile relationship is always clear, I know that I have to protect myself, I have to attack. On the other hand, God only knows what goes on in the mind of a friend. Absolute trust and strong affections harbor rancor, trickery, and betrayal. Perhaps that's why, over time, male friendship has developed a rigorous code of conduct. The pious respect for its internal laws and the dire consequences that come from violating them have a long tradition in fiction. Our friendships, on the other hand, are a terra incognita, unknown even to ourselves, a land without fixed rules. Anything and everything can happen to you, nothing is certain. Its exploration in fiction advances arduously, it is a gamble, a strenuous undertaking. And at every step there is the risk, above all, that a story's honesty will be clouded by good intentions, hypocritical calculations, or ideologies that exalt sisterhood in ways that are often nauseating.

Schappell: Do you ever make a conscious decision to write against conventions or expectations?

Ferrante: I pay attention to every system of conventions and expectations, especially literary conventions and the expectations they generate in readers. But that law-abiding side of me, sooner or later, has to face my disobedient side. And, in the end, the latter always wins.

Schappell: What fiction or nonfiction has most influenced you as a writer?

Ferrante: The manifesto of Donna Haraway, which I am guilty of having read quite late, and an old book by Adriana Cavarero (*Relative Narratives; Storytelling and Selfhood*). The novel that is fundamental for me is Elsa Morante's *House of Liars*.

Schappell: One of the most striking aspects of the novels is the uncanny way you are able to capture the complexity of Lena and Lila's relationship without lapsing into cliché or sentimentality. The description of the relationship between Lila and Lena is ruthlessly honest, maybe even brutal, and yet for a woman reader—or at least for me—it's not only absolutely right but liberating.

Ferrante: In general, we store away our experiences and make use of timeworn phrases—nice, ready-made, reassuring stylizations that give us a sense of colloquial normality. But in this way, either knowingly or unknowingly, we reject everything that, to be said fully, would require effort and a torturous search for words. Honest writing forces itself to find words for those parts of our experience that are hidden and silent. On one hand, a good story, or, rather, the kind of story I like best, narrates an experience—for example, friendship—following specific conventions that render it recognizable and riveting; on the other hand, it sporadically reveals the magma running beneath the pillars of convention. The fate of a story that tends toward truth by pushing stylizations to their limit depends on the extent to which the reader really wants to face up to herself.

Schappell: The unsparing, some might say brutally honest way you write about women's lives, your depictions of violence and female rage, as well as the intensity of feeling and the eroticism that can exist in female friendships, especially those between young women, is astonishingly spot on. Liberating. Given that we know how fraught and full of drama female friendships are, why do you think we don't read more books that depict these intense relationships more honestly?

Ferrante: Often that which we are unable to tell ourselves coincides with that which we do not want to tell, and if a book offers us a portrait of those things, we feel annoyed, or resentful, because they are things we all know, but reading about them disturbs us. However, the opposite also happens. We are thrilled when fragments of reality become utterable.

Schappell: There is a "personal is political" brand of feminism running throughout your novels. Do you yourself consider yourself a feminist? How would you describe the difference between American- and Italian-style feminism?

Ferrante: I owe much to that famous slogan. From it I learned that even the most intimate individual concerns, those most extraneous to the public sphere, are influenced by politics; that is to say, by that complicated, pervasive, irreducible thing that is power and its uses. It's only a few words, but with their fortunate ability to synthesize they should never be forgotten. They convey what we are made of, the risk of subservience we are exposed to, the kind of deliberately disobedient gaze we must turn on the world and on ourselves. But "the personal is political" is also an important suggestion for literature. It should be an essential concept for anyone who wants to write.

As for the definition of "feminist," I don't know. I have loved and I love feminism because in America, in Italy, and in many other parts of the world it managed to provoke complex thinking. I grew up with the idea that if I didn't let myself be absorbed as much as possible into the world of eminently capable men, if I did not learn from their cultural excellence, if I did not pass brilliantly all the exams that world required of me, it would have been tantamount to not existing at all. Then I read books that exalted the female difference and my thinking was turned upside down. I realized that I had to do exactly the opposite: I had to start with myself and with my relationships with other women—this is another essential formula—if I really wanted to give myself a shape. Today I read everything that emerges out of so-called post-feminist thought. It helps me look critically at the world, at us, our bodies, our subjectivity. But it also fires my imagination, it pushes me to reflect on the use of literature. I'll name some women to whom I owe a great deal: Firestone, Lonzi, Irigaray, Muraro, Cavarero, Gagliasso, Haraway, Butler, Braidotti.

In short, I am a passionate reader of feminist thought. Yet I do not consider myself a militant; I believe I am incapable of militancy. Our heads are crowded with a very heterogeneous mix of material, fragments of time periods, conflicting intentions that cohabit, endlessly clashing with one another. As a writer I would rather confront that overabundance, even if it is risky and confused, than feel that I'm staying safely within a scheme that, precisely because it is a scheme, always ends up leaving out a lot of real stuff because it is disturbing. I look around. I compare who I was, what I have become, what my friends have become, the clarity and the confusion, the failures, the leaps forward. Girls like my daughters appear convinced that the freedom they've inherited is part of the natural state of affairs and not the temporary outcome of a long battle that is still being waged, and in which everything could suddenly be lost. As far as the male world is concerned, I have erudite, contemplative acquaintances who tend either to ignore or to recast with polite mockery the literary, philosophical, and all other categories of work produced by women. That said, there are also very fierce young women, men who try to be informed, to understand, to sort through the countless contradictions. In short, cultural struggles are long, full of contradictions, and while they are happening it is difficult to say what is useful and what isn't. I prefer to think of myself as being inside a tangled knot; tangled knots fascinate me. It's necessary to recount the tangle of existence, as it concerns both individual lives and the life of generations. Seeking to unravel things is useful, but literature is made out of tangles.

Schappell: I've noticed that the critics who seem most obsessed by the question of your gender are men. They seem to find it impossible to fathom that a woman could write books that are so serious—threaded with history and politics, and evenhanded in their depictions of sex and violence. That the ability to depict the domestic world as a war zone and the willingness to unflinchingly show women in an unflattering light are evidence that you're a man. Some suggest that not only are you a man but, given your output, you might be a team of men. A committee. (Imagine the books of the Bible...)

Ferrante: Have you heard anyone say recently about any book written by a man, It's really a woman who wrote it, or maybe a group of women? Owing to its exorbitant might, the male gender can mimic the female gender, incorporating it in the process. The female gender, on the other hand, cannot mimic anything, for it is betrayed immediately by its "weakness"; what it produces could not possibly fake male potency.

The truth is that even the publishing industry and the media are convinced of this commonplace; both tend to shut away women who write in a literary gynaeceum. There are good women writers, not so good ones, and some great ones, but they all exist within the area reserved for the female sex, and must address only certain themes and in certain tones that the male tradition considers suitable for the female gender. It is fairly common, for example, to explain the literary work of women writers in terms of some variety of dependence on literature written by men. However, it is rare to see commentary that traces the influence of a female writer on the work of a male writer. The critics don't do it, the writers themselves don't do it. Thus, when a woman's writing does not respect those areas of competence, those thematic sectors and the tones that the experts have assigned to the categories of books to which women have been confined, the commentators come up with the idea of male bloodlines. And if there's no author photo of a woman then the game is up: it's clear, in that case, that we are dealing with a man or an entire team of virile male enthusiasts of the art of writing. What if, instead, we're dealing with a new tradition of women writers who are becoming more competent, more effective, are growing tired of the literary gynaeceum and are on furlough from gender stereotypes. We know how to think, we know how to tell stories, we know how to write them as well as, if not better than, men.

Schappell: Because girls grow up reading books by men, we are used to the sound of male voices in our heads, and have no trouble imagining the lives of the cowboys, sea captains, and pirates of he-manly literature, whereas men balk at entering the mind of a woman, especially an angry woman.

Ferrante: Yes, I hold that male colonization of our imaginations—a calamity as long as we were unable to give shape to our difference—is, today, a strength. We know everything about the male symbol system; they, for the most part, know nothing about ours, above all about how it has been restructured by the blows the world has dealt us. What's more, they are not even curious, indeed they recognize us only from within their system.

Schappell: As a female writer I take offense at the idea that the only war stories that matter are those written by men crouching in foxholes.

Ferrante: Every day women are exposed to all kinds of abuse. Yet there is still a widespread conviction that women's lives, full of conflict and violence in the domestic sphere and in all of life's most common contexts, cannot be expressed other than via the modules that the male world defines as feminine. If you step out of this thousand-year-old invention of theirs, you are no longer female.

Schappell: When you set out to write the Neapolitan novels, did you know the entire arc?

Ferrante: No. I knew only the basic stages of the story and even those as if through a fog. But that's been true for all of my books.

Schappell: Do you normally have a very clear picture of what shape the work will take?

Ferrante: I never know exactly what shape a story will take. What is clear to me, always, is that the writing must never lose sight of truth as its ultimate goal. Page after page, the drive to capture what is true, and not what resembles the truth, shapes the work. If, even for a few passages, the tone becomes false—that is, too studied, too limpid, too regimented, too well-phrased—I am obliged to stop and to figure out where I started to go wrong. If I can't, I throw everything away.

Schappell: You have been praised for your spare, muscular prose. There are no pyrotechnics, the language never draws attention to itself, and the effect is powerful. Do you start in this more spare and dialed-back register, or is the work in earlier drafts messier and more emotional?

Ferrante: I tell stories about middle-class women who are cultivated and capable of governing themselves. They have the tools to reflect on themselves. The slow, detached language I use is theirs. Then something breaks and these women's boundaries dissolve, and the language with which they are attempting to say something about themselves also is loosed, unbounded. From that moment, the problem—a problem that is, above all, mine, as I write—becomes how to rediscover, step by step, the measured language they started with and, with it, the kind of self-governing ability that stops the characters from falling into depression, into self-degeneration, or into danger-ous feelings of revenge, aimed at themselves or at others.

Schappell: Was there one novel in the series that was more difficult to write? Is there one that you feel most connected to or proud of?

Ferrante: The entire story, in each of its four installments, was, for me, a satisfying labor. Perhaps because of the themes it addresses, the most difficult to write was the third. And, again owing to its thematic considerations, the second was the easiest. But the first and the fourth are the ones to which I ded-icated myself without reserve, every day mixing different gen-res, pleasure and pain, obscurity and clarity. I love them very much for this reason.

Schappell: Did you know from the beginning that there would be four books? If not, when did it become clear to you?

Ferrante: Six or seven years ago when I started working on these books I was convinced that a single, albeit long, volume would be enough. But when I got to the story of Lila's wedding, I realized that I was going to need an exorbitant number of pages. I never thought of them as separate novels. While there are four volumes, for me the Neapolitan novels are one compact story, one very long novel.

Schappell: What do you do to relax?
Ferrante: I devote myself to boring domestic chores.

Schappell: Do you ever find yourself working against a certain kind of writing or writers?
Ferrante: I am curious about work that is very different from mine. I devote special attention to books that I could never write myself. If something feels foreign to me, but not annoyingly so, I try to study it to understand how it was made and what I can learn from it. It has never occurred to me to argue with other writers.

Schappell: Are you making a conscious choice when you sit down to write to create characters who won't play by the rules of polite society, or is it as Grace Paley puts it, "It's not that you set out to oppose authority. In the act of writing, you simply do."
Ferrante: I deliberate a lot over what I would like to do with writing. I have always read a great deal in order to borrow what I need from tradition. But then when I start working I just write, without worrying if something seems too trivial or refined, comfortable or uncomfortable, obedient or rebellious. The problem is one and only one: to tell a story in the most effective way.

Schappell: Where do you actually physically work?
Ferrante: Wherever I can. The important thing is that it is a little corner somewhere. That is to say, a very small space.

Schappell: The subject of abandonment appears in a lot of your work. What is it about abandonment that strikes such a chord with you?

Ferrante: Abandonment is an invisible wound that does not heal easily. As a storyteller, I am attracted to it because it synthesizes the general precariousness of all we consider constant, the deconstruction of everything that seemed "normal." Abandonment corrodes those certainties within which we believed we lived safely. Not only have we been abandoned but we may not hold up when faced with the loss; we abandon ourselves, we lose the consistency that we have gained through the sweet habit of entrusting ourselves to others. So, to get through it, you must find a new equilibrium while at the same time acknowledging a new fact—namely, that everything you have can be taken from you, and with it your will to live.

Schappell: Have you ever abandoned a book? Why?

Ferrante: I have abandoned many books, and some when they were already completed. The reason is always the same: I put aside everything that, even if the pages are well manicured and beautiful, strikes me as lacking truth.

Schappell: The theme of erasure—erasing one's self, being erased by the culture—also reappears in the novels. What is it about disappearing, or being disappeared, that you find so compelling?

Ferrante: I have always been fascinated by those people who, faced with a world so full of horrors it can seem intolerable, claim that the human condition is unchangeable, that nature is a monstrous machine, that humanity has produced an endless cycle of inhumanity even when animated by good intentions, and then back away. The problem is not what other people do to you. The problem is to stand impotent before the horror that afflicts the majority of people, the most precarious of our fellow human beings. Every day we find ourselves faced with the intolerable, and no promise of utopia—whether it be political, religious, or scientific—is capable of calming us. Each generation is obliged to verify this horror anew for itself, and to discover that it is impotent. So either you take a step forward or you take one back. I'm not talking about suicide. I'm talking about refusing to engage, about removing oneself from the picture. The sentence "No, I will not," when it comes from the depths of the intolerable, seems to me to be weighty, full of meaning, with everything to recount.

Schappell: It's interesting that you yourself have—by choosing to keep details of your identity secret—in a sense erased yourself. Could you write as honestly if you were a public figure? Or does it matter not at all?

Ferrante: No, if you write and publish you are hardly erasing yourself. Indeed, I have my private life and as far as my public life goes I am fully represented by my books. My choice was something different. I simply decided once and for all, more than twenty years ago, to liberate myself from the anxiety of notoriety and the urge to be a part of that circle of successful people, those who believe they have won who-knows-what. This was an important step for me. Today I feel, thanks to this decision, that I have gained a space of my own, a space that is free, where I feel active and present. To relinquish it would be very painful.

Schappell: Still, I am curious why an author—especially one so successful and critically acclaimed as you are—would choose to remain anonymous?

Ferrante: I have not chosen anonymity. My books are signed. Rather, I have withdrawn from the rituals that writers are more or less obliged to perform in order to sustain their books by lending them their author's expendable image. And it's worked out fine so far. My books increasingly demonstrate their independence, so I see no reason to change my position. It would be deplorably inconsistent.

Schappell: The writer never wants the reader to feel his or her presence, never wants to call attention to himself, and yet a careful reader should be able to detect here and there a few of the creator's fingerprints. What direction might you offer the reader desperate to find you in the work (beyond telling him to piss off)?

Ferrante: As far as I know, my readers do not despair at all. I receive letters of support for my little battle in favor of the centrality of the work. Evidently, for those who love literature, the books are enough.

NOTE

The interview with Elissa Schappell, translated by Michael Reynolds, came out on the Web site of *Vanity Fair* (U.S.A.) in two parts. The first part appeared on August 27, 2015, under the title "The Mysterious, Anonymous Author Elena Ferrante on the Conclusion of Her Neapolitan Novels"; the second on August 28th, under the title "Elena Ferrante Explains Why, for the Last Time, You Don't Need to Know Her Name."

14

SYSTEMATIC DISCONTENT
Answers to questions from Andrea Aguilar

Aguilar: How long did it take you to write the four Neapolitan novels? Has the increasing success of the books affected you? Do you read reviews or what is published about you?

Ferrante: In general I read every critical piece carefully, but only when it seems to me that the book is sufficiently distant. In this last case it was impossible. *My Brilliant Friend* for me is a single long, very dense novel. But its publication in four volumes—one volume a year—meant that, while I was finishing the story, I was getting the reviews of the first volume and letters from readers. It was like refining and completing a book while it's already generating a range of opinions and expectations among readers. It's an experience I still have to reflect on.

Aguilar: How do you relate to Lena's struggles as a writer? After she publishes her first book, it takes her a while to get started again; she seems to lose herself after the publication of each of her books. A portrait emerges of the insecurities she has to overcome, of how she feels lost when she's looking for a subject for a new book. Do you share this feeling? How did you start writing the tetralogy?

Ferrante: I've always written a lot. I conceive of writing as a craft that needs constant practice. Practicing it to acquire competence has never made me anxious. Publishing, however, still makes me anxious. And in fact my decision to publish is accompanied by a lot of hesitation and only if the story seems to me very truthful. I know how to recognize literary truth. If it arrives, it arrives when I've used up all my resources for writing and no longer expect it.

Aguilar: In a conversation with Lila, Lena explains that she feels obliged to connect every event to the one before, so that everything is coherent in the end. Is that how you felt while you were writing this saga? The power of the story of these two women is truly remarkable, but there are also many characters around them, and in the background is the history of Italy. How did you work on the plot? You start off with Lila's disappearance, and Lena's decision to write originates in a sense of revenge, in a way, as though Lila wanted to leave no trace and Lena would not allow it. Did you have a clear idea of everything that would happen to Lila and Lena?

Ferrante: I never write with a carefully developed outline. In general, I know in a very cursory way the point of arrival and some important intermediary points, whereas I don't know anything about the countless small way stations—I identify those as I write. If it were not so—if I knew everything about the events and the characters—I'd get bored and forget the whole thing. And in fact that often happens. I go on for a long time, attending to the framework of the story and to the writing. Then I realize that I'm bearing a kind of false witness, and I stop. In this I'm very different from Lena. The obsession that everything should hold together coherently and beautifully seems to me a capital sin against the truth.

Aguilar: Going back to Lena's struggles as a writer—I read in The Paris Review *interview what you say about the ten years that it took to separate your writing from* Troubling Love—*I wondered if you think that women are more critical, more clear-eyed, and harsher regarding their own work.*

Ferrante: I don't know. I do think, though, that if a woman

writer wants to achieve her utmost, she has to impose on herself a sort of systematic dissatisfaction. We compare ourselves with giants. The male literary tradition has an abundance of marvelous works, and offers a form for everything possible. The would-be writer must know the tradition thoroughly and learn to reuse it, bending it as needed. The battle with the raw material of our experience as women requires authority above all. Further, we have to fight against submissiveness, and boldly, in fact proudly, seek a literary genealogy of our own.

Aguilar: Starting with the third book, and then, later, in the fourth, Lena goes on various book tours and gives interviews (one of them with tragic consequences, according to Lila), and her reputation as a public figure grows. Encountering her readers seems to help her define her public voice and her arguments. "Every night, I improvised successfully, starting from my own experience," Lena writes. Would it be fair to say that your writing proceeds in the same fashion?

Ferrante: No. Writing is different from any public exhibition. In these written responses, for example, I'm an author who addresses readers under the stimulus of your questions, which are also written. I'm not improvising answers, as in other types of exchanges, I'm not onstage. I set aside much, very much, of my individuality, which in different forms of communication I would display without any difficulties. Writing for me is an activity aimed at a single possible encounter: reading.

Aguilar: The reviews of Lena's book, as you write in Book 3, are not always positive. You also write about the promotional tours that she undertakes. Was it your intention to write ironically about the situation for writers today? Why did you choose to write extensively about Lena's public life as a writer? In doing so have you had further confirmation of your own position?

Ferrante: I am not being ironic about the status of the writer today. I confine myself to describing how it acts on my two protagonists: Lena lives it, alternating adherence with discouragement; Lila clashes with it through her friend, and sometimes submits to it, sometimes tries to use it, sometimes deconstructs it.

Aguilar: Did you at any point consider inserting passages from Lena's books? Readers know them only through Elena's memories, and the same thing applies to Lila's writings. Your novels seem in some sense to reject pure fact in favor of feeling and memory. Do you think these elements make the story stronger and somehow more realistic? Given the intense subjectivity of this story, can we say that the underlying enigma is whether the beauty and the marvelous qualities that Lena finds in Lila are only in the eyes of the beholder?

Ferrante: I almost immediately discarded the idea of deploying passages of Lena's books as well as of Lila's notebooks. Their objective quality doesn't count much for the purposes of the story. What's important is that Lena, in spite of her success, feels her works as the pale shadow of those which Lila would have written; in fact she perceives herself the same way. A story acquires power not when it imitates in a plausible way persons and events but when it captures the confusion of existences, the making and unmaking of beliefs, the way fragments from varying sources collide in the world and in our heads.

Aguilar: In the fourth book the city of Naples becomes increasingly important; it's described and studied. What is the greatest difficulty in attempting to write about Naples? Also, as the story progresses Lila seems to embody the city. Was this something that you had in mind?

Ferrante: Yes, but it's a thought I rejected; I didn't want Lila to be reducible to anything. I wanted, rather, the constant shifting of all the characters, from childhood to old age, to spill out onto the topography of the neighborhood and the whole city. Naples is hard to write about because it isn't linear, opposites shade into one another, its extraordinary beauty becomes ugly, its highly refined culture becomes ordinary, its famous cordiality turns into violence.

Aguilar: When Lena recalls the presentations she gives during the book tours, she seems to realize that she has used the lives of others. The same thing happens when she writes the novel about her childhood neighborhood. Do you think that fiction writing always involves some sense of guilt?

Ferrante: Absolutely yes. Writing—and not only fiction—is always an illicit appropriation. Our singularity as authors is a small note in the margin. The rest we take from the repository of those who have written before us, from the lives, from the most intimate feelings of others. Without the authorization of anything or anyone.

Aguilar: Who are your favorite women writers? And who are the women characters who have fascinated you?

Ferrante: The list would be very long; I'd like to spare you. I'd prefer to point out instead that in the course of the twentieth century the tradition of women writers became extraordinarily robust, and not only in the West. My generation, I think, is the first to stop thinking that to write a great book you have to be male. Today we can believe with assurance that it is possible to emerge from the literary gynaeceum in which we tend to shut ourselves, and to seek the comparison.

Aguilar: Which male character in the Neapolitan novels do you feel closest to?

Ferrante: Alfonso, Lena's schoolmate.

Aguilar: What do you think is so special about friendship between women? It's a subject that has barely been treated in literature; do you have any idea why?

Ferrante: Male friendship has a long literary tradition and a very elaborate code of behavior. Friendship between women, on the other hand, has a rudimentary map that has only recently begun to be made more precise, with the risk that the shortcut of the edifying cliché might obstruct the effort involved in taking difficult paths.

Aguilar: Lena displays an increasing disaffection for feminism (something that is in a sense personified in the character of her former sister-in-law). What do you think about feminism?

Ferrante: Without feminism I would still be a girl overburdened with male culture and a subculture that I touted as my own free thought. Feminism helped me grow up. But today I see and feel that the new generations are laughing at us. They don't know that our gains are very recent and hence fragile. All the women I've written about know this to their cost.

Aguilar: In the last book of the Neapolitan novels, Lena rushes through decades, and the rhythm seems to change. It's as if for you it was more difficult to write the story the closer it gets to the present. Was it hard to end the series? Do you still think about your characters?

Ferrante: It's too soon to feel truly distant. In fact, it's as if I were still writing. About the present it's hard to say—it's by nature volatile. If I described it, I did so imagining it as a precipice, the evaporating spray of a waterfall. And yet the hardest volume to write wasn't the fourth but the third.

Aguilar: The protagonists of your books are always women writers. Why? Another subject that recurs often is motherhood: is it hard to write openly about it?

Ferrante: Women write a lot, and not as a job but out of necessity. They resort to writing especially in moments of crisis, to explain themselves to themselves. There's a lot about us that hasn't been told completely, in fact a lot that hasn't been told at all, and we discover it when daily life gets tangled up and we need to put it in order. Motherhood seems to me precisely one of those experiences which are ours alone and whose literary truth has yet to be explored.

Aguilar: Your works are in a way pervaded by a sense of fate, and even of classical tragedy. How much have classical Greek works influenced you?

Ferrante: I did classical studies, and as a girl I translated a lot, for my own pleasure, from Greek and Latin. I wanted to learn to write, and it seemed to me an extraordinary exercise. Then I no longer had enough time, and I stopped. You say that my education is evident in my books, and I would happily believe you. But I must say that I've always thought of my women as enclosed within historical-cultural boundaries, and not trapped by fate.

Aguilar: Are you working on a new book?

Ferrante: Yes, it's rare for me to go for long periods without writing. But to finish a book doesn't happen often. And when it does happen, I don't publish willingly. Writing puts me in a good mood, publishing doesn't.

NOTE

The interview with Andrea Aguilar appeared in *Babelia/El País* (Spain) November 11, 2015, under the title *Elena Ferrante "Escribir es una apropiación indebida."*

15.
WOMEN WHO CROSS BORDERS
Answers to questions from Liz Jobey

Jobey: *When did you start to write?*
Ferrante: In late adolescence.

Jobey: *You have said that for a long time you wrote without the intention of publishing, or even without having others read what you were writing. What function did writing have for you in the beginning?*
Ferrante: I wrote to learn how to write. I thought I had things to say but at every attempt, depending on the mood I was in, I felt I lacked either talent or adequate technical skills. I generally preferred the second hypothesis, the first scared me.

Jobey: *Your novels are concerned with women's lives, and with how women react to men, both privately and in society. Was this your aim when you decided to publish—to speak to women about women's experiences?*
Ferrante: No, I didn't have a plan then, and I still don't. The only reason I decided to have *Troubling Love* published was that I felt I had written a book I could permanently detach from myself without later regretting it.

Jobey: *There was a ten-year gap between your first book,* Troubling Love, *and your second,* The Days of Abandonment. *Was there a particular reason for that gap?*
Ferrante: Actually, there was no gap. I wrote a great deal in

those ten years but nothing I felt I could trust. The stories I wrote were overworked, very controlled but without truth.

Jobey: There are very few positive male characters in your books. Most of the men are weak or boastful or absent or bullies. Is that a reflection of the society you grew up in, or does it reflect the imbalance of power between men and women in the wider society? Has that imbalance improved or changed in recent years?

Ferrante: I grew up in a world where it seemed normal that men (fathers, brothers, boyfriends) had the right to hit you in order to correct you, to teach you how to be a woman, ultimately for your own good. Luckily, today much has changed, but I still think the men who can really be trusted are a minority. Maybe this is because the milieu that shaped me was backward. Or maybe (and this is what I tend to believe) it's because male power, whether violently or delicately imposed, is still bent on subordinating us. Too many women are humiliated every day and not just on a symbolic level. And, in the real world, too many are punished, even with death, for their insubordination.

Jobey: Your novels seem to be concerned with boundaries—emotional, geographical, social—and what happens when those boundaries are crossed or broken down. Is that something that particularly affects women of a certain age or class, or does it apply to all?

Ferrante: Limits are still drawn around women—I'm talking about women in general. This isn't a problem if one is dealing with self-regulation: it's important to set limits for oneself. The problem is that we live within limits set by others, and we feel guilty when we fail to respect them. Male boundary-breaking does not automatically entail negative judgments; it's a sign of curiosity and courage. Female boundary-breaking, especially when it is not undertaken under the guidance or supervision of men, is still disorienting: it is loss of femininity, it is excess, perversion, disease.

Jobey: You refer to characters "dissolving" boundaries as a way of describing emotional breakdown. Is that a feeling you recognize—in yourself? In others?

Ferrante: I have seen it in my mother, in myself, in many women friends. We experience too many bonds that choke our desires and ambitions. The modern world subjects us to pressures that at times we are unable to bear.

Jobey: The narrators in your novels find motherhood difficult. It devours them, reduces them, they long to escape it, and when they do, they feel liberated. Do you feel women would be stronger if they didn't have to bear the burdens of motherhood?

Ferrante: No, that's not the point. The point is what we tell ourselves about motherhood and child-rearing. If we keep talking about it in an idyllic way, as in many handbooks on motherhood, we will continue to feel alone and guilty when we come up against the frustrating aspects of being a mother. The task of a woman writer today is not to stop at the pleasures of the pregnant body, of birth, of bringing up children, but to delve truthfully into the darkest depth.

Jobey: The Neapolitan novels have similarities of character and plot to your three earlier novels. Are you, in some ways, telling the same story?

Ferrante: Not the same story but definitely the same features of a single malady. Life's wounds are incurable and you write them and rewrite them in the hope of being able, sooner or later, to construct a narrative that will account for them once and for all.

Jobey: Should we assume the story to be your story—as readers clearly do—or is that a failure of imagination on their part, a symptom of the modern trend that always looks for the author in the work?

Ferrante: The four volumes of the Neapolitan novels are my story, yes, but only in the sense that I am the one who has given it the form of a novel and used my life experiences to inject truth into the literary invention. If I had wanted to recount my own story, I would have established a different pact with the reader, I would have signaled that I was writing an autobiography. I have not chosen the path of autobiography, nor will I choose it in the future, because I am convinced that fiction, when it works, is more charged with truth.

Jobey: Could you explain why you decided to keep your identity hidden—to maintain an "absence," as you put it, from the business of publishing and promoting your books?

Ferrante: I believe that today it's a mistake to fail to protect writing by guaranteeing it an autonomous space, far from the demands of the media and the marketplace. My own small cultural battle, now two decades long, is aimed mostly at readers. I think authors should be sought in the books they put their names to, not in the physical person who is writing or in his or her private life. Outside the texts and their expressive techniques, there is only idle gossip. Let's restore authentic centrality to the books themselves and, if it's appropriate, discuss the possible uses of idle gossip as promotion.

Jobey: Do you feel that fame will always cause damage to a writer's work—or to the work of any creative person?

Ferrante: I don't know. I simply believe that today it's a mistake to let one's person become better known than one's work.

Jobey: Do members of your family and your friends know

you are the author of your novels? Are there people you feel would be upset, or would make your life difficult, if your identity as the author of your novels were known?

Ferrante: At first I worried I would cause suffering to the people I care for. Now I no longer feel the need to protect my loved ones. They know writing is my life and they leave me alone in my little corner. The only condition is that I should do nothing to make them feel ashamed.

Jobey: How do you work with your English-language translator Ann Goldstein? Can you assess whether the voice that comes in your translated works is your "true" voice?

Ferrante: I trust her completely. I believe she has done everything possible to accommodate my Italian into her English with the best intentions.

Jobey: One of your self-criticisms—about The Days of Abandonment—*is that you fear some parts might have "only the appearance of good writing." What, for you, is the difference between "good" writing and "true" writing—or, at least, the kind of writing you feel you produce at your best?*

Ferrante: A page is well written when the labor and the pleasure of truthful narration supplant any other concern, including a concern with formal elegance. I belong to the category of writers who throw out the final draft and keep the rough when this practice ensures a higher degree of authenticity.

Jobey: You have said, talking about women writers today, that "we have to dig deep into our difference, using advanced tools." Are there other writers who do that? Could you give some examples of women writers you admire—or writers in general?

Ferrante: The list would be too long. The present landscape of women's writing is wide and very lively. I read a lot and the pages I love most are those that make me exclaim, "Here's something I would never be able to do." With those pages I am putting together my own personal anthology of regret.

Jobey: I know that many women write to you after reading your books. Do men?

Ferrante: At first there were more men than women. Now women outnumber them.

Jobey: When you have finally published a book, do you need a period of recuperation, of recovery? [Are there periods when you don't write at all]

Ferrante: No. There is always something on my mind that bothers me, and writing about it puts me in a good mood.

Jobey: You have said that to reveal your identity now would be "deplorably inconsistent." But do you nevertheless feel under pressure from your success? How does it feel when you walk into a bookshop, or an airport, and see a wall of your books on sale?

Ferrante: I carefully avoid such spectacles. Publication has always made me anxious. My text reproduced in thousands of copies strikes me as a form of presumption, makes me feel guilty.

Jobey: Do you feel that your identity is gradually being revealed? To unmask you now, for some literary journalists, would be considered a scoop.

Ferrante: A scoop? What nonsense. Who would be interested in what remains of me outside my books? The attention paid to them seems too much already.

Jobey: You have said that Lenù could not exist as a writer without the character of Lila. Is that true for you, too?

Ferrante: I perceive writing as if it were motivated and fed by the accidental bumping of my life against the lives of others.

In this sense, yes, if I became impermeable, if other people no longer sowed disorder in me, I think I would stop writing.

> *Jobey: Are you writing another book?*
> Ferrante: Yes. But—right now—I doubt I will publish it.

NOTE
The interview with Liz Jobey, translated by Daniela Petracco, appeared in the *Financial Times* (U.K.) under the title "Women of 2015: Elena Ferrante, Writer."

16.

THE SQUANDERING OF FEMALE INTELLIGENCE
Answers to questions from Deborah Orr

O*rr: Usually, at this point in an interview, the writer sketches the subject and her surroundings. Under the circumstances, Elena, can I ask you to do this yourself, please?*

Ferrante: I can't. I don't know how.

Orr: Can we assume, then, that you see Elena Ferrante as a somewhat mysterious person, without a home, without a family, who exists inside your head?

Ferrante: No, Elena Ferrante is the author of several novels. There is nothing mysterious about her, given how she manifests herself—perhaps even too much—in her own writing, the place where her creative life transpires in absolute fullness. What I mean is that the author is the sum of the expressive strategies that shape an invented world, a concrete world that is populated by people and events. The rest is ordinary private life.

Orr: Do you think it's harder for women—especially mothers—to keep their creative lives and their private lives separate?

Ferrante: Women, in all fields—whether mothers or not—still encounter an extraordinary number of obstacles. They have to hold too many things together and often sacrifice their aspirations in the name of affections. To give an outlet to their creativity is thus especially arduous. It requires strong motivation, strict discipline, and many compromises. Above all, it entails quite a few feelings of guilt. And in order not to cut out a large part of one's private life, the creative work should not swallow up every other form of self-expression. But that is the most complicated thing.

Orr: Your novels are intimate, often domestic, but always with a strong sense of the socioeconomic forces under which your characters have been formed. Can you tell us a bit about the issues that have forged your own political consciousness?

Ferrante: I don't have any special passion for politics, it being a never-ending merry-go-round of bosses big and small, all generally mediocre. I actually find it boring. I confuse names, minor events, political positions. But I have always paid careful attention to social and economic conflicts, to the dialectic between high and low. Maybe it's because I was not born or brought up surrounded by affluence. Climbing the economic ladder has been very hard for me, and I still feel a great deal of guilt toward those I left behind. I also had to discover very quickly that class origins cannot be erased, regardless of whether we climb up or down the sociocultural ladder. Even when our circumstances improve, it's like the color that inevitably rises to one's cheeks after a strong emotion . . . I believe there is no story, however small, that can ignore that coloring.

Orr: It's widely assumed that you use a pseudonym not only to protect your own privacy but also that of a real Neapolitan community from which you draw your inspiration. Is that assumption correct?

Ferrante: Yes, it's one of the factors that motivated me.

Orr: What were the other factors?

Ferrante: The wish to be freed from all forms of social pressure or obligation. Not to feel tied down to what could become one's public image. To concentrate exclusively and with complete freedom on writing and its strategies.

Orr: Do you have a sense of how people in the community feel about the books?

Ferrante: No. But it must be said that I no longer protect myself from the world I grew up in. Rather, today I try to protect the feelings I have for that world, the emotional space where my desire to write first took hold, and still grows.

Orr: Philip Roth says that "discretion is, unfortunately, not for novelists." How far would you agree with him on this?

Ferrante: I prefer to call it illicit appropriation rather than indiscretion. Writing for me is a dragnet that carries everything along with it: expressions and figures of speech, postures, feelings, thoughts, troubles. In short, the lives of others. Not to mention the ransacking of the enormous warehouse that is literary tradition.

Orr: In My Brilliant Friend, *the patronage of a schoolteacher helps the main character Elena from an early age. But the teacher rejects her best friend Lila. Was the schoolteacher unfair in favoring Elena, or did she understand that Lila was a person who would always want to rely only on herself and make her own way?*

Ferrante: The school notices both Lila and Elena. But both feel constrained. Lila is the kind of person who cannot bring herself to accept boundaries except to break them, but then gives up under the strain. Elena learns immediately to make use of the school environment, as she will later learn to make use of the many other spaces she occupies in the course of her life, at the same time gathering and covertly putting into circulation some of her friend's strength.

Orr: Staying with the protagonists of the Neapolitan Quartet, Lila is a highly original thinker, and also susceptible to dissociative fugues. Would it be right to view Lila as a savant, gifted in a way that Elena isn't?

Ferrante: No. The structure of the narrative is such that neither Lila nor Elena can ever be definitively locked within a formula that makes one the opposite of the other.

Orr: The contrasting characters of the two women make for narrative drama. But did you see them as archetypes you wanted to examine for particular reasons?

Ferrante: Maybe that's true—it definitely happened with Olga in my second book, *The Days of Abandonment*, but in this case I didn't feel that either Lila or Elena could be reduced to some sort of original model that would ensure her coherence.

Orr: From the start, Lila and Elena have very different attitudes toward men and sex. Do you view Lila's disinterest as the source of her power over men? Or does the contrast between the two women serve a different purpose?

Ferrante: I think our sexuality is all yet to be recounted and that, especially in this context, the rich male literary tradition constitutes a huge obstacle. The ways Elena and Lila behave are just two different aspects of the same arduous and almost always unhappy adjustment to men and their sexuality.

Orr: Is it fair to say that the world depicted in your work offers few respectable ways out of a quite narrow, quite compromised life other than academic and intellectual success, for the men as well as the women?

Ferrante: No. I care a lot for Enzo's character; his journey is a hard one, but worthy of respect. And anyway, it's above all the narrator, Elena, who considers culture, education, as a way to pull herself out of misery and ignorance. Her journey is seemingly successful. But profound changes take generations; they must involve everybody. At times Elena herself feels that individual lives, even the most fortunate, are ultimately unsatisfactory and in many ways at fault.

Orr: Has that changed since the nineteen-fifties, when the Neapolitan story cycle starts, or do you think it's become more entrenched—the idea that only obvious exceptionality among the "lower classes" should be rewarded?

Ferrante: This is how it's going to be as long as class disadvantage and privilege exist. I have met truly exceptional people in whom the stubborn urge to climb the social ladder is absent. And so the most serious problem is that in deceptively egalitarian societies such as ours, much intelligence—women's especially—is squandered.

Orr: Would you describe the relationship between Lila and Elena as competitive? And is that something you see as important to women's place in the world?

Ferrante: No, competition between women is good only if it does not prevail; that is to say if it coexists with affinity, affection, with a real sense of being mutually indispensable, with sudden peaks of solidarity in spite of envy, jealousy, and the whole inevitable cohort of bad feelings. Of course, this makes for a very tangled skein of relationships, but that's fine. Our way of being is—for historical reasons—much more tangled than that of men, which is accustomed to using simplification as a quick way to solve problems.

Orr: Despite Elena's material success, Lila emerges as the dominant character. The reader understands that this may be an aspect of Elena's self-deprecating narration—she may simply feel dominated by Lila. Is it possible that you'd ever be tempted to let Lila tell her own story?

Ferrante: No. In the first draft there were long episodes written by Lila but I later excluded this path. Lila can only be Elena's tale: outside that tale she would probably be unable to define herself. It's the people who love us or hate us or both—who hold together the thousands of fragments we are made of.

Orr: Which of the two women do you feel most affection for?
Ferrante: I love Lila a lot; that is, I love the way in which Elena tells her story and the way in which Lila tells her own story through her friend.

Orr: Do you ever feel that your anonymity limits your ability to shape the debate inspired by the books?
Ferrante: No, my work stops at publication. If the books don't contain in themselves their reasons for being—questions and answers—it means I was wrong to have them published. At most, I may write when I am disturbed by something. I've recently discovered the pleasure of finding written answers to written questions such as yours. Twenty years ago, it was more difficult for me; I'd try but eventually give up. Now I see it as a useful opportunity: your questions help me to reflect.

Orr: The choice of Elena as your pseudonym and also the name of your protagonist in the Neapolitan novels invites people to assume they are romans-à-clef. Is this a literary device or a genuine hint to your readers?
Ferrante: Using the name Elena helped only to reinforce the truth of the story I was telling. Even those who write need that "willing suspension of disbelief," as Coleridge called it. The fictional treatment of biographical material—a treatment that for me is essential—is full of traps. Saying "Elena" has helped to tie myself down to the truth.

Orr: One of the wonderful things about your novels is that they're strongly and richly narrative, leaving the reader to come to her own conclusions, or at least feel that she's coming to her own conclusions, about the mass of issues raised. Was it a conscious decision, to show rather than tell?

Ferrante: Yes. What is important in storytelling are the characters' actions and reactions, the spaces in which they move, the way in which time flows over them. The narrator composes a score; readers perform and interpret it. A story is an anomalous kind of cage, one that traps you within its strategies and yet, conversely, makes you feel free.

Orr: What are the most important things you'd like to see readers learning or thinking about as a consequence of reading your books?

Ferrante: Allow me not to answer this question. Novels should never come with instructions for use, least of all when drawn up by those who write them.

Orr: Do you aim to speak primarily to women in your writing?

Ferrante: One writes for all human beings, always. But I am happy that my readers are first and foremost women.

Orr: Why?

Ferrante: We, all of us women, need to build a genealogy of our own, one that will embolden us, define us, allow us to see ourselves outside the tradition through which men have viewed, represented, evaluated, and catalogued us—for millennia. Theirs is a potent tradition, rich with splendid works, but one that has excluded much, too much, of what is ours. To narrate thoroughly, freely—even provocatively—our own "more than this" is important: it contributes to the drawing of a map of what we are or what we want to be. There's a quote from Amelia Rosselli—one of the most innovative and unsettling Italian poets of the twentieth century—that dates from the nineteen-sixties. Years ago I adopted it as a literary manifesto that is at once ironic and dead serious. It's an exclamation: "What black deep activism there is in my menstruation!"

Orr: Your female characters seem locked in a fight between past and future, traditional and modern, conventional and unconventional. It's a plight familiar to most women of recent generations. Where do you think women are now, in Italy and globally?

Ferrante: I believe all of us, of whatever age, are still in the thick of the battle. The conflict will be long, and even if we think we have left behind the culture and language of patriarchal society once and for all, we just have to look at the world in its entirety to understand that the conflict is far from over and that everything we have gained can still be lost.

Orr: Ambivalence—about success, money, career, motherhood, marriage—suffuses your books. Women have made progress. But what are the battles that feminism still has to win? And does it have to change its tactics to do so?

Ferrante: First of all, we must never forget that there are vast areas of the planet where women live in the most terrible conditions. But, even in those areas where many of our rights are safe, it's still hard to be a woman who challenges the way in which even the most cultured and forward-thinking men represent us. We are at a crossroads. We vacillate between rooted adherence to male expectations and new ways of being female. Although we are free and combative, we accept that our need for fulfilment in this or that field should be ratified by men in authority, who co-opt us after having evaluated whether we have sufficiently absorbed the male tradition and are able to become its dignified interpreters, free of female issues and weaknesses. Instead, we must fight, so as to bring about change that is profound. This will be possible only if we build a grand female tradition that men are forced to measure themselves against. It's going to be a long battle, centered on women's industry in every field, on the excellence of female thought and action. Only when a man publicly recognizes his debt to a woman's work, without the condescending kindness typical of those who feel themselves superior, will things really start to change.

Orr: What can you tell us about what you're working on now?

Ferrante: I never tell anyone the stories I have in my head. I would lose the desire to try and write them down.

Orr: Last question—will you accept the sincere thanks of this very grateful reader?

Ferrante: I must thank you, rather. When readers send me words such as yours, I am the first to marvel at *My Brilliant Friend's* good fortune. What is actually inside a book is a mystery above all for its author.

NOTE
The interview with Deborah Orr, translated by Daniela Petracco, appeared in *The Gentlewoman* (U.K.) February 19, 2016, under the title "Elena Ferrante: In a Manner of Speaking."

17.
IN SPITE OF EVERYTHING
Answers to questions from Nicola Lagioia

Lagioia: *One of the most powerful aspects of the Neapolitan Quartet is the way in which the interdependence of the characters is rendered. In the relationship between Lila and Elena, each manages to enter the form of the other, which continues to act, as an actual form of autonomous life, beyond the bounds of the physical presence that produced it. Each time Lila vanishes from the horizon of Elena's experiences, she nevertheless continues to act in her friend, and presumably the opposite is also true. Reading your novel is comforting because this is what occurs in real life. The people who are truly important to us, the people we've allowed to break us open inside, do not stop questioning us, obsessing us, pursuing us, and, if necessary, guiding us, even if they die, or grow distant, or if we've quarreled. This phenomenon, it seems to me, alters even the construction of memories. The way we reread the novel of our life depends partly on how those crucial people act silently within us (modifying the junctions). Because of the way you manage to convey these mechanisms, the Neapolitan Quartet seems to me an utterly modern novel.*

But in the four books this interdependence extends throughout the entire world of the two friends: Nino, Rino, Stefano Carracci, the Solara brothers, Carmela, Enzo Scanno, Gigliola, Marisa, Pasquale, Antonio, even Professor Galiani. Despite the fact that their rules of mutual attraction are not so intense as those that bind Elena and Lila, they all remain in the same orbit. To escape each other is impossible; they constantly reappear in

365

one another's lives. Certainly they quarrel, they betray each other, in some cases they nearly kill each other. They say or do things that in other contexts would be reason enough to cut off relations forever. And yet that almost never happens. There is always a small opening (I think, for example, of Marcello Solara, who continues to be cordial toward Elena even after her attacks in L'Espresso*). It seems that only death—or extreme old age—can break their bonds.*

When you think of what these bonds are made of, it might seem to be a curse—but shouldn't it also be considered a blessing? The alternative is to risk absolute solitude. In some cases I confess I have envied these characters.

Ferrante: Where do I start? In my childhood, my adolescence. Some of the poor Neapolitan neighborhoods were crowded, yes, and rowdy. To gather oneself, so to speak, was physically impossible. One learned very early to have the greatest concentration amid the greatest disruption. The idea that every "I" is largely made up of others and by the other wasn't theoretical; it was a reality. To be alive meant to continually collide with the existence of others and to be collided with, the results being at times good-natured, at others aggressive, then again good-natured. The dead were brought into quarrels; people weren't content to attack and insult the living—they abused aunts, cousins, grandparents, and great-grandparents who were no longer in the world as if it were quite normal. And then there was the dialect and there was Italian. The two languages referred to different communities, both jam-packed. What was normal in one wasn't normal in the other. The bonds that you established in one language never had the same substance as those in the other. Customs varied, the rules of behavior, the traditions. And if you sought a middle ground, you would assume a false dialect that was a sort of trivialized Italian.

All of this shaped me (us), but even now there is no particular order or hierarchy to its influence. Nothing has faded, everything is here in the present. Of course, today I have small quiet places where I can gather myself—but I still feel that the idea is slightly ridiculous. I've described women at moments when they are absolutely alone. But in their heads there is never silence or even focus. The most absolute solitude, at least in my experience, and not just as a narrator, is always, to paraphrase the title of a very good book by Hrabal, too loud. To the writer, no person is ever definitively relegated to silence, even if we long ago broke off relations with that person—out of anger, by chance, or because the person died. I can't even think without the voices of others, much less write. And I'm not talking only about relatives, female friends, enemies. I'm talking about others, men and women who today exist only in images: in television or newspaper images, sometimes heart-rending, sometimes offensive in their opulence. And I'm talking about the past, about what we generally call tradition; I'm talking about all those others who were once in the world and who have acted or who now act through us. Our entire body, like it or not, enacts a stunning resurrection of the dead just as we advance toward our own death. We are, as you say, interconnected. And we should teach ourselves to look deeply at this interconnection—I call it a tangle, or, rather, *frantumaglia*—to give ourselves adequate tools to describe it. In the most absolute tranquility or in the midst of tumultuous events, in safety or danger, in innocence or corruption, we are a crowd of others. And this crowd is certainly a blessing for literature.

But when we consider the materiality of days, the daily struggle of living, it's hard to play this game of reversals: curse/blessing, blessing/curse. I would feel like a liar if I considered the legacy of my neighborhood a positive one. I understand that the enduring interconnectedness of the world I've described may seem to be an antidote. There are many moments, in the Neapolitan Quartet, where the environment in which Lila and Elena are submerged seems, in spite of everything, gentle and welcoming. But one mustn't lose sight of that "in spite of everything." The ties to the neighborhood are confining and harmful, they corrupt and they abet corruption. And the fact that one can't cut them, that they reappear after every apparent dissolution, is not a good thing. The sudden emergence of bad manners from within good ones, followed again by a smile, still seems to me the symptom of an unreliable community held together by opportunistic complicities, and thus a community careful to ration rage and hypocrisy in order to avoid an all-out war that would require conclusive choices: you're on this side, I'm on that.

No, therefore, what unites the throng of the neighborhood is, in actuality, inevitably corrupt and, in my view, a curse. Naturally, however, that throng is made up of individual people, and people always have, amid innumerable contradictions, their humanity, which is extremely precious and which any story must take account of, if it doesn't want to fail. Especially since people move between good and bad almost without realizing it. The neighborhood is imagined in this way, and Lila and Elena are made of the neighborhood's matter, but a fluid matter that drags everything along in its wake. I wanted them, against the closed, fixed state of the environment, to be mobile, so that nothing could truly stabilize them and they themselves would pass through each other as if they were air—but without ever freeing themselves from the gravitational pull of their birthplace. They, too, had to feel it, above all and in spite of everything.

There, perhaps it's precisely that "in spite of everything" that is difficult to explain. You have to pay attention to the "everything," you mustn't forget it, you must recognize it in its every disguise, even if the emotional ties, the habits acquired in childhood, the smells, the tastes, the sounds charged with dialect seduce us, soften us, make us waver, make us ethically unstable. Maybe capturing the fluidity of existences on the page means avoiding stories that are too rigidly defined. We're all subject to continuous modification, but, to escape the anguish of impermanence, we camouflage it, until old age, with countless impressions of stability, the most important of which emanate precisely from narratives, especially when someone tells us: that's how it happened. I don't particularly like that kind of book; I prefer books in which not even the narrator knows how things happened. For me, telling a story has always meant reducing the techniques that present facts as incontrovertible milestones and reinforcing those that emphasize the instability. The long story of Elena Greco is marked everywhere by instability, maybe even more than the stories of Delia, Olga, or Leda, the protagonists of my earlier books. What Greco lays out on the page, at first with apparent assurance, becomes increasingly less controlled. What does she really feel, this narrator, what does she think, what does she do? And what does Lila do and think, and whoever else bursts into her story? In the Neapolitan Quartet, I wanted everything to take shape and then lose its shape. In her effort to tell the story of Lila, Elena is compelled to tell the story of all the others, herself among them, encounters and clashes that leave very varied impressions. The others, in the broad meaning of the term, as I said, continuously collide with us and we collide with them. Our singularity, our uniqueness, our identity are continuously dying. When at the end of a long day we feel shattered, "in pieces," there's nothing more literally true. If we look carefully, we *are* the destabilizing collisions that we suffer or cause, and the story of those collisions is our true story. To tell that story is to describe interpenetration, turmoil, and also, to be precise, an incongruous mixture of expressive registers, codes, and genres. We are heterogeneous fragments that, thanks to impressions of unity—elegant figures, beautiful form—stay together despite their arbitrary and contradictory nature. The cheapest glue is stereotype. Stereotypes calm us. But the problem is, as Lila says, that even just for a few seconds, stereotypes can lose their boundaries and drive us into panic. In the Neapolitan Quartet, at least in intention, there is a careful calibration of stereotype and dissolving boundaries.

Lagioia: Although Lila, when she goes to see Pasolini with Nino, shows her appreciation for him, there is not even the shadow of a Ninetto Davoli[9] type in the Neapolitan Quartet. Not to mention a Gennariello, full of innocence and inner beauty— the very archetype of certain Neapolitan boys that Pasolini (described by Nino, in that same scene, as a "fag" who makes "more trouble than anything else") depicted in Lettere luterane (Lutheran Letters). *What I mean to say is that in your novel the subproletariat has no redemptive power. Though the underclass is historically on the side of right, in practice it is always brutally on the side of wrong. It's hard to admit, but those who grew up in those environments or who know them well can't help but appreciate, even love and be moved by the absolute truth of the scenes you describe.*

There are critics who have compared you to Anna Maria Ortese and to Elsa Morante—correctly, in my view. And yet your underclass is more like the terrible human horde described by Curzio Malaparte in La Pelle (The Skin) *than that described in Ortese's* Il mare non bagna Napoli (The Sea Doesn't Bathe Naples). *Is that type of plebeian class truly irredeemable?*

Ferrante: I don't know about Malaparte, I should reread him. I've never felt any conscious affinity with *The Skin*, which I read long ago. But I have to admit that I've always felt that Gennariello, as well, is very distant from my experience. It's the chapter from *The Sea Doesn't Bathe Naples* titled "The

---

[9] Ninetto Davoli: an Italian actor (b. 1948) who appeared in many films directed by Pier Paolo Pasolini.

Involuntary City" that, at different stages of my life, seemed to me a necessary point of departure, if I was ever going to try to describe what I thought I knew about my city. But it's always hard to talk about literary influences: a halting verse, two forgotten lines, a beautiful page that at the time we didn't appreciate—often, through hidden pathways, these come to matter more than the literary emblems that, in good faith, we flaunt in an attempt to impress. But what can I tell you? My intention, at least, was not to show that Lila and Elena are born and grow up within a terrible human horde. But there is no neighborhood Gennariello, either. In any case, Pasolini himself believed Gennariello to be a miracle of his own imagination, an exception among so many disgusting fascists, as he wrote. The plebeian city I know is made up of ordinary people who don't have money and who seek it, who are of the underclass and yet violent, who do not have the intangible privilege of a good education, who mock those who think of saving themselves through education and yet still consider education valuable.

Lagioia: For Lila and Elena, studying is crucial. Getting an education is the only really worthy way to escape the condition of inferiority. Despite the many troubles they confront in the course of their lives, rarely do the two friends lose faith in the power of learning. Even when studying doesn't lead to any practical outcome, Elena and Lila don't question its importance in the construction of every individual. What do you think of Italy today, full of university graduates who are adrift? It's true that some of these youths don't have the almost desperate relationship with education that Lila and Elena do, and it's true that for the next generations (for Dede and Elsa, for example) there might be other tools with which to cross the shadow line. And yet, all in all, education doesn't strike me as a tool of emancipation like any other.

Ferrante: First of all, I would not reduce education to a mere tool of emancipation. Education has mainly been considered essential to social mobility. In post-World War II Italy, education cemented old hierarchies, but it also allowed for a modest assimilation of the deserving, so that to some extent those who remained at the bottom could say to themselves: I ended up here because I didn't want to study. Lenù's story, but also Nino's, demonstrates this use of education for upward mobility. But in the story there are also signs of dysfunction: some characters study and yet still they stumble. In other words, there was an ideology of education that no longer functions today. Its failure has become obvious: the directionless graduates are dramatic evidence that the long crisis in the legitimization of social hierarchy based on the credentials of an education has come to a head. But the story also demonstrates another way of understanding education: Lila's. For Lila, deprived of the opportunity to complete her education—at a time when this was crucial especially for women, and for poor women—and projecting onto Lenuccia her own ambitions of sociocultural ascent, education becomes the manifestation of a permanent anxiety about intelligence, a necessity imposed by the relentlessly chaotic circumstances of life, a tool of daily struggle (a function to which Lila tries to reduce even her friend, "who has studied"). While Lena, in short, is the tormented omega of the old system, Lila embodies the crisis and, in a certain sense, a possible future. How the crisis will be resolved in our own tumultuous world, I'm not sure—we'll have to see. Will the contradictions of the educational system become increasingly evident, signaling its decline? Will education be refined and accessible without any connection to the ways we earn a living? Will we have more cultured diligence and less intelligence? Let's say that in general I'm captivated by those who produce ideas, rather than by those who comment on them. I'd feel better in a world of imaginative creators of grand ideas—even if this seems to me, admittedly, a formidable goal.

Lagioia: If it's true, as I've read in more than one article, that My Brilliant Friend *presents no possibilities for transcendence (at least in the way transcendence is rendered in most twentieth-century literature), what do we make of Lina's* smarginature, *her episodes of dissolving boundaries? That is to say, the crucial moments when the world comes unglued before Lina's eyes, when it goes off its axis, appearing in its unbearable nakedness: a chaotic and shapeless mass, "a sticky, jumbled, reality" without meaning. They are revelatory instants, and the revelations are consistently terrible. Rather than the flashes of illumination experienced by the Dostoyevskian epileptics, these episodes call to mind one of the last chapters in* Anna Karenina, *when the protagonist observes from her carriage the streets crowded with people, and is convinced that life has no meaning, that love doesn't exist, that we are creatures hurled into chaos and governed by forces that the last shreds of illusion would call bleak— and that, even worse, those forces simply are what they are, no more or less meaningful than the law of gravity. Soon afterward* Anna Karenina *throws herself under a train.*

I can't understand (and I won't ask you) whether Lina's anguish derives from the fact that, during the episodes of dissolving boundaries, the universe appears to her inexorably devoid of meaning, or from an awareness that that trance state offers the broadest view granted to man, a view from which one intuits that, on the contrary, "meaning" (and therefore the possibility of peace, of happiness) exists in the abstract, but is eternally not only unattainable but also indecipherable to our senses. What interests me concerns, rather, the fiction. "Unreal things," as Lina calls them, "which with their physical and moral solidity pacified her." Unreal things are barriers against the disorder and violence that surround us. From this point of view, literature is an unreal thing, as is law or philosophy. On the one hand, this assumes that we are condemned to unhappiness, because all that can soothe us is an illusion, a belief in the truth of an unreal thing. But on the other hand I wonder whether it is not, perhaps, simply our nature to create "unreal things" that might let us reach our ultimate goal: true communication with each other and with the world?

Ferrante: I'm always surprised when someone points out as a flaw the fact that my stories contain no possibility of transcendence. Here I'd like to move on to a statement of principle: since the age of fifteen, I haven't believed in the kingdom of any God, in Heaven or on earth—in fact, wherever you place it, it seems dangerous to me. On the other hand, I share the opinion that most of the concepts we work with have a theological origin. Theology helps us understand the origins of the dregs we even now resort to. As for the rest I don't know what to tell you. I'm comforted by stories that emerge through horror to a turning point, stories in which someone is redeemed as confirmation that peace and happiness are possible, or that one can return to a private or public Eden. But I tried to write a story like that, long ago, and I discovered that I didn't believe in it. I'm drawn, rather, to images of crisis, to seals that are broken, and perhaps the dissolving boundaries come from these. When shapes lose their contours, we see what most terrifies us, as in Ovid's *Metamorphoses*, Kafka's *Metamorphosis*, and Clarice Lispector's extraordinary *Passion According to G.H.* You don't go beyond that; you have to take a step back and, to survive, re-enter some good fiction. I don't believe, however, that every fiction we orchestrate is good. I cling to those that are painful, those that arise from a profound crisis of all our illusions. I love unreal things when they show signs of firsthand knowledge of the terror, and hence an awareness that they *are* unreal, that they will not hold up for long against the collisions. Human beings are extremely violent animals, and the violence they are always ready to use in order to impose their own eternal, salvific life vest, while shattering those of others, is frightening.

Lagioia: The Neapolitan Quartet is full of memorable quarrels. The fights, the angry outbursts of the various characters are rendered magisterially—they're almost contagious. Every so often while reading I felt like pounding a fist on the table for the sole purpose of physically emphasizing some verbal explosion of Nunzia Cerullo or Elena's mother. I've always been struck by how certain poor people in Italy ignite. The repertoire is incredibly vast. Swear words, vomited up without a pause. Fierce, absurd accusations. Hair-tearing. Increasingly fantastic curses. My maternal grandparents were small independent farmers, while my paternal grandfather was a truck driver. I heard them rail at each other, or, more often, at themselves or at fate, in a manner I've rarely found in other places (though it happened more frequently in the cities than in the countryside). Sometimes I really miss it. I don't believe those bursts of rage are common to all oppressed peoples. In France, in England, things function more or less the same way. But in some Asian countries (Thailand, for example) the poor, at least on the outside, get angry with fate in a much less violent way.

So, on the one hand, I understand that the spectacle of foul language can be sad and degrading, even bestial. On the other hand, I would ask you: isn't it also a wail of civilization, the instinctive understanding of poverty as injustice?

Ferrante: Here let's return to the quarrels. And yes, let's say that with poor people the quarrel is a threshold. The threshold is an interesting rhetorical device; metaphorically, it represents a suspension between two opposing sides, and it effectively summarizes the time we live in. With the concept of class consciousness and class conflict defeated, the poor, the desperate, whose wealth consists only of angry words, are kept, by means of words, on the threshold—between the degrading explosion, which makes them like animals, and the liberating one, which humanizes and initiates a sort of purification. But in reality the threshold is continuously breached, it becomes bloodshed, a bloody war among the poor. Or it leads to reconciliation, but in the sense of a return to acquiescence, to the subservience of the weak toward the strong, to opportunism. The wail of civilization arises, if you like, from the intuition of one's own dignity that accompanies the necessity for change. Otherwise, the quarrels of the poor are simply another version of the capons of Renzo Tramaglino.[10]

Lagioia: Forgive me for returning to Malaparte. At a certain point I remembered a passage in The Skin *where he writes: "What do you hope to find in London, Paris, Vienna? You will find Naples there. It's the fate of Europe to become Naples."*

I couldn't help associating it—albeit in a mirror-image way—with some of Lenuccia's insights: "Naples was the great European metropolis where faith in technology, in science, in economic development, in the kindness of nature, in history that leads of necessity to improvement, in democracy was revealed, most clearly and far in advance, to be completely without foundation. To be born in that city—I went so far as to write once, thinking not of myself but of Lila's pessimism—is useful for a single thing: to have always known, almost instinctively, what today, with endless fine distinctions, everyone is beginning to claim: that the dream of unlimited progress is in reality a nightmare of savagery and death."

This distrust of history recalls the ultimate distrust of the cosmos, or of nature, that the narrator talks about at the start of the third volume: "I had fled, in fact. Only to discover, in the decades to come, that I had been wrong, that it was a chain with larger and larger links: the neighborhood was connected to the city, the city to Italy, Italy to Europe, Europe to the whole planet. And this is how I see it today: it's not the neighborhood that's sick, it's not Naples, it's the entire earth, it's the universe, or universes. And shrewdness means hiding and hiding from oneself the true state of things."

---

[10] The main character in Alessandro Manzoni's *The Betrothed*.

I would stop at history. The Neapolitan Quartet is also a sorrowful hymn to the illusions of the second half of the twentieth century, or perhaps of all modernity. I was frightened recently by the declaration by some historians that the forty years from 1950 to 1990 (the period in which inequalities diminished, social mobility became a reality, and the masses were often protagonists) could be read, in the grand scheme of things, as a small moment of discontinuity in a larger picture where vast inequalities are the rule. The twenty-first century began with the violent widening of the gap between rich and poor. Do you think that the second half of the twentieth century was really only a digression? Isn't it, rather, more realistic to think that the future remains, as ever, unwritten?

Ferrante: Yes, I think that's true: the future is always unwritten. But history and stories are written, and they are written from the balcony of the present, looking out on the electrical storm of the past; that is to say, there is nothing more unstable than the past. The past, in its indeterminacy, presents itself either through the filter of nostalgia or through the filter of preliminary impressions. I don't love nostalgia; it leads us to ignore individual sufferings, large pockets of misery, cultural and civil poverty, widespread corruption, regression after minimal and illusory progress. I prefer acquisition to acts. The forty years you cite were in reality very difficult and painful for those who started from a position of disadvantage. And by disadvantage I also mean, above all, being a woman. Not only that: starting in the seventies, the masses that endured inhuman sacrifices to climb a few rungs up the social ladder were already experiencing the torments of defeat, as were their children. Not to mention a sort of latent civil war; so-called world peace, always at risk; and the beginnings of one of the most devastating technological revolutions, which paralleled one of the most devastating deconstructions of the old political and economic order. The new fact is not that the millennium

begins with the widening of the gap between rich and poor—
that is a given, let's say, part of the system. The new fact is that
the poor no longer have any horizons in life besides the capitalist system, or any horizons for redemption besides religion.
Religion now manages both earthly resignation, in anticipation
of the kingdom of God in heaven, and insurrection in the
name of a kingdom of God on earth. Theology, which I mentioned earlier, is taking its revenge. But, as you said, nothing is
written, and what will happen can only surprise us. I'm not
fond of the technicians of prediction. They work on the past,
yet they see only the past that is comfortable to see. Navigating
by sight is less progressive and impulsive but more sensible,
especially when there are a lot of whirlpools. To me living on
the edge of chaos seems inevitable, it's the fate of those who
feel—and a writer has no choice but to feel it—the precarious
balance of all existences and of all that exists. It's right, and
stimulating, to always keep in mind that while on that
precipice things still function somewhat, elsewhere nothing
functions, and the distant imbalance is the sign of an imminent
collapse.

Lagioia: The end of The Neapolitan Quartet *seems to coincide with the end of a certain idea of Italy. Something that had
been revived in the immediate aftermath of the war is beginning
to seem worn out. I wonder if this is really true, or whether it's
just that Italy often seems to be dangling above some type of
abyss—perhaps because, at times, as in the preceding quotation
from Lenuccia, it does risk anticipating, concisely and nakedly,
discourses that other countries of the world then digest rhetorically in a less immediate and less shocking way. We frequently
find ourselves with no ground under our feet. Basically, if the*
Neapolitan Quartet *had ended in the summer of 1992, after the
death of the two Italian anti-mafia judges Giovanni Falcone and
Paolo Borsellino, there would have been a similar sense of being*

at the end of the line. The same could be said for 1994, or after the earthquake of 1980. Or this time, on the contrary, is our country turning (or has it finished turning) the page forever?

Ferrante: I don't see the end of the line of anything. I don't like either pessimists or optimists; I try only to look around. If the goal is a life that is tolerable, if not happy, there is no end of the line; rather, there's a constant reconsideration of the route, which concerns not only single lives but—as I told you—generations. Neither you nor I—nobody—is restricted only to this "time-now" or even to "recent decades."

Lagioia: We are the country of amoral family-ism. The family is the first social nucleus we experience and, often, also the last. The fact that we have historically been so uninterested in the common good beyond the door of our own home does not, I think, contradict the fact that the family is also a place of extremely violent clashes. For Lila and Elena it's like that, continuously. Blood ties continue to want to be cut and, at the same time, to possess us. We agree that every rite of passage has a price. But is freeing oneself from the family impossible in Italy, even today, without passing through an absolutely useless amount of violence and suffering?

Ferrante: The family is violent in itself, as is everything that is based on blood ties—that is to say, the ties we don't choose, ties that impose on us responsibility for the other even if we never chose to take it on. Feelings are always excessive in the family, both the good and the bad: we exaggeratedly confirm the former and exaggeratedly deny the latter. God the father is excessive. Abel is as excessive as Cain. Bad feelings are especially unbearable when someone related to us provokes them. Cain kills in order to cut the blood tie. He no longer wants to be his brother's keeper. To be the keeper is an intolerable task, a wearying responsibility. Principally, it's hard to accept that bad feelings are provoked not only by the stranger, the rival—

the one who is on the other shore of "our" body of water, who is not on our soil and does not share our blood—but, perhaps with even greater compulsion, by those who are close to us, our mirror, the neighbor we must love, ourselves. Emancipation without trauma is possible only within a nucleus in which the self-referential has been opposed from the start and one has learned to love the other not as oneself—a tricky formula—but, rather, as the only possible way of experiencing the pleasure of being in the world. What corrupts us is the passion for ourselves, the urgent need for our own primacy.

Lagioia: Someone who is truly rooted in life doesn't write novels. The relationship between Elena and Lila seems to me archetypal, from that point of view, in the sense that many friendships and rivalries function according to this dynamic. It is, if you will, the dynamic that binds artists to their muses, although the muses in this particular case are anything but ethereal. On the contrary, they are earthly to their core, committed to confronting life, to clashing with it wholeheartedly. It's Lila who feels the things of the world in a more visceral way. And yet, for that very reason, she cannot bear witness in the way Elena can. Although Elena fears that sooner or later her friend will manage to write a marvelous book, a book capable of objectively restoring the balance between them, that can't happen.

The implacability of such a rule is so recurrent that it makes me uneasy. To feel guilty about something that, if it suddenly had no more reason to exist, would be transformed into a threat. That is one of the paradoxes that seem to bind Elena to Lila. How can one try to undo it, or live with it? To bear witness on behalf of someone who will not do so herself might seem either a generous act or one of enormous arrogance. Or again—and this is the most painful hypothesis—it becomes a weapon to render the people we love harmless, even if it means that we crush them. What relationship do you have with writing from this point of view?

Ferrante: Writing is an act of pride. I've always known that, and so for a long time I hid the fact that I was writing, especially from the people I loved. I was afraid of exposing myself and of others' disapproval. Jane Austen organized herself so that she could immediately hide her pages if someone came into the room where she had taken refuge. It's a reaction I'm familiar with: you're ashamed of your presumptuousness, because there is nothing that can justify it, not even success. However I state it, the fact remains that I have assumed the right to imprison others in what I seem to see, feel, think, imagine, and know. Is it a task? A mission? A vocation? Who called on me, who assigned me that task and that mission? A god? A people? A social class? A party? The culture industry? The lowly, the disinherited, the lost causes? The entire human race? The elusive subject that is women? My mother, my women friends? No—by now everything is simple, and it's blindingly obvious that I alone authorized myself. I assigned myself, for motives that are obscure even to me, the job of describing what I know of my era, that is—in its simplest form—what happened under my nose, that is to say the life, the dreams, the fantasies, the speech of a narrow group of people and events, within a restricted space, in an unimportant language made even less important by the use I make of it. One tends to say: let's not overdo it, it's only a job. It may be that things are like that now. Things change and the verbal vestments in which we wrap them change. But pride remains. I remain, I who spend a large part of my day reading and writing, because I have assigned myself the task of describing. And I cannot soothe myself by saying: it's a job. When did I ever consider writing a job? I've never written to earn a living. I write to bear witness to the fact that I have lived and have sought a means of measuring myself and others, since those others couldn't or didn't know how or didn't want to do it. What is this if not pride? And what does it imply if not, "You don't know how to see me and see yourselves, but I see myself and I see you?" No, there is no way around it. The only possibility is to learn to put the "I" in perspective, to pour it into the work and then go away, to consider writing the thing that separates from us the moment it's complete, one of the many collateral effects of an active life.

NOTE
The interview with Nicola Lagioia (Italy) appeared on April 3, 2016, in *La Repubblica* (Italy), under the title "Perché scrivo. Elena Ferrante sono io" ("Why I Write. Elena Ferrante c'est moi").
Following is the e-mail exchange between Nicola Lagioia, Sandra Ozzola, and Elena Ferrante that accompanied Lagioia's questions.

February 3, 2015

Dear Elena Ferrante,
Thank you for agreeing to this conversation. But first I want to thank you for having written a work as beautiful, potent, and humane as the Neapolitan Quartet. The way this work raises the bar—or puts it back where it ought to be—makes those who do not hold themselves to that standard culpable.
As you'll see, my questions are more like reflections, or the beginning of a conversation. They're my response to the books, and I hope you might consider them starting points for further conversation on the friction between our world and the world you've created. It's been wonderful to be in the company of your voice.
Fondly and with admiration,
Nicola Lagioia

February 27, 2015

Dear Nicola Lagioia,
I don't know how to apologize. I very much appreciated your observations and your questions, I attempted to answer them, but I have to admit that, at least for now, I haven't succeeded. First I had a nasty flu that prevented me from answering, and now there's this

business of the Strega Prize.[11] I feel such a sense of unease and distrust these days that I can no longer write even half a word without fearing that, once published, it might be distorted or purposely taken out of context and used in a malicious way. So I stopped working on the answers; I can't do it with serenity. Instead I'm reading your *Ferocity* with great enthusiasm. I seem to find on every page confirmation of the great, truthful passion for literature that I immediately perceived in your questions and the way you explained them. I will certainly continue with the interview, if only because of the trust you inspire and for the pleasure of talking to you. But not during this especially depressing period. I hope that you're not angry with me— I would be sorry for it.

Elena Ferrante

February 28, 2015

Dear Elena Ferrante,

In Italy there is nothing literary about literary gossip: it's merely wearisome. Among other things, I myself did not know, when I sent you the questions, that Einaudi would nominate me for the Strega, and I suppose you didn't know about your nomination, either. Immediately after learning about our nominations, I thought: maybe our talk could be seen as a liberating moment of fair play between two nominated writers who prefer simply to talk about literature, because that is the only thing that interests them. I also understand, however, that there are those who are ready to seize the slightest opportunity to spread gossip and stupidity. Yet I won't stay away from the reading on March 13th. I will go with great pleasure to read some pages of the Neapolitan Quartet at Libri Come. If at some point in the future you'd like to resume our conversation, I'd be pleased. Gossip passes, good books remain, and it's never too late to talk about them.

Fondly,
Nicola

---

[11] Italy's best known literary prize. Both Ferrante and Lagioia were finalists for the 2015 prize. Lagioia's *Ferocity* won.

September 30, 2015

Dear Nicola, our author asks us to forward you these answers to your wonderful questions/non-questions. It seems to me that a very interesting dialogue emerges. But she asks that for the time being it not be published. Warm wishes from all of us,

Sandra

Dear Nicola,

I had promised you I would try to answer your questions once the tension of the Strega was over. Now I have done so, but I ask you not to publish anything, for the moment. Some of the answers are disproportionately long, on some points they're confused, and I'm afraid that here and there I've been rash. I'm sending you the text anyway, but only because every promise is a debt and because I have great respect for you.

I was happy to proceed by themes, as you suggested. But I tried, within the limits of the possible, to keep the discussion away from the Neapolitan Quartet. Like all books—whether good or bad—the Neapolitan Quartet is an elastic organism, and for readers it should remain so: open to every impression. I often quote with pleasure the page that Barthes, commenting on Balzac's *Sarrasine*, dedicated to the role of the S and the Z. Whether it's a solid critical piece or highly fanciful nonsense, that page is an extraordinary demonstration that a text is full of possibilities and that not just the sentence, not just the name, but even the individual letters of a story exist precisely to ignite the mind of the reader. To ruin its flexibility by providing, as the author, the "right interpretation," is therefore a mortal sin. Every time I do it, I regret it. And yet surely, even in this case, I've done it here and there. Maybe we should always assume that what the author imagines he has written is no more or less valid than what the reader imagines he has read. By this I don't mean that your observations are off base; I'm only trying to separate my book from my thoughts about it, and from what I wrote in this specific case.

Elena

October 1, 2015

Dear Sandra,

Please thank Elena Ferrante for me. Many of the answers seem to me not only good but important, because they take on the theme of literary writing (the approach to the page on the part of a writer) in a manner that's hard to find in the cultural debate, especially in Italy.

As for possible future publication: let's do what seems best to Elena Ferrante. If she wants to adjust, polish, clarify the argument, that's fine, of course. For me literary needs always take precedence over journalistic ones.

Fondly,
Nicola

ABOUT THE AUTHOR

Elena Ferrante is the author of *The Days of Abandonment* (Europa, 2005), *Troubling Love* (Europa, 2006), *The Lost Daughter* (Europa, 2008) and the Neapolitan Quartet (Europa, 2012-2015). She is also the author of a children's picture book illustrated by Mara Cerri, *The Beach at Night*.

FOR THE FUTURE OF ISRAEL

Shimon Peres and
Robert Littell

FOR THE FUTURE
OF ISRAEL

THE JOHNS HOPKINS UNIVERSITY PRESS
BALTIMORE AND LONDON

Published 1998. Originally published by Editions Denoël, Paris, 1997

Printed in the United States of America on acid-free paper

9 8 7 6 5 4 3 2 1

The Johns Hopkins University Press
2715 North Charles Street
Baltimore, Maryland 21218-4363
The Johns Hopkins Press Ltd., London

Illustrations courtesy of the Government Press Office, State of Israel.

Library of Congress Cataloging-in-Publication Data will be found
at the end of the book.

A catalog record for this book is available from the British Library.

ISBN 0-8018-5928-X

TO DANIEL ABRAHAM, a man who dreams peace
and practices wonderful friendship

*A Greek sage asked, What is the difference
between war and peace? He answered,
In wartime, parents bury their children,
in peacetime, children bury their parents.*

SHIMON PERES

Contents

Preface

I left my journalism (I was one of a handful of foreign affairs writers for *Newsweek* magazine) behind me several decades ago and have been engaged ever since in the eternal struggle with what Anthony Burgess precisely described as the "intractable enemy language," which is a fancy way of identifying myself as someone who makes his living as a novelist. When Cynthia Liebow, my editor at Denoël, the French publisher of my novels, asked me in the summer of 1996 if I would be interested in interviewing Shimon Peres as part of the Denoël series "Conversations with . . . ," I hesitated. I was about to start a new novel and feared that if I orphaned it, even for a few months, it might sulk and head for the hills. But the chance to have protracted talks with a world-class statesman and Nobel Prize winner such as Shimon Peres, someone I had admired from a distance, was something I couldn't walk away from. Which is how I came to make the delicious journey back into what looks like journalism — but journalism filtered through a fiction writer's anastigmatic lens.

Let me explain. The journalist is necessarily a prisoner of events; he concentrates, first and foremost, on what happened.

As a result, he generally manages to bring the event itself into focus while the characters involved often remain slightly blurred and just beyond the reader's finger tips. A novelist has other fish to fry. What intrigues him — what mesmerizes him — is character; or more exactly, the character of character. For me, the object of these conversations was to draw a pointillist's portrait of a man who happened to have been at the heart of one of the most astonishing political and human events of the twentieth century: the return of the Jewish people to their ancestral land and the creation, against all odds, of a Jewish state. I wanted to get under Shimon Peres's skin; I wanted to see the world through his eyes; I wanted to inch closer to the character of character.

I suspect that Mr. Peres sensed the direction from which I would come at him; why else would he have agreed to be interviewed by a writer of fiction rather than one of the many professional journalists with distinguished Middle East credentials? In any case, he had to know where I was heading when I started my first question with: "One of my literary heroes is F. Scott Fitzgerald."

I met with Shimon Peres during the last week of 1996 in the Tel Aviv office that the Israeli government makes available to former prime ministers. My first impression was of someone incredibly fit and energetic for seventy-three. After I'd seen him in action for a few mornings — his already crammed schedule included almost daily automobile expeditions to Jerusalem, a two-hour round trip from Tel Aviv, to attend Knesset sessions or meet with political friends or foes — I asked one of his staff, a woman considerably younger than Mr. Peres, how his associates managed to keep up with him. "We don't," she told me with a grin. She was clearly proud of her boss.

Mr. Peres is at his desk by 7:15 in the morning every day except the Sabbath. The day I first met him was the exception to the rule; he didn't get in until 7:30 because his ever-present bodyguards, intent young men with tiny Dick Tracy–like phones jammed into their cars and pistols on their belts, had spotted a suspicious automobile parked outside his apartment and wouldn't let him leave until they had checked it for explosives. I'd been warned that Mr. Peres is reserved and formal, both in dress and manner, with people he doesn't know. It turned out to be an understatement. There was no small talk. We shook hands and settled catty-corner to each other onto two couches. He asked his secretary to bring tea in a glass, Russian style, for him and a cup of coffee, black, for me. He wrapped his thick fingers around the glass as if to warm them while I wrapped my questions around him, hoping he would warm to the conversation. "Can you take me into the *shtetl* you knew?" He nodded imperceptibly; he could and did.

The interviews went on for five mornings, two hours each morning. (I interviewed Mr. Peres again in Paris in September 1997 in order to update the American edition of the book.) By the second morning, Mr. Peres was beginning to let his guard down; the radiant smile that is capable of illuminating what are essentially melancholy eyes flashed more often and his laughter punctuated his responses. By the third interview I could sense he was beginning to enjoy himself. He arrived that morning with his tie tucked under his shirt collar but unknotted, sank onto the couch in a comfortable sprawl—and the stories, recounted in a deep, soft, melodious voice, started to flow.

Shimon Peres is endowed with a prodigious memory. He has the ability to make scenes he witnessed sixty-five years ago come alive with details that make a novelist's mouth water. His responses—often lengthy, always subtle—came instantly on the heels of my questions, leaving me with the feeling that he was more philosopher than politician; that he had systematically thought through a vast number of matters over the course of a lifetime of introspection. He stuck stubbornly by people he considered friends — the late French President François Mitterrand comes immediately to mind — and declined on more than one occasion to fault people who were dead. When I met with Mr. Peres, he was still the leader of the Labor Party and attempting, without success as things turned out, to prod the Likud prime minister, Benjamin Netanyahu, into forming a national unity government, with Peres as one of its ministers. In or out of political office, Shimon Peres was clearly comfortable with power but, as far as I could tell, he exercised it without a trace of arrogance.

I can write here what I could never bring myself to say to Shimon Peres in person for fear of jeopardizing the detachment that is essential for interviews of this kind: I came away from these conversations with a conspectus of an extraordinary personal biography as well as fifty years of passionate Israeli and Jewish history. Beyond that, the conversations offered me insights into how a fundamentally pragmatic and often poetic visionary comes to grips with a broad range of immensely complex issues, which is another way of saying I caught a glimpse of the character of character. In short, while I learned a great deal from Mr. Peres, I also learned a great deal about him, for which I am very grateful.

ROBERT LITTELL

Life has two stories,
the physical one
and the dream one.

FIRST CONVERSATION

ROBERT LITTELL. One of my literary heroes is F. Scott Fitzgerald. Somewhere along the way he said that the best way to comment on large things is to comment on small things. So with your permission, Mr. Peres, I'd like to start at the start and talk about small things. You were born on August 21, 1923, in the *shtetl* town of Vishniva, in the heart of what is now Belarus, White Russia. To put it into time: 1923 was the year Transjordania, as it was then called, became an autonomous state, the year of Hitler's Munich "Beer Hall" putsch, the year Mussolini came to power. Your family name was Persky. You left for Palestine at the age of 11, so the image of Vishniva must be engraved in your memory. All of my life I've heard tales of the *shtetl;* for me it is a mythic, mysterious, romantic, and occasionally brutal place. Can you take me into the *shtetl* you knew?

SHIMON PERES. You know, a famous Jewish philosopher by the name of Yankelewitz said once that Jewish life in the Diaspora was similar to a voyage in a subway—you travel underground, you don't see the scenery, and nobody sees you in the train. It's only now, in modern times, that Jewish life is being conducted as if it were a voyage in a bus; you can see from within the outside scenery, and you can see from the outside that people are sitting in the bus. A *shtetl* in many ways was the subway of Jewish life; it was totally disconnected from the outside world. Let's have a good look at it—I mean, in a way, it was a dream and in a way it was a pleasure. It was a pleasure because it was disconnected from the rest of life. It wasn't a normal place to live. And a dream because we weren't living there mentally. Our hearts were in Israel. The *shtetl* was like a passing station. Vishniva wasn't a very large place—twelve hundred people, something like that. I think it possessed maybe one street, one and a half streets. It had wooden buildings, it didn't have electricity, it had two synagogues, it had a [Zionist] school which was called Tarbut. *Tarbut* in Hebrew means "culture." And at school we were taught Hebrew and Yiddish. There was already a generation gap—the generation of the more orthodox Jewish life, the more religious, and the more modern Jewish part of it. I saw it in my own family. My grandfather, who had a great impact on my life—the father of my mother—

R.L. The Reb Meltzer?

S.P. Yes. He was a product of the greatest yeshiva in Jewish life, which was near Vishniva. It's called Volozhin. He studied together with our national poet, Chaim Nahman Bialik,[1] in the same yeshiva. And my grandfather was very religious, very strict. He was the leader of the community. He had a beautiful voice— on Yom Kippur evening he would conduct the prayers. He made a living by making boots from wool, not from leather. There was a small place where they produced them and he used to work. My father, on the other hand, was already second generation, by which I mean a totally modern Jew. He didn't respect Saturday, he wasn't as religious. I was so much influenced by my grand-

1. 1873-1934: Ukrainian-Jewish poet and novelist who wrote mainly in Hebrew.

father that when my father bought the first radio in town, which worked on batteries—we didn't have electricity—and he tried to play it on Saturday, I broke it, I destroyed it.

R.L. Did he punish you? Was he furious with you?

S.P. No, I was never punished by my parents. I was always forgiven. I think they thought that they had a nice boy, so to speak. And they respected all my wishes, all my inclinations. So I was never punished in my life.

R.L. You studied Torah at the feet of your grandfather. For a moment I'd like you to put on the Talmudic hat you wore as a child in the *shtetl*. In Genesis we read that God created the earth and the seas and the grass and seed and the sun and the moon and fish and fowl and cattle, and after each creation he "saw that it was good." On the sixth day he created male and female in his image, but, intriguingly, he did not specifically say that this creation was good. Was God harboring second thoughts about having created man and woman?

S.P. I don't think so. I think this eternal contradiction is needed in order to maintain a continuation of human kind. Think what would happen if God had given reproduction to just one party, say man or woman. They might have become tired or self-satisfied, and they might have stopped reproducing. This ongoing tension is one of the incentives for reproduction; we spend our lives with men chasing women and women chasing men. In Hebrew, woman is *isha,* and man is *ish.* The spelling is very interesting. *Ish* is spelled with an *alef, yod,* and *shin:* איש. When it comes to *isha* you don't have the *yod,* but you have a *he—alef, shin,* and *he:* אשה. The combination of the *yod* from *ish* and the *he* from *isha* makes *yod he*—יה—or *ya,* which is the first syllable of the sacred name of God. So when the two come together, you have a heavenly meeting.

R.L. On the first six days God created the universe with what appears to be an effortlessness. Yet on the seventh day he rested. Why did God rest on the seventh day, Mr. Peres?

S.P. He said that he had accomplished enough—accomplished without having completed. He left something for us to do. Flaubert once said there is a division of labor between God and man: God is responsible for the beginning and the end and we are responsible for the in between. So God gave us a beginning, he gave us an end, and the end is in his hands. And in the meantime he told us to struggle and work hard, and he gave us a day off so that we can rest a bit and pray to the Lord. Saturdays are not only a day of rest but also a day of prayer. At that time people weren't working six or seven hours a day, they were working from sunrise to sundown, and the work was physical and extremely tiring. Computers didn't exist, robots didn't exist. So God saw man with his shortcomings and thought maybe he had to give him a chance to rest every now and then.

R.L. To get back to the *shtetl*—

S.P. We already had there all the parties which exist today in Israel. In this small *shtetl* we had the Likud, which was at that time called Betar;[2] Ha-shomer Ha-tza'ir,[3] which today is Meretz, the most extreme. We had the beginning of Labor and all the parties—

R.L. The schisms were already there?

S.P. Yes. I had it in my family, because my uncle was the head of the Betar, and my aunt was the head of the Ha-shomer Ha-

2. An acronym for Brit (which means "alliance") Trumpeldor, Betar was the right-wing Zionist youth movement of Vladimir Jabotinsky's Revisionist Party, which was the grandfather of today's Likud; Betar also refers to the town south of Jerusalem where Bar Kochba made his last stand against the Romans.

3. "The Young Guard," the youth movement and kibbutz movement of Mapam, the left-wing labor party that was one of the co-founders of Meretz.

tza'ir. So we were living very vividly. The greatest day was when books or oranges arrived from Israel and we used to smell the papers that covered the oranges. When somebody left for Israel we all went to the railroad station and there we witnessed the great departure. It was a great occasion — people were crying and embracing . . .

R.L. So your body was in Vishniva, but your head was somewhere else?

S.P. Exactly. And my uncle, too, was a man who impressed me very much, but he had cancer — he would lie in the garden under a trellis and I would come and spend a lot of time with him. So as you can see my world wasn't a real one. I mean, I had very little to do with the geography of the surroundings, which were not necessarily Jewish and had little to do with Jewish life. The landscape was gentile. And my heart was in Israel. All this [Vishniva] was a passing occasion. The language we spoke was Hebrew and Yiddish and at home a little bit of Russian —

R.L. Was there a kind of civil war in your home, on your street, in Vishniva, between those who spoke Hebrew and those who spoke Yiddish? What I'm getting at is that Yiddish speakers tended to assume that the Jews would remain in the Diaspora, while Hebrew speakers looked to Palestine.

S.P. The divisions were along generational lines rather than according to [political] camps. We used to say: why do the Jewish people use two languages, Hebrew and Yiddish? Hebrew was called *leshon ha-kodesh*, the holy language, and Yiddish was the daily language. So we would say that in one language the Jews would praise the Lord, in the other we would argue with him. And we have had to argue with the Lord on many occasions. Because sometimes we felt, like Professor [Yeshayahu] Liebowitz, that while the poor are on the side of the Lord, the Lord is on the side of the rich. The *shtetl* wasn't a world of contradictions, it was a world of wonders. You know, everybody wandered around, nobody felt himself fixed enough. And this very small area, strangely enough, produced some important people. The head of the Jewish Agency, Nahum Goldmann, was born and raised there. A famous author called Buki Ben Yogli was born there. A famous rabbi, Meir Berlin,[4] and the minister of finances, Yehoshua Rabinovich. So you can see how deeply engaged *shtetl* Jews used to be. Clearly, there was a tension between the Betar and the Ha-shomer Ha-tza'ir, but you know, both of them looked more like boy scouts than true political parties. In our *shtetl* Communism was considered a crime in the hearts of the people. It was like an assimilation. If somebody were to become a Communist—

R.L. It implied that he was planning to stay there and work to improve the lot of the Jews in Russia, as opposed to emigrating to Palestine to create a Jewish state.

S.P. Yes. Exactly.

R.L. A survivor of the Holocaust named Pinhas Epstein once wrote: "Whoever was in Treblinka will never get out of it, and whoever was not in Treblinka will not get into Treblinka." I suspect this is true for all deep experiences. With that in mind, let me ask you this: has Shimon Peres—the world statesman, the Nobel laureate, the intimate of presidents and prime ministers— been able to get completely out of the *shtetl*, or is there a corner of a lobe of your brain still back there studying Torah at the Vishniva Yeshiva?

S.P. Yes, yes, there is something like that. You know, this world of wonders never left me. To look for something which

4. Who Hebraicized his name to Bar Ilan before his death.

was outside myself, outside my immediate surroundings, living at the place and living somewhere else at the same time—that probably resides with me to this very day. And then the idea that life has two stories, the physical one and the dream one, the one that you physically live in and the other that you are mentally engaged in, this probably remains with me. Nor can my attitude toward religious Jews escape the early experience. I mean, when I see a rabbi with a beard, it clearly reminds me of my grandfather. When I negotiated with the rabbis in Israel about my exemption from military service—with the twelve rabbis all around me—really, the image was of my grandfather.

R.L. If Hitler hadn't had other plans for them, would the Jews still be there in the *shtetl,* looking like relics of another century?

S.P. I think so, at least many of them. You see, half emigrated to Israel and half remained there.

R.L. I've always been awed by our ability to mimic in our skulls the pitch of voice and patterns of speech of family, of friends. I myself can summon the voice of my father, who is long dead. Which voices from Vishniva can you hear in your head? And what do you hear them saying?

S.P. The greatest prayer in Jewish life is on Yom Kippur, which is Kol Nidre, and my grandfather used to sing it. I can still hear the song, the melody and the terrible tension—you know, on that occasion I felt as if I was leaving reality and going to heaven, watching Satan and watching the angels and with all my strength asking the Lord to forgive us our sins, and not forgiving myself the sins I'd committed which I was aware of. It was like taking off from reality to a heavenly place, full of dangers, full of awe, full of excuses, full of pardons. Then I think my mother inherited the voice of my grandfather. She used to sing Russian songs and Yiddish songs and Hebrew songs, which I still can remember.

R.L. Was it from Reb Meltzer that you came to think of high foreheads—which you yourself have—as a gift of God and a sign of wisdom?

S.P. That was the talk of the family. We would judge a person by the size of his forehead.

R.L. Do you still notice a person's forehead when you are introduced to someone?

S.P. No. I've changed my mind about high foreheads.

R.L. What percent of Vishniva's population was Jewish?

S.P. All of them were Jewish. No one was not Jewish. We saw the gentiles who came to buy and sell on the market day, which was a Wednesday or a Thursday.

R.L. You lived in a ghetto, then?

S.P. I lived in a subway. We saw the river or the trees, but we hardly saw gentiles.

R.L. What is it about Jews that—since the Venetians, in 1516, created the first ghetto in the section of Venice where there was a foundry, which is *ghetto* in Italian—the world has felt more comfortable caging them in ghettos?

S.P. The world hated the Jews.

R.L. The world hated many people over the centuries, but only the Jews have been crammed into ghettos.

S.P. Yes. The basic idea, I think, is that the Jews were different, strangers. I mean, the message that the Jews carried was ahead of its time—against slavery, against cruelties, against wooden gods. And the Jews, too, were like a fire. They were not compromising. Very little. A Jew could assimilate, but not compromise. The minute he compromised he would stop being considered Jewish. And the Jews were always in a minority and swimming against the stream and talking nonsense in the eyes of gentiles. You see, the Jews from earliest times preferred ethics to esthetics, and that looked like a betrayal of human taste, of human normalcy. All the different codes and commandments, all the moral judgment—we were too much of a challenge. I think the French encyclopedia described the Jews as the people who didn't let the world fall asleep. It's true, but the Jews, too, were unable to fall asleep. I mean it was a sleepless tribe . . .

R.L. You have spoken of your abiding passion for the Hebrew language. You surely remember that Eliezer Ben-Yehuda, the father of the Hebrew revival, was shunned—I'm using the word in its Amish sense—by the ultra-Orthodox Jews, who thought that Hebrew should not be used except when studying Torah or praying to God. Was this quarrel between Ben-Yehuda and the ultra-Orthodox the beginning of the schism between the secular Israelis and the ultra-religious Jews today?

S.P. Yes, I think so. You see, for the religious Jews Hebrew was the language of prayer—you prayed in Hebrew. You didn't speak in Hebrew. It was really considered a holy language that shouldn't be used on a daily basis.

R.L. David Ben-Gurion,[5] at a Histadrut Conference in February 1945, came to the podium after a Yiddish speaker had recounted the story of the Vilna ghetto and raised a storm by remarking that Yiddish was a "foreign and grating" language. Was your attraction to Hebrew matched by your feeling uncomfortable with Yiddish?

S.P. Yes. You must understand something which was very typical and very deep in Ben-Gurion. He never forgave Jewish history for being in exile. The exile was shameful in his eyes. The two thousand years that we were in the Diaspora, separated from the holy land—he thought that not only had we given up our

5. 1886–1973: Born in Poland, he emigrated to Palestine in 1906; an early and ardent Zionist, he founded what is today's Labor Party, steered the country toward independence in 1948, and became Israel's first prime minister.

land, but we'd adopted terrible habits. He thought it spoiled the
Jewish character. Yiddish was the symbol of the Diaspora. So the
struggle was not just against a language, but against everything
that represented the Diaspora and exile. At the beginning they
wanted to make Yiddish the official language of Israel, but Ben-
Gurion jumped and fought like hell. There was an organization
by the name of the Bund.[6] I think that either Trotsky or Lenin, I
don't remember which, said that the Bund's Zionists were afraid
of becoming seasick—but they were not only afraid to cross the
sea, they were afraid to cross the barrier of language.

R.L. When you lived in Vishniva there was a Jew from your
village who was murdered by anti-Semitic thugs in a nearby
woods. After you came to Palestine, a Jew was murdered by
Arabs in the Herzl Forest near Ben-Shemen—his name was
Chaim, and he was the watchman in the Herzl Forest. When you
were fifteen and living in Ben-Shemen, you said you could feel
the hatred emanating from the neighboring Arab villages. Sho-
lom Aleichem has a play called "It's Hard to Be a Jew." Did you
grow up thinking it was hard—even dangerous—to be Jewish?

S.P. There was a vast difference between the two murders.
In Vishniva, when I was smaller, I felt almost totally helpless.
Victimized. The murder was a terrible shock. We were unable
to defend ourselves, neither could we trust the police of the gentiles. We were exposed to this danger. Our defense was being
separated from the rest of the world. In Ben-Shemen it was different. We had rifles, we could defend ourselves. We thought that
the Arabs were violent, but we didn't think that we were helpless.
I myself at that time had already been sworn into the Haganah
and I was on guard with a rifle in my hands every night. So the

6. A European Jewish socialist movement founded in Russia in 1897, not to
be confused with the pro-Nazi German-American organization of the 1930s.

feeling was certainly different. In Vishniva we were shocked, in Ben-Shemen we were outraged, not shocked.

R.L. Early Zionists like the British playwright and novelist Israel Zangwill had a curious slogan: Palestine, they would say, is a land without people, and the Jews are a people without a land.

S.P. Theodor Herzl[7] said that too.

R.L. At the time of World War I and the Balfour Declaration, a British census listed some 700,000 Arabs in Palestine and about 70,000 Jews. Palestine certainly wasn't a land without people. You yourself have said that the "clash with the Arabs" had "not been taken into account in the Zionist blueprint." How do you explain this failure of vision on the part of the early Zionists?

S.P. When Zionism was born they were looking at the Ottoman empire. Who was thinking at all about Arabs? Don't forget that the Arabs did not demand their own independence until the First World War. The national rebirth of the Arabs, too, came very late. So Herzl thought that he had to negotiate not with the Arabs, but with the Ottoman empire. And he tried to. There was an Arab population here and an Arab population there, but there weren't Arab states. There was the very broad concept of the Ottoman empire. So the Arabs were unnoticeable. Nobody counted them. People didn't think about them.

R.L. We're speaking about Zionist leaders who were incredibly visionary—it still represents a failure of vision.

S.P. They were unaware of it, I tell you. They really were unaware of it. Look, the power of Zionism was partly ignorance. You cannot have a dream if you are fully informed. I think that Judge [Felix] Frankfurter[8] remarked about General Eisenhower,

7. 1860–1904: Hungarian Jewish journalist who was the founder of modern Zionism and organizer of the first Zionist World Congress in Basel in 1897.
8. 1882–1965: Associate justice of the U.S. Supreme Court from 1939 to 1962.

there are some gaps in his ignorance. So this was a gap in our
ignorance.

R.L. The Balfour Declaration — we're talking 1917 — recognized the right of Jews to a national home for the Jewish people,
but specified "without prejudicing the rights of non-Jews."
How could a Jewish homeland have been established without
prejudicing the rights of the non-Jews who didn't want the Jews
there to begin with? Was what you have called the clash of the
Jewish national renaissance and the Arab national renaissance
inevitable?

S.P. Let's face it — at that time there were no Arab states. There
was no division. When you look at maps of the Middle East, they
were partly resolved in negotiations between the French and the
British — the Sykes-Picot treaty [1916] — and partly between the
British and the Egyptians. The [border] lines are going straight
as though somebody took a cake and cut it with a knife. So there
wasn't any Arab entity in it at the time. Churchill came up with
the concept of dividing Palestine into two parts, so the idea may
have prevailed that the Arabs would be on one side of the Jordan
River and the Jews would be on the other side. Nobody had too
clear an idea about it. But there wasn't an Arab map. The map
was either Ottoman or, later on, British. After one of his meetings with Stalin, Roosevelt happened to cross Palestine; it took
him ten minutes. At that time they were talking about partition.
So Roosevelt remarked, What do you suggest, five minutes for
the Jews and five minutes for the Arabs?

R.L. I think the world grasps the degree of Arab responsibility for the Arab-Jewish confrontation. But to what degree was
this Zionist mind-set that you're describing responsible for the
vicious circle of violence that has still not been resolved today.
This failure of Zionist vision —

s.p. They were very naive. They thought that they would come and bring a blessing to the Arabs. They didn't imagine any clash with them. They thought that they would bring enlightenment and modern life and education and health, so that it would be a blessing rather than chaos.

R.L. Elie Wiesel[9] has written: "The opposite of love is not hate, it's indifference. The opposite of life is not death, it's indifference." Weren't Zionists indifferent to Palestinians?

s.p. No, they didn't have the slightest idea what Arabs were. They had never seen an Arab in their lives before they came to Palestine. It was like reading science fiction — it was ignorance, not indifference.

R.L. The founder and headmaster of your school at Ben-Shemen, a charismatic *Yekke*[10] named Siegfried Lehmann, argued that Zionists ought to offer far-reaching concessions to the Arabs to achieve a modus vivendi with them. Did Dr. Lehmann convince you?

s.p. No. I was against him. I was already by then a Ben-Gurionist. There was a group which was called Brit Shalom — Alliance for Peace — and it comprised some of the most important people in our life. Martin Buber.[11] Judah Magnes, who was the president of Hebrew University.[12] Albert Einstein. Lehmann was in that group. And we looked upon them as a dangerous group, politically speaking, because they were ready to give up

9. The Nobel Peace Prize laureate and Rumanian-born American writer is a survivor of Auschwitz and Buchenwald; his 1958 autobiographical novel *Night* recounts the horrors he witnessed in the death camps.

10. The more or less affectionate Israeli term for a German-Jewish immigrant.

11. 1878–1965: Austrian-born Judaic philosopher whose 1923 classic *I and Thou* posits a direct personal dialogue between the individual and God.

12. From its founding in 1925 until his death in 1948.

Jewish sovereignty. They thought that we could live under the Arabs, or at least that we could live in a bilateral state.

R.L. You must have had some heated arguments.

S.P. I had a terrible argument with Martin Buber himself. And I attacked him like a young man who doesn't have God in his heart. I was close to twenty by then. Buber said that after the war not many Jewish people would remain alive and that we don't have a future, and I said that this was nonsense. That was the second time I had an argument with Martin Buber. The first time was when I edited the paper at Ben-Shemen, and I attacked the way they were teaching the Bible, and Lehmann was so shocked that he invited Martin Buber to teach us a lesson about it, and again I took a very extreme position and had a terrible argument with Buber. This whole group of intellectuals was against Ben-Gurion, against statehood, against Jewish sovereignty. They thought the main challenge was to make peace with the Arabs, with the Palestinians. Lehmann was already in that group and I belonged to another group.

R.L. The Balfour Declaration of 1917 recognized the right of the Jews to a national homeland, but in 1922 the British issued a "White Paper" backing away from that promise. The Passfield White Paper of 1930 recommended a halt to Jewish immigration to Palestine. Another White Paper circulated in 1939 repudiated the Balfour Declaration outright, envisioning the creation of a state that would be predominantly Arab with Jewish immigration restricted. In 1947 the British finally dumped the problem into the lap of the United Nations, which then partitioned Palestine into a Jewish and an Arab state. Do you think that the post–Balfour British betrayed the Jews?

S.P. Well, as a famous Englishman once said, Great Britain never had friends, only interests, and the various White Papers reflect the different interests in the foreign policy of Britain. I mean, one shouldn't look with a romantic eye upon this sort of commitment. Times change. People can change as well. And I think that at the beginning the British weren't aware of a possible Arab reaction. For them, the Arabs became more important and crucial as time went on.

R.L. If the British had lived up to even a part of their Balfour commitment, hundreds of thousands of Jews might have escaped the Holocaust because they would have had a place to go. Do you feel any bitterness toward the British?

S.P. I feel bitterness, yes, but I feel more bitterness about ourselves. I think the Jewish people should have replied to the call of Herzl in greater numbers. You know, between 1882, when the great immigration from Russia and Eastern Europe started, until 1914 and the First World War, almost three million Jewish people left Eastern Europe. Of that, I think only 50,000 came to Palestine. If 200,000 had come instead of 50,000, the whole future would have been different. Declarations are declarations, and you can be bitter about them. But deeds are deeds. I am among the Jews who, before looking to put the blame on somebody else, continually ask, How much should we blame ourselves? There is a tendency among many nations to always put the blame upon others. In our concept, it is for us to know ourselves. Otherwise we shall be lost.

R.L. At the time of the 1948 War for Independence, one of the attacking armies, the Arab Legion of Jordan, was trained and led by British officers. The British joined the Americans in imposing an arms embargo on the new Jewish state. I've heard many stories of British officers handing strategic Taggart forts over to Arab army units as the British pulled out of Palestine; the fortress at Latrun is an example. Were the British at heart pro-Arab and anti-Jewish?

S.P. Most of them were pro-Arab, and not only in '48. You know, the Arabs appealed to a certain romantic streak in British character.

R.L. Lawrence of Arabia.

S.P. Lawrence, yes. The tents. The desert. The hospitality. The submission. Jews are tough and not very hospitable. They're a stubborn people. So I think many British felt easier with the Arabs than with us.

R.L. Was there any justification, in your opinion, for the Stern Gang's murder of Lord Moyne, the British minister of state in Cairo, in 1944?

S.P. It was a terrible mistake. A terrible mistake. It didn't solve anything. It was the nature of our movement not to kill innocent people. I think it was an *escapado* [escape] in the wrong direction. And finally what did it accomplish? It produced some headlines and some tears among the members of his family. It was a mistake.

R.L. Is the British Foreign Office in particular, and Britain in general, pro-Arab and anti-Israel today?

S.P. I'll tell you, Britain has lost a great deal of its importance. Dean Acheson[13] once said about Great Britain that they lost their empire and didn't find a role. So they are less important. There were times—under [Douglas] Hurd, under [Margaret] Thatcher, for example—that they have shown sympathy toward Israel. Under [Harold] Wilson, too. The same can be said about [James] Callaghan. Strangely enough, the person who opposed Israel more than anybody else was [Ernest] Bevin.

R.L. The British Labour Party was very pro-Israel until it came to power in 1945, at which point Foreign Secretary Bevin turned hostile to Zionism. How do you explain this about-face?

S.P. Bevin was a trade unionist who all of a sudden became

13. 1893–1971: American secretary of state from 1949 to 1953 under President Truman.

a representative of a national force, so he forgot where he came from. De Gaulle once said, how can you run France when the left is against the state and the right is against the people? So Bevin went over from being with the people to being with the state, and since he was a man of absolute convictions and powerful in the Attlee government, he went out of his way to demonstrate the patriotism of the Labour Party at the time.

R.L. At one point the British offered the early Zionists a Jewish homeland in Uganda, but they turned it down. The handful of Jews who survived the Holocaust might well have gone to live in a Jewish state no matter where it was. The same holds true for the Jews who flee the former Soviet Union today. Do you think a Jewish state could have worked in Uganda?

S.P. No. One must go back to the Jewish faith. Ben-Gurion claimed, and I agree with him, that Judaism is not a religion, a faith, the difference being that religion is an organization, it's a hierarchy, you have the Lord, you have a vicar, you have a whole structure, whereas between the Jew and the Lord there is no intermediary that we recognize at all. Judaism is comprehensive and integrated. It has a set of recognizable commitments, which is to believe in the existence of one Lord, who is invisible; to believe in a certain language, which is Hebrew; to be devoted to a certain land, which is Israel. There is no distinction between nationhood, religious statehood or geographic commitment, language, history—it all is a universal commitment—

R.L. It's one package.

S.P. One package. You cannot be completely Jewish without speaking Hebrew—that was our concept at the time; you cannot be fully Jewish without believing in one Lord in heaven; you cannot be Jewish if you don't live in the state of the Jewish people, where Judaism was born. This concept gave an air of holiness to the land, particularly to Jerusalem and other places. So it wasn't just to have a shelter, but to have a coming-back to a home. They tried to have a Jewish state in Russia, a Godless Jewish state —

R.L. One of Stalin's dumber ideas.

S.P. Yes. It was a total failure.

R.L. One could say that Stalin was a total failure.

S.P. André Malraux said something very penetrating about Stalin. He said that he knew everything but innocence.

R.L. In 1934 you emigrated to Palestine. Again, to put it into time: 1934 was the year Von Hindenburg died and Adolf Hitler won 88 percent of the plebiscite to become president of Germany; Sergei Kirov was assassinated in Leningrad, marking the start of the ruthless Stalinist purges of the 1930s; in America, Shirley Temple made her first full-length film; in China, Mao Tse-tung began his "Long March" of 6,000 miles to Yenan; in Germany, a book entitled *Power and Earth* by a German geographer named Karl Haushofer argued that Hitler's Reich had a natural right to all of Eurasia; and Heinrich Himmler, age thirty-three, was appointed head of the German concentration camps. You were only eleven years old at the time, but do you remember being aware of any of these events?

S.P. Some of them, yes. Shirley Temple, for example! You know, in Palestine we were under the spell of the assassination of Chaim Arlosoroff, of the Jewish agency.[14] He was on the beach at Tel Aviv with his wife and somebody came along and shot and killed him.

R.L. A Jew killed a Jew?

S.P. Some said a Jew, some said an Arab. The Labor movement claimed it was the Revisionists, that he was killed by a man

---

14. A prominent Zionist Labor leader in Palestine, he was assassinated in 1934 at the age of 33.

named Abraham Stavsky.[15] There was a great split in our lives because of this. There were accusations that the assassination was masterminded and executed by what is today the Likud. To this very day nobody knows who killed him. For me, the thing that dominated that year was an urge to come to Palestine. It changed my whole life.

R.L. Did you feel the dark cloud of the Nazis on the horizon?

S.P. Not yet. Later on. I think the first time I felt it was in '35, '36, when the refugees from Germany began to arrive.

R.L. I once heard Levi Eshkol[16] describe how he walked from Russia to Palestine. How did you get to Palestine?

S.P. We went by a carriage drawn by horses to the railroad station. The whole *shtetl* was assembled, all of our relatives, everybody crying, everybody waving, and we took a train from Vishniva to Constantinople. And there were my mother and my brother and myself, the three of us, and from Constantinople we embarked on a small steamship called the *Kosciuszko* — it was named after the Polish general who was considered one of the liberators of Poland — and on this ship we came to Jaffa. Jaffa was the most unbelievable scene I had ever seen in my life. Tremendous noise and activity — we saw the Arabs with red tarbushes on their heads for the first time.

R.L. Here you were, a Zionist coming to Palestine for the first time, and you set foot in the Jewish homeland and saw Arabs in an Arab city. What impression did this make on you?

S.P. We knew Jaffa was an Arab city. We knew there were Arabs in it. We knew that they could be very dangerous or very servile. But they were considered by us neither a nation nor a people. They were so-called Arabs. I was surprised by the

15. Stavsky was acquitted of the crime by a British court.

16. 1895–1969: Prime minister from 1963 to 1969.

way they looked, the way they behaved—it was exotic, men-acing, charming, like coming to an entirely different world. It was something like landing on the moon, if the moon had had people.

R.L. I have always been fascinated by the story of the Hebrew revival, led by Eliezer Ben-Yehuda at the turn of the century. The Irish tried to revive Gaelic at roughly the same time. But the great Irish writers of this century—Joyce, Beckett, Yeats, Shaw, O'Casey—wrote in English. Why did the Jews succeed in reviving Hebrew, in making it the language of its literature and its marketplaces, where the Irish failed?

S.P. One of the reasons was that for us to return to the home-land was the same thing as returning to the language. The return to the homeland and the return to the language were on an equal footing. I mean, we couldn't imagine that we could return to the land without returning to the language. A holy land and a holy language. Second, Hebrew was the language of our prayers. And third, the revival of Jewish life was done in Hebrew. The Tarbut chain of schools were teaching in Hebrew, like the one in my own *shtetl*. Also, the first great authors and poets of Jewish life had already started to write in Hebrew—Bialik and others.

R.L. Irish writers at the turn of the century attempted to write in Gaelic—

S.P. And then we had the character of Ben-Gurion. He wouldn't hear of anything but Hebrew as a national language.

R.L. Curiously, I never came across a description of your bar mitzvah in your books.

S.P. I had a bar mitzvah, of course, but I never had a bar mitz-vah celebration. At that time I was already totally secular and totally shy. I didn't want to have a party. And my parents didn't insist.

R.L. In Palestine, you joined the socialist youth movement and wound up at the agricultural school at Ben-Shemen. It was about then that you decided to change your name. Your first choice was not Peres, which means eagle, it was Ben-Amotz, a reference to the prophet Isaiah, who was the son of Amotz. Why did you decide on Peres? Why didn't you stick with Ben-Amotz?

S.P. The reason I abandoned Ben-Amotz was very strange. There was a teacher at Ben-Shemen who spoke [Hebrew] in rhymes all the time. He'd say something like, a table without olives is like a cemetery without dead people. All the time. We had a literary trial in the school; he was the defense attorney and I was the prosecutor, and he was so mad at me that he started to make rhymes on my name, and he said, Ben-Amotz that fell in the mud and a thorn was put in his nose . . . There was more, so I decided it was a dangerous name and I gave it up.

And then we went by foot from one part of the country to the other. We were fourteen boys. We went from the Mediterranean to Aqaba and Eilat. It took us sixteen days. It was a mixed group of the youth movement and the Palmach — the Palmach was the [elite] armed force of the Haganah. We had among us a zoologist, because we wanted to learn a little bit about plant life in the desert. And then we saw on a tree a nest of eagles. When I started to climb the tree the eagle took off. "Here is a *peres*," the zoologist said, using the modern Hebrew ornithological term for eagle that comes from Leviticus. And then he said, "You have to change your name to Peres." That's where I got my new name.

R.L. The socialist group to which you belonged founded Kibbutz Alumot in Poriya, above the Sea of Galilee. From there you joined the headquarters of the largest Jewish underground organization, the Haganah — that was 1947 — and you became head of personnel. The Haganah became the nucleus of the Israeli army upon independence. In those early days, did you take an active anti-British role?

s.p. Yes. I participated in demonstrations against the British presence. I was sworn into the Haganah when I was in Ben-Shemen, when I was fifteen years old. We had a cache of arms in Ben-Shemen, and the British came to search. They arrested the head of Ben-Shemen, Lehmann, and many teachers. And we were sitting on the floor to cover the cache of arms. We made believe we were having a lesson, and the cache we were sitting on wasn't discovered. But they discovered arms in other places. And the entire management and faculty of Ben-Shemen were arrested and put on trial. I participated in many demonstrations in Tel-Aviv against the British which had elements of violence—shooting in the air, these sorts of things.

r.l. At the start of World War II, there were some Jews in Palestine known as the "activists"—those who thought that Jews should take advantage of the British predicament and attack them, or at least not help them. And there were those, like the Irgun leadership, who argued that the main enemy was fascism, that the Jews should join in the fight against Hitler and deal with the British after the war. Which side were you on?

s.p. I was among the activists. But the definition of the activists was made by Ben-Gurion. He said, "Let's *oppose* the British as though we're not fighting the Germans, and let's *fight* the Germans as though we are not opposing the British."

r.l. I'd like to broach an agonizing subject: the Holocaust. President Roosevelt managed to give a so-called fireside radio chat every week of the war until his death without ever mentioning the word "Jew." On June 30, 1942, the *New York Times,* a Jewish-owned newspaper, ran a six-paragraph story under the headline "1,000,000 Jews Slain by Nazis, Report Says" on page seven—a fact that the *Times* itself bitterly regrets. For me, the American attitude toward the Holocaust was best summed up by Assistant Secretary of War John McCloy, who advised against sending bombers to destroy Auschwitz on the grounds that the bombing "might provoke even more vindictive action by the Germans." The painful truth is that some Jews who managed to escape to American shores were sent back to die in Hitler's death camps. American immigration quotas were not opened so that those who might have made it out of the inferno would have had a place to go. How do you account for the failure of the Americans and the British to pay public attention to the Holocaust? How do you account for their failure to save as many Jews as possible by opening immigration quotas for those who could have escaped?

s.p. In one word, I think it's unforgivable. But I don't have an explanation. There are many things I cannot explain. For example, the failure [of the United States in 1948] to support the Jewish state of Israel in her self-defense. They didn't give us rifles to defend our lives. There was a double standard about the Jewish people throughout history until the creation of the State of Israel. Only with the creation of the state did anti-Semitism become a non-Jewish malady. Until then it was a malady shared by both Jews and non-Jews. But I don't have an explanation. There are two or three possibilities. First, I'm not sure that all of us grasped the size of the tragedy that the Jewish people were going through, both because the information wasn't readily available [at first], and then because our minds could hardly grasp it when the information did become available. And then I can say: there was a threat [in Palestine] to our whole existence. And it wasn't as though England was sure and safe, and France was sure and safe, and the Middle East was sure and safe. There was a heavy cloud hanging over our existence all the time. We were not free to disregard our own need of self-defense. I mean, the early years of the Second World War were terrible. It looked as if we were going to lose it, as if Hitler was going to win everything. But otherwise I cannot explain it [the American attitude].

R.L. You're not willing to entertain the idea that Roosevelt and the American establishment were guilty of latent anti-Semitism? What I'm driving at is that there are historians who suggest that the lack of reaction on the part of the Allies to the Holocaust convinced Hitler that he was doing the world's dirty work for it. Roosevelt didn't raise his voice, the pope didn't raise his voice —

S.P. Maybe. Maybe. Yes. It was strange, it was paradoxical. On the one hand they accused the Jewish people of running the world. On the other hand the world didn't give a damn about the Jewish people. It's a bitter contradiction. But both attitudes existed.

R.L. To me it's painful but logical that the American Jewish leaders — living in the Diaspora, with all the insecurities that that implies — didn't scream from the rooftops. But why didn't the Jewish leaders in Palestine scream from the rooftops?

S.P. The information reached us quite late. There is now a book being published on the subject that shows that Ben-Gurion tried very hard to raise the issue — unsuccessfully.

R.L. How? With whom? Where?

S.P. Publicly. By making statements, announcements. By sending paratroopers. The British were willing to cooperate with us to see what was happening to Jewish life abroad by sending a group of [Jewish] paratroopers, including the famous Hannah Senesh, to occupied territories in Europe.[17]

R.L. Did you know her?

17. The Hungarian-born Szenes, as her name was spelled in Hungarian, escaped from the Holocaust to Palestine, then volunteered to parachute back into Central Europe. She was captured while crossing the Yugoslav-Hungarian border, tortured and executed in the closing days of the war.

s.p. Yes. I knew her personally. We befriended each other. She was also in the youth movement. We had a seminar in which she participated. I was the instructor.

R.L. Was she already writing poetry at that time?

s.p. I didn't know if she was writing. She was very introverted. She wasn't the sort of girl to show off. She was very strong-minded.

R.L. And she and a few other Jews parachuted back into the Holocaust from which they had escaped—

s.p. It was a joint venture between the Haganah and the British army. So we tried to see what could be done. But we weren't well informed.

R.L. Looking back, you don't accept that the Jewish leaders in Palestine, and David Ben-Gurion in particular, could have done more—I use the expression "scream from the rooftops," but you see what I'm getting at?

s.p. At that time we were trying to see how to defend our own lives. We didn't know what was happening in Europe.

R.L. One doesn't preclude the other. You can defend yourself with your rifles, and scream from the rooftops at the same time.

s.p. We didn't have the full picture. It was some time before we became aware of the Holocaust. Only in the last two years of the war did we begin to understand what a tragedy it was. By the time we knew, it was already too late to do anything.

R.L. What a painful subject.

s.p. It is a painful subject. I don't think it was lack of caring. It was rather lack of knowledge. Under very demanding circumstances.

R.L. Do you think there could be another Holocaust?

s.p. It's hard for me to imagine. Because of the existence of Israel. And also because of the experience of Nazism.

R.L. We have holocausts with a small *h*. I'm talking about the recent ethnic cleansing of Muslims in Bosnia. Fifty years after the Jewish Holocaust, the world and Europe sat and watched ethnic cleansing—

s.p. It's not the same thing. They didn't have gas chambers, it wasn't organized by a state. It was more of a civil war.

r.l. We can't quibble over whether there was a death factory or not—

s.p. You know, in Yugoslavia what happened recently happened for the second time. It happened during the Second World War too, between Tito and [Draza] Mihajlovic.[18] There were more people killed in Yugoslavia by the Yugoslavs than by the Germans. So this is an ongoing war. It was an attempt to force different ethnic groups and different religions to coexist. But it wasn't a matter of a master and a slave. Yugoslavia is made up of differences. They could have overcome them democratically, or through the use of force. And Tito used force.

r.l. In Louis Malle's brilliant film *Au revoir les enfants,* there is a scene in which a Gestapo officer arrests a Jewish boy hiding in a French Catholic school. As the officer crosses the classroom toward the Jewish boy, he passes a photograph of Pope Pius XII on the wall; in the photograph the pope is looking the other way. In an article discussing the differences between the Yiddish version and the French version of Elie Wiesel's classic on the Holocaust, *Night,* Naomi Seidman, a professor of Jewish studies at the Graduate Theological Union in Berkeley, California, argues that Jewish Holocaust literature "has been framed to offend Christians as little as possible." Her point seems to be that both Christians and Jews let Christians off the hook for their failure to face up to Christian anti-Semitism and its role in the Nazi Final Solution. Do you let Christians off the hook?

18. The Serbian guerrilla leader executed after the war by Tito for collaboration with the Germans.

s.p. No. I think the problem is: where does convenience stop and ethics begin. What happened to Europe and to Christianity was that convenience overpowered their basic values. They didn't understand Hitler. They didn't want to understand Hitler. It was inconvenient to understand Hitler. And from this inconvenience they created a global policy, both in England and in France. Usually democracies are very reluctant to recognize dangers. It makes their life very inconvenient. That is why, on the one hand, democracies are not aggressive and don't take initiatives to start wars, but they are not defensive enough when they face a danger. So, I mean, closing the eyes, saying I didn't understand, I didn't know, it's not so terrible, it's part of the game.

Churchill was a pain in the neck for them because he saw things rightly and he said it loudly. And you could see how the whole of Europe submitted to the whim of a madman. Even his craziness had a certain attraction in their eyes. And Hitler was aware of it. And he really supplied the necessary food to put them to sleep. Anti-Semitism always existed—latent, clear, loud—and usually the attitude toward anti-Semitism was that very few stood up against it. There were many who said, well, it's a problem, it's a malady, let's look for doctors to cure them. And the others said, well, there is something to it. So it's not that Hitler created anti-Semitism, but he took advantage of the existence of anti-Semitism.

r.l. Let's speak specifically about the Catholic Church and Pope Pius XII. Aren't we letting him off the hook—

s.p. The church clearly should be blamed for its attitude throughout the Hitler period, and particularly for the anti-Semitism. I think a church without a spirit is not actually a church. It's a hierarchy. The church doesn't have armies. If it has anything, it has virtues. And if it doesn't mobilize its virtues, it's like a demilitarized—a demoralized—organization.

R.L. Let's talk about France for a moment. Many people think the French still haven't come to terms with the fact that France was a collaborationist country, that a legally elected French Parliament installed Marshal Pétain, who promulgated the *Statut des juifs,* which defined who was Jewish in the eyes of the French state and then systematically excluded them from top positions in the civil service and officer corps as well as jobs in teaching, journalism, radio, film, and theater; that the great majority of the 76,000 French Jews sent to death camps were rounded up by the French *milice* [militia] on orders of the legal French government in Vichy. French is a language you speak well. France is a country you know well. Do you think the suggestion that France has not come to terms with its past is valid?

S.P. Only after the war, after the defeat, did France return to itself. Before that, it was divided as a country can be divided, between Catholics and Protestants, between the rich and the poor, between Paris and the provinces. And each of these parts of France had its own mentality. Let's take the French left that was led by many Jewish people—Léon Blum, Daniel Mayer, Jules Moch, and many others. The French socialist movement was the only one, except for the Italian, that tended to be more revolutionary than democratic; namely, they were Marxists. No wonder that there was such a powerful Communist group in France. As Guy Mollet[19] once said, the problem in France is that left is east and right is west. Because the French Communist Party got orders from Russia. And the minute the Russians collaborated with the Germans, the French Communists fell under the spell of the Russians. It's a shame. It's a shame.

19. 1905–75: French socialist leader and former resistance leader; as Président du Conseil (the equivalent of prime minister before the Fifth Republic), a post he held from 1956 to 1957, he negotiated the first comprehensive security understanding with Israel.

But let me go back a little bit. Jean Jaurès, who was a founder of the French Socialist Party and who, as you know, was assassinated in 1914, was among the ones who protested against the Dreyfus trial.[20] He called it the mobilization of the moral cavalry. The Dreyfus trial was a watershed in Jewish life. Because then there was an argument among Jewish people, What went wrong with Jewish life? Why is there anti-Semitism? Why are the Jews so hated? And there were two basic intellectual answers; the argument came to a head at the Dreyfus trial. One held that the Jews were suffering because the world was badly constructed. It was made up of classes, of religions, of nations, and there was no way to correct Jewish life without correcting the life of the world. And then they started to cook up a classless society, a godless society, a nationless society to change the world. And the other answer said no, the Jews are suffering because they are wrong. We have to correct the Jewish life. They have the wrong profile: they don't have a state of their own, they don't have an army of their own, they don't have an identity card of their own. We were living in between the holes of the lives of other people. And that brought us to the Zionist solution. So the people with the first answer became revolutionaries, socialists, even Communists. And the others became Zionists. Herzl was at the Dreyfus trial—

R.L. There's the famous story of his hearing the French demonstrators shouting anti-Dreyfus, anti-Semitic slogans.

S.P. Yes. He took the Zionist way. And Léon Blum was at the time an aide of Jaurès—he was impressed with Jaurès and took the other side. But I want to say that the left, including the Jewish

20. Captain Alfred Dreyfus, an Alsatian-Jewish French Army officer, was falsely convicted of treason in 1894 on the basis of forged evidence; anti-Semitism played an important role in the case. His case became a *cause célèbre*, both in France and worldwide. Dreyfus was eventually exonerated and freed from Devil's Island.

part of it, was on the fence—they felt that as long as we remained Jewish we were a problem; they felt that we had to change the world. And for that reason many Jews became Communists. And particularly the ones who were under the spell of the Russians. They closed their eyes. It's a shame. Now, the French Catholics, strangely enough, are much more ignorant about Jewish life. You wouldn't believe it. They know so little about Jewish history. From [Charles] de Gaulle,[21] to [Georges] Pompidou,[22] to [Valéry] Giscard d'Estaing[23]—

R.L. What about François Mitterrand? [24]

S.P. No. Mitterrand was an exception to the rule. He was the only one who was knowledgeable. I remember visiting de Gaulle with Ben-Gurion. It was a brilliant day in Paris. And after lunch—where de Gaulle said that Israel was "our ally" and "our friend"—we were sitting around small tables in the garden of the Elysée having tea, and around the table where I was sitting sat de Gaulle, Ben-Gurion, and Michel Debré, who was then prime minister. And de Gaulle turned to Ben-Gurion and said, "Mr. Prime Minister, tell me your hidden dreams. I know you are short of territory. You are a very small country. Would you like to have the desert of Sinai? Would you like to have the mountains of Moab in Jordan? You don't have water. Would you like to have the Litany River [in Lebanon]? Tell me, I won't tell anybody." Ben-Gurion was occasionally quite naive and innocent, and he said, "Mr. President, if you had asked me fifty years ago, I would have given you a map. If you ask me this question today, my hidden dream is to have more Jews, not more

21. 1890–1970: Leader of the Free French forces during World War II, he became the first president of the Fifth Republic, serving from 1959 to 1969.

22. 1911–74: French president from 1969 to 1974.

23. 1926– : French president from 1974 to 1981.

24. 1916–96: French president from 1981 to 1995.

territory." De Gaulle was shocked. He said, "More Jews! What for? Why do you need Jews?" And then de Gaulle stood up and called "Couve. *Venez ici.*" [Maurice] Couve de Murville²⁵ was sitting nearby. And de Gaulle called Guy Mollet over to the table. And he said, "You know what the prime minister of Israel wants? More Jews! More Jews! Would you believe it?" Then de Gaulle asked Ben-Gurion, "And where will they come from?" And Ben-Gurion said, "From America." So de Gaulle said, "Will they give up their Cadillacs?" Ben-Gurion said, "Yes. Also from Russia." De Gaulle said, "From Russia?" Ben-Gurion said, "Yes. Communism will fall down and the Jews will be able to leave it. The intelligentsia in Russia will never agree to remain forever under Communism." De Gaulle said, "Where else?" Ben-Gurion said, "From France." "From France? Who will leave France? Have any Jews left France already?" So Ben-Gurion said, "Yes. Adolphe Cremieux."²⁶ Adolphe Cremieux was the minister of justice who created the first agricultural school in Israel. So de Gaulle said, "Cremieux was crazy. Who else?" Ben-Gurion said, "Rothschild." So de Gaulle said, "Rothschild is not a Frenchman, he's an Austrian."

You know, it was funny. He didn't get the idea. Once de Gaulle told me in a private conversation he never believed Jews could suddenly become farmers and soldiers in Israel. I mean, it was so strange listening to him. Really. The man was a genius, but he was totally uninformed about Jewish life. Read his memoirs. And then, when Giscard d'Estaing came here [to Israel] I had a long talk with him. He was never taught to understand who the Jewish people are, what the Torah is. He was totally unaware of its importance. So I mean, the Catholics, by inclination—for

25. 1907– : Foreign minister at the time, he later served as prime minister from 1968 to de Gaulle's retirement in 1969.
26. The head of the French-Jewish Alliance israélite universelle in the 1870s.

them Jewish life was a faraway wind that they couldn't identify. Unlike the Catholics, the Protestants were much more knowledgeable. [This is because] the Catholics were educated in the New Testament, the Protestants in the Old Testament.

R.L. During the Second World War there was a largely Protestant village in France called Le Chambon-sur-Lignon, which saved thousands of Jews. The village's pastor, whose name was Trocmé, was later honored by the State of Israel as a "righteous gentile."

S.P. Yes. The Protestants were like the Calvinists in Holland. They were educated in the Old Testament. So they had a feeling [for the Jews]. The Catholics of France were historically touched by anti-Semitism. For them Jews represented a revolting image. The French countryside didn't have many Jewish people. And the Jews themselves were very much assimilated. Very much. When Israel started its relations with France I asked the [French] Jews to open a line of communication to the Elysée. None of them was ready. Finally it was I who asked de Gaulle's people to invite the Jewish people for lunch with Ben-Gurion.

Before the election in 1955 — I don't remember the date exactly — I made a tour with all the leaders in France, including Guy Mollet. And he asked me, "Did you hear the rumor that I am an anti-Semite?" And I said, "Why are you asking?" "Because there are rumors that I'm an anti-Semite," he said. "It's not true. I was competing with Daniel Mayer for the leadership of the Socialist Party — to see who would succeed Léon Blum. And because I was against Daniel Mayer, they said that I am an anti-Semite. That's nonsense." And then Mollet told me, "Look, most of the French newspapers are in the hands of your compatriots. Can you help me a little bit with the newspapers?" At the end of the week, a picture of Mollet appeared on the cover of *Paris Match*. He called me up and said, "Thank you very much." I told him, "Believe me, I don't deserve the slightest credit." He said, "Don't tell me stories." He didn't buy it.

R.L. It reminds me of the story of the meeting between Ben-Gurion and John F. Kennedy right after Kennedy's election, when Kennedy, aware that Jewish-owned newspapers had supported him, asked, "What can I do for your people?"

S.P. You know what Ben-Gurion replied? He told Kennedy, "Be a great president."

R.L. Let's return to François Mitterrand for a moment. During the last years of his life, details came out that must be very disturbing for a Jew—I'm talking about his connection with the collaborationist Vichy government during the war, I'm talking about his long-time friendship with René Bousquet, who was named by Pierre Laval as head of Vichy France's police during World War II and was responsible for the deportation of tens of thousands of Jews. There is a strong suspicion that Bousquet was never prosecuted because of Mr. Mitterrand's protection. How do you deal with this dark cloud over Mitterrand?

S.P. First of all, I wasn't aware of it. I know what I know and I didn't know what I didn't know. But I want to tell you the following story. When I met Mitterrand his best friend was Georges Dayan. They were together in the P.O.W. camp in Germany. Dayan was not only Jewish, but proudly Jewish. On two occasions Mitterrand sent him to me to straighten out different matters. Then on many occasions we had intimate dinners and lunches, and around the table Mitterrand was the only non-Jewish person—there was Jacques Attali,[27] Saltzman, and many other Jewish people.

R.L. This almost comes under the heading of: some of my best friends are Jews.

27. One-time Mitterrand aide, one-time chief executive of the European Bank for Reconstruction and Development.

S.P. They weren't his best friends. They were his intimate
aides. They weren't accidental friends.

R.L. But Bousquet was a friend too?

S.P. Maybe. Also, Mitterrand was the only one who really
knew the Bible by heart. And he made some remarks that were
really penetrating. To give some examples: he told me that nobody attended Joshua's funeral when he passed away. I didn't pay
much attention to this detail, but then he told me why he didn't
like Jeremiah.

And then on a personal note I want to tell you something
which moved me very much. We arranged a lunch. I arrived and
found Mitterrand in a sentimental mood. He embraced me. We
had a walk in the garden. He was very intimate, very open. And
then I was told by his doctors that they had discovered the seriousness of his cancer three or four days before this lunch and
they wanted to operate, and he said no, I want to have lunch with
Peres. And he postponed the operation two or three days. I don't
know anybody else who would have done that.

And then two or three times I was at Latche, his retreat in
the Pyrenees, and usually the talk was about Jewish subjects;
Mitterrand was very active on the question of Jewish dissidents
in Russia. I met Mitterrand for the first time at the home of
Mendès-France.[28] We had lunch together, Mendès, Mitterrand,
and myself. He was an admirer of Mendès. I remember Mendès telling me that this man was the best "pianist" in the French
parliament. So I mean, I saw Mitterrand in a different time.
He was the only French president I have known who was really
keen on the Bible, who knew Jewish history, who worked with
Jewish people, who was fascinated by Jewish life. Once I asked
him, "Why do you travel so much?" And he said, "I probably

---

28. 1907–82: Prime minister from 1954 to 1955.

have some drops of Jewish blood in my veins." He was a very complex person. That I know. I didn't detect in him any trace of ignorance or hatred. But I did find a profound interest in Jewish history.

He visited Israel on many occasions. He came incognito. As a president, he visited Israel—the only French president to visit Israel [until Jacques Chirac's visit in 1996]. Maybe he did have some dark spots in his biography; that doesn't change my judgment about him. I never found that he bluffed me.

There's another story. I was invited to his inauguration as president. I didn't go, and later on he asked me why. And I told him the true story. [Menachem] Begin[29] decided to bomb the nuclear reactor in Iraq on the very day of Mitterrand's inauguration. And I went to Begin and I told him, "Look, it's not done. It's a French reactor. You cannot do it on such a day. It will be taken as a provocation." Begin agreed to postpone it, but I wasn't sure he would. So I decided to remain in Israel to make sure. Later on Mitterrand told some friends, "Where would you find a friend like Peres?"

R.L. Let's cross the border into Italy. Benito Mussolini passed a series of anti-Jewish laws in 1938. Although some Italian Jews wound up in the death camps, in general Italian Jews fared better than French Jews. I know of one story that illustrates the difference between the French attitude toward Jews during World War II and the Italian attitude: when the French Vichy *milice* tried to arrest Jews who had taken refuge in the mountains behind Nice, which was then a zone occupied by the Italians, they were held off at the points of bayonets by Italian soldiers. How do you explain the fact that Italian Jews suffered less than French Jews?

29. 1913–92: Right-wing Likud prime minister from 1977 to 1983.

S.P. The Italians are basically incapable of being cruel. Their spirit is more musical than vindictive. It has to do with their character and nature. They are much more liberal, much more humane, much more permissive, and then Italy is a country where seriousness has some limitations. They are afraid that if you overstep you will stop being humane. In all walks of life. Even in war. The French say there is a very thin line between the sublime and the ridiculous. Mussolini stood on this very thin line. He was poised between the sublime and the ridiculous. Nobody could take him seriously. They say that he pulled off a great bluff. I read a book about him which said that even the trains in Italy never really arrived on time under the Fascists. It was a bluff. And then he had a mistress for a very long time who was Jewish — they published her biography two or three years ago. A very interesting story. So the Italians are afraid to be serious.

R.L. Even when it comes to persecuting Jews?

S.P. On every subject. And then the Jews in Italy were not too numerous — they never played an important role in Italian government. I can hardly recall any important Jewish person in the politics of Italy. And also anti-Semitism was foreign to the Italian makeup, because let's not forget that Italy is itself a mixture. The Italians cannot say that they are an Aryan nation, because southern Italy is more Mediterranean —

R.L. France is as mixed as Italy.

S.P. You don't have in France a real Mediterranean area. But Naples is really Mediterranean. The whole southern part of Italy. No wonder that today they want to divide Italy between north and south. The Jews were good doctors, good architects, good traders. But they didn't go into politics.

R.L. They kept a low profile?

S.P. Yes. Even among the rich, they weren't very important. You don't have an Italian Rothschild, for example. You don't have an Italian Disraeli.[30] You don't have an Italian Ferdinand Lassalle.[31]

R.L. How about Germany? Elie Wiesel, testifying at the trial of Klaus Barbie[32] in Lyon in 1987, said: "Those men who killed with submachine guns in the Ukraine . . . afterwards they would go home and read a poem by Heine." This is the nagging question I've heard all my life: how could a civilized country like Germany, which produced a Bach and a Beethoven and a Goethe, produce the Holocaust?

S.P. To this very day it's hard to explain. The Germans can be easily disciplined, and what the French call "grandeur" the Germans call "supremacy." And Hitler promised them they would be the supreme race, that he would get rid of the secondary races that contaminated the German race. Heine himself was often attacked. He said in one of his books that the Germans invented the printing press to spread foolishness and they discovered iron to produce chains. Heine was the one who forecast the Holocaust. He spoke in terrible terms about the arrival of a sort of a *führer*. He said movingly, "Since the Exodus, freedom has always been spoken with a Hebrew accent."

Germany has had its ups and downs. Hitler came to power in a nation that was frustrated economically and politically. After the First World War the Germans didn't have the right to build an army. The Europeans really didn't judge the Germans correctly—they said that a small warship cannot produce a large war, only large warships can; they said that limiting the caliber of cannons was a guarantee against war; and they limited the

30. 1804–81: British statesman of Jewish origins, he was baptized a Christian in 1817, served as prime minister in 1868 and again from 1874 to 1880.
31. 1825–64: A founder, in 1863, of the first workers' political party in Germany, the forerunner of the Social Democratic Party.
32. Gestapo chief in Lyons during World War II.

[German] army. And internally, Germany was broken. And then came a man who said, I will introduce order, I will give you supremacy, I will get rid of all these limitations. But the lengths to which they went were unprecedented. I don't think it can be explained completely. It shows that a nation can become a group of animals under given circumstances. It's very worrying.

R.L. Could it happen again?

S.P. I don't think so. Today it's hard because of television, because of the transparency that exists. Dictators who don't have the capacity to blind their people cannot last. Today it's difficult to blind the people because of the media. Even the Iron Curtain could not withstand the strength of the silver curtain. And on top of that the world has been changed by the nuclear bomb. If somebody were to come today and try to do what Hitler did, he would be bombed out.

R.L. In recent years we've seen Jewish cemeteries across Europe desecrated—Carpentras in France being the most notable example. In Austria, the far-right Freedom Party is within striking distance of winning the next parliamentary election. France's Jean-Marie Le Pen, who publicly referred to the Holocaust as a "minor event" in the history of the Second World War, got 15 percent of the vote in the last presidential election, and his extreme right-wing National Front scored even higher in some local elections in the south of France. In Italy, Gianfranco Fini, the leader of the old neo-Fascist movement, has become a major player in national politics. Croatia, with a long history of anti-Semitism, recently reprinted an edition of the loathsome anti-Semitic *Protocols of the Elders of Zion*.[33] Given Europe's extremely high unemployment and immigration problems, does

33. A notorious anti-Semitic book, first published at the turn of the century and purporting to expose a Jewish plot to dominate the world.

this resurgence of far-right or proto-fascist parties worry you?

S.P. I am concerned. I am concerned. I don't say that this is the end of anti-Semitism. I don't say that this is the end of racism. But the all-embracing complete takeover on the model of Hitler looks to me today almost impossible.

R.L. Notwithstanding the Warsaw ghetto uprising, also the uprisings in Treblinka and Sobibor, for a long time some—I'm tempted to say many—Israelis had mixed emotions about the Jews who died in the Holocaust and the Jews who survived. It was almost as if there were something shameful about being a Holocaust Jew—the image that leaps to mind is the one of Jews digging the ditches into which they were shot, or lining up for the gas chambers. You lost relatives in the Holocaust— your grandfather, your family in Vishniva disappeared in this inferno. Yet you are an Israeli Jew, the generation of Moshe Dayan[34] and Yitzhak Rabin,[35] archetypal warriors. Did you ever harbor doubts about the heroism and dignity of the Jews who went to their deaths stoically—not battling against the Germans, protecting their children as best they could, in some cases even killing their own children in order to spare them the horrors of the death camps?

S.P. To be fair, I don't think they had much of a choice. We disagree with the way they were living, so we disagree with the way they were dying. We didn't want them to remain in the Dias-

34. 1915–81: Chief of staff during the 1956 Sinai campaign, defense minister at the time of the 1967 Six-Day War, he served as foreign minister from 1977 to 1979.

35. 1922–95: As chief of staff, he was the architect of Israel's stunning victory in the 1967 Six-Day War; he went on to become Israel's first native-born prime minister, serving in that post from 1974 to 1977, and again from 1992 until his assassination in 1995. From 1992, Peres served as Rabin's foreign minister; together the two of them opened secret negotiations with the Palestinians in Oslo that led to the signing of the Oslo peace accords.

pora. We wanted them to come over here. They could have come here—

R.L. They couldn't have come here. The British wouldn't have let them in. American immigration quotas were closed—

S.P. No, no. I'm talking about before Hitler. I mean, there were many ways open [to emigrate to Palestine]. A very small portion of the Jewish people came to Palestine. Herzl was sensational in his vision, but very limited in the realization. Only 3 percent of the Jewish people responded to Herzl and went to Palestine.

R.L. So you do harbor doubts—

S.P. About their choice [before the war]. But during the Hitler era they didn't have a choice. To be fair, I don't see they could have done much. Very little.

R.L. I've seen it suggested that Europe and America solved their post–World War II Jewish problem—what to do with the several hundred thousand Jewish survivors of the Holocaust—by dumping the problem into the lap of the Arabs. Do you agree with this interpretation?

S.P. No. They didn't do it [create the State of Israel]. We did it. Israel was not an American-European solution, it was a Jewish solution. Let's be fair.

R.L. To what degree does the State of Israel owe its existence to the Holocaust? Israel gave that impression by requiring, until about two years ago, all foreign dignitaries to visit Yad Vashem, the Holocaust museum in Jerusalem. Do you think there would have been a state if there had been no Holocaust?

S.P. I think that Ben-Gurion would not have pushed for sovereignty so soon if it had not been for the Holocaust. And he wouldn't have agreed to so many territorial compromises if he had not been in a hurry to save Jewish [Holocaust survivors'] lives. That clearly played a major role in his pushing for independence when he did. The Holocaust was the greatest event and experience in Jewish history. I mean, the size of the tragedy was really shocking. And it has shaken the whole Jewish existence fundamentally. So clearly the Jewish state is an expression of this tragedy. I don't say this is the only reason for the creation of the Jewish state, because there were generations of pioneers who came before the Holocaust. There was what we call the first immigration [*aliyah*], the second immigration, and the third immigration.

R.L. Nazi gold and money, part of it stolen from Jewish victims of the Holocaust and reportedly including gold fillings from the teeth of Jews murdered in death camps, found its way into Swiss bank vaults during World War II. It seems clear, too, that the Swiss acted as middlemen for the Germans in sending some of the Nazi wealth on to Spain and Portugal and Latin America. Jewish groups estimate that Swiss banks today hold as much as $7 billion belonging to the heirs of Holocaust victims. After searching their records for months, the Swiss banks claimed that the real figure was a tiny fraction of that, but after much prodding, the government and the banks offered to set up a compensation fund for Nazi victims.

S.P. I think the Swiss must be perfectly open about this affair. There cannot remain the slightest doubt about their returning to the last penny everything that belongs to Jewish people individually and to the Jewish people collectively.

R.L. Do you think they will do this?

S.P. If there is enough pressure, yes.

R.L. What happened in Vishniva during World War II?

S.P. They executed all the remaining people — put them in a synagogue, my grandfather at their head, and burned them alive. And then they burned down the whole town. Nothing was left. When I visited Vishniva, nothing remained but a heap of stones, which serves as the collective tomb for the Jewish people who were burned to death in the synagogue. You know, I went back to try and find out ... the place that I was born and raised ... I mean, not a single one of the old houses was left. They built some new homes in their place. Finally I found the place, because I remembered that in our courtyard there was a fountain, so I went there and I took out the ... how do you call it? ... the container of water, and I tasted the water. That was the only thing that reminded me of my childhood. The taste of the water hadn't changed ... otherwise nothing was left.

R.L. The Holocaust obviously had an enormous impact on the religious beliefs of Jews. There is a prominent American rabbi and intellectual by the name of Arthur Hertzberg—

S.P. Yes, I know him.

R.L. He wrote memorably, "The Messiah who did not show up at Auschwitz is not going to show up on Eastern Parkway,[36] or in the parking lot of a West Bank settlement." Has the Holocaust affected your religious beliefs? Your belief in God? Your philosophy of good and evil?

S.P. No. I think of God as a challenge and not as a savior. What I mean by this is that if there is a God in heaven, He forces me to be a person of values and virtues, but I don't feel that He runs an insurance company. So in a way [the belief in God] is an attempt to better the human race. But I don't believe a God will save me. That I don't believe. He challenges me? Look, the concept of God—that each of us was born in His image—is actually a return to ourselves. We are not outside God, we are part of Him. The Lord in His loneliness has invited us to join Him. So I

36. The street in Brooklyn on which Rabbi Menachem Mendel Schneerson, the spiritual leader of the Hasidic Lubavitcher sect whom many of his followers believe to be the Messiah, lived until his death in 1994.

wouldn't recognize any contradiction between reason and holiness. I don't accept it. I am ready to believe in holy things as long as I am reasonable. I wouldn't permit myself to give up reason just because I have an explanation that it is a religious obligation.

R.L. About three and a half years ago, in the crematorium at the heart of Auschwitz, a young German neo-Nazi was haranguing everyone within earshot, in English, telling them that nothing had happened at Auschwitz; that the Jews had won the war and written its history; that Auschwitz had been a work camp with swimming pools. The story of this confrontation appeared in the *New York Times* on December 15, 1993. It identified the neo-Nazi as Bela Ewald Althans, said to be the "führer" of a new generation of extreme rightists. The article identified the only person to challenge him and call him a liar as "a young American" because the *Times* didn't know his name. I do. The young American was my youngest son, Jesse. My story is leading to a question: How do you explain the phenomenon of Holocaust denial? What is the psychology behind it?

S.P. I don't explain it. They are psychopaths. Look, it is very difficult for me to consider maladies as a healthy phenomenon. Sick is sick. A sick person is sick. You know, it's a shame for us to take them seriously. They are disturbed people. They are sick people.

*Enemies are
the raw material
of partners.*

SECOND CONVERSATION

R.L. In 1948, you were on the side of those who agreed with Ben-Gurion, who argued for immediate statehood rather than holding out for a larger or "Greater" Israel, even though the United Nations partition plan offered the Jews a minuscule state that didn't include any part of Jerusalem. Ben-Gurion, clearly in a hurry, as you've pointed out, to succor as many survivors of the Holocaust as possible, decided that time mattered more than space. There must have been a lot of soul-searching going on at the time. Did you harbor any doubts that Ben-Gurion was right?

S.P. No. I was completely taken with Ben-Gurion. In 1946 there was a Zionist congress in Basel, and the labor group elected two young delegates, Moshe Dayan and myself. We went to the congress and discovered that the majority of the delegates were against partition, which meant that they were against establishing a Jewish state immediately, against fighting the British, against illegal immigration. Ben-Gurion was desperate. He thought a majority in the party opposed him. I was sitting with a friend of mine, Arie Bahir, who was one of the founders of Kibbutz Afikim in the northern part of Israel, and for a while secretary of the Labor Party—he was one of the supporters of

Ben-Gurion. Ben-Gurion trusted him very much. While we were sitting together in the hall listening to the arguments, Mrs. Ben-Gurion arrived and said, "He went crazy!" So we asked her, "What's happened?" She said, "He's decided to leave the congress." So Arie told me, "Let's go and see what can be done." Ben-Gurion was staying at the Drei Könige, which is the hotel where Herzl used to stay. We went over and knocked on the door of his room. No reply. Again we knocked. Again no reply. Finally we opened the door — we were a little worried. And we saw Ben-Gurion standing in the middle of the room packing his valises. So we said, "Shalom, Ben-Gurion." No reply. Then he turned to us and said, "Are you coming with me or not?" I said, "Where are you going?" He said, "It's a rotten congress. Nothing will come out of it. They don't understand the call of history. They are no longer leaders, they are bureaucrats. I'm going to create a new movement of young people, of idealists, that will understand the urgency of our time, the meaning of it. Are you coming or not?" Arie looked at me and said, "You shall answer." I said, "Yes, we are coming with you. But before we all leave, you shall come with us to the congress and see. If you have a majority, we will all stay. If not, we will all go." So he agreed.

And he came and the rest of the night we had a stormy meeting. Ben-Gurion was out of his mind. He attacked everybody. He shouted. The plenum was chaired by Golda Meir.[1] She really had a tough time. Finally there was a vote and Ben-Gurion had a tiny majority. Now clearly I felt he had the tools — it was not a matter of being pleasant or not pleasant. It was a matter of, If not now, when? And I felt completely with him. I trusted him. I felt he was a really honest man. He never adopted a position

1. 1898–1978: Russian-born American schoolteacher who emigrated to Palestine in 1921 and served as prime minister from 1969 to 1974.

in order to make an impression. He came to a conclusion and he put it on the table. I became a Ben-Gurionist at a very early stage of my life and never changed my mind. I understood his reservations about the Diaspora, about Communism, about the rightist movements—he wanted to leave everything and go back to the Bible. He thought that everything that happened to the Jewish people after the Bible corrupted our life. He thought that the Bible is the place where heaven and earth meet—the values of heaven and the realities of earth.

R.L. You were standing alongside Ben-Gurion on November 29, 1947, when the United Nations General Assembly adopted the partition resolution, creating a Jewish and an Arab state. Ben-Gurion said: "Today they are dancing; tomorrow they will have to shed blood." What were your emotions at that moment?

S.P. I was caught up in the joy. In my heart I thought maybe Ben-Gurion was a little bit jealous, because he was so restrained and bitter, and here the whole nation was dancing—it was such a tremendous victory for Israel.

R.L. Did you worry about the dangers?

S.P. I trusted Ben-Gurion. I thought he exaggerated a little bit, but I was wrong—

R.L. Ben-Gurion was right. In the early hours of statehood, Israel was attacked by five Arab armies, including the British-trained Arab Legion of Jordan. Egyptian planes bombed Tel Aviv. The situation must have looked dark. Was there a time when Ben-Gurion wondered if the new state would survive?

S.P. Maybe deep in his heart, but he didn't show it. He was determined. He never showed the slightest inclination to change his mind. He was very tough, like a stone. The more complicated the situation became, the more reassured he appeared. He was a genius.

R.L. Did history make Ben-Gurion, or did Ben-Gurion

make history? Would there be a Jewish state today without Ben-Gurion?

S.P. I wonder. I'm not sure. I think in this case the man made history. There are some occasions where men have made history. Gandhi, for example. You cannot say that history made Gandhi; Gandhi made history. And I think this is the case with Ben-Gurion—he made history.

R.L. Very early on you moved into the crucial realm of arms procurement. With America and Britain imposing an arms embargo on the fledgling state, and Russia either joining in that embargo or, later, siding more and more with the Arab states, you bought the major part of your arms—old German Messerschmitts, heavy machine guns, rifles—from Czechoslovakia, which was a Communist state and a Soviet satellite at the time. Why did the Czechs sell you arms? Why did Stalin permit it?

S.P. There were two reasons. First of all, we paid very dearly for the arms in hard currency, and Czechoslovakia was short of money. That was a good enough reason, too—let's not forget it. Second, I think they felt that these arms were aimed against the British, not only against the Arabs, and Stalin thought the situation wasn't too bad. Let's not forget that [Andrei] Gromyko [2] voted for the creation of the Jewish state. This [support for Israel] was the Communist bloc position vis-à-vis the Western bloc. He made quite a moving speech, Gromyko, at that time.

R.L. Things changed later.

S.P. Stalin eventually became a sick person. A real paranoid. The paranoia matched his organizational talents. If a paranoid doesn't have great organizational powers, he's not as danger-

2. Soviet ambassador to the United Nations at the time of partition.

ous. But when you combine a talent for organization with the sickness of paranoia—it's a terrible combination. Stalin was probably the greatest paranoid in history. Recently a biographer I admire very much, Henri Troyat, published a book on Ivan the Terrible, who lived five hundred years ago. When you look at Ivan the Terrible and Stalin, you are amazed by the similarity. Ivan the Terrible was the first edition of Stalin. Troyat tells unbelievable stories—there was a countess with a deep *décolleté* who was married to Ivan's son. Ivan approached her and said, "What sort of a dress is that?" She answered, "That's my taste." So he slapped her on the face. Ivan's son came over and started to shout at Ivan that he didn't have the right to do that. So Ivan took his—how do you call it?—the long stick with a sharp edge?

R.L. Spear? Lance?

S.P. Yes, lance. And he threw it at his own son and wounded him deeply. And for three days and three nights Ivan sat next to his bed crying like a baby. And when the French doctor couldn't save his son, Ivan burned the doctor alive. I mean, the cruelty, the suspicion—it was like in an insane asylum. And that was also true with Stalin. The lie about the plot of the Jewish doctors. The killing of the whole membership of the Politburo. It's terrible. Occasionally one may think that you cannot be a leader unless you are a little bit sick.

R.L. There's an old joke that even paranoids have real enemies. It was certainly true in Stalin's case.

S.P. Yes.

R.L. You were instrumental in opening the so-called back channel to buy arms from France and thus get around the arms embargo that menaced Israel. This is something even your political enemies give you credit for. A right-winger phoned into a radio talk show here in Israel recently. He ranted on along

the lines of: "Who is this Peres—he didn't even hold a rifle." [3]
To which the talk show host, also a right-winger, replied, "On
questions of security, people should take their shoes off before
Peres." [4]

S.P. The business about not holding a rifle is nonsense—I held
a rifle from the age of fifteen. During the War of Liberation they
wanted to give me the rank of a high officer and I refused.

R.L. Why?

S.P. I refused because even without the rank I had the highest
rank. There was nobody above me. I could move around and
do whatever I wanted. I established informal authority. I didn't
need rank. I thought it would limit me.

R.L. Throughout your political career the lack of a formal
military rank has haunted you. Looking back now, don't you
wish you had accepted? If only for political reasons.

S.P. Yes. Yes. Maybe.

R.L. Let's go back to the arms purchases from France. I understand why Israel bought arms from France. But why did France
agree to sell arms to Israel?

S.P. There were several reasons. After the war France strongly
identified herself with the fate of the Jewish people. I've already
described how France was divided during the war into four or
five different parts. After the war France was divided into two
camps, the collaborators and the *maquis*. Everybody wanted
to be on the *maquis* line, and to be on the *maquis* line you had
to be pro-Israel. I will never forget having dinner at the home
of the chief of staff, General Ely. I was sitting to the right of his
wife, Madame Ely. And all of a sudden she turned to me and

3. A reference to the fact that Peres was a soldier, never an officer in the
Israeli army, a criticism often raised by Peres's opponents.

4. A reference to Moses removing his sandals at the burning bush because
he was in the presence of God.

said, "Did you know that I was in a concentration camp together with Jewish people?" And I was really surprised. So there was an inclination to help the Jewish state.

And then there was the Gaullist part of it — to show that France was the equal of Great Britain and Russia and America, Israel could become a "client" of France. That was the de Gaulle concept. And the third reason was Algeria. Nasser was considered to be a supporter of the FLN.[5] Guy Mollet told me that he was afraid of every phenomenon prefaced by a "pan" — pan-Germanism, pan-Slavism, pan-Arabism. He said that Nasser was an apprentice of Hitler.

And then there was also the French arms industry, which was interested in doing business with us. I was a logical person. I knew that there were only four countries in the world that produced the sort of arms we needed. The first was the United States — to this very day I can't understand why the United States recognized the State of Israel and refused to give us rifles to defend our lives.

R.L. Did you ever talk to Henry Kissinger about it?[6]

S.P. I talked to Averell Harriman.[7] He invited me to his house for lunch and we were going over the history of Israeli-American relations. It was the first thing I asked him. He said it was a mistake. He said America didn't want to get herself involved in a war. Kissinger gave me the same answer.

R.L. You were saying that there were only four countries in the world —

S.P. Yes. And then Great Britain in our eyes was very pro-

5. Front de Libération, which led the 1954 Algerian revolt against French rule that led to Algerian independence in 1962.

6. American secretary of state from 1973 to 1977.

7. 1891–1986: American financier and diplomat, U.S. secretary of commerce from 1946 to 1948.

Arabic. And Russia was clearly pro-Arabic at that time. So the only country that could have helped us was France. My problem was that the whole Israeli establishment in Israel was Anglo-Saxon. They didn't believe in France. Ben-Gurion never forgave France for losing the war. We had a military attaché in France, General David Shealtiel—whenever he went into Ben-Gurion's office, Ben-Gurion never forgot to ask him why France had lost the war. And Ben-Gurion thought that de Gaulle was a burden, a heavy cross—the Cross of Lorraine, as they say. All of them were oriented to Great Britain; Moshe Sharett[8] had reservations about France, so did Golda [Meir], so did [Dov] Joseph,[9] and in a way so did Ben-Gurion.

I will tell you a little story. When de Gaulle published his memoirs, I went to Ben-Gurion and told him, "Look, it's a rich book, it is more impressive than the memoirs of Churchill from the point of view of style and character." And I told him that I had asked a publishing house in Israel to translate it into Hebrew, because it was an important book for the officers in our army. The publishing house said it was ready, but asked who would write the foreword to the book. So I told Ben-Gurion, "I'm asking you to write the foreword." He said, "Me? Never! Who is de Gaulle? What did he do? France lost the war. He misbehaved with the British." So I wrote the foreword for the first edition of the book. Only with the second edition—after Ben-Gurion had met de Gaulle and had come to know him—did he agree to write a foreword.

Now I came [to France] totally ignorant—I didn't know

8. 1894–1965: Israel's foreign minister, he became prime minister in 1954 when Ben-Gurion retired to the Negev kibbutz of Sde Boker, serving for a little more than a year.

9. 1899–1980: Military governor of Jerusalem during the 1948 war, he served in a succession of cabinet posts under Ben-Gurion and later Levi Eshkol.

the language, I didn't know the country, I was inexperienced. And I came and said let's work with them. People [in Israel] thought this was too much. They didn't like what I suggested. And when we started and the [French] minister of defense asked for this to be a relationship between the two ministers of defense, our ambassador and our foreign minister wanted to kill me — they thought that this was an intervention in foreign policy by somebody who was nobody.

Now we had many starts. We went from very strange starts to very fascinating results. A friend of mine, an Israeli industrialist, came to me and said, "Look, I have a friend, Georges Elgozy, who is Jewish and is the economic advisor to [the then French prime minister] Edgar Faure. Let's see if he can be of help." I called Elgozy up and he said, "Come over to my apartment for a cup of tea." I came in with our [Defense Ministry] representative in Paris, Yosef Nahmias, who was laughing at me — he thought the whole story was a joke. We came into a beautiful apartment. All the walls, even the closets, were filled with famous paintings. Picasso. Chagall. I never saw anything like it. And in the middle of the room sat an old lady, as if on a throne, and Elgozy said, "I shall be ready to talk with you after my mother has had a look at you." I went over to his mother. She took my hands and looked at them and she said, "Georges, it's okay." So Georges said, "If my mother says it's okay, okay. Come over to the Hotel Matignon at 10 o'clock.[10]

The next day Nahmias laughed at me. He said, "Are you an idiot? You think this man is serious, with all the paintings and the mother?" I said, "What are you afraid of? Let's go over to the Hotel Matignon and we'll see." We went over at 10 o'clock the next morning. We said we wanted to see Mr. Georges Elgozy.

10. The official Paris residence of French prime ministers.

Nahmias was sure they would say there was nobody there by that name. But the guards had an order. "Yes, he's expecting you. Come in." And we went in and found Georges Elgozy, the economic advisor to the prime minister. And he asked us what our problems were. Then he took us to see the prime minister, Edgar Faure, who spoke like a machine gun, very fast; he was a little bit impatient, but when Elgozy explained to him the problem [of Israeli arms procurement], he said, "Why not?" And we returned to Elgozy's office and from there he called everyone in France — the industries, the ministries — and he said he was acting on behalf of the prime minister. And it opened all the doors. *All the doors.*

Another beginning was under the government of Mendès-France. I want to tell you that Mendès-France was very courteous — he invited Dayan and decorated him with the *Légion d'Honneur* for his role in fighting with the French army in Lebanon [during World War II]. This was the first open recognition of the Israeli army in France. Mendès-France's Minister of Defense was General [Pierre] Koenig. I called up General Koenig, who invited me to the Ministry of Defense on Sunday, which was very unusual. Koenig was a great believer in Israel. I told him we had [arms] requests. And he told me, "Send me over the list and I shall study it and see what I can do." I told him, "By tomorrow at ten o'clock you will have it." I sent the list. At five minutes past ten I got a call from General Koenig. He said, "Where is the list? You told me it would be here at ten o'clock. It didn't arrive." I checked; our messenger had had a slight motorcycle accident. It shows how eager Koenig was to help us. We became dear friends.

Once I told Guy Mollet, "Look, I know our socialist friends. You are very pro-Israel when you are in opposition, but the minute you are in power you are completely undependable — you will let us down. You will forget about us." Our ambassador at the time told me that if there was one person who didn't have a chance to come to power it was Guy Mollet. After the election, it so happened that Mollet became the prime minister. He called me up and said, "Shimon, you remember what you told me? That if I came to power I would forget about you? You're wrong." And he invited me for dinner. I came from Tel Aviv. It was a Friday night. Asher Ben Natan, who was our representative in Paris, drove like crazy. We arrived fifteen minutes late at the Hotel Matignon. And Mollet said, "Look, whatever I promised you—here I am." With Guy Mollet I felt at home, and we started working together.

R.L. Was the end point of this cooperation France's agreement to supply Israel with a nuclear reactor?

S.P. We started with the planes, the tanks, and the guns. We wound up with a deep friendship between our two countries, a golden age that lasted for a decade. We had France, so we had French arms.

R.L. Let's talk about the Suez war of 1956. It always seemed to me that Israel was pulling the French and British chestnuts out of the fire. But I never understood what was in it for Israel until I read about the negotiations between you and the French just before the Israelis agreed to participate in the war. If the French had not agreed to give you the nuclear reactor at Dimona, would Israel have come in on the side of the French and the British? Was the Dimona reactor a quid pro quo?

S.P. I thought that it was a good time to ask for the nuclear reactor, but it wasn't a condition. You know, all my life in dealing with politics I have been very careful not to make conditions. I think it's a mistake. You have to choose the right moment, the right reason, the right occasion. Because if people are not ready, a condition will simply outrage them. And when it is the right moment, you don't need a condition. We had agreed, for the

Suez operation, that we would fight our own war. We did not intend to liberate the Suez Canal. We fought to open the Strait of Tiran, to bring an end to terror, to destroy aggressive arms.

R.L. President Kennedy once asked you the unaskable question, Did Israel have an atomic bomb? Your answer to him was that Israel would never be the first country to introduce atomic weapons into the Middle East. Atomic weapons have been introduced into the Middle East by Saddam Hussein —

S.P. He tried to.

R.L. That's the same thing. So I'd like to ask you the unaskable question. I have never understood why, if the atomic bomb is a deterrent, and you clearly see it as that, Israel doesn't come clean and openly admit it has nuclear weapons.

S.P. It's enough that there is the suspicion; the suspicion is a deterrent. So why should we go further than that? The suspicion is strong enough.

R.L. So you won't go further than that today?

S.P. I don't think it's necessary. If it were to come out more clearly, it would encourage the others to get the same weapon.

R.L. Can we talk about the '67 war? In your memoirs you said that you submitted a proposal to Moshe Dayan when he was appointed defense minister immediately before the Six-Day War that would have deterred the Arabs and prevented the war. You said also that you couldn't give details for reasons of state security. Can you — will you — talk about it now?

S.P. Not yet.

R.L. An eminent Israeli philosopher and biochemist, Yeshayahu Liebowitz, who died two years ago, said immediately after the Six-Day War: "This brilliant victory will be a historical and political disaster for the State of Israel." Liebowitz was making the case that occupying great chunks of Arab territory and administering — I'm using the polite word here — the occupants would "impair the character of the Jewish state and corrupt the moral fiber of its people." Looking back, was the character of the Jewish state, was the moral fiber of its people and its army, corrupted by the almost thirty-year occupation of Gaza and the West Bank?

S.P. It affected it. We escaped in time. The Oslo agreement was the escape. We tried earlier, but weren't successful. After the Six-Day War the Eshkol government, with the participation of [the right-wing leader Menachem] Begin, published a declaration saying that for a full peace, we were ready to withdraw from Egyptian and Syrian territories to international boundary lines. There was no reply. And at that time we didn't think there was a partner on the Palestinian side [to talk to]. Arafat was considered a terrible person. Nobody was ready to meet him and talk with him. Then Dayan came out with the idea of "open bridges," namely; that we would not necessarily be an occupier. And it worked. The bridges were opened to Jordan and the Palestinians could conduct their own economic life with relative freedom.

R.L. So you don't think Israel was corrupted —

S.P. In the end, no.

R.L. Perhaps corrupted is too strong a word. What word would you use? Was morale hurt?

S.P. Yes. I mean, the position the Labor Party took was that we intend to govern the life of the Palestinians and we were looking for an occasion to bring an end to it. And finally we did end it. It was a regrettable experience, being an occupier. But I don't think it really corrupted us.

R.L. But I have spoken to Palestinians who claim that, in retrospect, what appeared to be an enormous Israeli triumph in the '67 war was in fact a Pyrrhic victory. Their reasoning goes this way: before '67, the struggle was pretty straightforward — between the Jews who had washed up on Arab shores and the

Arabs in the neighboring countries who didn't want them there. After 1967, after Israel conquered Jerusalem, the third holiest city in Islam, after it humiliated three Muslim armies and Muslim pride and Muslim faith, the conflict turned into a struggle between the world's fifteen million Jews and a billion followers of Islam. Beyond that, Israel suddenly found itself lord and master over roughly two million Palestinians—which is something you yourself have described as a morally precarious position. With the advantage of hindsight, do you think there is a grain of truth to this Arab line of reasoning, that the '67 war was a Pyrrhic victory for Israel?

s.p. It's part of the story, but not the whole story. Because as a result there began to be a readiness on the part of the Arabs to make peace with Israel. I think their readiness was partly a result of their impression that they could not beat Israel, and this feeling came from the Six-Day War. So, like many phenomena it's not clear-cut.

R.L. Often what looks like an enormous victory, with time looks like less of a victory. The Gulf War is another example. It looked like an incredible American triumph at the time, but now we're beginning to see another side of it—the weakening of the Saudi royal family that resulted from the stationing of American troops on Saudi soil.

s.p. Every war is fought twice: once on the battlefield, then in history books. When you go to war you should always remember that it is a double fight, and you shouldn't judge the results just by what happens on the battlefield, but also by how it will be seen after the dust of battle has settled. The Gulf War brought an end to the Iraqi attempt to occupy Kuwait. That will be the verdict of history.

R.L. Let's talk for a moment about the 1982 Israeli invasion of Lebanon, and the three-year quagmire in which Israel found itself in the wake of that invasion. Was Lebanon Ariel Sharon's war?[11] Did Mr. Sharon really manage to suck Israel into Lebanon without telling the Cabinet about his plans?

S.P. In a way, yes. Sharon had a very naive prime minister. Menachem Begin hardly touched the ground. He floated. I think that Sharon wanted to copy the Dayan Sinai campaign, and one of the brilliant strategies of that war was to start at the end—to land the parachutists at a far point and move backwards—

R.L. You're referring to the parachute drop onto the Mitla Pass in Sinai in '56—

S.P. Yes. The Mitla Pass. Sharon wanted to do the same thing. For him Junia, north of Beirut, was the Mitla Pass.

R.L. But Sharon had already made his reputation in the '73 war, when he led Israeli units across the Suez Canal. He didn't need more military fame—

S.P. Fame is not rationed. Once you get it you want more.

R.L. On September 14, 1982, Bashir Gemayel, a Christian who had been elected president of Lebanon the previous month, was assassinated. The next day Christian forces bent on revenge massacred eight hundred Palestinians, including women and children, at the Sabra and Shatilla refugee camps in south Beirut. It was later established that the Christian militiamen had passed through Israeli lines to get into the camps; that Israeli soldiers, stationed on rooftops overlooking the camps, witnessed the shootings and didn't intervene. The Israeli commission that investigated the atrocity decided that Ariel Sharon, then minister of defense and now the minister of national infrastructure in Mr. Netanyahu's Cabinet, bore "personal responsibility" for

11. A former army general and one of the heroes of the 1973 Yom Kippur War, Sharon was the minister of defense in Prime Minister Begin's government at the time of Israel's invasion of Lebanon.

not preventing the massacres at Sabra and Shatilla. How do you assess Israeli responsibility for these atrocities?

S.P. I organized at the time the greatest demonstration of the war to protest the massacres. I thought it was a tragic mistake. We were very uncomfortable with the relationship that developed with the Lebanese; we gave them the impression that we were ready to fight for them. You see, I personally knew two of the leaders on the Christian side in Lebanon. One was Bashir Gemayel, the son of Pierre Gemayel; the other was Danny Chamoun, the son of Camille Chamoun. They were fighting all the time. When I was defense minister, I met the sons quite often. When they were at my home once I asked them to promise that as sons, they would not continue the fight of their fathers. And they did promise. But then we continued talking and I told them that if a catastrophe were to occur to the Christians, we would be on their side — we could not stand aside at the time of a holocaust or a genocide. But otherwise please remember you will have to fight for yourselves. Don't count on us to fight your war. And please don't go to war unless you are sure you are ready — not that we [Israel] are ready, but that you are ready. So don't jump. I think that Begin and Sharon were so enchanted with the Christians that they went along with them too much. And actually the Christians did expect us to fight their war for them. Which we couldn't.

R.L. They went to war hoping to suck Israel into it?

S.P. Yes.

R.L. But Sabra and Shatilla — is that an open wound for Israel?

S.P. At the beginning we thought that maybe our soldiers were involved, but they weren't.

R.L. They weren't directly involved.

S.P. Yes. In the end, there was an [Israeli] investigating committee that drew very strong conclusions about it.

R.L. To move on—in 1949, Mr. Peres, you and your wife, Sonia, and your daughter lived in New York, where you attended the New School for Social Research, after which you attended Harvard for four months. What did you study at the New School and at Harvard?

S.P. At Harvard, I took a course called Advanced Management Program. It's a very interesting course because you actually learn as much from the students as you do from the professors. The course is aimed at training people who are in very high positions in companies or the army or elsewhere—the level of vice presidents. Our seminars, or bull sessions as they were called, covered a series of case studies. And there for the first time I really met people from all walks of American life, from industry, from unions, from the army, and also some foreigners. Harvard didn't usually accept students under the age of forty or under a certain level of management into this seminar, but we claimed that we were a young country, so two of us were accepted, the commander of the [Israeli] air force, General Aharon Remez, and myself. And these were four extremely happy and fruitful months for me. It all made a great impression on me. It was there that for the first time in my life I drank whiskey—I had never tasted whiskey before—because they had cocktail parties twice a week so people could get acquainted.

At the New School for Social Research I studied economics and history and English. When I was accepted at the school I didn't know a single word of English. And the first lesson, I will never forget it, was about the role of psychology in economics. I came home late. I didn't know what psychology was, so I took the dictionary and looked through all the *s*'s and all the *c*'s and I couldn't find it. I was brokenhearted by my inability to find the translation of the word. The next morning I asked some friends and they explained it to me. Then I started to study English intently, and after three or four months I began to get some *A*'s in English as well.

R.L. It was during this period that you discovered America. You were the deputy head of the defense ministry's mission in America. You combined work with studies. Can you give me your impressions of America and its people—their strengths, their weaknesses?

S.P. First of all, what I liked in America was the respect for work. It is a very labor-oriented country. And no matter what you do, as long as you work, you're respected. So from the man in the elevator up to the top manager of the company, people are proud of their jobs—they take them very seriously, they don't waste time, they work hard. That was one of the great things that impressed me.

The second thing was the capacity of the United States, of the American people, to adapt to new ideas. I will never forget that when I came to the United States I read about an American student who had heard about a train with wheels so large that if somebody were to fall underneath the car he would not be killed. So the student went over to the station and lay on the tracks to see if the engine would really pass over him and he would live through it. This curiosity about new ideas was the second thing that impressed me.

The third thing was the human relations. Even if it is not always sincere, there is ongoing encouragement. People say nice things about each other. In America, the smallest compliment is to say that you are "brilliant." I mean, everybody in America is brilliant. And everybody is great. The average American is above average. And everything is "wonderful." Have a wonderful day. Everything is the biggest and best. Whether it is accurate doesn't matter. You know, only in America can you hear, I had a *wonderful* day, a *wonderful* morning, a *wonderful* event. It's a way of encouraging people. The difference between America and France is that in France it is very difficult to make a friend, but once you make one the friendship lasts for the rest of your life. In America it takes you five minutes and you know the names of the children, which psychiatrist they go to, and what the troubles and relations in the family are. But maintaining the friendship is very demanding.

Another thing I liked very much was the cleanliness in America. The tablecloths in the restaurants, the sheets in the hotels—I mean, this absolute white color.

R.L. I find that the French invariably describe something as "*pas mal*" where the Americans say "fantastic." It's almost as if the French are afraid of becoming too excited, too enthusiastic—

S.P. The difference is that in France you have intellectuals, in America you have celebrities. A celebrity can be a boxer or an author or a film star or a criminal. In France you have to be an intellectual. But what I also liked about the United States is that there is a responsible elite there. The people who publish the *New York Times,* the people in foreign affairs, the people in the universities. When I came to America—it made a great impression on me—it was at the time when President Truman fired [General Douglas] MacArthur.[12] Then they accused [Dean] Acheson of being behind the firing, and Acheson testified before Congress for days on end. The entire proceedings were published in the *New York Times.* I read it like a novel. The man was outstanding. I think Acheson was one of the greatest foreign ministers in this century, a real intellectual. I very much liked his book *Present at the Creation.*

At the New School, one of the professors—he taught once a

12. 1880–1964: Allied commander in the Southwest Pacific during World War II, later commander of the United Nations forces during the Korean War until he was fired in 1951 by President Truman in a policy dispute.

month—was Judge [Felix] Frankfurter. And it so happened that the first lecture I heard him give was his eulogy for [the British socialist] Harold Laski, who had just passed away. Laski had been a great friend of Supreme Court Justice [Oliver Wendell] Holmes. Laski and Justice Holmes corresponded for twenty or thirty years—they used to write daily letters to each other. And there were two books published that contained their correspondence. Judge Frankfurter was a short man. He was almost the same size as Berl Katznelson,[13] my own teacher. And when I heard Frankfurter, if I had closed my eyes it would have been like listening to the eulogy that Berl Katznelson gave for Chaim Arlosoroff, the young fellow who was murdered on the beach at Tel Aviv in 1934. There was such a great similarity between Frankfurter and Katznelson—the way they thought, the way they spoke. I was fascinated by Frankfurter's brilliance, his penetrating mind. Another teacher that I remember very well was Reinhold Niebuhr.[14] He was the intellectual leader of American Protestantism, and he gave lectures on the Judeo-Greek influence on Western civilization. I learned as much about Judaism from Niebuhr as I did from anybody else in my life.

R.L. Did you get a whiff of racism in America during this period?

S.P. Very much so. We were living not far from Harlem—we went through it many times. I remember at that time they used to say that in America the South hated blacks in general, but white Southerners were very nice to individual black people. But

13. 1887–1944: A contemporary of David Ben-Gurion, he was, along with Ben-Gurion, one of the most influential voices in the Zionist and socialist movements in Palestine; Peres first met Katznelson when he delivered a series of lectures at Ben-Shemen.

14. 1892–1971: American theologian who wrote primarily about morality and Christianity's refusal to confront social problems.

in New York whites were for the blacks in general, but disliked them individually. I was very impressed by Lincoln—by his role in giving liberty to the slaves.

R.L. Wasn't it Ben-Gurion who admired Lincoln's Gettysburg Address?

S.P. Yes. Ben-Gurion explained it in the following way. Dictators also say they are *for* democracy, *for* the people. Being *of* the people—again, many rulers are *of* the people. But you need a combination of the three—being *for* the people, being *of* the people, and being *elected by* the people—to have real democracy. And that was what Ben-Gurion saw in Lincoln's 152 words: the most precise definition of what democracy stands for.

R.L. Where exactly did you live in New York?

S.P. On Ninety-sixth Street and Riverside Drive. We had a very large apartment—six or seven rooms. We organized a small kibbutz in our apartment. Other Israelis shared the apartment with us. We really had a collective life, like on a kibbutz. We prepared breakfasts and lunches together.

R.L. Yitzhak Rabin had a stormy relationship with American Jewish leaders. He accused them of being overly intrusive in Israel's international affairs. Do you agree with Mr. Rabin's assessment that the American Jewish lobby "mistakenly thought that it was, if not the Israeli government, at least the Israeli foreign ministry?"

S.P. I don't think so. I don't think these were Rabin's feelings, either. It was an outburst more than a constant position. American Jewry by and large played a very positive role in the formation of Israel. I don't have these sorts of reservations.

R.L. When Mr. Rabin came to Washington to sign Oslo II, he spoke at a closed-door meeting to two hundred American Jewish leaders and intellectuals and philanthropists. In his talk he castigated right-wing Jewish groups and individuals in America for opposing the Oslo agreements. American-born extremists seem to be in the front ranks of those who oppose returning so much as a square inch of the West Bank to the Palestinians. Why are American Jews, both in America and in Israel, so opposed to Oslo?

s.p. First of all, we're talking about a minority. I don't believe that this [opposition to Oslo] represents the entire spectrum of American Jewish opinion. Don't forget that from 1977, with a short interruption, Israel was governed by the rightist people — the government of Begin, the government of [Yitzhak] Shamir.[15] We came back to power in 1992. So the American Jews were supporting the position of the government of Israel —

r.l. I was thinking of the extremist right-wing Rabbi Meir Kahane, who extolled the virtues of Jewish violence; I was thinking of Kahane's disciple Baruch Goldstein, the American-born and American-educated Qiryat Arba settler who, in 1994, murdered twenty-nine Muslims in the mosque at the Cave of the Patriarchs in Hebron.

s.p. Yes, yes. Kahane, Goldstein — it's a terrible story, but I wouldn't blame it on all American Jews. I wouldn't go in for generalizations. The vast majority of American Jews were not in their camp.

r.l. Israel, with your approval, acted as the middleman in dealings between President Reagan and so-called moderates in Iran, the aim being to free American hostages held by Shi'ite groups in Lebanon. The quid pro quo was delivery of advanced arms by America to Iran. Israel, on America's behalf, secretly

15. 1915– : One of the founders, in 1973, of the conservative Likud party, he succeeded Menachem Begin as prime minister in 1983. He served as prime minister in a national unity government from 1986 to 1990, and as prime minister of a Likud-led government from 1990 to 1992.

delivered a planeload of weapons, and the first hostage, the Reverend Benjamin Weir, was freed. Weren't the Americans doing precisely what the Israelis always said you should not do in hostage situations, which is to say, rewarding the hostage-takers, which only encourages more hostage-taking? During the Entebbe hostage crisis, you argued long and loudly in the Cabinet against rewarding the hostage-takers.

S.P. In Entebbe we had another option. In the case of Iran, I don't think the Americans had another option. The Americans also approached not only us—they also approached the Palestinians to negotiate for the hostages. To trade hostages for arms was an American decision, not an Israeli decision. I felt very strongly at the time that if the Americans asked us to be instrumental, we owed it to the United States to comply. With a full heart. I thought it was almost an occasion to be of service on a human scale to the United States. Don't forget there was another point. We went on the assumption that in Iran there were three different factions, what they used to call line A, line B, and line C. It wasn't simply giving arms to those who captured the hostages, it was the hope of encouraging a possible change in Iran.

R.L. The idea that there were moderates in Iran with whom the West could deal was ridiculed later—

S.P. Maybe. But at the time that was our assumption. We didn't want to help the ones who took the hostages, we wanted to help the ones who wanted to change the tendencies of Iran.

R.L. If I can change the subject—my Israeli friends tell what is supposed to be a joke, which goes like this: What is anti-Semitism? The answer is, hating Jews more than necessary.

S.P. That story is attributed to Churchill.

R.L. I didn't know that. In any case, it seems to me more sad than funny. It implies that anti-Semitism is here to stay and that

Israelis are willing to accept a certain amount of anti-Semitism as long as it doesn't get out of hand. Anti-Semitism has been a fixture in the world for two thousand years. Is it here to stay?

s.p. You know, the strange part of it is that there is anti-Semitism even if you don't have Jews —

r.l. Poland.

s.p. Poland. I mean the Jews all died, but anti-Semitism is alive, which is a very strange phenomenon. Which shows, in my judgment, that anti-Semites are sick people. It's a sickness. It's one of those prejudices that goes from one generation to the next, and prejudices don't have to have reasons or evidence. They have an existence of their own, like any other mental illness. Today we feel very strongly that anti-Semitism is a gentile malady, not a Jewish malady. We don't feel we have anything to do with anti-Semitism. We don't feel that we have to change in order to be liked. Not at all. We think that anti-Semites have to change in order to become healthy. It's not only anti-Semitism — you have Le Pen, you have the different rightist groups, which are a sickness in society. And each society in which this happens has to take the necessary measures to cure itself.

r.l. My oldest son is an admirer of the oeuvre of the French writer Louis-Ferdinand Céline, who was a great anti-Semite and a great collaborator during World War II. I refuse to read Céline because of his active and ardent anti-Semitism at a time when Jews were being killed for the crime of being Jewish. My son says I'm missing out on one of the great writers of the century. I throw in my son's face a quote from Tzvetan Todorov, a French intellectual of Bulgarian origin. "La beauté de leurs oeuvres ne leur procure aucune immunité morale" [The beauty of their works does not give them moral immunity]. Neither I nor Tzvetan Todorov can convince my son that an artist's anti-Semitism discredits his art. Here I'm thinking also of Ezra

Pound, of T. S. Eliot, to name just two. How can you convince people not to read Céline?

S.P. Well, I read Céline, too. One must distinguish very clearly between being talented and being morally right. There are many vicious people who are extremely talented, and you must be sophisticated enough to distinguish between viciousness and talent. I read Céline with a taste of revulsion in my mouth, but I must admit that some of his descriptions of the military and the war were very powerful, very convincing. But it shows that people who are talented do not necessarily have the talent to distinguish between right and wrong. And maybe the talent to distinguish between right and wrong is the greatest talent. It is not the accumulation of impressive words and sentences that makes life right or wrong, but the distinction between the two. I would take Céline like a bottle that has a label on it: "Be careful, it's poison."

R.L. Cigarette smoking can be dangerous for your health?

S.P. Yes. With this label on it I would say, Okay, go ahead and read it, why not?

R.L. Perhaps we should move on to current events now. Relations between Mr. Netanyahu and Mr. Arafat—between Israel and the Arab world—are clearly in a state of crisis. President Kennedy once reminded us that the Chinese word for crisis is composed of two characters.

Wei   Gi

The first character, pronounced *wei*, represents danger, the second, pronounced *gi*, represents opportunity. I think any idiot can see the dangers inherent in the present crisis, namely that the reconciliation between Israel and its Arab neighbors will reach a dead end when the two sides begin to discuss the future of Jerusalem, or the status of the Jewish settlements on the West Bank and in Gaza, or the final boundaries of Mr. Arafat's Palestinian entity. Since you are, by your own account, an eternal optimist, perhaps you could spell out the opportunities — assuming the Chinese are correct in their definition of crisis.

S.P. I can answer briefly or I can answer at length. What do you want?

R.L. Whichever answer you think is the best.

S.P. You see, I definitely decided to pursue the peace process when I reached the conclusion — I was warned also by my friend Amos Oz[16] — that Yasir Arafat had become so weak that he might fall. And I kept asking myself what would happen if he were to fall from power. Because in order to make peace you must have a partner more than a plan. If you have a plan and you don't have a partner, you have a piece of paper that's of no value. Only when you have a partner can you try and find the proper plan. (I shall say a word also about the plan.)

Now enemies are the raw material of partners. Dangers are the raw material of hope. How to overcome them? How to take an enemy and make a friend of him? How to take a danger and turn it into an opportunity? And then, you know, it's as difficult to meet the enemy face to face as it is to confront a danger. Because you are trained, it's in your blood, it's in your mind. And then when you finally meet the other person, you are surprised to learn that he is a human being like yourself.

Because, you know, the problem is that when you have an enemy and you have a danger, you have a one-sided dialogue with yourself. When you dialogue with yourself you're terribly

---

16. 1939– : Israeli novelist best known for *My Michael* (1968).

brilliant. You win all the arguments. Somebody asked in a famous American poem, What is a pier? A pier is a frustrated bridge. It has just one end. And in life, the problem is how to make a pier into a bridge. It is dangerous when you have only one end, but if you have two ends you have the opportunity to go somewhere. It's a very difficult process because once you start to negotiate, you discover there is another party. It's like married life—after the wedding night you have family life, which is a totally different story because, until your marriage, you lived as a single person. But when you marry you are two on a daily basis, and it is very hard for each of the two to get along. So you begin to look for compromises and make concessions.

And then you discover that your own people are beginning to ask: What are you doing? We have had such a happy life—because to live in danger gives you "happiness." Everything is clear. You don't have to make concessions. You don't have to make compromises, you see. It is only when you try to get out of it that you discover the other side of the danger, but you also discover the other side of the opportunity. Now what usually makes me optimistic is that when you go through a crisis, people think that it is the end of the world. A crisis is actually a passing phenomenon. Basically I believe that there is nothing perfect in life, including viciousness. No perfection. Which means that you can always find an opportunity in the worst situation.

R.L. So your starting point for Oslo was the weakness of Mr. Arafat?

S.P. Yes, the weakness of Arafat and the danger that he would disappear. I mean, his disappearance was in my opinion a greater danger than his existence.

R.L. But doesn't Mr. Arafat's weakness represent a fatal flaw in the peace process? What I'm driving at here is that only a weakened and isolated Arafat could have been lured to the peace table, only a weakened and isolated Arafat would have made the concessions necessary to attain an accord. On the other hand this same weakened and isolated Arafat could not deliver on the security aspects of the accord which, for Israel, was one of the mainstays of any PLO-Israeli agreement. You needed a weak Arafat to negotiate an accord, but a strong Arafat to deliver on the accord.

S.P. But once we met him he became more powerful. The Oslo meeting gave him strength. You see, his weakness pushed him to see if something could be done, and he found nothing. The people who opposed him became very strong. The minute we met him the whole picture changed.

R.L. You and the late Prime Minister Yitzhak Rabin never spelled it out, but the world—and the Palestinians—believed you were moving toward a two-state solution. Mr. Rabin's aides have been quoted since his assassination as saying that the late prime minister considered that Oslo II in practice created a Palestinian state. Not long ago Mr. Netanyahu's people launched what in America we call a trial balloon, hinting that a Palestinian state is within the realm of possibility, which is something Likud never said before. In your view, did Oslo II create a Palestinian state in everything but name? Is a Palestinian state inevitable?

S.P. You know, I have gone on record in favor of a Jordanian-Palestinian confederation because I thought we were living in a triangle and you had to refer to each of the angles. If you only refer to two of the angles in the triangle and you ignore one of the three, you may face problems later on. Here I may reveal something that has never been told before. I actually suggested to Arafat that Gaza would become a Palestinian state and the West Bank would remain autonomous. One part [Gaza] would be a full state and the other part [the West Bank] would be an autonomy attached to this Palestinian state. I thought this would permit the Palestinians to negotiate [a Jordanian-Palestinian confederation] with the Jordanians from the point of view of statehood. But the Palestinians were reluctant at the time. So I never thought that autonomy was the less [important] station on the road. I think it is a station on the road to a permanent solution, but not itself a permanent solution. Yet I felt all the time and I still feel that we have to reveal our full vision gradually. If we reveal it ahead of time not only will we encounter unnecessary opposition, but we will give away before negotiations what we should keep for our fallback position.

R.L. When you and Mr. Rabin started out with Oslo, how did you—in your private discussions—see the peace you were attempting to construct? Was it going to be a peace that integrated the Palestinians and the Israelis, economically and as a people? Or would the peace you envisioned have separated them?

S.P. I can answer for myself. I saw it as separate politically and integrated economically. I distinguish between the two. I thought economically we should become a Benelux because in the modern age you cannot really draw borders in economic terms. But I thought they were entitled to have their destiny and we were entitled to have our destiny in the political sense. So I was thinking about a triangle that would comprise the Jordanian, Palestinian, and Israeli economies and a border that would separate us politically.

R.L. It is generally accepted that unless both sides begin to trust each other, a lasting peace—a total solution to the problem—is out of reach. The interim accords (Gaza and Jericho) were designed to put off the hard issues (Jewish settlements, Jerusalem, borders, Palestinian refugees, the nature of the Palestinian entity) to give both sides time to build up trust and confidence in each other. This is a clear failure.

S.P. Why is it a clear failure? We created trust—

R.L. It seems to me that there is less trust today than when you started the peace process.

S.P. When we left power [after losing the election to Mr. Netanyahu in 1996] the trust was full. I think even today we enjoy a great deal of trust among the Arabs. Among the Palestinians.

R.L. You don't accept that there is less trust now?

S.P. I think that the present government made many mistakes and lost trust. And for that reason they made the Palestinians even more cautious. But with us it [the peace process] could have gone a long way.

R.L. Is the Netanyahu government using Islamic fundamentalist terrorism as an excuse to put an end to the Oslo peace process that it never liked in the first place?

S.P. No. They're not as sophisticated as that. You see, I'm not so sure they want to put an end to the Oslo agreement. Maybe it's even more convenient for them to say, "We were forced by Oslo." If they have to make a choice, it will be very difficult for them to choose Oslo. But since Oslo exists, it's not bad for them to have as an excuse. The maneuvering around Oslo is because of the restraints in his own Cabinet which I've described already. He is a master of his survival and the prisoner of the consequences of his survival. It's a strange situation.

R.L. More and more Americans appear to be coming around to the view that, with the end of the Cold War, United States vital interests are not really at risk in the Israeli-Palestinian conflict. Would you agree?

S.P. I don't accept that. Because the greatest danger for many parties, including the United States, is a combination of Muslim fundamentalism with long-range missiles and non-conventional warheads shaking up the Arab status quo and taking over countries which are oil producers. This is the worst scenario I can think of. The effect on the economies of the United States and

Europe would be tremendous. So it's a little casual to say, let them play around. It's not bad to play around if you don't have nuclear bombs and you don't have missiles. Once you have them, well, my God, be careful with the game.

R.L. In light of all that's happened in the Middle East in the last six months—all the terrorist bombs that have exploded, the stalemate in peace negotiations—do you still believe in the possibility of creating what you've called "the new Middle East"?

S.P. The answer is a hundred percent yes. There is a new world and the Middle East will be forced to become part of it sooner or later. Today even old leaders have young viewers of television. They are watching what's happening in the world and they keep asking, How about us? So it's only a matter of time. I was pressing forward in order to save lives and sacrifice and damage, not because I had any doubt about the ultimate arrival of the new Middle East. I thought that to shorten the time of the arrival would be a great service to young people, to mothers, to a nation.

R.L. Let's talk for a moment about the Palestinians as a people. The Scottish essayist Thomas Carlyle, writing in 1841, said: "The Arabs are Oriental Italians. A gifted noble people; a people of wild strong feelings, and of iron restraint over these." In some Arab countries—I'm thinking of Kuwait before the Gulf War, for example—it was the Palestinians who made things work. I've even heard Palestinians referred to as the Arabs' Jews. What do you see as the strengths and the weaknesses of the Palestinian people?

S.P. Undoubtedly they are a talented people, and under the right circumstances they can become a modern people—as modern as any other people in the world. They have several shortcomings. One is that they have never been a people—there never was a Palestinian people until very recently. They have never experienced the taste of statehood—there never was a Palestinian state. And they were eaten up by violence and terror, as well as tribal and family divisions, which makes it very hard for them to unite. But then I think they are fast learners—they can be quite ingenious. I mean, they could excel in all walks of life if they were to come to normalcy. They are on their way to normalcy. To compare them with the Jewish people would be apt if you remember that the Jewish people didn't have normalcy either. By normal, I mean running a state and becoming responsible. Another shortcoming is their sensitivity to respect and honor. They are very sensitive to their self-respect. This is [for them] almost consideration number one. But having land is their highest priority. This in an age in which science is more important than land, which is something they haven't grasped yet.

R.L. There are Jews, too, who put more value on land than on other things. I'm thinking of the right-wing Jewish settlers on the West Bank.

S.P. They are wrong, too. But you know, in many of the discussions I had with the Palestinians, they said: "You took land away from us." I told them, Let's try to look at it differently. It's not the amount of land that counts, but how much the land will yield. Because together we have learned that from the same dunam [one-quarter acre] of land you can produce seventeen times more than you could previously. So maybe one dunam is worth seventeen dunams. And I'm not inventing this figure, because in twenty-five years agricultural production in Israel has gone up seventeen times. So if you needed 170 dunams before, maybe today with only ten dunams your production is greater and better. But that will come with age.

And then the family life [of Palestinians] is very, very strong. If you come into an Arab village you will find beautiful homes and apartments, but the village itself is a little bit neglected. So collective responsibility is secondary to family responsibility. But Palestinians are quick to learn. And they are on their way to pass from one era to another.

Every transitional voyage has its fascinating side and its complicated side. Look, we [Israelis] created something and, on second thought, I'm not sure that we were right—and this was experts on Palestinian affairs. People ask me if I am an expert on Palestinian affairs. I say no, because I think basically we have to behave vis-à-vis them and vis-à-vis ourselves as human beings. I mean, the idea that we were dealing with something that was special and different is wrong. An Arab mother loves her children as a Jewish mother does. An Arab industrialist wants to be successful as a Jewish industrialist does. I think that if I am appreciated in the Arab world today, it's because they feel deep down that my attitude was humane and not partisan, for good and for bad. I felt that this was a meeting between human beings, not between specialists for one kind of human being and specialists for another kind of human being. I've wondered all my life if these descriptions by the experts were really creating differences more than helping us to overcome them. You know, Ben-Gurion always used to say that all the experts are experts for things that have already happened. We don't have experts for things that may happen. And our vocation is to see things that may happen and not to analyze things that have already happened.

R.L. During your 1996 campaign for reelection, you vowed that Jerusalem was indivisible and eternally Jewish. Your opponent, Mr. Netanyahu, said precisely the same thing. The difference between you and Mr. Netanyahu was that most Israelis believed he meant it, but few believed you meant it. Did you mean it when you said that Jerusalem was indivisible? Or did you imagine—do you imagine today—some formula by which Jerusalem could remain Jewish and still be the capital of a Palestinian state?

s.p. Politically, I don't see room in the present Jerusalem for two capitals. And I wouldn't agree to dividing Jerusalem the way Berlin was divided. I distinguish between the spiritual side and the political side. Spiritually, yes, Jerusalem can be open to all believers. Look, some people didn't believe me [with respect to the indivisibility of Jerusalem]. That was because of propaganda against me. The Likud spread the rumor that I was going to divide Jerusalem. And people take insinuations more seriously than guarantees.

r.l. Assuming the Palestinians could be coaxed into an accord that left Jerusalem in the hands of the Israelis, how can there be a lasting solution to the Jerusalem question that doesn't satisfy the Palestinian side as well as the Israeli side?

s.p. You know, in my life I have learned that when you have two alternatives and you think, My God, how can I convince one side to accept the other alternative, you will discover there is a third alternative that hasn't yet been noticed. And this is the domain of creativeness. So surely the existing alternatives will not be accepted simultaneously by both sides, but I trust in creativity to find the solution. Include a solution that says, Okay, we have given in on 90 percent of the issues, let's live in peace while 10 percent of the issues, including Jerusalem, are not agreed upon. I had very tough negotiations with Arafat on Hebron, on the Tomb of the Patriarchs. I told him that for us, it's a holy place — the second holiest place after the Wailing Wall in Jerusalem. And Arafat said, Look, for me it's also a holy place. It's an ancient mosque of great importance. And we argued and argued and argued. Finally we agreed to conclude it in the following way: since the two parties couldn't agree on the future of the Tomb of the

Patriarchs, we would keep the status quo. So actually we agreed to live in disagreement. So I mean, nobody thought about this possibility, but it became a solution.

R.L. What brought the PLO to the negotiating table at Oslo? The weakness of Arafat, which you've already spoken about? The Gulf War? The breakup of the Soviet Union?

S.P. Everything combined. The PLO made many mistakes. The terrorism didn't lead to any solution. On the contrary, it led to the building of an anti-terrorism network all over the world. Then the PLO foolishly took the side of Saddam Hussein. Then the collapse of the Soviet Union. Then the fact that the Arab countries negotiated with Israel without paying attention to the PLO — let's not forget that the most important Arab country, Egypt, signed a peace agreement with Israel without the Palestinians. They had to face the possibility that we would reach an agreement with Jordan without them. So all told, they felt that this might be their only option — to sit with Israel and see what could be achieved. In a strange way Israel more than the Arab countries became their best bet.

R.L. What brought Israel to the negotiating table at Oslo? Would Israel have gone to Oslo without the intifada?

S.P. Yes. A hundred percent. That was our choice. We were not going to rule the Palestinians against their will. We were always looking for a way to liberate them from our occupation and to liberate ourselves as occupiers.

R.L. I have Israeli friends who argue that Israel is talking with the wrong people, that it should have dealt with leaders of the intifada, which is to say Palestinians from the administered territories, what you referred to as "the inside," and not with the PLO leaders based in Tunis since their expulsion from Beirut, what you called "the outside." When I speak about "the inside,"

I mean people like Faisal Husseini, heir of a famous nationalist family and perhaps the most respected Palestinian in the Israeli-occupied territories, or the Palestinian academic Sari Nusseibeh.

S.P. The idea that we were talking to the wrong people is nonsense. There were insiders and outsiders, but not with respect to authority. Clearly authority rested in the hands of Arafat. He was the great maneuverer. At the time we were involved in bilateral negotiations and multilateral negotiations. In the beginning Rabin suggested there would be a division of labor between the two of us. I would be responsible for the multilateral, and he would be responsible for the bilateral. The bilateral talks in Washington[17] were going nowhere. When I heard about Abu Ala'a,[18] I decided to test him to see if he was really serious. In the multilateral negotiations, there was a group dealing with the issue of refugees, and the Palestinians appointed a member of the Palestinian National Council to head their team on refugees, and that embarrassed us very much. So I sent Abu Ala'a a message that said, Look, you're embarrassing us by appointing a member of the PNC. Can you change it? And he changed it. And the minute he changed it, I said to myself, Okay, I can work with this man.

R.L. And that little signal led to the ultimate success of the Oslo back channel?

S.P. Yes.

R.L. Did you ever ask Mr. Arafat himself what brought him to the Oslo negotiating table?

S.P. Yes. He said he was in search of it all his life. He sent us

17. The official channel, with Israel talking to Palestinians who were supposed to be independent of the PLO, but in fact were not.

18. The PLO representative at the multilateral back channel talks in Oslo.

many feelers indicating that he wanted to meet. There was the chancellor of Austria Bruno Kreisky,[19] for example—

R.L. Who was Jewish.

S.P. Oh, yes. He once told me that Arafat wanted to negotiate with me. You know, there was also Léopold Senghor.[20] He invited me to participate in the meeting of an international socialist bureau that took place in Dakar. We didn't have formal relations with Senegal at the time. When I arrived I was surprised to see the president and the whole government waiting for me at the airport. It was pretty funny. All of them were standing at the foot of the ladder that opened up to first class, but I was traveling in tourist class. So when all the passengers came down from first class, they were a little bit shocked because they thought for a while I was not on the plane. When he greeted me, the president said, Look, you are my guest. You will stay with me in the palace and I will take you there in my car. When we left the airport, the president said, Look, not far from here there is a small villa where Arafat is staying. Let me take you to the villa. Nobody will know about it. So I told him, Mr. President, I bought a round-trip ticket. I have to return home. If it were to become known that I had seen Arafat, how could I go back home? And if there were to be an act of terror, what would I say? So I refused. That was a Thursday evening. I returned to Israel Sunday. And on that day there was one of the ugliest acts of terror ever committed in Israel—a PLO group captured a father and two children and broke the heads of the children with stones. And I thought to myself, My God, if I had met Arafat on Thursday and come home

19. 1911–90: A lifelong socialist who was chancellor of Austria from 1970 to 1983.

20. 1906– : African statesman and poet and the first black member of the French Academy, he served as president of Senegal from 1960 to 1980.

on Sunday and it had become known, I wouldn't have been able to return home.

R.L. It's been suggested that both Israel and the PLO are more fearful of Jewish and Arab right-wing fundamentalism than of each other. Do you think there is any truth to this?

S.P. Again, it's overgeneralized. I think that Arafat thought in his heart that he could break the Muslim fundamentalists, that he could split them and win them over. He didn't think it was a lost cause. Even today he thinks this. The problem is to distinguish between the fundamentalists who use arms and the fundamentalists who don't use arms. The Jewish fundamentalists basically don't use arms. They vote, but they don't shoot.

R.L. Except for Baruch Goldstein.

S.P. Yes, but this is not a movement. This is a single person. It's a shame, but it was done by an individual. The one who assassinated Rabin — it's the same story. So let's distinguish between individual criminals and movements.

R.L. Before the recent elections, the Israeli security services, whose reputation was hard-hit by their failure to protect Mr. Rabin, tracked Yahya Ayyash, the so-called engineer responsible for Hamas suicide attacks, to Gaza, booby-trapped his cellular phone, and killed him. You were the prime minister at the time; they surely couldn't have done this without your approval. It was this assassination that spurred Hamas to retaliate with suicide bombings on Israeli buses and in Tel Aviv, killing sixty-two Israelis. Looking back, it is difficult not to see the assassination of Ayyash, which led to the Hamas suicide attacks that mortally hurt your chances of reelection, as a dramatic miscalculation on your part. With the passage of time, do you agree?

S.P. We had definite information that Ayyash was in the Gaza Strip. I spoke personally to Arafat. I told him, you have to put your hands on him. And he said—he always called me "Your Excellency"—"I assure you that Ayyash is not in the Gaza Strip. I have all the information in the world that he left the Gaza Strip." Then we had evidence that Ayyash was actively preparing another attack. It wasn't a matter of revenge. The decision to liquidate him prevented this terrorist act.

R.L. It was a preventive strike—

S.P. A hundred percent.

R.L. Can we talk about Hebron for a moment—one hundred thousand Palestinians, a great many of them Hamas members or sympathizers, and four hundred or so Jewish religious zealots who believe, like the late Rabbi Meir Kahane, in the forcible expulsion of the Palestinians from the West Bank. This is an explosion waiting to happen. After Baruch Goldstein murdered twenty-nine Palestinians in the Hebron mosque in 1994, did you and Mr. Rabin miss an opportunity to remove the Jewish fanatics from Hebron? You could have argued convincingly that you were doing it for their safety, something the great mass of Israeli citizens at the time could have understood.

S.P. You know, I don't want to go into it. I hate to pass judgment on things that belong to the past, because you can't change them. You can only put the blame on somebody. But I can tell you that the subject was before our eyes and for one reason or another, things weren't realized. Basically it was the responsibility of Rabin and he should speak for himself. He cannot speak for himself.

R.L. Starting with the most recent election, the Israeli prime minister was elected by direct vote, something which obviously altered the political system that existed before. Mr. Netanyahu seems to be concentrating a great deal of power in his own hands—in short, he is coming to resemble an American president. Isn't this a delicate moment to be ironing out the relationship of the prime minister with the Knesset [the Israeli parliament] and the Cabinet?

s.p. It's a terrible mistake we have made, changing the system. Because you cannot elect a president without having a presidential system. The American president has his own checks and balances. He has an independent Congress — the Senate, the House of Representatives — and they have full authority on many issues, including the budget. Here they took away the authority of the parliament and they have invested it in the hands of the prime minister, so the checks and balances are in danger. Imagine what would happen if the American president were a member of the Senate; were at the same time the leader of the majority of the Senate; would have the right to nominate senators to his Cabinet. He would co-opt the Senate. So I mean, what you need is a complete system; you cannot just pick out pieces. The United States Constitution is very carefully constructed to distribute power, to control power, to use power. Here some thoughtless, supposedly great experts on elections have introduced a system that is detrimental to democracy and to the distribution of power. And the future worries me very much.

r.l. I have an Israeli friend who met you in the post office of Zichron Ya'akov when you were campaigning for Yitzhak Rabin in 1992. As my friend shook your hand, he told you that he was voting for Mr. Rabin, but bitterly regretted that you were not heading the Labor ticket in Mr. Rabin's place. In the most recent election, my friend, a long-time liberal, voted for Mr. Netanyahu. How did you lose his vote?

s.p. Did you ask him?

r.l. I did. But I'm interested in your answer.

s.p. I don't think I lost many votes. I got over a hundred thousand votes from the [followers of] Likud. So if there is a small group that left Labor, it is balanced by the fact that many of the Likud voters voted for me.

R.L. There was a sizable element in the Israeli electorate that preferred you as a person. My Zichron Ya'akov friend says that, intellectually, in terms of vision, you are head and shoulders above everyone else. Yet he voted against you. He was frightened by the secrecy surrounding the Oslo negotiations —

S.P. He was frightened by the terrorism.

R.L. He was frightened you were going too fast.

S.P. Yes, but he's seeing what happens when you go too slowly. Look, the problem in democracy, and in the polls, is that the results always look absolute, while the feelings [of the voters] are never absolute. Even if a person votes for you, he's 51 percent for you, not 100 percent. And everybody has a floating vote in his heart. All it takes is for one thing to happen and the 51 becomes 49 or the 49 becomes 51. Because people are made up of so many doubts and questions. So it's no wonder that some people changed their minds. Particularly after the four terrorist attacks that took place in Jerusalem, Tel Aviv, and Ashkelon. People asked, how can you trust the Arabs when they throw bombs in the squares of Israeli cities. And then the religious [Jews] voted in bloc against us — not necessarily against me.

R.L. Were the people who voted against you essentially voting against Arafat, which is to say they didn't see him as an acceptable partner in peace negotiations?

S.P. Partly, yes. Also the Likud turned on its propaganda machine, saying that you can have peace for nothing. Which is nonsense. Saying that you can have security before peace. Which again is nonsense. Look, yesterday two of our soldiers were killed in Lebanon again. Saying that Labor is in a hurry; that Israel has to slow down. If you slow down, the anti-peace forces accelerate, as they did in the last six months. And then they said that I would divide Jerusalem — it was a smear campaign. And a smear campaign convinces some people, particularly the floating vote.

R.L. The first time you met Ben-Gurion — you hitched a ride to Tel Aviv in his car in the early days of the state, if I remember correctly — he told you that Lenin was Trotsky's inferior in terms of intellect, but Lenin became the leader of Russia because he was decisive — he decided on peace and paid the heavy price that peace required.

S.P. I, too, paid.

R.L. And Mr. Rabin paid.

S.P. Yes.

Ben-Gurion surrounded by young leaders of the Jewish state. On his right, Dayan; on his left, Peres; between Peres and Ben-Gurion, Rabin. Ben-Gurion "thought that the Bible is the place where heaven and earth meet — the values of heaven and the realities of earth."

Left to right: Teddy Kollek, mayor of Jerusalem, Ben-Gurion, Dayan, and Peres. "The more complicated the situation became, the more reassured [Ben-Gurion] appeared. He was a genius."

With Sadat and Shamir: "Let's not forget that the most important Arab country, Egypt, signed a peace agreement with Israel without the Palestinians."

With Rabin: "We had been fighting for so many years, it wasn't easy to wind up a lifelong struggle with such a warm embrace. It wasn't easy for him or for me."

"You have to be strong in order to make peace, and not in order to be strong."

With Mitterrand: "The French Catholics . . . know so little about Jewish history. . . . Mitterrand was an exception to the rule."

With Shamir: "I saw many people who won elections and didn't know what to do with their victory."

With Pope John Paul II: "You cannot speak about religion as if it were a frozen phenomenon."

With the Christian leaders of Jerusalem: "I think internationalization of Jerusalem is a remote dream more than a real position of the Vatican."

Before enlarged photograph of Golda Meir: "It was a regrettable experience—being an occupier. But I don't think it really corrupted us."

With President Ezer Weizman: "We live in a world without borders, but all the borders are still in our minds."

"The great thing about Judaism is that it is very optimistic because it is based on the idea that you can improve every person, you can better every nation, you can bring an end to wars, to poverty."

With Sonia: "I tried to do my very best to conquer her heart. Among other things, I read to her by moonlight chapters from Marx's *Das Kapital*."

With Sonia: "Every person who has loved and does not have the strength to continue loving takes another step toward death."

With his grand-daughter: "We felt it was our obliga-tion to the younger generation."

With Bedouins: "The only known occurrence of the status quo happened in the Bible when Joshua ordered the sun to stop shining."

With King Hassan II: "They can fall. They can also overcome the fundamentalist threat. I don't believe in determinism in history."

With Clinton: "As far as Israel is concerned, he is a real friend. He has paid four visits to our country, more than any other American president. He went the longest way to support us, to support the peace process."

With Mubarak and Clinton: "This is the first time that Egypt has escaped the delta and the pyramids and entered a new age."

With Palestinians: "You have for the first time a geographic address, you have a Palestinian Authority, you have a negotiating position, you have a future."

With King Hussein: "He's really caught between so many fires that for him, not to get burned is a major achievement."

With an Ethiopian immigrant: "Memory has been our land for two thousand years."

John Major (*top, left; left to right*): King Hussein, Peres, Bill Clinton, Hosni Mubarak, Boris Yeltsin, Yasir Arafat, and King Hassan II during a conference on terrorism. As Harry Truman said, "If you can't stand the heat, stay out of the kitchen."

With Arafat: "When it comes to facts, he prefers to become a sort of Chagall — things can float around."

With Rabin: "Occasionally the two of us were surprised to see that without even talking beforehand we had the same attitude, the same reaction, to people, to events."

Before Rabin's tomb: "I was shocked to the depths of my heart. Nothing else . . . there was no consolation."

With Robert Littell (*in white*).

*The debate about
the frontier is
without frontiers.*

THIRD CONVERSATION

R.L. Thomas Friedman, writing in the *New York Times,* reported that in the recent election, King Hussein preferred Mr. Netanyahu to Shimon Peres. Were you aware of this preference? And how do you explain it?

S.P. I was aware of it. I'm not sure I can explain it. For me it's very hard to explain mistakes. I think he made a mistake. Two or three things disturbed him. First, he didn't like our negotiations with the Palestinians. He may have thought that Netanyahu would be tougher on the Palestinians. The second was he thought I was trying too seriously to establish relations with the Syrians. And that again maybe wasn't very much to his liking. And then he thought that I devoted too much time to the Palestinian agreement and too little time to the Jordanian agreement. So it was probably a combination of these things.

R.L. Is an independent Palestinian entity—I won't even use the term *state*—ultimately a threat to Jordan, with its population made up of 70 percent Palestinians and 30 percent Bedouins, with the army and the government in the hands of the Bedouin minority?

S.P. The king says no. He says he prefers a Palestinian state.

Look, I think there are different feelings at different periods of time. Right now I think the Jordanians have clearly decided to divorce themselves from the [West Bank and Gaza] Palestinians and would like to see a Palestinian state. They think [that in Jordan] they were able to create what they call a Jordanian personality that comprises also the Jordanians who were originally Palestinian. I think there were times when the Jordanians would have gone for a confederation with the Palestinians. But then Arafat did something which put an end to that idea. He apparently suggested that he and King Hussein alternate as the head of the confederation—

R.L. Did he suggest this to the king's face?

S.P. That's the story.

R.L. That's called chutzpah, isn't it?

S.P. Yes. I think that put an end to the idea of a Palestinian-Jordanian confederation.

R.L. You have spoken often about the danger that a Palestinian entity could try to swallow the Jordanian entity and form one large Palestinian state that, especially if it fell into the hands of the Muslim fundamentalists, could threaten Israel.

S.P. Yes. My own preference would be to see a Palestinian-Jordanian confederation, but it's in their hands. And right now the two parties say that they prefer to have separate states.

R.L. Mr. Netanyahu has been quoted as saying that he has a very clear idea of the direction he wants to go in, and so the world pokes among his words and actions, and the requirements of his various constituencies, to try and discover what he really has in mind. Is Mr. Netanyahu, who never held a Cabinet post before his election as prime minister, lurching from crisis to crisis out of inexperience, or does he have an agenda and a game plan?

S.P. I'm not sure that he has an agenda, much less a strategy.

I think he wants to be very successful in whatever he does. The agenda is to be successful. And he thinks that the road to success is on the tip of the tongue of the person — that he can be eloquent, that he can talk his way to success. And for that reason he makes so many speeches. And finally the speeches themselves begin to complicate things because a speech can always be nicer than the reality, and the gap that is being created between the eloquence of his words and the stuttering reality hurts the credibility of the person. That's what's happening to him.

R.L. After the explosion of two suicide bombs in the Jewish market in Jerusalem, Mr. Netanyahu once again pushed Mr. Arafat to crack down on Islamic fundamentalists. Instead, Mr. Arafat seems to have gone in the other direction, publicly embracing a Hamas leader in Gaza. How do you read these tea leaves, Mr. Peres? Do you take this as a sign that Mr. Arafat has written off all hopes of reaching an agreement with the Netanyahu government and that the peace process, for the moment, is dead?

S.P. No. I think this is Arafat's reaction to Netanyahu's attempt to paint him as an agent of Israel. I mean, the minute Mr. Netanyahu said, I am giving you a list of two hundred people to put under arrest, he was telling the Palestinians that he was giving orders to Arafat. When Netanyahu said, I will stop providing you with money unless you fight terrorism, which was another misjudgment, I think the message back from Arafat was: I'm independent, I'm not your agent, and contrary to what you think, I'm not afraid to embrace Hamas. You see, we [Rabin and Peres] tried to look upon Arafat as a partner. Netanyahu, knowingly or unknowingly, looks upon him as an agent. Arafat cannot exist as an agent. You cannot give him orders. You have to offer him incentives, too. Many people have asked me if Arafat is trustworthy. What do they mean by that question? He didn't

become a Zionist, neither will he become a Zionist. It's nonsense. He's the leader of the Palestinians, and that's what he will
remain. We can meet as partners for peace, but we cannot make
out of him an instrument to realize our policies.

R.L. Mr. Netanyahu often loudly complains that the Palestinian Authority is not democratic. At the same time he demands that the Palestinian Authority clamp down on Muslim
fundamentalists, and he doesn't appear to be particularly concerned whether this is done with jurisprudence or without. In
their heart of hearts, what do Israelis really want, Mr. Peres, a
democratic Palestinian entity, or an autocratic Arafat presiding
over that entity in such a way that Islamic fundamentalists are
suppressed without quibbling about due process?

S.P. Basically, I would prefer a democratic Palestinian entity. I
think that [Palestinian] freedom is the best guarantee for [Israeli]
security. Furthermore, I think it's very hard to achieve 100 percent of peace unless you give 100 percent of freedom. Let me
analyze our story. We have had two sorts of terror: the intifada,
and the suicidal terrorism by Hamas. The intifada was stopped
by Arafat and we tend to forget this. When it comes to Hamas,
I'm not sure that even with a 100 percent effort on his side he
could bring a 100 percent end to terrorism. Mr. Netanyahu made
a terrible mistake when he said that he would provide security
before peace. For peace you need a majority. For terrorism a tiny
group of people can do whatever they want. You know, when
Arabs who are Israeli citizens say to me, we gave you 95 percent of our vote, I tell them, yes, I'm grateful, but four bombs
that were thrown in Jerusalem and Tel Aviv and Ashkelon, alas,
had a greater impact on the voters than your support. It shows
that the majority of the people cannot match the minority who
throw bombs. And when you say, I will not make peace unless all

the bombs disappear, you encourage the terrorists to continue. Because you hand over the fate of peace to a group of maybe a hundred, two hundred, three hundred people who are ready to sacrifice their lives. Our formula was: let's fight terrorism as if we weren't conducting peace negotiations; let's continue to negotiate as if we didn't have terrorism.

R.L. According to recent newspaper reports, Mr. Netanyahu seems to be floating the idea of offering the Palestinians roughly 40 percent of the West Bank (and not a state), divided into enclaves separated from each other by Israeli-controlled roads and settlements and strips of Israeli-annexed territory. In your opinion, is the 40 percent merely an opening position designed to lower Palestinian expectations, or are Mr. Netanyahu and Likud simply planning to make an offer the Palestinians have to refuse in order to try and blame the eventual breakdown in negotiations on the Arabs? In other words, what is Mr. Netanyahu's game plan?

S.P. In my judgment the numbers reflect the composition of his coalition. He thinks that this is the maximum he can squeeze from his own government. So it's really a response to his own coalition rather than to the Palestinian side. He cannot make a single move without jeopardizing his coalition; every morning he has to count the number of ministers and deputies who are still on his side. My opinion is that there is no chance on that basis to achieve peace. But if he decides there is no chance for him to survive [politically], it will go further than that. I've said that Netanyahu has support, but he doesn't have supporters, because many of his own people are very critical of him. But since nobody wants to leave the government, and he doesn't want to dissolve the government, the support remains in this strange hiatus — support without supporters.

R.L. You seem to be suggesting that, short of toppling Mr. Netanyahu, the only way to bring a change of policies is to change the composition of the Netanyahu government. Is this what you're aiming for now?

S.P. Yes. That's what I think we have to do.

R.L. For quite a while Jewish individuals and Jewish organizations have been quietly buying up property in the Arab quarter of the Old City, as well as in the Arab sections of Jerusalem such as Silwan. I saw several of these Jewish enclaves with my own eyes, with Israeli flags draped over their second-floor balconies. How do you feel about Jews buying property in Arab neighborhoods?

S.P. I feel very bad about it. They shouldn't intervene in such a negative way, especially at such a delicate moment. The people who supply the money live in Miami, and we in Israel will have to bear the consequences of these purchases, we and our children. You see, even money can become a tyrannic phenomenon. What is a tyrant? A person who tries to influence a situation by power. Money is also power. In a democratic state, the voters should decide, and not a small group of rich people who use their money to limit Israel's choices.

R.L. Would you agree that some of the money used to buy property in Arab sections of Jerusalem comes from American Jews willing to fight to the last drop of Israeli blood?

S.P. I wouldn't like to be so impolite, but there is something to what you are saying.

R.L. Last spring the Palestinian Authority announced that it would impose the death penalty on Arabs convicted of selling land to Jews. Shortly afterward, a Palestinian real estate dealer named Farid Bashiti, aged 70, was lured to Ramallah and murdered, and the word spread that he had been executed for selling land to Jews. Several other Palestinians suspected of having sold land to Jews have been found dead since then. What are your thoughts on this, Mr. Peres?

S.P. It is a terrible thing. Basically, I'm against the death penalty under all circumstances. I think only the Lord has the right to give life and take away life. Human beings don't have the right to take away life because they can do it mistakenly, and it's a mistake that cannot be corrected. I understand that the Palestinians have retreated from this policy—they've understood themselves that this is a terrible thing, that it lowered their standing in their own public opinion, and in American public opinion. I hope they won't make this terrible mistake again. You cannot say that owning real estate is more important than owning life.

R.L. I took the killing of Palestinians for selling land to Jews to be an expression of enormous frustration on the part of the Palestinian Authority. They don't know which way to turn—

S.P. What's interesting here is to note that when the PLO was a terrorist organization, it didn't pay attention to public opinion. The minute they became a political body, they could no longer close their eyes to the reaction of the world, and the reaction was unequivocally negative.

R.L. Can you comment on the significance of the Hebron deal that Mr. Netanyahu signed with Arafat? Do you consider the Hebron deal that Mr. Netanyahu worked out—it took him seven months—to be more than marginally different from the original Hebron agreement that you worked out?

S.P. Netanyahu claimed that he was forced to implement the Oslo agreement and tried to introduce some changes in it. The changes worked both ways, in favor of Arafat as well as in favor of Netanyahu, and are altogether insignificant; more semantics than substance. Netanyahu's renegotiation that took seven months was a waste of time and caused a loss of good will. In the end he had to sign the Oslo agreement, and by doing so he brought an end to the ideological position of the Likud Party that forbids giving up an inch of territory.

R.L. Have you met Mr. Netanyahu since the election?

S.P. Yes.

R.L. I know that you delivered the oration at the funeral of his brother, Jonathan Netanyahu, who was killed leading the 1976 Israeli commando raid on Entebbe. You quoted 2 Samuel 1: 19–26, King David's lament for Jonathan: "The beauty of Israel is slain . . ." Did your heartfelt regret at the death of Yoni Netanyahu have any effect at all on your personal relations with his brother, the present prime minister?

S.P. I think so. I think our personal relations have a background of very warm feelings toward me by the whole family. Politics consumes relations, you know. So right now we're on opposite sides of the [political] story. He criticizes me, I criticize him, but there is an element of warmth that comes from those days.

R.L. Do you think Mr. Netanyahu could be obliged by events to form a national unity government?

S.P. Maybe. You see, people say that in time of war you need a national unity government. So why not the same to prevent war? A war that doesn't take place may be the best war.

R.L. When you announced that you would not be Labor's candidate for prime minister in the next election, due to be held in 2000, the Israeli columnist Nahum Barnea, writing in *Yediot Ahronot*, a daily newspaper, said of you: "The news of his political demise is premature." Was he right? Would you serve in a national unity government?

S.P. If it were to be clearly a government for peace, yes. I shall serve peace. I am not interested in serving in a government per se. If I think that my participation would advance peace, yes. If my participation would only be a chair in the Cabinet, the answer is no. I'm not interested.

R.L. Could you serve in the same government as Ariel Sharon?

S.P. If we had an agreed-upon agenda, yes.

R.L. Mr. Sharon is a famous hawk. You are worlds apart when it comes to your views on a Palestinian state or the degree of Palestinian sovereignty over that state.

S.P. I don't know. He says that when I am speaking about my conception of the new Middle East—the need to have a full peace, and my economic vision—he shares my views. But he disagrees with me about what roads to take to arrive at that vision. So we have to explore this.

R.L. Mr. Sharon would certainly disagree with any lines that you would draw on a map.

S.P. He himself said he favors a national unity government. And he said he understands that a national unity government must be made by the two main parties [Likud and Labor] changing their lines.

R.L. In June 1997 you stepped aside as head of the Labor Party and Ehud Barak[1] became the party leader. It is Mr. Barak who will represent the Labor Party at the next general election. What are your relations with Mr. Barak?

S.P. I played a major role in bringing him to this post. It was Rabin and myself who decided to bring him into the Cabinet after he was chief of staff, at the beginning as minister of the interior, and then when I became prime minister I made him the minister of foreign affairs. During the election he served as my chief of staff. So clearly we're no strangers. I believe there are some differences of opinion between the two of us, namely, I don't think we have time to wait for the next election [due in the

1. A brilliant and highly decorated army officer who rose through the ranks to become army chief of staff.

year 2000]. I think decisions must be taken before that. I'm not sure that the [Netanyahu] government will fall right away, so we have to look for other solutions.

R.L. Like a national unity government?

S.P. Probably, yes.

R.L. Is Mr. Barak in favor of a national unity government?

S.P. Not yet. He may be in the future.

R.L. What are some of the other differences between you?

S.P. I would favor taking a clearer stand vis-à-vis the Palestinians. I think Mr. Barak is looking more to the center and I'm not convinced that this is the right way. You see, generally what has happened is that the religious parties have become extremely powerful in the [Netanyahu] government. Today, in my judgment, it is the Likud that serves the religious parties more than the religious parties serving the Likud. The religious have a veto power. Although in fact most Israelis are secular, not religious. This secular front was split between the right [Likud] and the left [Labor], which means that both the right and the left were courting the religious parties [to have a majority in the Knesset], and the religious gained strength in disproportion to their real weight. I thought that a national unity government could change this balance, you see — create a normal majority.

R.L. If Mr. Barak becomes prime minister, what role do you see yourself playing in his government? Foreign minister? Elder statesman? Or a voice crying from the wilderness of retirement?

S.P. Everything depends upon the state of peace. I'm not seeking a post, I'm fighting for a cause. And I will make up my mind in accordance with the requirements of peace. I mean if Barak becomes prime minister and we have peace, then I will be a satisfied elder statesman. If there isn't peace, which in my opinion is critical to the future of the State of Israel, I shall continue to fight like a young man.

R.L. The conventional wisdom holds that Shimon Peres is the dreamer and Benjamin Netanyahu is the pragmatist. There are some observers who are beginning to think that your dream — which is that without an accommodation with the Palestinians, Israel will remain a garrison state; a garrison state will never thrive, and might not survive — looks suspiciously pragmatic. And Mr. Netanyahu's pragmatism — his image is that of someone who prefers the status quo ante but will reluctantly settle for the status quo; all process and no peace — looks suspiciously like a dream. Between the two of you, who is the dreamer and who is the pragmatist?

S.P. For most of my life I was accused of being a pragmatist and an executor, a person without a dream, a person without a vision. So for me it's refreshing to see them accuse me of being a dreamer and not an implementer. All my life they said that I was heading a group made up of doers who don't care about anything else. So I don't buy it. I don't think you can put life in a refrigerator and say that we will wait for the next occasion. Nobody can freeze life. It's nonsense. Life moves one way or another. And what you can do is try to channel it in one direction or another. You cannot stop it. So even if Netanyahu decides on the status quo, how can he achieve it? Are the Muslims going to listen to him? Are the Arabs going to listen to him? Are the superpowers going to listen to him? Will the Arabs stop buying arms, will they stop threatening, will they stop terrorism? It's nonsense. I mean, the only known occurrence of the status quo happened in the Bible when Joshua ordered the sun to stop shining and the moon to stop moving. But that was the single occasion in all of human experience. Since then we have never had a status quo.

R.L. If an accord with the Palestinians is not worked out to the satisfaction of both parties, is war inevitable?

S.P. Yes. Yes. I'm not sure that war will be the next step. They will start with terrorism and boycotts and condemnation. But at the end of the road there may be another confrontation.

R.L. Even as you pronounce the word, you say it with a sigh.

S.P. Yes.

R.L. Do you think the future of the State of Israel is in jeopardy?

S.P. You see, if we do not have a partition in fact, we will become a binational country. We will be killed by demographics. If we become a binational state we cannot prevent the Palestinians from becoming citizens. To remain a state of the Jewish people, we need a non-Jewish state as our neighbor.

R.L. Israel will become like South Africa under apartheid.

S.P. If we become a binational state we shall eventually endanger our [Jewish] majority. So the whole description of territories vis-à-vis peace is not real. The real problem is demography against geography.

R.L. The breakup of the Soviet Union was an event that had a profound impact on the strategic balance in the Middle East, and led to the emigration of 700,000 Russian Jews to Israel. What caused the disintegration of the Soviet Union?

S.P. The incompatibility between the system and the times. Marxism, which is the materialistic side of life, passed away because history is not materialistic, but intellectual. Because you can make out of science and technology and information more than you can make out of land and natural resources and numbers. The best examples of this are Japan and the Soviet Union. I compare Japan with Israel. Japan is eighteen times the size of Israel. Like Israel it doesn't have enough water, it doesn't have oil, it doesn't have natural resources. It is far away. And yet both Japan and Israel are a success. The Soviet Union was a thousand times the size of Israel. Israel is twenty-four thousand square kilometers, the Soviet Union was twenty-four million square kilometers. Exactly a thousand times larger. Not only did they have a vast amount of land, but they had unlimited water resources. There are three million lakes in the Soviet Union. In Israel we have two lakes, and one is dead. They have a hundred thousand rivers, twelve of them the most formidable in the world, including the Don, the Dnieper, and the Volga. Israel has one river, the Jordan River, which is blessed with history more than with water. And yet Russia is short of food and Israel exports food.

One of the stories I like to tell is that after we renewed our relations with the Soviet Union, the first thing the Russians bought from us was cows. Why cows? Because it came out that an Israeli cow produces three times as much milk as a Russian cow. The same cow with the same horns. The difference is in the system. The moral of the story is that you can get more milk from the system than you can from the cow. Which again shows you that it's not the cows, but the system that matters — it's not the material side of life, but the technological side, the scientific side.

The Communist system could have continued for a while longer if it hadn't been for the media. The fact is that the media overcame the barriers. The Communists lost their capacity to blind their people. And once the people opened their minds, Communism began to die. Communism is a system that can exist only with closed eyes and closed ears. If you open them up — finished! When young people in Moscow began to watch television, you couldn't say time and again that New York is a lost place and London is a concentration of poor people and Paris has breadlines. Nonsense.

And not only was their concept old, but so was their management. An old system run by old people. And they started to pass away one after the other. [Yuri] Andropov. [Konstantin]

Chernenko. [Leonid] Brezhnev before them — he was sick for ten years. It was like an old house filled with sick or senile people. That led them to elect [Mikhail] Gorbachev[2], who was at least healthy and young. And Gorbachev had some nice qualities. He was the first Russian leader who didn't try to put the blame on his predecessors, but instead put it on the system.

So I mean, "nothing is more powerful than an idea which reaches its time." The whole idea of materialism, the whole idea that you can create a world without a Lord, a world without a nation, a world without classes, a world without crime, and instead of a Lord you can have a dictator — it doesn't make sense. The extraordinary thing about Russia, and you see it with our immigrants, is the unbelievable contradiction between the intelligence of the people and the lack of intelligence of the system. Never did such an unintelligent system produce so many intelligent people. They were very good in education, very good in the arts, in literature, in the theater, in music.

But the system had an element of self-destruction, and for a very simple reason — it didn't respond to the needs of the nations that live there. Even if you focus on a single nation, the Russians, the system didn't serve their interests. They described it as a dictatorship of the proletariat, but the system didn't respond to the needs of the proletariat. At last it went to the Politburo, and the Politburo also didn't answer the needs of the members of the *nomenklatura*, but only the needs of the top men. And in the last analysis, it was a system where only the top person really enjoyed

2. 1931– : A Nobel Peace Prize laureate, Gorbachev was General Secretary of the Communist Party from 1985 until he was ousted in a palace coup by Boris Yeltsin in 1991; during his years in power Gorbachev introduced *perestroika*, the restructuring of the Soviet economy and bureaucracy that eventually led to the collapse of the Soviet system and the breakup of the Soviet Union.

anything. The rest were slaves. So by definition the system had to create a revolt.

R.L. What were Mr. Gorbachev's intentions? Did he want to reform the existing system in order to make it work? Or was his goal the overthrow of the existing system?

S.P. I think that basically he wanted to reform the existing system. He deeply understood that unless he could change the system, Russia would fall to pieces. I read his book and I was extremely impressed by his understanding, which occasionally was rather theoretical, of the need to change. He was very realistic when he was speaking about the need to change, and very theoretical when he imagined the changes he wanted to introduce. So at least half of the way was realism and half of the way was lack of real experience.

R.L. Did the revolt, the breakup, when it came, take you by surprise?

S.P. Yes. I thought it would happen, but I didn't know when. When it happened it was very surprising.

R.L. At a conference of Commonwealth heads of government, President Nyerere of Tanzania, commenting on the mutual hostility of the then superpowers, once noted that when elephants fought, the grass beneath their feet was crushed. Lee Kwan Yew of Singapore remarked that the result was much the same when elephants made love. My question is, How can tiny Israel keep out from under foot of the elephants?

S.P. The answer is that elephants are a disappearing phenomenon. Every year we have fewer and fewer elephants in our life. And that will continue to be the case. You see, you cannot have an elephant in a world where the economy is without borders. Competition replaced domination. The Internet is more important than countries—a system of information like a wind blowing over the globe. Nobody can arrest a wind. So you can-

not arrest information. It's a different world. I wrote an article
entitled "The End of the Hunting Season in Human Life." I
mean, we were hunting when we ate animals and lived on the
land. No longer. You can produce almost anything artificially.
And for that reason I think that all those concepts of power are
a thing of the past. Bill Gates, with his industry [Microsoft] is
more powerful today than a country. He cannot use his power,
but he can make money. But what sort of damage can he do? So
he's an elephant without legs —

    R.L. Could we describe him as a giraffe?

    S.P. Maybe he's a giraffe, yes.

    R.L. I'd like to return to the man you have called a legend
in his own time — Yasir Arafat. His greatest accomplishment to
date may be that he survived — he survived Levi Eshkol, Golda
Meir, Yitzhak Rabin, Menachem Begin, Yitzhak Shamir, Shimon
Peres, Shamir again, and Rabin again. Until Oslo, Mr. Arafat was
clearly Israel's public enemy number one. Did Israel ever try to
assassinate him?

    S.P. I don't think so. We could have, but we didn't. On the
retreat from Lebanon,[3] he was within rifle range of our army. I
think Begin gave the order not to kill him.

    R.L. Why? Since Ariel Sharon went into Lebanon to eradicate
the PLO, the story is very curious.

    S.P. First of all, there was an agreement that we should let
him leave Lebanon unhurt. So it would have been a violation of
a commitment. And second, we thought that maybe his death
would cause more trouble than anything else. He was a symbol.
You must be very careful not to eat symbols.

    R.L. I saw a film clip of you and Mr. Arafat during one of your
many meetings after Oslo. You were telling him not to take his

---

3. In 1982, when the PLO was forced out of West Beirut by the Israeli
invasion of Lebanon.

complaints to the press, but to phone you first. It seemed to suggest that you had more or less become his mentor, his teacher. Could you characterize your relationship with Mr. Arafat?

s.p. I don't think I became his mentor. I think he learned to trust me. So I could tell him very honestly what the shortcomings were and how they could be corrected. And I did it with tact. I would never do it in front of other people, in order not to insult him. But privately I was very open with him.

r.l. What does he know about international affairs? Has he read Dr. Kissinger's book on nuclear escalation? What does he know about game theories and common knowledge theories?

s.p. I think that most of his intelligence was the result of listening more than reading. He is a very great traveler and he has met a lot of people and heard a lot of speeches, so he is like those people who have educated themselves by hearing more than by reading.

r.l. Is he very intelligent?

s.p. What do you mean? Intellectually?

r.l. Does he have a good memory?

s.p. Yes. Let me say the following — he has a good memory for certain things. He remembers a lot of names, a lot of events. He doesn't submit to the discipline of history. He doesn't feel himself obliged by facts — he can create his own interpretations of facts. He is a master of the facts, not a slave to them. He doesn't feel that he must be concerned with details. But he has a good memory, he has a good grasp. He is a little bit reluctant in a conversation in English because he feels that his English is far from perfect, and he is not sure he understands everything you are telling him. But if you compare him to Hafez al-Assad,[4] who is so provincial, he is really cosmopolitan. Arafat has been at cere-

4. 1928– : The leader of the 1970 military coup that made him president of Syria.

monies all over the world and he knows how to behave and he grasps a bit of French, and so on. I mean, he's quite phenomenal from that point of view.

R.L. Does he have a staff that generates position papers so that he has a sense, when he does something, of where it might lead?

S.P. He has writers who prepare important speeches for him. But he trusts his own instincts. He lets his people negotiate, and to show his authority he will stop them or order them to retreat from what they have agreed to.

R.L. Is Mr. Arafat religious?

S.P. Yes. He considers himself as coming from the line of the Prophets. He is a very religious man.

R.L. You mentioned before that French Catholics don't have a great understanding of Jewish life and Jewish history. Does Mr. Arafat understand Jewish life and Jewish history?

S.P. He thinks he is a great expert on Jewish history.

R.L. Has he read the Torah?

S.P. I don't know if he has read it, but from time to time he quotes it — all of us are the sons of Abraham. When we were talking about the tomb of Rachel,[5] he almost made her a member of his family. Very strange. He said that Abraham was an Iraqi. I mean, when it comes to facts, he prefers to become a sort of Chagall — things can float around.

R.L. He thinks he is a great expert on Jewish history, but is he?

S.P. I wouldn't say so.

R.L. Does Mr. Arafat know about the Holocaust? I'm not asking if he knows that it took place; I'm asking if he knows about it in a deep way. Does he know the role the Holocaust plays in the Jewish psyche?

---

5. In the Old Testament, the second wife of Jacob and the mother of Joseph; she is considered to be one of the four Jewish matriarchs.

S.P. I'm not sure. I mean, he is fully occupied with what he considers the Palestinian tragedy.

R.L. During the negotiations that followed the original Oslo Declaration of Principles, Mr. Arafat seemed very intent on obtaining the trappings of statehood: a Palestinian police in bright blue uniforms, a Palestinian port, a Palestinian airport, a Palestinian currency, Palestinian stamps, passports, license plates. Did he mistake the trappings of statehood for the thing itself?

S.P. I don't think so. I think he achieved quite a lot. Look, statehood means a great many symbolic things, like a stamp and a flag and a uniform. And for him maybe these things mean a great deal.

R.L. Does Mr. Arafat take pleasure in what he has achieved?

S.P. Once during a conversation Arafat told me, Look what you did to me. I was such a popular person and you made a controversial man out of me. Before, everybody had my photo in his hands and kissed it. And now look how many people are criticizing me. I said to him, When you look at this century, there were two leaders of the Palestinians. One was the Grand Mufti of Jerusalem, Haj Amin el-Husseini, who was the leader of the Palestinians for forty-three years. He organized the first gangs that attacked the Jews, killing women and children. He went as far as a leader can go — he visited Hitler. And he was so popular he even ordered the Palestinians to leave their homes [in 1948], promising them that they would return after the triumph of the Arab armies. So he created the refugee problem. The more popular he was, the more tragic your people became. What did he bring to them? Then you followed in his steps. You were using the same techniques for twenty-one years — violence, terror, trying to boycott Israel. You were extremely popular. But what did you bring back to your people? Now you are controversial, but look what you have. You have for the first time a geographic address, you have a Palestinian Authority, you have a negotiating position, you have a future. So which is better, to be controversial and bring bread and butter back to your people, or to be popular and just offer pictures?

R.L. How did Mr. Arafat respond?

S.P. He smiled.

R.L. Missile technology has obviously changed the strategic situation in the Middle East. Israel can now be attacked by countries with which it has no frontiers. Peace with the Palestinians could foreclose the possibility of a war with a distant Arab ruler who, for reasons internal to the Arab or Islamic world, would like to be seen as the conqueror — or the punisher — of the Jewish state. Was it this consideration that changed strategic thinking in Israel, and your thinking in particular?

S.P. We are going over from geographic measurements to ballistic ones, so today it is not just the proximity of your neighbor that counts, but the range of the missiles that other countries possess. This change of arms surely made an impression. But if I had to write my own autobiography, I would say it was the road that began in Dimona [6] and wound up in Oslo. I worked for forty years to create a good deterrent so that we could go for peace. I never did it in order to go for war. And I kept telling myself, Look, in order to make peace, you must be strong. But never forget that many nations have said that, but the minute they became strong they lost their appetite to make peace. I kept telling myself: Remember, you have to be strong in order to make peace, and not in order to be strong. So I worked constantly in my heart for this purpose until it was realized. All the rest, in my judgment, were intermediary events until we reached the point

---

6. The Negev site of Israel's nuclear reactor.

where we could rely on our own deterrent, and from that point jump to peace.

But I also foresaw the advent of the missiles. A couple of weeks ago *Le Monde* published on its front page the first agreement that I signed with the Dassault Company in France for the production of the most important missile that we have had, the Jericho missile. I gave it that name. That was thirty-four years ago. It was only published now. You asked before whether I was a dreamer or a pragmatist. I'm a dreamer who created pragmatism, who changed realities. It's not that I spent my life dreaming. I knew that you dream at night, but when the morning comes you have to translate the dream into reality.

R.L. Do you think that with or without Shimon Peres, peace with the Palestinians is inevitable?

S.P. In principle it's inevitable, but if some mistakes are made we may lose it.

R.L. I'd like to explore with you the often-heard suggestion that only a Nixon could open relations with Communist China; only a de Gaulle could give Algeria its independence; only a Menachem Begin could return the Sinai to Egypt in exchange for peace, and order the Israeli army to remove the Jewish settlers in Sinai by force; that only a rightist leader like Mr. Netanyahu can make peace with the Palestinians and sell that peace to the Israeli public.

S.P. All this is nonsense. First of all, a man who may have made peace as much as de Gaulle did was Mendès-France, who was a leftist. He brought an end to the war in Vietnam and pushed Tunisia toward independence. All this in a very short period of time. So what can you learn from that? It was Attlee[7]

7. 1883–1967: British Labour Prime Minister from 1945 to 1951.

who dismantled the British Empire. If you examine every case you mentioned, you will see it's wrong. Take the agreement with Egypt. We [the Labor Party] made the first two agreements with Egypt. Begin made the third one. The first one covered the separation of forces [after the 1973 Yom Kippur War] by which we pulled back from the Suez Canal. The second was the partial agreement which led to our retreat to the middle of the Sinai. And if we had remained in power we would probably have made the third one too. Then we made peace with the Palestinians without the right [wing]. We made peace with Jordan without the right. All these ideas [that only the right can make peace] are legends.

R.L. It's been said that you and Mr. Rabin were going up the wall because of the many violations by Mr. Arafat of the Oslo accords. The Gaza-plus-Jericho accord, to cite one instance, gave Mr. Arafat a 9,000-member police force; at last count he seems to have something in the neighborhood of 30,000. To cite another instance: when Mr. Arafat returned to Gaza in triumph, he was said to have hidden people on the Israeli most-wanted list in the trunk of his car. He procrastinated about annulling the thirty-three articles of the Palestine National Covenant that directly or indirectly call for the destruction of Israel. What marks would you give to Mr. Arafat for fulfilling the Oslo accord obligations?

S.P. First of all, these stories are not accurate. People are exaggerating. We agreed to 9,000 and maybe he has 15,000, not 30,000. He didn't have any most-wanted people in his trunk; he had people we were looking for, but not the most important ones. And not in his trunk. As for the Covenant — it's nonsense. Look, he wrote a public letter to Rabin saying everything that contradicts the Covenant; saying that he recognizes Israel, its right to exist, its right to live in peace. He denounced terrorism and violence and said that all these disputes must be solved by dialogue. What are they talking about? And then he sent us a letter that he is annulling the Covenant.

But you know, the problem with the Likud—it's a party of talks and speeches. They don't stop speaking. Their policies are made of paper and their judgment is built on paper. Benny Begin [8] is the greatest critic of Arafat. The nickname of Arafat is Abu Amar. But I call Benny Begin Abu Amar. Why? In Arabic *Abu* means *father of* and *Amar* means *builder,* but in Hebrew *amar* means *he said.* Begin is always quoting what Arafat said, until he himself has become an Abu Amar, the father of *he said.* Words have a different role in different societies. In some of them, including Arabic, they can be an ornament rather than a commitment.

R.L. With respect to Hamas and Islamic Jihad, Mr. Arafat seems to have belatedly fulfilled the Palestinian promises made in Oslo—that they would crack down on terrorists. There have been hints in the press that Mr. Arafat has thwarted terrorist attacks. Can you give me details?

S.P. Oh, yes. He discovered the whole structure and organization of Hamas in the Gaza Strip. The Palestinian police killed twenty of them. They're really working very determinedly. They arrested the three persons who killed the Jewish mother and her son in Ramallah.

R.L. Mr. Arafat is clearly not the democrat that the world, perhaps naively, hoped for. We know of seven Palestinians who have died while being questioned by the Palestinian police. Jibril Rajoub, the head of Palestinian Preventive Security in the West

8. The son of the late Prime Minister Menachem Begin, Benny Begin resigned from Mr. Netanyahu's Cabinet to protest against the Likud decision to pull the Israeli army out of four-fifths of Hebron and hand the city over to Mr. Arafat.

Bank, has been accused by Amnesty International of tortur-
ing prisoners. The eighty-eight-member Palestinian Legislative
Council that was supposed to act as a check on the Palestinian
Authority executive is completely ineffective. Corruption is
said to be widespread within the Palestinian Authority and the
Palestinian police. We know of attempts to stifle dissent or anti-
Arafat stories in the Palestinian press. I have a Palestinian friend
in a West Bank town who complained bitterly about Mr. Arafat
to me, but noted that he would not dare say in public what he
was telling me for fear of being beaten up by the Palestinian
police. In light of all this, how do you justify doing business with
Mr. Arafat?

s.p. Well, I admit that it's not a perfect democracy and not
a perfect socialism. You can see how far away they are from
the goal of perfect democracy and perfect socialism, but if you
compare them not with the final goal but with the point they
started from, you can see a great deal of progress. That you
have to admit. The fact is that they have had elections and those
were free elections. And Arafat was elected and the eighty-eight
members were elected and they act as a parliament. This is a
new experience in Palestinian life, a new experience in Arab life.
Compared with other Arab countries, the Palestinians are far
ahead.

Then I want to say something about socialism: I attended a
meeting of intellectuals in New York and one of them challenged
me and said, "Socialism is like a luxury liner that sank, the
Titanic—it hit an iceberg and it sank. This is what happened to
socialism." I told him, You're wrong. Socialism is not a ship, but
a sea. Can a sea sink? Never. You can have different voyages on
the sea, but the sea itself continues to exist even if the ship sinks
in it. I said, Socialism is not a voyage, and not a dogma. Socialism is a civilization, an attitude toward the most important issues

in our life. Peace. Justice. Equality. Humanity. Now, when you
have war, to be a socialist means to be for peace. And when you
take the PLO, the mere fact that they went over from terrorism to
dialogue, from being pro-terrorism to becoming anti-terrorism,
is an advancement. So it depends where you begin your measurements. If I begin from the point of departure, I must say that
they have made a voyage. If I look at the port of destination, they
still have to sail a long way. In one of our talks, Arafat told me:
"Democracy! My God, who has invented it? It is so tiring," he
said. "You have to go from one meeting to another meeting." I
had sympathy for him. So you can see that everything depends
on the way you measure. That would be my answer.

R.L. You met with Chairman Arafat after Mr. Netanyahu
opened the archeological tunnel in the Old City of Jerusalem,
and the subsequent explosion of violence. Could you use that
meeting to show us what a meeting with Mr. Arafat is like. I
know he calls you "Your excellency." What do you call him?

S.P. I call him different names at different periods — it depends on the atmosphere of the meeting. He wanted to be called
President. And I called him Chairman. And then we agreed that
his name would be *Ra'is*, which in Arabic means both Chairman and President. *Ra'is* is like the Hebrew *rosh*, which means
head. There was a very nice ambiguity. We've had three meetings
[since the tunnel incident]. One was in Erez [the crossing point
between Israel and the Gaza Strip], another was in the Villa
d'Este on Lake Como, the third was in Nablus. Now a meeting
with Arafat always has a formal part, which has to do with the
way he addresses you — "Your Excellency." In Erez, we sit tête-
à-tête, one next to the other. In his office there are two chairs
which are being decorated more and more — it's very much like
in Washington where the president's most important guests sit
together. Arafat is extremely polite, and also quite thoughtful.

For example, he was very careful not to embarrass me by saying things which would be hard for me to swallow, such as criticizing Netanyahu. It's not simple. I can criticize Netanyahu at home, but I wouldn't like to criticize him under those circumstances. So Arafat was very careful in selecting his words. Then the problem with Arafat is always when he begins to speak French and he says, "*Après vous.*" That's a very "dangerous" moment, because he's so polite and always wants you to go ahead. Then he puts his hand around you and all the cameras begin to click, and you'll discover this very strange photo of you being embraced by Arafat.

R.L. Do you speak English or French to each other?

S.P. English. There are occasionally some French words, such as *caduc* [frail, insecure]. Somebody suggested it to him as a deus ex machina expression, a word that nobody really knows. He is very careful, very thankful, very appreciative. We go through the issues—what should be done, how things can happen. He puts his side very clearly, but in very restrained language.

R.L. During the violence that followed the tunnel incident, the Palestinian police, for the first time, turned their guns—which Israel had given them—on Israeli soldiers, killing fifteen of them. How did you address this with him? Did you criticize it?

S.P. I surely did. I told him that this aggravates the situation. He said that they were provoked, and that he gave very strict orders to prevent it. And then he said that he is taking all the necessary measures in order to fight terrorism. He thinks that the terrorists were aiming at him as well as at us. There shouldn't be the slightest doubt where he stands on it.

Then he also complained about the economic situation. And I came up with one or two ideas. In Israel we are building an institute for peace, which is a nongovernmental and nonprofit organization. What we want to do is further economic ties with the Palestinians. So we got an idea. There is a shortage of computer software workers in Israel and the people in the industry wanted to import workers from India to do the job. So I called up the people in the industry and said, Why not Palestinians? Let's take some youngsters in Gaza and build a school and train them in computers, in software. I talked with Arafat about it. He was totally enthusiastic. I asked him if he had any available buildings so we wouldn't have to buy them. He agreed to provide the buildings. I think I've found a donor who will give several million dollars for this purpose. The idea is that instead of having workers from Gaza coming to Israel and doing manual jobs, let's send work from Israel to Gaza and engage them in high technology. Arafat liked it very much. And we're working on it.

R.L. An Israeli journalist named Amira Hass recently spent three years in Gaza as a correspondent for *Ha'aretz*. "Gazans," she said, "look on us as three-dimensional and not one-dimensional creatures. They know us better than we know them." Do you think there is any truth to this?

S.P. All of us are shortsighted. We think about the Palestinians as different Israelis, and they think about the Israelis as different Palestinians. But none of us is really capable of going into the skin of the other side and understanding fully what is happening. I mean, the knowledge is somehow superficial, somehow conceptual; it doesn't have the strength of an instinct, it doesn't have the depth of a mentality. There is information that is available—like weather forecasts, like the national mood, like who is important and who is unimportant—but the real story of what makes a people tick is extremely difficult to grasp. I said jokingly that I'd heard that President Assad has a special person who translates Israel's two afternoon newspapers for him every day. There is no chance that he will ever understand Israel—if he judges us by the two afternoon newspapers he will always get the wrong idea.

R.L. I once went from Zichron Ya'akov to Ben-Gurion Airport in a taxi driven by a man who had lost an arm fighting alongside Moshe Dayan in the 1956 war. The driver told me: If Arafat were to regain the territories lost in the Six-Day War—Gaza, the West Bank, even the Arab part of Jerusalem—you can bet that he or his successors would come back in, say, five or ten years and demand what they lost in the '48 war. Mr. Arafat's famous May 1994 Johannesburg speech, in which he compared the Oslo accords to the "Peace of Quraysh"—a reference to the peace the Prophet Muhammad made with the tribe of Quraysh so that he could build up his forces, at which point he wiped out the Quraysh—didn't help matters. What would you tell this taxi driver to calm his fears?

S.P. I would say that history is not made by making demands, but by referring to facts. The fact is that Gaza is an Arab community. It was never really in our hands in recent history. Tel Aviv is a Jewish community. It is not in their hands. So to say that Arafat got Gaza because he made demands—it's nonsense. He got Gaza because Gaza is Arab. In Israel today we have four-and-a-half-million Jewish people and a million non-Jewish people, and this is a plain fact. It cannot be divided on demand. It is not subject to salami tactics because it is not a salami. All of these stories are very superficial and shallow—

R.L. These are frightened people—

S.P. People who are frightened are not thinking clearly. They speak out of fear.

R.L. You have written very movingly about learning the Talmud with your grandfather. You said he taught you that if you see only one side of an issue, you have not studied it properly. Does Mr. Arafat see the Israeli side of the issue?

S.P. Not completely. Partly. He has learned some basic things, for example that for Israel, security is a major issue. And he knows that when it comes to security, he has to take that into consideration. Then let's not forget that Arafat considers himself a great general — he once described himself as the only general of the twentieth century that has never lost a battle. Well, that's a little bit exaggerated. And he considers himself a great engineer. You know, his conception of himself is quite interesting. So when security comes up, he becomes a general who understands strategy and tactics and when you sit around the maps, he's a different person. But whether he understands our moral commitment, I'm not sure. So he grasps what is necessary for the negotiations. And he's a smart negotiator. He negotiates according to his own rules, not according to our rules. I mean, it's not only that you have two sides in the negotiations, but you have two sets of rules in the negotiations. And they are not necessarily compatible. You know, the art of negotiation is creativeness even more than bargaining. To find a surprising solution that nobody had thought about —

R.L. That's why I asked you about Jerusalem — whether you didn't have in mind exactly that: a creativeness about Jerusalem, a solution nobody had ever thought about.

S.P. No. If I say it people will think that I'm ready to divide Jerusalem. I'm not ready to say it. The only thing I can say is that we have to find an original solution for the religious side of the issue without changing the political side. Jerusalem is politically closed, and religiously open.

R.L. How about Mr. Netanyahu — does he see the Arab side of the issue?

S.P. No. He spent a large part of his career outside Israel. He sees himself as a great authority on terrorism. On many occasions he looks at the Arab side through the eyes of an expert on terrorism. His book is devoted to the issue of how to fight terrorism. I am not sure that he understands [the Arab side].

R.L. I have seen it in print that Yossi Beilin, who played such a key role in the Oslo accords, signed a secret Memorandum of Understanding with the Palestinians three days before Mr. Rabin's assassination. The Permanent Status envisioned in this memorandum includes statehood for the Palestinians, the annexation by Israel of the 6 percent of the West Bank where roughly three-quarters of the Jewish settlers live, a superhighway connecting the West Bank to the Gaza Strip. It also envisages transferring large chunks of the Jordan Valley occupied by Israel to Palestinian rule within twelve years. Can you confirm whether such a Memorandum of Understanding exists?

S.P. No. There was nothing signed. I asked [one of Arafat's aides] and he told me those were general impressions. I think that when we sit down at the table, the Palestinians may take it as an opening position. But there was never such a memorandum signed, and I wouldn't approve it.

R.L. Mr. Arafat repeats over and over that he is not asking for the moon, but to many Israelis it seems as if that's exactly what he's asking for. I understand that one should not ask a negotiator to give away his position in advance. Still, could you draw the rough outline of a compromise between the Israelis and the Palestinians that might have a chance of succeeding with the various constituencies on both sides of the fence. In other words, can you outline a compromise based — as the formula went for the Oslo II agreement — on a "balance of interests" rather than a "balance of power"?

S.P. I can give you some lines of approach. The solution cannot be an orthodox one. Usually when we search for solutions we rely on accepted precedents and terms. The concept of sovereignty was introduced in the sixteenth century, but since then sovereignty has lost a great deal of its meaning. Because as in the Middle Ages, when we went from cities to states, today we are in the process of going from states to communities, or commonwealths. This is clearly true on the economic side, but it doesn't stop there—it goes from economy to strategy, and eventually from strategy to common passports and common currencies.

Now I think that the next step should be an agreement that will be based on three different borders or frontiers: a military one, an economic one, and a political one. The military border should be the Jordan River line, which means that no foreign army may cross the Jordan River and threaten Israel. And whatever territories are given back to the Palestinians will remain demilitarized. Also I think the Jordanian, Palestinian, and Israeli economies should cooperate. You cannot put an endless number of custom posts and barriers on such a small territory.

R.L. You're talking about a mini–common market?

S.P. I'm talking about a sort of Benelux.[9] Politically, any agreement should take into consideration the demographic layout. Wherever there are densely populated Palestinian areas it should be under the rule of the Palestinians, except for the security locations. It will be difficult, but not impossible, in my judgment. In the beginning it will look strange, but let's not forget that the Gaza-Jericho agreement—the nature of [Palestinian] autonomy—was also unprecedented. We created precedents, we

9. The Benelux Economic Union, the 1958 treaty between Belgium, Luxembourg and the Netherlands to promote the free movement within the union of workers, capital, goods and services.

didn't follow precedents. And for that reason it is very difficult to keep everything we agreed upon in line—we don't have any reference books, there is nothing to compare it to.

R.L. In the future, perhaps negotiators will use you as a reference.

S.P. If they are in a similar position. You see, the great story about the Israeli-Palestinian conflict is not so much the size of the land or the number of people, but the complex nature of the conflict. On such a small piece of land, with such a long history, with such a great conflict—it's very hard to find solutions. We came in at the last moment. Because in politics it's like in your own kitchen: you can break eggs and make omelets, but you cannot make eggs again from omelets. Bosnia, for example, is an omelet. We are being very careful now to stop the omelet-ing, so to speak, of the Arab-Israeli conflict. And to cut it exactly is not a simple matter. But that is what we have to do and what we will do.

R.L. The *Jerusalem Report* writers put out a book on Yitzhak Rabin called *Soldier of Peace,* and it's published in England by Halban. The book says that, contrary to what the Israeli government has always claimed, Ben-Gurion in 1948 ordered the expulsion of 50,000 Arab civilians from the twin towns of Lydda (today Lod) and Ramlah southeast of Tel Aviv; that two young Israeli officers, Yigal Allon and Yitzhak Rabin, executed the order. The book goes on to say that Mr. Rabin's memoirs, written thirty years after the event, recounted this incident honestly, but the Cabinet committee that checks ministerial memoirs for security breaches ordered the passage deleted. We spoke of France's failure to come to terms with its Vichy past. Has Israel come to terms—

S.P. It's not true. That's again *nouveaux* historians, so to speak—they talk nonsense. I was present, as Dean Acheson once said, at the creation. I was present when the thing happened. Ben-Gurion insisted that no Arab be thrown out. He called in the Mayor of Haifa, a city with many Arabs, and told him, "Don't throw them out." He gave orders all the way down the chain of command not to create an Arab refugee problem and not to expel the Arabs. That I heard with my own ears. I mean, it's not as if somebody had told me. I think what they're referring to — Rabin never said that Ben-Gurion *gave* him orders. He said *he was told* that Ben-Gurion gave orders. This is the whole story. I spoke with Rabin about it. Rabin never got orders of this nature.

R.L. But did Mr. Rabin and Mr. Allon expel 50,000 Palestinians from Lydda and Ramlah?

S.P. I don't think so. What happened was that Moshe Dayan, heading an armored force and racing ahead in a jeep, created such an impact that many of the Arabs began to move. But nobody expelled them by force.

R.L. But the reporters for the *Jerusalem Report* say that Mr. Rabin wrote this story in his memoirs —

S.P. I don't believe that that is what Rabin wrote. It must be checked very carefully.

R.L. Do you think there is any truth to the suggestion that you and Mr. Rabin built up Palestinian expectations to such an extent that any solution acceptable to the Israeli public would be a disappointment to the Palestinian public?

S.P. That's far-fetched. People exaggerate. It's a nervous look at the situation. The Palestinian expectations existed before we started our negotiations.

R.L. I've read that nearly all the concessions pried out of Mr. Arafat at Oslo II occurred when you personally met with him, and that you were tougher as the talks went on. I remember the story about Henry Kissinger's negotiating technique during the Egyptian-Israeli disengagement talks that followed the 1973

Yom Kippur War. In order to get the Israeli team to make concessions, Dr. Kissinger would take long naps in the afternoon
and then try to exhaust the Israeli negotiators by scheduling all-
night sessions. Did you have a technique for getting concessions
out of Mr. Arafat?

s.p. I wouldn't call it my technique. My approach was the following: I was very careful not to win too much, and not to win
anything unnecessarily. So whenever I could be generous, I was
generous immediately. I didn't appear as a trader. And on many
occasions I went a very long way, to the point where I was criticized by my colleagues. For example, adding Jericho to Gaza. Or
the nature of the Palestinian passport. Or the title of Arafat. Our
people raised hell with me for calling him *Ra'is*. Having agreed
to these three things, I could insist very strongly on things which
I believed were right. Arafat knew that I was sincerely for peace.
And whenever I took a very tough position I would go for a
tête-à-tête meeting with him. And there without any niceties I
would put our case very forcefully. Also I think I came with many
creative ideas.

I didn't lose any point on security. Never. Because I knew
that if I were to lose on a security issue, it would be very hard
for me to mobilize the good will of the security people and even
of Rabin himself. So I would listen very carefully to what our
military and our security people had to say. It doesn't mean I accepted everything they were saying. I could be tough with them
as well. Because don't forget that I started to work with gener-
als when I was twenty-eight or twenty-nine, and I was already
running the show then.

r.l. After the Romans had suppressed the Bar Kokhba revolt
of 132–35, many Jews took refuge in the spine of hills running
north and south from Jerusalem. Many of these same Jews were
converted to Islam in the seventh century. At the September

1995 signing of Oslo II in Washington, Mr. Rabin, in his speech, wondered aloud whether Mr. Arafat might have some Jewish blood in him. At the time Mr. Arafat laughed. Is the idea that far-fetched?

S.P. Well, all of us, according to Arafat, are sons of Abraham, so he must have some Jewish blood in him. I mean, these are the sorts of stories in which you will never reach a real conclusion. You can play with them. They are meaningless. It's impossible to trace them back.

R.L. It's an intriguing idea — to think that the Palestinians in the hills were Jews who fled from the Romans and later converted to Islam, in which case the Israeli-Palestinian conflict begins to look a lot like a civil war —

S.P. Who knows? Here you are passing over from history to legend. Legend is a different art. It's not facts, it's assumptions, it's imagination.

R.L. After Arafat, the deluge? Hamas? What?

S.P. No. There are Palestinians who can succeed him. And they may succeed him when the time comes. The number two man now is Abu Mazen, a highly civilized man who gained the trust of our people.

R.L. The indelible image of Mr. Rabin reluctantly shaking hands with Mr. Arafat in Washington has to be one of the great moments in the political history of the second half of this century. Mr. Rabin's incredible body language betrayed to the whole world his worries about the peace process, as well as his personal distaste for Mr. Arafat. You were standing next to Mr. Rabin at the time. Can you describe the handshake from your point of view?

S.P. First of all, let's remember that Rabin originally decided not to go to Washington at all. We agreed that I should go and represent Israel. I think the president of the United States insisted that Rabin come so that the signing would be on the highest possible level. And Rabin changed his mind at the very last moment. So he went with a sense of distaste. He understood that it was necessary [to shake hands with Mr. Arafat], but he wanted to postpone the moment or avoid it completely if he could. Finally when we came in [to the White House] he was very careful not to bring himself to the point where the handshake would be done ahead of time or in an uncontrolled way. He was particularly worried about the *après vous* embrace of Arafat. At the ceremony we were standing next to each other, and after he shook Arafat's hand he turned to me and whispered in my ear, "Now it's your turn." As though he had gone through a terrible experience. For him it was a very difficult moment. But he understood that he had to do it because that was part of our agreement. Later on I think he changed his mind about Arafat. He became more forthcoming.

R.L. Oded Ben-Ami, Mr. Rabin's spokesman at the time, once said that for Mr. Rabin, seeing Mr. Arafat was like going to the dentist. The anxiety before was much worse than the treatment.

S.P. Yes. Rabin had his ups and downs with Arafat. The downs were not so surprising, but occasionally there were some ups as well. I think it was part of Rabin's nature—an appreciation combined with a suspicion. On several occasions he was very fair in judging Arafat and in understanding his difficulties.

R.L. Let's home in on the peace process for a moment. A great many people suspected that as long as peace with the Palestinians wasn't a viable option, Israel as a country and Israelis as a people didn't have to bite the bullet: they didn't have to decide what an eventual peace would look like. In other words, Israel didn't have to decide what kind of society it wanted to be: a pragmatic secular Zionist society, or a Messianic redemption-oriented religious society living on all of the sacred soil that God bequeathed to Abraham. Oslo changed all that. Aren't Israel's political leaders in large measure responsible for not having defined what they wanted from a peace settlement, and in the process, defined what kind of state Israel was going to be, before attitudes on both sides of the divide hardened?

s.p. It's like somebody would tell you, You shouldn't leave the hospital because you won't have doctors to take care of you later on. I mean, it is not that Israel should have defined her nature in peace, but rather that war defined the nature of Israel as long as we were at war. And nobody could really say when it was going to end. Clearly when you have a war, people are united because of the threat. So Israel was united. And all the differences were reduced in size because of the need to stand together.

There were two events in this century that kept the Jewish people together. One was the Holocaust, the other was the threat of war that kept the Israelis together. What I am trying to say is that there is a limit to theory. It is, as they say, the events that create the theory on many occasions. Now, in Israel, if we are to have peace, we have to address several major questions. One is how we are going to maintain our moral standards, because I think what typifies Jewish life — I think I said it already — is the preference of ethics over esthetics. So we have to keep our ethical values. The other is to try and think very carefully about our democratic system. Democracy is not a collection of agreements, but a collection of disagreements. Look at the great democracies. Look at the United States. The blacks and the whites, the Protestants and the Catholics, the poor and the rich, the right and the left — whatnot. And the greatness of the U.S. Constitution is the injection of tolerance into a collection of disagreements and differences. For me democracy means two things. One is the right of every person to be equal. But equally important is the right of everybody to be different.

Getting back to Israel's situation, I believe we have to replace the unifying force of war with the unifying strength of
a constitution and institutions and even further, with norms,
with relations and ethics. For example, to take the relations between Israel's religious [Jews] and the secular [Jews], as long as
the relations between religious people and secular people are
person-to-person I don't see any difficulty. You can have people
in the same family who are religious, who are traditional, and
who are secular. But if you convert the religious into parties and
the secular into parties, then you have a real clash. Because if you
are an individual believer, the Lord is eternal and constant —
you don't have to pay Him a monthly salary, you don't have to
satisfy Him every day. But if you are a political party, you have to
bring home some important achievements every day. So when
religious people form a party, by definition they have to raise
their demands endlessly. By doing so they are sharpening the
differences. And I think that's the major problem — that we have
religious parties and secular parties, and the relations are between the parties and the parties are constantly sharpening their
differences. Imagine if in the United States you were to have a
Protestant party, a Catholic party, a Jewish party. Or France.
You wouldn't be able to run the country. So sooner or later we
will have to deal with this question. It would be better if the religious people were members of the different [secular] parties and
pushed [through the secular parties] to respect religion.

And then, too, there is the new system of election that re-
wards every split and penalizes every union. Instead of having
ideological parties in the parliament, with the new system you
are beginning to have pressure groups. You make a deal with
a candidate for prime minister and he pays you off later on. I
think we'll have to take a good look and ask ourselves how we
can prevent all the friction that stems from these differences. You

need oil in every mechanism where there is friction. And oil—
tolerance—must be constitutionalized and institutionalized in
the future.

R.L. Addressing the peace rally in Tel Aviv moments before
his assassination, Yitzhak Rabin said, "There is no painless way
forward for Israel." You yourself have juxtaposed "the hopeful
future" to "the painful present." Is that the destiny of the reborn
Jewish state—to have a hopeful future but a painful present?

S.P. Yes. A mother gives birth to her child after several
months. When it comes to the birth of a nation, it takes years
and years and years. Birth is a painful process.

R.L. Are you saying that fifty years after the creation of the
state, Israel is still going through its birth pangs?

S.P. Yes. Yes. Israel is not yet a finished country. Not a completed country.

R.L. At a dinner in Jerusalem the other night, a journalist
at the other end of the table said, "Thank God we have enemies or we'd be killing each other." Is a civil war between Jews
conceivable in Israel?

S.P. I don't think so. Since our military strength is based on
reserves, and people in every walk of life have rifles, I don't think
anybody would dare use these rifles one against the other.

R.L. Yitzhak Rabin thought the same thing. Not long before his assassination, he said during a television interview, "I
don't believe a Jew will kill a Jew." Historically, of course, he was
wrong. The Babylonian-appointed Jewish governor of Judaea
after the destruction of the First Temple, Gedaliah, was assassinated by Ishmael, son of Nethaniah (II Kings 25). Mattathias of
Modin, the father of Judas Maccabeus, slew an idol-worshipping
Jew in the Modin marketplace to start the Maccabean uprising.
More recently, in 1957 Rudolf Kastner was murdered in Tel
Aviv by Jews who decided he had "sold his soul to the devil" by

negotiating during World War II with Adolf Eichmann to save Hungarian Jews. Unfortunately, the list of Jews who have killed Jews is a long one. Still, in recent years, it seemed as if there was a fine line that deterred would-be assassins; as Mr. Rabin said, Jews didn't kill Jews. What went wrong?

s.p. The fanatics. Israel is the only country in the world that doesn't yet have a permanent frontier. And as long as you don't have a permanent frontier, you have an ongoing debate about where the frontier should be. And the debate about the frontier is without frontiers. It goes deeper and deeper. It becomes almost a national trauma. And you have, like you've always had in our history, some jealous people who are very dangerous. But finally it comes down to small minorities, which are manageable. I don't say that you can avoid every victim, that you can prevent every casualty. Strangely enough, because of war Israel is no less democratic militarily than politically. By this I mean that everybody serves in the army. Everybody has a rifle. And from that point of view, a day of war never postponed a day of democracy. And democracy characterizes even our armed effort. But as the Polish poetess Wislawa Szymborska wrote so beautifully — she's the one who just got the Nobel Prize for literature — "I would like to see the globe dressed in mufti, not in uniform." The day will come when Israel will be dressed in mufti — in civilian dress, not in uniform. Because the uniform is not our choice. The examples you give [of Jews killing Jews] come from a different age, when we didn't have television. Today television and blood don't go together. If a drop of blood, which in the past would usually not have been noticeable, appears on television, it becomes a national trauma. This is the reason the Americans lost the war in Vietnam. This is the reason the Russians withdrew their forces from Afghanistan and later on from Chechnya. The mothers cannot stand the drops of blood. Even the fathers. So to compare today with different ages is out of place. It's a different age.

R.L. When you were a child in Vishniva, there were anti-Semitic thugs who might have killed you. When you came to Israel and lived on your first kibbutz, there was rifle fire from marauding Arabs that might have killed you. And here you are, a Jew living in a Jewish state, and every time I come to your office you are surrounded by bodyguards—you yourself told me you couldn't leave your home for fifteen minutes this morning because your bodyguards wanted to check out a suspicious car parked in the street. How do you deal with the fact that there are Jews out there—not Arabs, but Jews—who disagree with you so violently that they would kill you if they could? Does it disappoint you—

S.P. I prefer to live without fear than to die because of the fear of death. You know, I take it as the cost of peace. All my life I thought to myself that the real leader must agree to be controversial rather than popular. If you want to be popular, you must try to be liked by everybody, and the only way you can be liked by everybody is to do nothing. But if you want to do something, you are controversial to different degrees. Some controversy ends up with smears, others with bullets. But that's not a reason to retreat or to be afraid.

I have said before and I can only repeat: both Rabin and myself were prime ministers and ministers of defense. We sent many young people to battlefields, to dangerous places. Many of them didn't return. What right do we have to be concerned about our lives? I know that the murderer [of Mr. Rabin] was undecided about whom to shoot first, Rabin or myself. I take it coolly as far as I'm concerned. I'm sure that Rabin would take it coolly, too. I mean, there must be an honesty and a seriousness in whatever you do. So maybe it is disappointing [that a Jew would want to kill me]. But I prefer that my generation risk its life instead of having our children risk their lives. A Greek sage asked, What is the difference between war and peace? He answered, In wartime, parents bury their children, in peacetime, children bury their parents. And the difference must be clearly understood by us.

R.L. Do you know the story of the Oval Office deliberations during the 1962 Cuban missile crisis? Curtis LeMay, the general in charge of the U.S. Air Force, recommended to President Kennedy that his bombers strike at the Russian missile bases in Cuba. LeMay is supposed to have said: Mr. President, in the event of a war with the Soviet Union, I can guarantee victory. At which point a voice — some versions of the story say it was Bobby Kennedy — was heard to ask, Would the general care to define the word *victory*? If there is another war in the Middle East — and you've said that war is possible — would Israel emerge the victor? If the answer is yes, could you define the word *victory*?

S.P. Israel can emerge the victor in the narrow sense, which is a military victory. But military victories are of a passing nature. It may add to the glory of the nation, but not to its well-being. There is just one victory, which is peace. The ends of war are a sort of victory that no war can provide. I admit that if you have a war, there is no alternative except to win it. But if you want to have peace, there is no way to achieve it without compromising. So between compromise and confrontation, the two of them have a cost. Ultimately the difference may be not so much in the cost, but in the result — in the difference between a military and a civilian victory.

The camel that carries sugar
to Mecca has to satisfy its
stomach by eating thorns.

FOURTH CONVERSATION

R.L. I'd like to return to the subject of Yitzhak Rabin. I imagine it must be difficult to speak candidly—for that matter, to speak at all—about someone who was assassinated and who today is seen as a martyr to peace. People who knew Mr. Rabin agree that he wasn't an intellectual—his forte wasn't philosophic or religious thought. Could you speak in a general way about his strengths and his weaknesses?

S.P. His strength was his real capacity to understand a situation, to grasp it, to analyze it and to draw conclusions. And when he reached conclusions he would express them without fear. And he was true to his conclusions—he didn't run away from them. On many occasions he was more spontaneous than intellectual. But it wasn't a capricious sort of spontaneity. And then I think he had a capacity for leadership. He had some outstanding talents: an excellent memory, an organized mind, an eye for people. All these things are very important qualities. On the other hand, he was quite pessimistic, with a tendency to become suspicious. To travel the road he did required so much carefulness and danger-avoidance, it [his tendency to be suspicious] became second nature.

But when we started to work together, I told him, Look, both of us have our weaknesses. You are overly pessimistic and I am overly optimistic, so maybe the two of us together can find the center and the balance. Which in fact is the way I felt. It took him a very long time to get rid of the suspicions he held against me. But once he did we cooperated, the two of us, like an unbelievable team. And I know that he paid some compliments to me behind my back which, I don't deny, meant a great deal to me. He said that he thought I was the most able person the Israelis had, something like that. And I tried to reduce every shadow of suspicion by being very careful not to leak anything. The way we worked was totally informal. There were just the two of us. No protocol. No aides. No witnesses. We relied on our memories and actually we didn't have a single misunderstanding. Once we agreed on something—I say this to his credit—the agreement was an agreement. And it withstood different difficult tests. Also, I was very careful not to claim credit. He was the prime minister, I was the foreign minister. Perhaps I am giving a little bit of credit to myself, but I think it was the true picture—I avoided confronting him on any issue except peace. He was very worried that I would put my candidacy again before the party, that there would be another struggle for power.[1] I told him, Look, if you go for peace, don't worry. If you depart from peace, worry. If you go for peace, you can be assured that I am not going to contend, because my real interest is peace and not power. And then finally we came to a point at which we openly discussed everybody and everything without any restrictions. I only remember one or two cases where this relationship failed to perform the way it should.

1. In 1992, Rabin narrowly defeated Peres in the race for the leadership of the Labor Party, and thus became prime minister when Labor won the general election.

R.L. Your description of Mr. Rabin as a pessimist and yourself as an optimist would seem to support the general perception that in dealing with the Palestinians, you forged ahead and Mr. Rabin acted as a brake on you. Someone close to him said that he was always conscious of the need to "bring Peres back down to earth." Is this perception correct?

S.P. I would say that on some occasions he was more analytical and I was more creative. But I was very careful to make sure that there was agreement between the two of us — that there was coordination between the motor and the brakes. It worked better than in any other situation I can think of where two people ran the same show. You know, it's very difficult to have two people standing at the helm, but it worked.

R.L. Everyone takes it for granted that Mr. Rabin, who was the architect of Israel's victory in the 1967 Six-Day War, was an excellent military leader; you yourself are on record as saying this. But you are also on record as saying that Moshe Dayan, whom the world considers to be a great warrior and an accomplished general, didn't think so. What were Mr. Dayan's reservations about Mr. Rabin?

S.P. Since both of them are no longer alive, I wouldn't like to go into it. Why should I make negative remarks?

R.L. A great deal of ink has been spilled trying to understand the relationship between you and the late prime minister. In many ways you and Yitzhak Rabin seemed to represent an attraction of opposites. Malraux was once asked to explain his relationship with de Gaulle. He sidestepped the question by replying: "Parce que c'était lui, parce que c'était moi" [Because it was him, because it was me]. Can you do better than Malraux? Can you explain the chemistry between you and Mr. Rabin?

S.P. Both of us felt that we were at the last stage of our lives and that our task should be to make all the hard decisions in order to save the younger generation from living with the dilemmas. We felt it was our obligation to the younger generation. We talked clearly with each other about not running away from the tough decisions. The minute Rabin agreed that peace would be our top priority—people can be divided by their interests or inclinations, but united by a vision—we had a unifying vision. You reach a point where even without analyzing it, you know what is serious and what is just a passing impression. And you develop a distaste for the impressive things which appear higher on the agenda than the real things, or for impressive people who are really empty. That comes with experience. Occasionally the two of us were surprised to see that without even talking beforehand we had the same attitude, the same reaction, to people, to events. And then we fought so much—my God. I think Rabin was satisfied that he had won the latest contest [for Labor Party leadership] and I was satisfied that I had won ideologically. Occasionally I have wondered what would have happened if it had been the other way around. I'm not sure that we would have made a team.

R.L. What would have happened?

S.P. I think Rabin would have continued to criticize me a great deal, and I would have had to make a big effort to pacify him. But as it turned out, history at the last moment made a good arrangement—he was number one in the hierarchy and I had a free hand.

R.L. If you had been elected Labor Party leader and prime minister in 1992, what job would you have given to Mr. Rabin?

S.P. He would have been number two. I think he would have become minister of defense.

R.L. Not foreign minister?

S.P. He wouldn't have liked to be foreign minister. You see, when Rabin was forced to resign in 1977 as prime minister,[2] he didn't tell me that he was going to announce that I would succeed him. As a matter of fact, I was surprised — why did he appoint me? Because there was a person closer to him, Foreign Minister Yigal Allon. Why did he appoint me and not him? I don't know. I can imagine — he won the party leadership by such a narrow margin that he thought I was the logical successor. I came back home and turned on the television and found out about it. I didn't have the slightest idea.

R.L. At the Tel Aviv peace rally just before he was struck down by the assassin's bullets, Mr. Rabin, who was not a demonstrative person, memorably put his arm around you on the podium, and many people interpreted this as a public acknowledgment of the rapprochement that had taken place between you. Did you see it in the same way?

S.P. Yes. You know, we had been fighting for so many years, it wasn't easy to wind up a lifelong struggle with such a warm embrace. It wasn't easy for him or for me.

R.L. You were with Mr. Rabin on the night he was assassinated — he was shot moments after you left the Tel Aviv peace rally. In fact, the bullets that fatally wounded Mr. Rabin might well have been fired at you as well — Yigal Amir, the assassin, hoped to kill both of you — if Mr. Rabin had not turned back at the last moment to thank the organizers of the rally and you had not gone on ahead without him. What thoughts, what emotions flashed through you when you realized Mr. Rabin had been shot?

S.P. I was shocked. I was shocked to the depths of my heart. Nothing else . . . there was no consolation.

2. After it was discovered that his wife had illegally kept a dollar account in an American bank from the time when he was Israel's ambassador in Washington.

R.L. You were in your car —

S.P. You see, we were supposed to go down the steps together [to where the cars were waiting]. Then the security people came over and said it was impossible. Rabin came up to me before that and told me that there was information that the Hamas was trying to plant a bomb at the rally. There was a little bit of tension because we didn't know exactly — we didn't suspect that a Jew would do it. And then Rabin told me he was going to stay in Tel Aviv, and I intended to go back to Jerusalem. As we were departing I asked him if he had thanked the organizers. He said, Oh my God, I forgot. And he went back to thank them. And I went down the steps and when I got to my car I asked his driver, who was standing behind my car, where Yitzhak was. He said, "There." So I looked and he was ten, fifteen meters from where I was. So I got in my car — I saw him coming down happily, no problem. When I shut my door I heard the shots. I asked my security people to stop, but they became very alarmed and they turned on the sirens and started to drive fast — they themselves didn't know if the shots had come from a Jew or an Arab — we heard the shots but we didn't see anything, we didn't even know if Rabin had been hit.

R.L. People in Israel remember Leah Rabin's memorable comment when the crowds gathered outside her apartment after the assassination of her husband. She said she was happy they were there, but reproached them for being silent when the opposition was vilifying you and Mr. Rabin. Last night I visited the site of Mr. Rabin's assassination here in Tel Aviv and spent an hour or so reading some of the poems and messages scrawled on every available surface. One graffito said: "We were silent and our silence killed you." The silence that killed Mr. Rabin — did it wound you?

S.P. Not really. One must distinguish between the natures of people who belong to the moderate side of life and people who belong to the extreme side of life. People on the moderate side of life not only take moderate positions, they behave moderately. If anything, moderates would prefer to criticize their own leaders, their own positions, because moderation has a certain amount of skepticism and reservations. Extremism has a great amount of blindness and blind admiration. So when you belong to a camp which is by definition a moderate camp, don't expect to have much of a hurrah or much support or much agreement. It is only after your death that all of a sudden the admiration is openly expressed. But when you're alive, admiration doesn't exist. So I'm not surprised. I'm used to living in this environment. And I don't expect much [vocal] support.

I must say that after I took over [as prime minister, after Mr. Rabin's assassination], I received such an outpouring of admiration, in Israel and all over the world, that I was almost embarrassed. But it's a belated sympathy. And I don't think we have to look for an immediate reward. You must have the capacity to meet frustration all along the way before you can see the results of what you have done. One of the proverbs that I like very much is an Arab proverb. It says the camel that carries sugar to Mecca has to satisfy its stomach on the long trip by eating thorns. Even if you have sugar on your back, you have to be ready to eat thorns on your way.

R.L. How do you deal with the fact that it wasn't a raving lunatic who murdered Mr. Rabin, but a calculating yeshiva-educated Golani combat soldier[3] who was convinced he was serving God's will and the people of Israel?

S.P. I think that this is a danger when somebody appoints himself as the representative of the Lord. The Danish philoso-

3. The Golani brigade is one of Israel's elite units.

pher [Søren] Kierkegaard cautions that when somebody says he has heard the voice of the Lord, check that it wasn't the voice of Satan.

R.L. Has Israel lost its way? Has it crossed a psychological fault line?

S.P. Let's distinguish between group violence and violence as an individual phenomenon. You have it [individual acts of violence] in history all over the place. Look at America, at how many presidents and outstanding people have been killed. And we have had it once or twice before [in Israel]. I mentioned Arlosoroff, who was assassinated. Kastner was assassinated. But nothing like this.

R.L. Ben-Gurion wasn't assassinated by the people who were furious at him for accepting a much smaller Jewish state than they were willing to accept.

S.P. It was a different time. I agree. Something has gone wrong in our society that we have to make a supreme effort to correct.

R.L. You saw Mr. Rabin in the hospital immediately after the assassination, and you described him as having an ironic smile on his dead lips. André Malraux said that death reveals the "grandeur tragique de la vie et son absurdité" [tragic grandeur of life and its absurdity]. Could this be what you saw on Mr. Rabin's lips — an acknowledgment of the absurdity of life?

S.P. I don't think so. I mean, it was an irony that comes with an unexpected occasion. All of a sudden everything disappears — it was taken away from you suddenly. His expression wasn't only ironic. It also had an air of tranquility, like someone smiling in the face of an unexpected tranquility.

R.L. When the killer Yigal Amir appeared in court, he invariably seemed very sure of himself, with what has been described as a cocksure smile permanently plastered on his face. The newspaper *Ma'ariv* even published a supplement that it said was dedicated to wiping the smile off his face. Is there anything you could say now to wipe that smile off the killer's lips?

S.P. Yes. All of a sudden he [Amir] felt he was a hero. In spite of his normal appearance, however, the man is disturbed. There is a deep craziness residing in this sort of person. Because whenever a person abandons the respect for life, he departs from normality. I mean, any justification to kill is insane. This is the final line that distinguishes between sanity and the world wherein one ceases to be a human being. The one who takes away human life is no longer a human being. This is especially true for Jews, where the respect for life is so great. And you know, strangely enough, during the fifty years of existence of the State of Israel, no single person was ever executed except Adolf Eichmann.[4] Over the years there were Arabs who killed children and women and men, and they were caught by us. But we never had gallows. And that wasn't just by chance. It was something basic and deep. And here a person [Amir] does what the state doesn't permit itself to do — he creates his own gallows. He must be taken out of circulation.

R.L. I wanted to ask you about capital punishment. In the early days of the Jewish state, during the 1948 War of Independence, a Haganah commander was convicted of spying for the British and was executed. Later Ben-Gurion opened a new inquiry into the affair, after which the executed man was found innocent and rehabilitated.

S.P. It's a terrible story. We had a man who was a legend in

4. The Nazi official who, as head of the Gestapo's Jewish section, was responsible for the murder of millions of Jews during World War II. In 1960 the Israeli secret services abducted him from Argentina; Eichmann was tried and hanged in Israel for crimes against the Jews.

our country. His name was Yehuda Arazi. You remember the story of the ship *Exodus?*[5] He ran the ship. He was also the man in charge of acquiring weapons in Italy. He was a free spirit, who could never be disciplined by anybody. I will never forget—his headquarters were in Rome. He came from Rome and drove straight from the airport to my office and said, Shimon, they're going to execute Toubiansky—believe me, he's innocent. I asked him, How do you know? He said, Look, I know the person; a Jew would never do these things in time of war. He would never betray his brothers. Arazi begged me to go and speak to Ben-Gurion. Which I did. But it was too late.

R.L. I'd like to talk to you about power. Henry Kissinger is supposed to have said, "Power is the great aphrodisiac." Why does any sane, normal person seek political power? Or, to put it another way, are the people who seek political power sane and normal?

S.P. People who seek power for its own sake are wrong. Power is an instrument. It's like an energy station. In order to have electric light you need a power station. You can use power to kill or you can use it to provide light. So it depends on what the purpose of the power is. Power per se is like a power station that does nothing. Why do you need it? It damages the environment, it's an illusion to the people. So I never thought about power in terms of naked power. I was never tempted by it, you know. I would like to attract people, but not to control them. I don't think I used power for its own sake.

I often think that even though I was criticized so much during my life, I was also tremendously helped even more often than I

5. In 1947 the *Exodus,* crammed with illegal Jewish immigrants to Palestine, was intercepted by the British and forced to sail to Haifa. There the passengers were forcibly loaded onto a prison ship and taken to British internment camps in Cyprus.

was criticized. People who are in power tend to forget the assistance of a voluntary nature that they have had. I can't complain. People say, Why didn't you answer? I can't tell them that if I try to answer the accusations, I will lose balance because I will not be able to compensate for the support. All told, I think I was more supported — I was given many more opportunities than any one man could ask for. So I mean, power per se looks a bit ugly to me. Power for its own sake is like rape instead of love. Maybe it's the same act, but it has totally different motivations.

R.L. St. Just said, "Nobody governs innocently." Even if you start out with the ideas you just expressed, does power inevitably corrupt?

S.P. I don't think so. I mean, you may have corruption in you, and you can be corrupted without having power. But you can also remain uncorrupted when you have power. After all, what is character if not the choice of controlling corruption, instead of corruption controlling you?

R.L. Does it take a lot of effort?

S.P. It takes a lot of self-control, and it must be constant. It is very dangerous to indulge in moments of self-pity.

R.L. How about self-knowledge?

S.P. Self-knowledge, too. You shouldn't leave the criticism about yourself to other people. You must use a certain amount of your intellectual energies in criticizing yourself.

R.L. A French or a German or a British leader makes decisions, but if he or she is wrong, the country will still exist. An Israeli leader makes decisions, about weapons procurement, about the allocation of resources — in Golda Meir's case in 1973 about whether to mobilize the reserves — and if he or she is wrong, the result is likely to be tragic for the Jewish state. It is easy to see how you personally agonized over decisions of military hardware procurement when, as minister of defense, you had to rebuild Israel's stocks and equipment in the wake of the 1973 Yom Kippur War. Where do you, Mr. Peres, find the courage or the nerve or the audacity or the vision to make crucial decisions — with the inherent risk that the State of Israel will one day cease to exist if you are wrong?

s.p. The answer is relatively simple — not making decisions is as dangerous as making them. Running away from a decision is also a decision, and 90 percent of the time it is the wrong decision. If you are afraid to make a decision — as Harry Truman said, "If you can't stand the heat, stay out of the kitchen." But if you are in the kitchen, you cannot just sit and watch the stove. You really have to do your job. And by running away from decisions you may become a catastrophe to your people. Immobility is the sort of philosophy that endangers many good opportunities to improve situations.

Usually I analyze a situation very carefully. And you know, there are also analyses that stem from experience, not just from calculations. You develop an instinct about what is right and what is wrong, who is right and who is wrong. When I listen to a report, I know deep in my heart that I have to know the nature of the reporter not less than the nature of his report, because the report is a function of his nature. And I know you must develop a quick eye for people. I would never talk about it, but my first impulse is to measure people. And there again, I've learned that, since on many occasions you will fail anyway, it is better to fail by trusting people than by suspecting them. On many occasions I failed because I put too much trust in people, but I don't regret it because by trusting people I also got support and assistance that I would never have gotten otherwise. So since you are going to make mistakes, make the right mistakes instead of the wrong ones.

r.l. Can we talk about Islam? Writing about the Afghan

Taleban movement, *Time* magazine said that the phrase "fundamentalist Islam" sounds like an air-raid warning to Americans.
To Israelis, too, except that the threat is closer to home. Should
we fear fundamentalist Islam?

s.p. We should be afraid of fundamentalist Islam. The Machia-
vellian description about movements that think goals justify
means applies here. This way of looking at things gives Islamic
fundamentalists permission to kill, to cheat, to terrorize, to bluff.
What they did to Salman Rushdie[6] is in a way what they want to
do to Israel. For them, Israel is a collective Salman Rushdie. They
are running terrorist organizations, they are killers, they are
cheating, they are lying. They think holiness permits anything.
Iran itself is constructed on three different levels: a government, a super-government, and a justification of government.
The government is [Hashemi] Rafsanjani and his Cabinet. But
there is a super-government run by the ayatollahs — they have
a budget, they have an army, they have a supreme commander
of the armed forces, they are not accountable to anybody, there
is no openness. It's like the Politburo was in the Soviet Union.
And they really want to conquer the world. They don't have
any patience with anybody who is not a fundamentalist. The
third layer is the justification of government. It's a holy license,
something like Communism — they do social work, they have
a very high opinion of themselves and their goals. But it's the
most hypocritical and dangerous system that one can imagine.
And it is particularly dangerous because this may be the first evil
movement in history that will acquire a nuclear bomb. Imagine
Hitler with a nuclear bomb. So they're extremely dangerous.

6. His allegorical novel *The Satanic Verses,* published in 1988, enraged many
Muslims. Iran's Ayatollah Khomeini sentenced Rushdie to death, forcing the
author into hiding.

In an age of such lethal arms and lethal ideas, this combination of ideology and weaponry is the worst that humanity has ever experienced.

R.L. Many countries appear to be ripe for fundamentalist plucking. Could Saudi Arabia, could Jordan (where the fundamentalists recently made electoral gains), could the Maghreb, Algeria and Tunisia, and eventually even Libya, fall to fundamentalism?

S.P. Yes. It's a possibility. They can fall. They can also overcome the fundamentalist threat. I don't believe in determinism in history.

R.L. The grievances enumerated by the fundamentalists are real and not imagined — pervasive poverty, inequitable distribution of national wealth, autocratic regimes.

S.P. Yes, but you know, the fundamentalists come into poor countries and make them poorer. The problem is that they are right in pointing out the failures, but they are wrong in proposing the solutions. Iranians under Khomeini became poorer, not richer. The fundamentalists may distribute some food, but they also distribute death. People [in fundamentalist countries] are not equal in their right to live, so what's the sense of being equal when it comes to the right to get food?

R.L. Will the masses in the Muslim world wake up to this?

S.P. Yes, probably because of television. That will be a restraining influence. But you see, the problem is that once a religion becomes a hierarchy it's very problematical.

R.L. Is it fair to make comparisons between Muslim fundamentalists and Jewish fundamentalists?

S.P. No. Because Jewish fundamentalists don't use violence and arms. It's not permitted.

R.L. It's not true. The Jewish fundamentalists in the settlements are armed.

S.P. They have arms legally, from the state. But they don't have separate organizations —

R.L. How about Kach?[7]

S.P. Kach is dangerous. But you cannot compare Kach to the Moslem fundamentalists because quantity is also a factor. Kach is several hundred people. If it is not a mass movement, it's a different story.

R.L. The distinguished Israeli journalist Amos Elon has suggested that the rise of extreme nationalist Jews would never have taken place "if the humane, moderate ideals of practical Zionism, the Zionism of Weizman and Ben-Gurion that built Israeli society, had not slowly withered away after the 1967 Six-Day War." Do you agree that moderate Zionism has withered away, or is there life in it yet?

S.P. Every time you have a new wave of immigration you have a new Israel. When you had people coming from Russia it was one Israel. People coming from Rumania created another Israel. People coming from North Africa created still another Israel. And now there's the new wave coming from Russia. What I'm getting at is that each immigration was different. The immigration from North Africa and Yemen was basically a messianic one, very religious or at least traditional. And they made their presence felt in the making of Israel. So it's not that ideas have changed, rather that the composition of the population has changed. And everybody has the right to be religious or secular or traditional. But this diversity of backgrounds has clearly had an effect on the outcome.

There are different sorts of Zionism. Zionism in Europe was

7. Disciples of the late ultra-right-wing American-born rabbi Meir Kahane who live, for the most part, in the West Bank settlements of Kiryat Arba and Jewish enclaves in Hebron, and have been linked repeatedly to violence against the Palestinians.

a response to anti-Semitism, to discrimination, to suffering, to insult. Zionism in North Africa or Yemen was basically messianic. It wasn't a reaction to their immediate condition, but an ongoing prayer that stayed with them for two thousand years. The first settlers from North Africa, according to our tradition, came on boats from Tyre even before the destruction of the Second Temple. So there were different wings that brought different birds.

R.L. The Messenger Mohammed, who was plainly familiar with the Old Testament, came to rule in Medina with the assent of the local Jews. In the earliest days of Islam, the Muslims turned toward Jerusalem when they prayed, not toward Mecca. Islam clearly felt more comfortable with Judaism than with Christianity, which it perceived as having betrayed pure Old Testament monotheism with its doctrine of the Trinity. There is a passage in the Koran that says: "There are unbelievers who say, 'God is the Third of Three.' No God is there but One God." Jews, for their part, clearly felt more comfortable with Islam than with Christianity; in the eleventh century, the Jewish sage Maimonides, in his *Epistle on Martyrdom,* wrote that Jews could convert to Islam to save their lives, but they weren't permitted to convert to Christianity under any circumstances. This being the case, why are Jews and Arabs at each others' throats? What is at the root of the enmity between them?

S.P. You cannot speak about religion as if it were a frozen phenomenon. Christianity has changed beyond recognition since the Middle Ages. It doesn't have the Inquisition, it doesn't have the hatred, the violence. I mean, the temper of Christianity became more democratic, more liberal. Whereas with Muslims it was the other way around. Islam became aggressive politically. In the time of Maimonides, it was much more open than it is today. And I am sure that the time will come when the Muslim religion will also go through a liberal stage. It's a matter of development. So you cannot speak about religions as if they were constant all the time. They are influenced by the winds of change in their nations, their people, and their age. This is true for almost every king and every pope. I believe in what Baruch Spinoza said, that the age decides the language. Every expression has a different meaning in a different era.

R.L. Not much attention is paid these days to the Armenian struggle against the Turks, the Kurdish struggle against both the Turks and the Iraqis, the Berber struggle against the Algerians, but the latest development in Hebron is hot news around the world. Do you see a grain of truth to the proposition that the Palestinians are lucky to have the Jews as their enemies, in the sense that if they didn't, no one would pay attention to them?

S.P. Maybe. It is clear that the Jewish people have a unique history. Jewish life always raises interest, suspicion, and admiration, because it looks as if the rest of the world was marching in one direction, under one set of rules, while the Jewish people were marching in another direction, under a different set of rules. So anything concerned with Jewish life, for good or for ill, automatically generates a great deal of interest. I read somewhere that according to United Nations statistics, the greatest sources of news in the world are the Americans, then the Russians and the Israelis. Well, it's clearly disproportionate when you look at the size of the countries and the depth of the issues. But it indicates a fascination that has continued through the ages and never stopped.

R.L. Does the fascination have to do with the fact that the Jews have been victims for two thousand years, and now, suddenly you have Jews who are not victims—that the world is focusing on the Jewish state to see what it will do with the power? Will the Jews—the descendants of prophets and psalmists who have been preaching morality for two thousand years — turn out to be no different from the Americans ethnically cleansing the native Indians, or the French Catholics flinging Protestants into rivers with stones attached to their ankles?

s.p. If the Jews had only been victims, they would have been forgotten a long time ago. They were victims in body and victors in spirit. What makes them fascinating is the fact that they have overcome all the suffering and pogroms and the Holocaust, and they have done this despite being dispersed and lost and beaten. They made a comeback. And not only a simple comeback, but a comeback with outstanding military achievements, as well as achievements in agriculture, in science and technology, and in education. The Jews provided the first demonstration of the superiority of quality over quantity. Clearly we didn't have quantity. So the only thing that could save us was the qualitative part of it — in war, facing superior armies; in agriculture, facing a desert; in science and technology, being on the cutting edge. And all the while keeping ourselves democratic.

And after such an interruption — such a long time — to return to the land and the language. And by the way, the return to the language was even more difficult than the return to the land, because strangely enough there are countries where the people never left the land, but lost their language. Look at the Romans, look at the Assyrians —

r.l. And the Irish, whom we talked about.

s.p. Yes. We are one of the only ones who still speak the language of our fathers. So there must be an inner strength to it. And in a way, the ones who carried us through history were the mothers rather than the fathers. The mothers thought that the intellectual side of the child was no less important than the physical side. The mothers insisted that the children continue to learn and study. And the world is fascinated by all this.

R.L. In the history of the Middle East, there never was a Palestinian state or a Palestinian people. Even the original 1948 United Nations partition plan that created two states spoke of an "Arab state" and not a "Palestinian state." The rise of Palestinian nationalism, the concept of a Palestinian people and state, came into being as part of the ideological struggle against Zionism, and the Jewish state that Zionism created. In conversations with you, has any Palestinian—has Mr. Arafat—ever talked about this curious debt to Zionism?

S.P. I don't think so. The Palestinians consider themselves part and parcel of the Arab world. But let's face it, while the Arab world came to stand at their side when war was announced [in 1948], they didn't stand so strongly with them when peace was announced. Actually, if the Arabs would do for the Palestinians what the Jewish people in the Diaspora did for Israel, the Palestinians wouldn't have the problems they do. I mean, Saudi Arabia alone could have taken care of the great deficit and economic problems of the Palestinians. So it is this relationship between support and refusal [of support] which has defined the Palestinian entity.

R.L. The Vatican has let it be known that it favors the internationalization of the Christian holy sites in Jerusalem. What is your opinion of internationalization?

S.P. I think internationalization of Jerusalem is a remote dream more than a real position of the Vatican. They are aware that this is not a potential solution. Why do they think that if they have, say, the Russians and the Chinese and the Indians and the Americans and the Europeans, Jerusalem will be better guarded? I mean, when they speak about the internationalization of Jerusalem, they are referring to a world that no longer exists. What was called Europe in the old days was the continent of Christianity; where Christianity stopped, Europe stopped.

Today when you look at the globe, the temptation to have Jerusalem internationalized, in my judgment, totally disappears. But the Vatican occasionally consults old maps and old situations.

I want to tell you an anecdote. When the pope first visited Israel, he said that he would like to come here through Megiddo,[8] which is in the northern part of Israel. We didn't understand why he wanted to come through Megiddo, particularly when there was no airport there. So the head of our police force went to check with the security people at the Vatican. And it came out that they had a map made before the creation of the State of Israel, and they had planned the trip according to this old map. We showed them that the situation had changed, the map had changed, and finally we also changed the entry point [into Israel] of the pope. I have never really heard from the pope, who is quite informed and *au courant* in affairs, this demand for internationalization.

R.L. The Holy See finally decided to establish diplomatic relations with the Jewish state in December of 1993 after decades of refusing to recognize Israel. The Vatican explained its refusal by saying that the borders of the Jewish state were disputed, but of course the Vatican had formal relations with many countries with disputed borders — Croatia is an excellent example. Why did the Vatican refuse to recognize Israel all those years? And why did it change its mind?

S.P. As they explain it, they have a Christian minority in the Arab world and they are very concerned about them. They are afraid that the Christian minority will be hurt. And the Christians really are having problems in the Middle East — look at Lebanon. I read somewhere that there was an exchange of letters

8. The setting of Armageddon where, according to the Bible, the final battle between the forces of good and the forces of evil will take place at the end of the world.

between Fidel Castro and Hafez al-Assad, the president of Syria. Castro asked Assad why he didn't let Lebanon alone to pursue her destiny. And Assad replied very tellingly. He said, We made a mistake by permitting the creation of a Jewish state; we shall not repeat the mistake by permitting the creation of a Christian state [in Lebanon] in the midst of the Arab continent. So the Vatican has always focused on the fate of Christian minorities spread all over the world.

R.L. But Israel was the great defender of the Christian minority in Lebanon.

S.P. Yes, but the Vatican wasn't concerned about the defense of Israel, but the threat of the Arabs [against Christian minorities] in Lebanon, Syria, Iraq, Jordan, and Egypt. And for that reason the Vatican always took a very cautious position concerning Israel.

R.L. It sounds as if you are describing a foreign policy based on appeasement.

S.P. Maybe. Maybe. But that was the case. But finally they came to the conclusion that if the Arabs were making peace with Israel, why should the Vatican wait? You know, when I met with the pope for the first time, in 1985 or '86, he told me that all of us are the children of Abraham and that we were making the same voyage in history. I told him, Yes, your holiness, but our ticket was the most expensive one.

R.L. I'd like to ask you about the Palestinian intifada. I'm very intrigued by the word *intifada* itself which, as you know, can be translated as a shrugging off or throwing off. How did the insurrection come to be called *intifada*, or *shrugging off*, which obviously refers to the shrugging off of what the Palestinians considered the odious Israeli rule, rather than a *revolution*?

S.P. The name wasn't an official one. Nobody thought it out. It stemmed from the same spontaneity as the movement itself.

I mean, the interesting thing is that the intifada started spontaneously. It started and spread like a fire. It wasn't planned and introduced by the Palestinian leadership. It grew out of the realities of life more than from orders of the hierarchy of the Palestinian movement.

R.L. Can we talk for a moment about these realities of life — the Israeli occupation of Gaza and the West Bank? From the Palestinian point of view, it was rough. There were more than a thousand deaths, there were humiliations, there were arms broken. Israelis in general tend to defend the occupation of Gaza and the West Bank as relatively mild. What is your point of view?

S.P. There are two things that one should never forget, which distinguished what happened here from the classic occupation. Our army didn't wake up one morning and decide to occupy these places. Our presence in the territories was the result of an attack upon us, not a result of our attack upon them. So it wasn't a choice, it was a function. Then I think that Moshe Dayan, who was the first to manage the territories, really had a feeling for the Arab side, and in a strange way our representatives in these areas not only served the military needs but also the needs of the civilian population. I myself was in charge of the economies of the territories in the '70s — Dayan asked me to take this on — and I really tried to think how to be of help, how not to oppress. We didn't look upon it as a business, neither did we look upon it as a purely military matter. We understood perfectly well that the human conditions must be considered very carefully. And for that reason we tried to introduce education and health and jobs, and we didn't do it expecting anything in return. We did it in order to create a different feeling. So the two points are different. The reason why we were there, and our reasoning about *how* to be there.

R.L. Early on in the intifada, Mr. Rabin, the then minister of

defense, may or may not have issued the famous order instruct-
ing Israeli soldiers to break bones. Mr. Rabin himself denied
having said this, but soldiers under investigation for breaking
bones testified that they had been following the defense minister's instructions. Either way, bones were broken. In 1988 a CBS
cameraman filmed four Israeli soldiers on a hill near Nablus
beating two Palestinian stone-throwers with rifle butts. In the
West Bank, an Israeli bulldozer buried four troublemakers under
a small mountain of earth. With the advantage of hindsight, do
you think that Israel's political leadership provided appropriate
guidelines to Israeli soldiers? Did Israeli soldiers perform as well
as could have been expected under difficult circumstances?

s.p. First of all, I believe Rabin's denial. I don't think he used
the words [break bones]. Maybe soldiers were under the impression that this was the policy, but I don't believe it; the policy was
much more careful and instructions were issued about the limits,
about what could or should be done in different circumstances.
It's extremely difficult when a soldier is in the street and somebody throws a stone at his head. What do you expect him to do?
Look at all wars. Look at all revolts. They create cruelty. Because
the right of defense is not of lesser importance than the tendency
to revolt. As the French say, *à la guerre comme à la guerre.* War
has its own logic, its own mentality—which I don't like. But
always the evil is in war itself, and not because war is such an
ungentlemanly confrontation. So you have to uproot the war instead of complaining about its consequences. But if it happened
[bone breaking], I think all of us regretted it and we wouldn't
support it. Never to hit an innocent person, never to use force
brutally—we thought it was a mistake, and we still think it's a
mistake.

r.l. I saw a BBC documentary in which you could be seen
talking to a room full of Palestinians. When a woman angrily ac-

cused the Israelis of killing Palestinians, you replied that Israelis who killed Palestinians were tried and punished. This is plainly not true. According to a *Washington Post* article dated November 20, 1996, there were 1,250 Palestinians killed by Israeli soldiers during the 1987–93 intifada. During that period, fourteen Israeli soldiers were tried and convicted after killing Palestinians in violation of army regulations that prohibit soldiers from using lethal force unless their lives are in danger. Eleven of the fourteen were given suspended sentences or ordered to perform community service. And there is the recent case of the four Israeli soldiers who were convicted of negligently shooting to death an 18-year-old Palestinian at a roadblock near the Palestinian town of Salfit. The Israeli military court sentenced them to one hour in jail, suspended, and fined them each one Israeli agora, which is slightly less than a third of an American penny. Looking back on how the Israeli military handled the intifada, would you agree that there was a double standard?

s.p. On the last example you gave, I think that the verdict was ridiculous. Either, or; either they were innocent, or why punish them so lightly? The fact is that the military authorities have appealed to the Supreme Court [to have the sentence increased] because of the light punishment. We don't take it lightly. Usually, the problem before the courts — not that I want to justify it — is how not to create a situation in which every soldier will have a lawyer at his side. The soldiers are also endangering their lives — they weren't there for pleasure. It's not a casino. And it's extremely difficult under fire to measure every movement. So that was the dilemma the court faced. But still, the fact is that fourteen soldiers were convicted.

r.l. Before intifada the Israeli army was generally seen by foreigners as a defensive and dissuasive force; after intifada it was seen — thanks to the thousands of photographs of young Palestinians throwing stones at armed Israeli soldiers—as a police force, an occupying army. Did intifada transform the Israeli perception of the role of the Israeli army?

S.P. I don't think so. Deep in their hearts the Israeli people understand that we cannot act as a police force. When an army meets a guerrilla it has a real problem. So the army, defending Israel militarily, maintained its image. Fighting terrorism is also very complicated. All of us feel extremely uneasy when we see our soldiers facing this. And the best answer is to change the situation. That's one of the reasons I felt so strongly that our soldiers had to leave Gaza. Why remain there? We'd been there for almost thirty years. Gaza didn't become Jewish. Nor could we solve the problem of the Arabs there. So why send our young boys to become targets for stones and hand grenades? It's foolish. So instead of asking if the army can confront young boys throwing stones, we must ask the question, why should this happen in the first place? They say if you have a swamp and mosquitos, you should drain the swamp instead of hunting the mosquitos.

R.L. I'd like to turn now to your views on the strengths and weaknesses of various personalities. Let's begin with Jordan's King Hussein. He was traumatized by the assassination before his eyes of his grandfather, King Abdullah, in July 1951 on Jerusalem's Temple Mount. Referring to King Hussein, you have quoted Shakespeare's famous phrase, "Uneasy lies the head that wears a crown." Did King Hussein ever speak to you about the assassination of his grandfather?

S.P. Oh, yes. Yes. It's not that I have quoted Shakespeare's phrase; the king himself has quoted it. The memories of his grandfather are very moving, very much in his mind. It's probably the paramount event, and the most deeply set, that he carries in his heart and mind. The king is a man of great eloquence and has a historic sentiment, not only historic judgment. He's really caught between so many fires that for him, not to get burned is a major achievement. Let's not forget he is one of the longest-ruling kings in our time. So he must have the capacity to survive and the capacity to lead.

R.L. Before and during the Gulf War, King Hussein openly sided with Iraq's Saddam Hussein, the man who had sworn to obliterate half of Israel with chemical weapons. How is it possible for Israel to see King Hussein today as a friend and even an ally?

S.P. You don't judge friends by their past, but by their future. If you judge friends by their past you will hardly ever have a friend.

R.L. How about Syrian President Hafez al-Assad? What's his game plan? Concerning the Golan, you made him an offer he couldn't refuse—land for peace—but he did. Is it possible he needs to keep Israel as the external enemy in order to remain in power? Does Assad prefer a state of no-war to a real peace?

S.P. I would say that he finds it extremely difficult to go from a state of war to a state of peace. Not that he doesn't want to leave the state of war, and not that he doesn't want to arrive at a state of peace. But to cross the bridge for him is terribly difficult. Actually what happened is that I got a message through the Americans that Assad would like to conclude peace by the end of 1996. And I said yes, I'm ready. Because originally the date for the [Israeli] elections was supposed to be November 1996, not May (which is when it took place). I said, Look, if you really want to conclude before 1996, okay, but I cannot go through the elections with [what amounts to] an open-heart operation without a commitment to close it again; I can't risk reaching the elections without having any conclusion. So I suggested that we raise the level of the negotiations to the top level. I suggested that we meet and that I would take his reaction to the suggestion as an indication of whether he really wanted peace. I sent Assad a message through the Americans in which I quoted André Malraux, who [like Assad] was also a pilot. Malraux said that mothers whose children are pilots are praying that their boys will fly low and slow; they don't understand that to fly high and fast is more secure. So I said to Assad, You're a pilot — what do you want to do, fly high and fast or low and slow?

And then I got a reply from the Americans saying that he was ready to meet, but he couldn't give me a date. So I told the Americans, Look, a girl without a date is like a date without a girl. I don't see the difference. If he wants to meet, let's have a date, and let's meet. The reason Assad gave [for not setting a date] was that we attached conditions that he couldn't meet — that aroused his suspicion. You see, everybody was saying what we were ready to give to him, but he felt that our demands were overwhelming. We asked several things. To some of them he agreed. The first thing I asked for after taking over from Rabin [after his assassination] was to make the Syrian-Israeli peace treaty an all-Arab-Israeli peace treaty, meaning that on the occasion of the signing of peace with Syria all the Arab countries would come together and bring an end to war. That he liked. But what he didn't like were three other points. One was our demand for the economic consequences of full peace. He thought we had an *arrière pensée* [hidden motive] about this. He didn't like our demands on the security arrangements [on the Golan]. He didn't like our demands on [the allocation of] water. So he moved very slowly. Too slowly. And he missed the boat.

R.L. French President Jacques Chirac seems to be a man of great contradictions. He was the prime minister under Giscard d'Estaing (1974–76) who sold the Osirak nuclear reactor to Saddam Hussein that Israeli planes destroyed in June 1981. At the

same time, Mr. Chirac was the first French president to openly
address the sensitive question of Vichy deportations of Jews
during World War II; soon after becoming president, he publicly acknowledged that "the criminal folly of the occupiers was
seconded by the French, by the French state." During a recent
visit to the Middle East, he clinked wine glasses with Assad and
publicly lectured the Israelis about the need to return the Golan
Heights to the Syrians, but he made no mention of Assad ending
what amounts to the Syrian occupation of Lebanon. How do you
explain these contradictions?

s.p. I think there is some tendency in Chirac's policies to follow the de Gaulle line. De Gaulle thought that France had a certain obligation to Lebanon; over the last thousand years France
was supposed to have been the provider for and the protector of
Lebanon. Now it's interesting when you compare the British and
the French, the British are always talking about British interests,
the French are always talking about *la présence française.* It's a
much more sophisticated link. And it has a dialectical Cartesian
phenomenon associated with it. I think that basically Chirac
considers himself to be a friend of Israel.

The last time we met he asked me why Israel was criticizing
him so much about his visit and behavior. I told him, Look, if
I may suggest something, it would be that the French position
should be that whatever is agreed between the parties will be
agreeable to France. Because what you're seeking is not a particular result, but the achievement of peace. And to achieve
peace you cannot impose your position, or any position — you
have to urge the parties to come to a position. I told him that
if I were French, I would be very careful not to introduce ideas
of my own because it antagonizes both sides — you appear to be
taking one side against the other. So you can say, for example,
that I am for full peace with the Palestinians that might include

a Palestinian state. But you shouldn't say, You have to adopt a Palestinian state right away, because by doing so you take away from us the ability to negotiate.

R.L. How did he react to this?

S.P. I think he appreciated my point of view. I told him, Every negotiation begins with an opening position and a fallback position. You want us to take your fallback position as our opening position. It doesn't make sense. And then there was the other argument, the question of competition with the United States. There is a prevailing feeling in Europe that Europe is paying the check and America is taking the glory. He asked me about that, too. I said, There are three different aspects to peace. One is the economic aspect; here everyone is doing whatever he thinks is right. And getting the credit for it. Then there is the diplomatic aspect; here clearly you cannot have two mediators at the same time, you cannot create a situation where the American mediator arrives in the morning, and in the afternoon the French mediator arrives. Finally, you discover that the Arabs and Israelis are mediating between Europe and America. So I told him that the best thing to do was to have an Atlantic policy. You already have an Atlantic policy, which is called NATO, which is basically directed against an enemy you have lost. The original reason for NATO no longer exists. On the other hand you have economic and political problems without having a proper Atlantic instrument. So create an Atlantic policy and work together. This may be the best solution.

R.L. Richard Nixon was known to have used anti-Semitic terms for Jews during private conversations. You met him a number of times, including at the end of his presidency and when he visited Israel in June 1974. Europeans tend to see Mr. Nixon as a brilliant foreign policy maven, the man who opened contacts between the West and China, and belittle his proven abuses of office, which eventually brought him down. How do you see him?

s.p. Not that I'm ready to justify his anti-Semitic outbursts, but I must say he also had anti-American and anti-European outbursts. He had his outbursts. People who think that he was a brilliant negotiator — I would say that one of the greatest things he did was to appoint Henry Kissinger as secretary of state. The fact that Kissinger was appointed suggests that Nixon was not truly anti-Semitic. Because this was the top post, the most sensitive one. Nixon was a complex man. I mean, he was full of — how would you say it? — feelings and sentiments and protest. He was not an easy sea, but a sea full of waves. Some of them could even sink a ship. He wasn't a calm person. And for that reason he reached the top and then fell down into the chasm. His destruction was of his own making. His talents brought him up and his failures brought him down.

r.l. Which brings us to Henry Kissinger. Interestingly, he was born the same year as you, 1923, but where you went to Palestine from Belarus in 1934, he came to the United States from Germany in 1938. Like you, he is a Nobel Peace Prize laureate. Would you comment on his strengths and weaknesses?

s.p. I think he is a brilliant and outstanding man. Let's not take it away from him. The gods have blessed him with great capacities. He is a real historian, he is an original analyzer, he has his own view of the world. And then he possesses a charm and a sense of humor, and a capacity to maneuver and create situations. In the last analysis, a statesman should be judged on his record. And Henry Kissinger's record is quite impressive. One cannot deny it. He is probably one of the two or three most outstanding people in the field of foreign affairs in the last half century. Again, things are never simple. He is supposed to be a cold-blooded person. I saw him very emotional on two occa-

sions. The first was at the airport when he departed from Israel
after he had had a terrible argument with Rabin. He had tears in
his eyes.

R.L. Was that when he was negotiating the Israeli-Egyptian
disengagement after the Yom Kippur war?

S.P. Yes. The second time I saw him with tears in his eyes was
when he was retiring from his post [as secretary of state]. I think
I was the last visitor to his office. He spoke so movingly about
Israel. He said, Where on earth have you ever seen such a small
country going through wars, keeping its democracy, developing its capacity to produce a tank and a plane and, he added
smilingly, a textile factory — that was a reference to Dimona, because our nuclear reactor was sometimes described as a textile
factory. And again I saw tears in his eyes. Also, the man did the
most unbelievable things for a Jewish person who had emigrated
to America. Nixon once told Golda Meir, Both of us have foreign ministers who are Jewish, but yours doesn't speak with an
accent — he was referring to Abba Eban.

Kissinger told us a number of stories which touched our
hearts. One was about his first meeting with Faisal, the king of
Saudi Arabia.[9] Kissinger came with a planeload of journalists,
many of whom were Jewish, and he wasn't sure they would be
permitted to enter the holy city. But they were. And each of them
was given a nice room in a very lovely hotel, and on the tables in
the rooms they found beautiful leather cases, and in the leather
cases were copies of *The Protocols of the Elders of Zion* to educate
them properly. And then Kissinger said that the king, standing
on a small stage, received him at twilight in a very impressive
ceremony — there were two hundred sheiks, all of them dressed

9. 1906?–1975: He reigned from 1964 until his assassination by a nephew in
1975.

in black *abbayehs* and white *kaffiyehs,* and two Bedouins holding swords in their hands led him down this avenue of sheiks toward the king. And Kissinger saw behind the king an illuminated painting of something, and he was thinking to himself, How shall I start this conversation with the king? So finally when he approached he said, Your majesty, I admire your taste in modern art. And then the king became very sour and he said, This is [a painting of] the Ka'aba, the stone at Mecca upon which Mohammed laid his head. So Kissinger started off with a faux pas. And then the king told him, Mr. Kissinger, I receive you here not as a Jewish person, but as a human being. To which Kissinger replied, Your majesty, some of my best friends are human beings. And the story went on and on. On top of everything else, Kissinger was really a great storyteller.

R.L. What about Ronald Reagan? In America, it has been said that he asked his aides to summarize any issue, no matter how complex, on an eight-by-ten index card. King Hussein once told you that President Reagan had asked him about fishing in the Dead Sea — where, of course, there are no fish. You have said that you genuinely liked the man Reagan, and appreciated "his refreshingly innocent reactions when the going got complicated." This certainly sounds tongue in cheek. You are quite critical of Prime Minister Begin for not being on top of the situation during the Israeli invasion of Lebanon, and quite complimentary toward King Hussein for invariably being on top of the subject under discussion. Why do you let Mr. Reagan, the leader of the free world and the Western Alliance, off the hook? Isn't it possible for an Israeli leader to be critical of an American president?

S.P. Sure it is. But let me say about Reagan two or three things. Number one, he was far more able than people gave him credit for. He had a good memory, he was not bad at polemics at all.

I think people underrate his capacities. He would never have become president if he had been such an empty person. Let's not forget that he became the governor of California, then president. He won several elections. So it cannot be just an accident. At the beginning I think he had much more [capacity] than people attributed to him. And secondly, he was a real friend. I mean, the [concept of the] bad guys and the good guys, as they say, resided in his thinking. If he considered you a good guy, he stood unhesitatingly on your side. And what I liked about him was his air of modesty. You came into his office — you never felt someone standing there in a formal manner. He was very, very modest. And he had his own way of thinking. He was a great collector of Russian jokes. I remember every time we came we used to hear a nice anti-Russian joke from him. I can even remember the last one. Stalin and Roosevelt and Churchill were meeting at Yalta. They were supposed to have dinner together, but Roosevelt, who was sick by then, retired to his bed. Only Stalin and Churchill remained. So they were eating and drinking and talking and drinking and talking. The next morning Churchill approached Stalin and said, "Joe, last night we drank too much and we talked too much. We have to do something about it." And Stalin replied, "You know, I have exactly the same feeling. Actually, there were three of us, you, me, and the interpreter. But don't worry too much, the interpreter has already been executed."

R.L. Is President Clinton at heart a friend of Israel's?

S.P. Yes. I like Clinton very much. I think he is a very sophisticated man with a great capacity to learn. He has had a real dilemma. On several occasions I discussed this dilemma with him. He is the first president since World War II who hasn't had the Russians as an enemy. And you know, when you don't have an enemy you can hardly conduct a foreign policy. You cannot come to the Congress and ask for money. They say, What for?

Where is the enemy? Clinton faces dangers, which are hard to define, rather than enemies, which are easy to point out. And he has had to convert a long American tradition of making Communism the major consideration of an American administration to something else. And not only that, he also lost the competition of the other superpower. So all of a sudden he found a stingy Congress which focused on domestic issues and forgot many other issues. And everything was complicated by the Vietnam memories that make it extremely hard for any American president to send American soldiers abroad. I think he has learned quickly, and a great deal, from his experience.

As far as Israel is concerned, he is a real friend. He has paid four visits to our country, more than any other American president. He went the longest way to support us, to support the peace process. He had special relations with Rabin and very good relations with me later on. We trusted each other fully. A nice anecdote I can tell is that after we signed the agreement with King Hussein on the lawn of the White House, the president took me aside and asked, "Shimon, how come you finally reached an agreement with King Hussein?" I told him, "Mr. President, it was because of a mistake you made." He said, "Me? What sort of mistake did I make?" I told him, "You told all of your aides and officials to make it clear to the king that you would not forgive him the foreign debt that Jordan owes to the United States. But then when you met, you forgot what you told your aides and you gave Hussein the impression that you were willing to forgive the debt if he concluded the peace treaty with Israel." Clinton said, "Shimon, if you have another situation for me to make a mistake, call me up."

R.L. In Germany we are beginning to hear the first rumblings of the possibility of a post-Kohl era. Will you comment on German Chancellor Helmut Kohl?

S.P. Kohl is a happy politician. I never saw a man who enjoys his role as much as Kohl does. But again, Kohl has suffered from underestimation, which now is being corrected. He is much more thoughtful than people give him credit for. His ambition was to become the longest-serving chancellor in German history. He has already passed fourteen years—more than [Konrad] Adenauer.[10] And he has very good instincts. When you look at German policies, which are very interesting, Adenauer built the bridge between the West and Germany. [Willy] Brandt[11] built the bridge between Russia and Germany. And Kohl took the two bridges and united the two Germanies into one. But then, being rather wise, he said that he didn't want Europe to have a strong Germany, but rather a Germany that belongs to a strong Europe. Which shows quite an imaginative approach to the destiny of Germany.

R.L. [Former] British Prime Minister John Major appears to be reaching the end of his rope. How do you account for his lack of popularity?

S.P. I don't know John Major as well. The three or four meetings we have had were very pleasant. I found him always perfectly well prepared for every meeting, an extremely pleasant person. I never heard a foolish remark come from him. And I can hardly analyze why he suffers from such indifference from his own voters. Maybe it's because of the length of time the conservatives have been in power.

R.L. How about Russian President Boris Yeltsin?

S.P. I have met him twice. I don't know another leader who acts from the head and from the stomach with the same strength.

10. 1876–1967: The first post-war chancellor of West Germany, he served from 1949 to 1963.

11. 1913–1992: A Nobel Peace Prize laureate, he served as chancellor of West Germany from 1969 to 1974.

You never know what comes out of the stomach and what comes out of the head.

R.L. By stomach you mean gut. A gut reaction?

S.P. In Hebrew, we say stomach. Gut reaction, yes. Yeltsin is more surprising than constant. And it's interesting, in terms of Russian history, that what actually made Yeltsin so famous was five minutes standing on that tank. Stalin had to kill millions of people to establish his leadership, but Yeltsin did it in five minutes by climbing on a tank. Again it shows both the courage of the man and the strength of television. It's also a contradiction — when there was the coup against Gorbachev, Yeltsin remained loyal. And then he brought him down. So it's a contradiction. He can be very friendly when you meet him, or he can ignore you completely. Again, it's a gut reaction more than a calculated one.

Memory has been
our land for
two thousand years.

FIFTH CONVERSATION

R.L. Perhaps we can talk about things which are closer to home. How did you meet your wife?

S.P. When I was at Ben-Shemen, I was sworn into the Haganah, and we had guard posts to defend the village against invasion and shootings. I was assigned to the position that was near the house of Sonia, my wife. Night in, night out I used to stand guard there. And there I saw her for the first time one morning, and it was love at first sight. She came out barefoot and dressed in a very modest way, and she had—how do you call it?—pigtails and a classic Greek profile. I fell in love immediately. And then I tried to do my very best to conquer her heart. Among other things, I read to her by moonlight chapters from Marx's *Das Kapital*—I thought that this would impress her deeply.

R.L. Do you speak Arabic?

S.P. I used to. But I have forgotten it.

R.L. Have you read the Koran?

S.P. Yes, I have read it both in English and in Hebrew.

R.L. One finds many of the Old Testament stories retold in the Koran—the Garden of Eden, the story of Ibrahim (as the Muslims call the patriarch Abraham) leaving the land of Ur, though in the Koran he is going to sacrifice Isaac's half brother, Ishmael, at the Ka'aba, and not Isaac on what became the Temple Mount in Jerusalem, so tradition tells us. How do you view the overlapping of these tales?

s.p. I think the Bible is more varied and more sophisticated. It has many escapes—*escapados,* as they call them—from the norms of life. In Spanish it's called *escapado* when a man leaves with another woman. In English, it's an escape. There are many stories in the Bible with a twinkle in the eye. About Solomon, about David, about Joshua. The Koran is without twinkles.

r.l. Can you describe your religious beliefs? Do you believe in God? In life after death?

s.p. I believe that God resides in our hearts no less than He resides in heaven. For me, God is the real consciousness of life. And the idea that we are born in His image calls for a moral commitment. I don't think that God is a great mechanic that sits somewhere and plans and makes man and makes this and makes that. But I do believe that God is a great spirit, a great wisdom. And I think the whole world would be poorer without Him, and each of us would be poorer without Him. And the fact that He is invisible greatly helps me to live in peace with the mystery of His existence. He is a moral resident in our lives more than the master of our affairs. As for the afterlife, I doubt it very much. I think in a way death is a liberation. Suppose we were to live forever; what would we do with our lives? It is better to end life by reproducing than to maintain yourself endlessly. I don't complain about being a passing phenomenon provided that I can use my time and place properly. I don't have any complaints about death. Nor do I have any fear of dying.

r.l. Malraux said famously: "The twenty-first century will be spiritual or there will be no twenty-first century." Do you agree?

S.P. I think it's a mistake, because it can be both—it can be spiritual and not spiritual at the same time. I think the idea that the world is made up of contradictions is also the idea that it's made of balances. Wherever you go you will face twin phenomena. Everything comes in pairs, whether in an electric current or in the weather or in the mind or in the feeling or in the happening. So happily enough the world is symmetrical and complementary, not one-sided. We have two hands and two eyes and two legs and two faiths and two fortunes, we have birth and death.

R.L. And two lobes of the brain.

S.P. Yes. So I mean the idea that it's either/or—I don't buy it. The world is both symmetrical and endless. There is no end to the smallest thing and no end to the largest thing. And for that reason we are constantly searching in an attempt to reach the end which is the beginning, but we are incapable of finding it. Whenever we think we've found what we consider the smallest cell or particle, we discover it's nonsense. We thought that the atomic particle was the smallest, and then we went into it and discovered that down below there is not matter at all, but currents or movements or waves. A dancing cosmos. Which, by the way, is chaotic—a macarena without rules. It confuses our minds. And for that reason until now we have not been able to get rid of the simple symmetry and we have been unable to penetrate the end which is the beginning, or the beginning which is the end.

R.L. The American poet e.e. cummings, who wrote his name in small letters, has a line that says: "Progress is a comfortable disease." The American writer Henry Thoreau said pretty much the same long before cummings: "Men," he declared, "have become the tools of their tools." Do you agree?

S.P. I don't think so. I think that life is not made of repetitions, but of mutations of progress. I mean, I accept the Buddhist concept that when you cross the river, you never cross the same water twice because it flows. Life flows. And we cannot stop it. And we cannot turn our backs on it. You cannot go backward. The Lord gave us eyes in our foreheads so that we could go forward. He did not give us a spare set of eyes in the back of our heads so that we could go in both directions with the same equipment. We are equipped for progress. We are not equipped for regression. The problem is that our minds have memories that are too strong. Many of the things that still exist in our minds—we cannot forget them. The power to think and the inclination to remember wind up occasionally with memory overpowering thought. For example, we live in a world without borders, but all the borders are still in our minds. And when we move from one place to another we need a mental passport, because we cannot cross the borders that are fixed in our minds. I mean, this is the funniest part of it—life is moving faster than our intellectual capacities. We are always late. You know, intellectually we are not in a car, we are in a boat. When you drive a car the driver sits in the front, when you drive a boat the driver sits in the rear. So all the time the boat is way ahead of where the driver is.

R.L. The Jews claim to have introduced the concept of monotheism into Western thinking—Deuteronomy 6, the *Shema Yisrael,* is cited as the first unequivocal statement of monotheism. Freud in *Moses and Monotheism* argued that monotheism was a step backward, in the sense that monotheism went hand in glove with intolerance; with the belief in one God came the notion that those who worshipped other gods were, in fact, worshipping false gods. This implied that the worshippers of false gods had to be educated or corrected or punished, or in some cases eliminated. Over the centuries, a great many people have been killed

in the name of somebody's one and only god. Do you agree with
Freud? Was monotheism a step forward or a step backward for
mankind?

s.p. Cruelty, killing, assassination all existed in the world
when there were many gods. The difference is that when we talk
about monotheism, we are talking of the image of the Lord, and
when we are talking of the pluralistic gods, it's the imaginary
lords. One God is an image that concerns all of us. When you
have twenty gods, all of them are imaginary gods. We were not
born in their image, they were made in our image. To make a
sculpture and say that it represents the Lord—it's so primitive. I
mean, it's an insult to the human mind and the human spirit that
you carry your small wooden god in your pocket. My God, how
primitive can the world be? So the first departure from primitivism to sophistication is the departure from wooden gods and
many gods to an invisible God. And then, over the centuries tolerance came, even with monotheism. There was an age of cruelty
and an age of liberalism, which goes on today. It has nothing to
do with religion; religion itself is going through different ages.

r.l. Are you familiar with the old tradition of the missing
letter in the Hebrew alphabet? A thirteenth-century Cabalistic
text, Sefer HaTemunah, teaches that one letter of the Hebrew
alphabet is missing. Every defect in the universe is supposed
to be mysteriously connected to this missing letter. The name
and pronunciation of the missing letter will come, like the Messiah, in the future. When this missing letter falls into place in the
alphabet, chaos will become order, so the tradition tells us. Have
you ever heard the faint whisper of a Hebrew consonant that
does not seem familiar to you?

s.p. No, I don't believe in all those stories. You know, the
greatest thing about the Messiah is that he didn't arrive. If he
were to arrive, he would be criticized so much that he might run

away. The Messiah, somebody once said, is the greatest diplomat the Jewish people ever had for the simple reason that he didn't come. And this missing letter is another story—it's nonsense.

R.L. Jews have a tradition of writing messages to God and wadding them between the stones of the Wailing Wall. Did you ever leave such a message?

S.P. Yes.

R.L. Would you say what you wrote on it?

S.P. I said: Spread above our heads the tabernacle of peace [Hashkiveinu prayer]. And then also on another occasion I wrote: Justice, justice you have to pursue [Deut. 16:20].

R.L. It is impossible to read your memoirs or books about you without noticing one quality that stands out: your sense of loyalty to people. You are loyal to a fault to Ben-Gurion; you can barely bring yourself to criticize his stubbornness when he feuded with Levi Eshkol and tried to oust him as prime minister, to name one instance. You are loyal to Moshe Dayan; you can barely bring yourself to hint at defects in his character. You are loyal to François Mitterrand despite what you describe as the "dark spots" of his Vichy past. Why is loyalty so important to you?

S.P. I hate the hatred of men. I find we are so quick to criticize and so slow to support. Now I'm aware that each of us has weaknesses. There is nothing new about that. But when I discover people's good qualities, they are very dear to my heart. And particularly when people are unduly criticized. And particularly when they are dead and don't have a chance to defend themselves. As the Indian poet Vikram Seth wrote: "Love me when I am dead. Don't let me die." So I, remaining alive, feel that I have to speak of their good qualities because they themselves are silent. And you know, people in general tend to be extremely stingy. And I do not see any reason why I should not be generous. I feel I am strong enough and convinced enough to be generous. People have been generous toward me, and that creates an obligation—you have to be thankful to them. I don't have very much money. So I mean, what I can be generous with is my attitude toward people. I don't see any reason why I should be stingy.

R.L. Are you personally conscious of having made history, of having, by your existence, by your presence, by your actions, diverted, however slightly, the river of history?

S.P. Not really. Not really.

R.L. A great many people think otherwise. Aren't you being too modest?

S.P. I don't want to appear to be modest. I don't claim to be a modest person. But I have my doubts about what constitutes history. So in another hundred years four boring students will write a thesis about the year 1996 and they'll make a reference to Peres—it's not such a big deal to me. If I can save the life of a single child this year it's more important than to have a chapter in history next year. I have lost my patience with history. I want to tell you a very telling story. When Eshkol passed away some of us went to Ben-Gurion and said, "Look, it's finished. The man is dead. You should attend his funeral." Ben-Gurion became very angry and said, "I will not attend his funeral and I don't want him to attend my funeral."

R.L. I have seen it suggested that Israelis have split personalities. The Torah—with its tales of Joshua conquering Canaan, or David triumphing over Goliath, or Deborah leading Israel against the Philistines—tells Jews that they are warriors and lions. The Holocaust, on the other hand, appears to convey the message that Jews are victims and lambs. I have seen it suggested that Jews carry the Torah in their heads and the Holocaust in what you in Hebrew call their stomachs and we would call the guts; that the two traditions war with each other inside the Jew. Do you detect a grain of truth in this generalization?

S.P. No. I think that life is very complex. All the attempts to submit life to classification are artificial. Everything is so mixed and so varied that you have all of those ingredients in the same personality, whether it's a person or a nation. There were times when the Jews were lions. There were times when the Jews were victims. And there were times when they were both lions and victims. Or there were Jews during the same time that were lions and other Jews that were victims. You can generalize about just one thing and that is faith in relation to the future. Only the future can be unequivocal. The past is always mixed.

R.L. Elie Wiesel, speaking of Jews, once said, No other people has such an obsession with memory. Do you agree that Jews are obsessed with memory? That memory has a moral power?

S.P. I agree that Jews are obsessed with memory because they lost their land. Memory has been our land for two thousand years. So memory was, in a way, a replacement. When it comes to other memories, I am afraid that there is an attempt to purify them; they never arrive as raw material. Because memory is what we say it is. We cannot really revive the whole situation, with its deviations and mistakes and scenes. Memory is a moral conclusion, because you try to take out from memory the moral side.

R.L. You filter memory for morality?

S.P. Yes. You filter it.

R.L. There is a passage in the Babylonian Talmud that says: "Of the ten measures of beauty that came down to the world, Jerusalem took nine." Do you agree?

S.P. Yes.

R.L. Why do you live in Tel Aviv?

S.P. I live in Tel Aviv because I spent a great part of my life

in the Ministry of Defense, and it is the only ministry of the
government which is still in Tel Aviv. That was the original reason. Tel Aviv is the heart of the reserves, and the army is built
on the reserves. So here I made my place to live and bought my
apartment. But I have spent a great deal of my life in Jerusalem.
I lived there for twelve years, even more. And I liked Jerusalem
tremendously. But I want to tell you something — a person like
me can't go around buying and selling apartments. I cannot go
into any financial dealings. And both Sonia and I are extremely
careful when it comes to financing and money. To sell and buy
an apartment is quite an operation in our life, you know. And we
have preferred to live as we do, in the same modest apartment for
the last twenty-six years. Because although during fifty years of
political life I was often the object of criticism and the center of
controversy, there is one thing that nobody could ever challenge
me on, and that is our financial honesty. The apartment I live
in — my brother, who was a builder, sold it to me for a reasonable
price. When we bought it it was a low price, today it has a high
value because the area has changed. But we don't want to speculate. We don't want to buy, we don't want to sell, we don't want
to move. So we have stayed in the same place.

R.L. You were quoted in the French newspaper *Nouvel Obser-
vateur* as saying: "Ce n'est pas le pouvoir qui m'intéresse, c'est
la poursuite du processus de paix" [It isn't power that interests
me, but the pursuit of the peace process]. If in fact you are out of
active politics, which may well be the case, how do you see your
role in pursuing and encouraging the peace process? What can
you do from the sidelines?

S.P. First of all, I believe that my voice will be heard and taken
into consideration. I'm not going to become silent. And then
I think that I am going to devote a great deal of my time to the
building of three institutes, two that already exist and a third

that I have in mind to build. One which we are building now is an institute for peace, which is called the Peres Institute, and it will deal with the economic aspects of peace in order to introduce economic ideas, to offer economic ties, and to have think tanks. It will be nongovernmental, nonprofit, nonpartisan and attached to the university. And we have started to build the endowment fund; we already have the initial seed money. Right now the institute is being headed by the person who was our main negotiator in Oslo — Uri Savir, who was the director general of the foreign ministry. It will also analyze the Oslo process. It will be, so to speak, an intellectual pragmatic contribution to the continuation of peace.

The second project, which was set up a long time ago, and which I support and am very much involved with, is an institute devoted to de-desertification — fighting desert. It's located in the Ben-Gurion University at Sde Boker.[1] I am trying to collect the money necessary to support this project because I think that desertification of the land is like the ignorance of the people — these are the two main reasons why a region becomes poor and lost. And I hope that I shall participate in building a third institute, perhaps on the frontier between Jericho and Israel, which will deal with the biotechnology of agriculture; it will be a joint venture for the Arabs and the Palestinians and us. The idea came from a Frenchman who is a scientist, and I cherish it and am trying to see what can be implemented. So I'm not going to be idle. And I think I will use whatever I may have in the way of experience or attention [focused on me] to devote myself to peace. I would also like to devote part of my time and experience to educate beginners, young people.

1. The kibbutz in the Negev to which Ben-Gurion retired.

R.L. Can we talk for a moment about the Israeli Arabs, the roughly 950,000 Arabs who live in Israel proper and are citizens of Israel. Are they loyal to the State of Israel, or might they one day opt to detach chunks of, say, the Galilee and join a Palestinian entity, assuming such an entity exists?

S.P. I have confidence in them. I basically trust their loyalty to the state. Look, let facts speak for themselves. The Israeli Arabs went through five wars against Arab states with us and there was scarcely a single occasion of treachery. So let's give them credit for it.

R.L. It's difficult to read written accounts of the period before and during the War of Independence, or any period for that matter, without noticing that a great percentage of Israel's leaders came from the kibbutz movement. And of course, the officer corps of the army, not to mention the special units, the paratroopers, consists disproportionately of kibbutzniks. Kibbutz casualties in Israel's wars have been way out of proportion to the casualties among the general public. What is it about the kibbutz environment that produced and continues to produce highly qualified and highly motivated leaders?

S.P. It's a wonderful experience. It equips you with a sense of collective responsibility. This is the greatest voluntary attempt to make concern for yourself secondary to collective responsibility. There is no other form of life that without coercion makes you such a full member of a society—watching the others, being watched by the others, having an eye for interpersonal relationships on a daily basis and on a novel basis, investing so much in the education of the children, and having a permanent commitment to a modest life, having a permanent commitment not to spend, not to show off. And being governed by the spirit of pioneering—whatever you do, you often do for the first time.

We came to a land that was harsh and we fought for our existence. The kibbutz is a human experience that Martin Buber
once described as the least evil human experiment.

R.L. A great deal has been written about the decline of the
kibbutz movement. Is it burning out or can it be rejuvenated?

S.P. It must change with age. You know, when the first kibbutzim came in, there were several ideas. One was that we Jewish
people have to return to manual work — to cultivate the land
with our own hands. And by the way one of the reasons for this
was that we didn't want the Arabs to become our "natives." We
ourselves would do our manual work. But today you irrigate
with computers, you plow with tractors. It's becoming high-
technology agriculture. Usually agriculture is a joint venture
between the Lord and man. And one of the partners is totally unreliable. He brings you drought, He brings you cold, He brings
you heat. So we have had to have the intervention of science to
compensate for the unreliability of the other partner, which is
nature. And then today most of the kibbutzim are engaged in
industry.

I want to tell you a story. I was trained in a kibbutz called
Geva in the Jezreel Valley. And there if you woke up a minute
after sunrise you were considered a criminal. And if you came
back home before sunset, again you were a criminal. I mean, we
were hard-working, very indoctrinated pioneers. I was working
there, among other places, in the barn milking cows. And I said,
Look, the future cannot remain just agricultural. We have to
think about industry, and so on and so forth. They thought that
I was a criminal. Talking in the heart of the kibbutzim, in the
midst of all this agricultural commitment, about industry was
like talking in the synagogue about eating pigs' feet.

Okay. Later I became the minister of transportation and communication. We had a lot of trouble with the public telephones.

They were broken down. So I remembered that during a visit to Paris I had seen for the first time a magnetic ticket to use the metro. I wrote a letter to the management of the railways in Paris and asked if they thought we could adopt a magnetic card for the telephone as they had for the trains. They said yes, they thought it was possible. But then to my great surprise they said they didn't make the magnetic tickets themselves, they imported them. So I asked for the address of the company that produced them. And then I got back a reply. It said that the producer of the magnetic tickets was Kibbutz Geva in the Valley of Jezreel. So I went to my kibbutz and saw the place where I used to milk cows, and there I found electronic machines and the kibbutzniks were milking the magnetic cards. So that was one change. The other thing that changed over the years was that, at the beginning, the kibbutzim were usually located very near the frontier, but then later the frontier was pushed back.

R.L. Which took away the essential quality of being a pioneer?

S.P. Yes. The idea of cultivating your land with your own hands and at the same time defending your country—that changed.

R.L. The Harvard sociologist Daniel Bell once told me about a piece of graffito he found scrawled on the wall of a bathroom at the very intellectual and mathematics-oriented University of Chicago. The graffito went like this: "In every civilization known to man, the ratio of horses' asses to horses is greater than one." A person in your position gets to meet more people than most. Has it been your experience that the horses' asses outnumber the horses?

S.P. I never gathered any statistics, but probably there are some. And may I add to that, one of our famous authors, David Grossman, said that the problem in our lives is that foolishness doesn't age.

R.L. The verdict is in on the economic system that went by the name of Communism. It didn't work. But because Communism didn't work doesn't mean capitalism — whatever that word means — works. Recently Juergen Schrempp, the Daimler-Benz chairman, attempted to reduce sick pay benefits, cut thousands of jobs from the company's unprofitable divisions and liquidate the century-old AEG electronics division. Mr. Schrempp has since backpeddled, but at the time he justified all this by saying that the only thing that mattered was "profit, profit, profit." His *cri de coeur* — profit — appears to be the rallying cry for the great majority of the large, and often profitable, companies in America and Europe that are downsizing at the expense of their employees. In your opinion, does the free market economic system we call capitalism work?

S.P. I've said on different occasions that what we really need is to make money like capitalists and distribute money like socialists. I agree that profit should be a major consideration. But what is profit? And how do you make a profit? Just by saving money? Maybe you can make more of a profit by raising the standard of living of people; by doing so, you increase the demand [for products], you increase job opportunities. The idea that profit calls for cuts and not for growth is idiotic. And for that reason I think that Communism and market-oriented economies are both one-legged phenomena. You cannot stand forever on one leg. You have to move with your two legs.

Communism was a great philosophical mistake that goes back to Marx. He thought that future economies would be based on materialism. Now we know that economies are based on intellectualism, on science. Marx was outstanding in criticizing capitalism, but he was totally ineffective in proposing an alternative. The alternative he proposed was from the outset full of self-destruction. And finally Communism blew up Communism.

The most important quotation I took from the Gorbachev book is that only Communists can destroy Communism. He's right.

Now, market economies that remain indifferent to social needs will also fall down. Because what are we living for — money? We need money in order to make a living, and we need more money to make a better living. But more money for the few doesn't make any sense in an age of television. You can commercialize products, but not human beings. So I think that finally a balance will arrive somehow, somewhere, particularly when this gentleman you are quoting forgets which age we live in. We live in an age in which capitalism has adopted maybe 50 percent of the ideas of socialism. There is no more of the naked capitalism that used to exist at the beginning of mass production in America. But when you look back and compare the two revolutions — of Lenin and Ford — I think the revolution of Henry Ford[2] was more successful. Because in the end Lenin made slaves out of the workers, and Ford made consumers out of them. The more they earn, the more they consume, the more even Ford will become successful.

R.L. The verdict is also in on the political-social system called Communism. The evil empire, as Ronald Reagan called it, didn't work either. But because political Communism didn't work doesn't mean that political capitalism — again, whatever that means — works. The American Secretary of State Dean Acheson left us, on the year of his death in 1971, some food for thought. "Democracy," he said, "is only tolerable because no other system is." Would you argue with him on this point?

S.P. You're comparing two things, Communism and capitalism, when what we really have to compare is dictatorship and democracy. It doesn't matter if a dictatorship is socialist or

2. His mass-produced Model T Ford became the first widely affordable automobile in the United States.

capitalist. The dictator is the evil element. And again, it's not capitalism or socialism, it is democracy that provides the main source of human existence — freedom. That's the only commodity that the Lord didn't charge us for, and we keep wasting it. The only limitation on freedom is the freedom of the other person. But basically, the real competition is between the rulers who tend to be totalitarian and the leaders who understand that they have to be facilitators. This is the great ideological conflict.

R.L. Your grandfather taught you that if you see only one side of an issue, you have not studied it properly. But aren't people who see many sides of an issue at a permanent disadvantage to those who see only one side of an issue? What I'm getting at here is that if you see one side, you can act with incredible certitude, while if you see several sides, you may, like Hamlet, hesitate.

S.P. Not necessarily. We are provided as human beings not only with eyes to see the two sides, but with a mind to make a selection. Even when you see the two sides of the picture, you have to compare. And maybe the result will not be perfect, but it may be the lesser of two evils. So in between perfection and evil there will be quite a game of choice. And personally, as I told you, I don't believe in perfection. Neither positive nor negative perfection. I think the greatest criminal is not perfect. Even he will finally be brought to trial. So why do you need a mind in addition to your eyes if you don't have to weigh the things you perceive on the scale of your judgment?

R.L. So what your grandfather was saying, if I have it right, is to see two sides, but then choose between them. And the refusal to make a choice is also a choice.

S.P. The refusal to make a choice — that's Hamlet's weakness. When Hamlet says, "To be or not to be," he makes the mistake of thinking the choice is "or." That's not a choice. This is an arresting connection between two choices, but it's not a choice in itself.

R.L. So in the end, Hamlet wasn't very sophisticated.

S.P. Surely he wasn't very sophisticated. But Shakespeare doesn't claim that he was. Shakespeare refers to him as a spent spirit — a spirit that has lost its capacity to move.

R.L. Maybe that's because Hamlet was reacting from his stomach or gut, and not his head.

S.P. Again, you have a stomach and you have a head. You have to use both. If you have all these parts of your body and you don't use them, you are a self-appointed invalid. We weren't condemned to be invalids.

R.L. A Russian Jew who emigrated to Israel after World War II drove me to the Golan Heights after the 1967 Six-Day War. Coming back he stopped on the empty road to watch the sun set. As darkness settled around us, sparks of lights flickered on in the Jezreel Valley. In the darkness the lights looked like stars, except that they were far below us, not far above. My guide said to me: "Imagine you are a nineteen-year-old Syrian soldier sitting up here in these trenches that the Russians built — you are illiterate, there is no electricity up here on the Golan, and night after night you watch the lights of the Jewish kibbutzim flash on below. It must seem like the Western world saying" — excuse my language, Mr. Peres, but I'm quoting the guide directly — "fuck you, fuck you, every time another kibbutz turns on its lights." The conventional wisdom holds that the struggle between the Palestinians and the Israelis is over land. But isn't it also a question of honor? Isn't Israel a thorn in the side of Arab dignity?

S.P. Yes, maybe. But dignity is also conservatism. And again, in order to keep dignity you cannot freeze the rest of the world. We didn't turn on the lights in order to provoke them, in order to hurt their eyes. But if we didn't do it, we would go backwards.

R.L. You're talking about that from the Israeli point of view—

S.P. I also want to say to the Arabs, You can do like us. And they're doing it. They're building colonies, they rebuilt one of their cities. You see, nothing has just one meaning. It can have a double meaning. I met with President Mubarak[3] several weeks ago in Sharm el-Sheikh and he told me what the Egyptians were doing—they reclaimed four million dunams of land, they cut an irrigation canal from the Nile to western Egypt, they are going to develop an industrial center between Ismailia and Cairo. And then he told me—and that I saw—that they were converting the Sinai peninsula into an attractive tourist center. And Osama-el-Baz, his aide, said that the Egyptians had learned a great deal from [my book] *The New Middle East*—from what I was talking about in the book.

I told him, Look, for many years the perception about Egypt was that it was a nation that grows very rapidly because of a high birthrate, and yet was confined to the Nile delta, which is the only fertile land. And every once in a while you found another sphinx or another pyramid and you made news. This is the first time that Egypt has escaped the delta and the pyramids and entered a new age. And I told him, I think you have to publicize this, because everyone has the impression you are concerned only with the delta and the pyramids and arms. Here you have begun to develop your country.

And I must say to Mubarak's credit, they have reduced the birthrate from 3 percent to 2.1 percent, which is quite an achievement. They have economic growth of 6 percent. It's quite revolutionary. I told him that in a way Egypt is the China of the Middle East—in other words, the most populated land. You can live in

3. 1928– : Succeeded as president of Egypt after the 1981 assassination of Anwar el-Sadat.

backwardness and still start to adopt modern technology and marketing. And the same goes for Syria. There is a limit to symbolism; at a given time you must be more serious than a symbol. If you have a flying flag and a declining country, what do you have? — a piece of fabric. So you cannot just watch the flags. You have to refer to the realities.

R.L. So if I understand you correctly, what you are saying is that if Israel is an affront to Arab dignity, it's the fault of the Arabs and not the Israelis.

S.P. Right. To live in backwardness is not so dignified, in my judgment. And you see, when some Arabs say that you [Israelis] want to dominate our lives, I answer, Don't be foolish — nobody wants to dominate poverty. I told Mubarak the following story: Imagine if Disraeli were to come today to Queen Victoria and tell her, "My Queen, I've brought you some gifts — Bangladesh, Pakistan, Ghana." She would throw him out of the room and say, "Go to hell, who needs it? What for? Give me a good laboratory. Give me a good idea." Who is looking to conquer people or land these days? What you really want is to use science and conquer nature. Today we wouldn't go, unless we were attacked, to conquer the Golan Heights for the sake of having more land. Even now many of us don't intend to keep it; we believe peace is higher than a mountain. So you see, your whole story has maybe a poetic value, but no more than that.

R.L. I have heard several Israeli intellectuals refer to you as a tragic hero — a hero because of your enormous contributions to the Jewish state over a period of fifty years, tragic because the voters wouldn't let you finish what you started: the Oslo peace process. Do you accept this characterization of yourself as a tragic hero?

S.P. If you judge me by the elections, maybe that's a tragedy. But if you judge me by my achievements, maybe it's a success. I really don't know how to summarize it. I saw many people who won elections and didn't know what to do with their victory. I saw other people who lost elections and knew what to do with their loss. So things are not simple. I had a very active and full life and I intend to continue. I have to change with the circumstances and, as they say, age is very intransigent — you cannot argue with it. I feel healthy and strong and very involved and concerned.

R.L. Politicians are notorious for their natural reluctance to admit mistakes. Will you break the mold, Mr. Peres? What mistakes did you make along the way?

S.P. Since I am not talking about my achievements, I will not talk about my mistakes either. It's a very long list —

R.L. You mentioned one already, which was your refusal in the 1940s to accept a commission in the Israeli army.

S.P. I've committed many other mistakes, but I have a tendency not to recall them because I cannot change them, and others cannot draw lessons from them. So why do it?

R.L. The theory is that one learns from mistakes.

S.P. I don't know if you do learn from mistakes. Even if you learn from them, it doesn't prevent you from making others. It's an endless process of trial and error. It's a little bit naive to think that if you learn from one mistake, you have learned about all mistakes. The mistake you learned from you may not repeat, but then you have many opportunities to make other mistakes. I mean, since you are always acting in a field which is not clear — there are many guesses and assumptions, and you have to face a future which is unknown — you don't walk on a definite map. Only geography has maps. Politics does not. So you have to rely a great deal on your character, your intuition, and your knowledge. It won't save you from making mistakes. And also you are very much influenced — you are attacked by different inclinations: pity, self-pity, aggressiveness, over-aggressiveness. I do not believe that there is anyone who is totally self-controlled. So I wouldn't judge any person, including myself, by mistakes, because this is part and parcel of our nature. I would prefer to see on which occasions he was able to take off, rather than fall down. This is the great story of life.

R.L. You and Mr. Rabin risked everything for peace. He paid with his life, you paid with the loss of a friend and the loss of an election. If you could do things over, what would you do differently?

S.P. Maybe I would try to conduct a tougher electoral campaign. I was impressed by the ideas of some of the staff who said that the purpose of the campaign was to win over the floating vote, and for that you need a "soft" campaign. Looking back, I think it might have been a mistake.

R.L. You have a daughter, Zikki, who teaches psycholinguistics; a son, Yoni, a veterinarian; another son, Hemi, an air force pilot and now an industrialist. Do you have grandchildren?

S.P. Six.

R.L. Do you have the same authority over your children and grandchildren that your grandfather, the Reb Meltzer, had over you?

S.P. Probably yes. But they have established the authority more than I have. It wasn't an attempt on my part. They listen carefully to what I say — I don't have to make any effort. It comes naturally. As far as I'm concerned I don't seek authority. I offer and seek love.

R.L. Could you define Judaism? Is it a religion? A nation? A book? A way of looking at history?

S.P. None of them. Judaism is a faith. Religion in almost all cases is an organization. A hierarchy. Look at Christianity. You have the Lord and the vicar and you have different ranks of priests. Look at the Shi'ites—it's the same. Even Buddhism is constructed with very much of a hierarchy. These are very strong organizations with rules and norms. Judaism, by definition, is not an organization, and not a hierarchy. The Lord has never appointed a Jewish vicar. The Lord has never appointed different ranks among the Jewish clergy. So what typifies Judaism is the direct contact between man and the Lord without interference, without intermediaries. Even when it comes to performing a marriage, according to the Torah you don't need a rabbi. You need two witnesses. That will do the job. There is no call in the Torah to wear a hat or what we call a *kippah.* There is in the Torah an injunction not to charge an excessive rate of interest. Some Jews emphasize the ceremonial part of it, the cult, instead of the content, which is a mistake.

Now when it comes to the philosophy of the faith, the great thing about Judaism is that it is very optimistic because it is based on the idea that you can improve every person, you can better every nation, you can bring an end to wars, to poverty. The prophecy is oriented toward optimism, not an attempt to justify whatever exists or to live with it. And Judaism combines an affinity for the universal and the national, because in the Hebrew tradition there is no difference between a nation and a religion. It involves the belief in a single Lord who is invisible, who made each of us in His image. And it involves a commitment to a land and a language, to a moral code, to ten commandments, to a universality in our responsibility. So while being a nation and a faith at the same time, we are also universal. While we are located in one place, we must have global aspirations. So it's different from other religions. And it's very little concerned with power, with beauty, with strength, and very much concerned with the human condition and a moral code.

R.L. Do you think there is any truth to Sartre's proposition:

"The Jew is one whom other men consider a Jew . . . it is the anti-Semite who makes the Jew." In other words, whatever a Jew is, he owes his identity as a Jew to those who hate Jews "more than necessary."

S.P. Judaism wasn't born in hatred, Judaism was born in faith. Judaism was born as a nonconforming way of life that was against the idea of wooden gods, against the idea of slavery, against the idea of oppression. When you are nonconformists, you clearly mobilize all the conformists against you. So it isn't that the conformists created the nonconformists, but the other way around. That's the reason I disagree with Sartre.

R.L. Chou En-lai was once asked about the impact of the French revolution on France.

S.P. He replied that it is too early to judge.

R.L. I see you know the story. He formed his hands into a pyramid with his fingertips touching and repeated the question, then thought about it a while before finally saying, "Too soon to tell." We have a bit more perspective when we try to weigh the impact of Judaism on the Western world, it's been three thousand years since King David set up shop in Jerusalem. Could you form your hands into a pyramid and give the question a shot — what impact has Judaism had on the Western world?

S.P. Well, as long as life continues, there is no final judgment. But we can judge what has happened up to now. It is clear that no other nation as small as the Jewish nation has had such a tremendous impact upon the entire world, all of civilization. I mean, what we're seeing is clearly a demonstration of quality being superior to quantity. I don't remember who said it, but someone once remarked that Christianity came about because the Jews were not patient enough with Judaism. Maybe there is something to that. I don't know. But Judaism has had a great impact on Christianity, on the Moslem world, on the philosophy of

the Western world. Judging by the number of people involved—
the number of Jews who shaped the Torah—Judaism has had an
unbelievable impact. What typifies Judaism is the tremendous
impact of individual Jews such as Moses, Jesus, Marx, Freud,
and Einstein—you don't have anywhere else such a collection of
tremendous figures who have so greatly changed the lives of so
many people.

R.L. Other peoples—the Philistines, the Moabites, the Am-
monites, the Edomites, to name just a few—have disappeared
from the face of the earth. But this dispersed people that for
two thousand years—for fifty generations—wandered the earth
without a nation-state of their own, without a language of their
own, are still here, in Israel, the land of their ancestors, where
they speak the language of their ancestors. This despite attempts
by the Babylonians and the Romans to disperse them, by the
Roman Emperor Hadrian to banish them from Jerusalem, by
the French and the Spanish to convert or expel them, and more
recently by the Nazis to exterminate them. What is it about the
Jewish people, what qualities of mind or heart or spirit, that
accounts for their longevity?

S.P. The lack of happiness, and the belief that it is possible to
attain happiness—the combination of the two. The great contradiction between the status quo and the Promised Land—the
Jews always have a motherland and a Promised Land, a land at
which they haven't yet completely arrived. So they always are
concerned with the future, they always are engaged in a search.
We weren't born to be satisfied. We're a dissatisfied people, a
people that makes demands on itself, a people that the only
electricity it knows is high-tension—there is no low-tension in
Jewish energy. And a belief that the brain is not an instrument
of pleasure, but an instrument to search for new opportunities,
new shores, new journeys. In a way Genesis was a beginning, but

never an end. The Jewish people are an ongoing Genesis. They're still not out of it — there were so many imperfections in what was done in the first seven days that we have to continue to work for the rest of our lives and the rest of eternity.

R.L. Israel has come a long way since the 34-year-old Viennese journalist named Theodor Herzl covered the Dreyfus trial in 1894 and heard mobs in Paris cry "Death to the Jews." Today it is a thriving country of five million Hebrew speakers. Do you worry that a culture based on five million Hebrew speakers in Israel, and perhaps twelve million Jews in the Diaspora who tend to intermarry and assimilate so rapidly that Mr. Rabin referred to the phenomenon as a "holocaust" with a small *h*, will not be able to withstand what you have called "the pervasive, corrosive effects of the global television culture"? In short, do you worry about the disappearance of the Hebrew language and the Jewish people?

S.P. To start with, this is the largest number of Hebrew-speaking people that has ever existed. At any given period throughout Jewish history there have never been more than three million Hebrew speakers in the world. So having five million is quite a sensation; it's almost double what we used to have. We have more Hebrew-speaking Jews, as Amos Oz remarked, than Danish-speaking Danes. I think that on one hand there is clearly the danger of an invasion of the lowest common denominator, which is being broadcast by television and other media — it's a real problem.

On the other hand, since political sovereignty is losing its strength, cultural sovereignty will be more cherished. I am concerned about cultural invasion no less than military invasion. Because people like to be different. I mean, every person wants to distinguish himself. So does every nation. And if you can't distinguish yourself on the map, you have to distinguish yourself in the dictionary in order not to disappear. Maybe the dictionary will be the future geography of mankind, and language will be as important as land, maybe more so. So while I'm worried about the corruption that comes from the power of the media — I don't say that the media are only corrupting — they have another important role: undoubtedly the media challenge dictatorships.

But I do believe we're not at a bad beginning, particularly because Hebrew is not only a language, but a philosophy, too. It represents quite nicely the philosophy of the Jewish people, with a great impatience for the present, with a great love for the past, and with a striking orientation toward the future. In Hebrew you don't have all the different past-present models — the imperfect, the pluperfect, the subjunctive. Hebrew is a language of the past and the future, with a very pale recognition of everything that is in between. Philosophies or languages, everything which is intellectual, may emerge in the future as more real than real estate.

R.L. You are drawn to poetry. You courted your wife, Sonia, by reading her poems as well as passages from *Das Kapital.* As a young man you wrote poetry. I'd like to offer you an intriguing quote. The English novelist W. Somerset Maugham said that the poet "makes the best of us look like a piece of cheese." Do you sometimes feel like a piece of cheese, Mr. Peres?

S.P. The famous French poet Paul Valéry said that the difference between prose and poetry is like the difference between walking and dancing. With prose you begin at a certain point and you wind up at another point. With poetry you dance. And all the beauty of art is invested in poetry. Since I think the world would be extremely dull if it were a strictly scientific organization without artistic feelings, I admire poetry. Recently I came across this book of Rumanian poetry [translated into Hebrew], and I found there some poems that speak for themselves. I shall translate for you: "Every person who doesn't have the strength to love is for me a fountain of deep sadness." Isn't that beautiful? "Every person who has loved and does not have the strength to continue loving takes another step toward death." Then it says: "When I shall no longer have the strength to love a person, you who know that you are entitled to be loved, please don't kill me." The name of the poet is Geo Bazza.

R.L. Depending of course on how things develop, these conversations may be seen as marking a watershed in a political career that has spanned half a century. Most of your contemporaries have passed from the scene — David Ben-Gurion, Levi Eshkol, Golda Meir, Moshe Dayan, Menachem Begin, Yitzhak Rabin. You are among the last of your generation. You've come a long way from the days when you strapped on your wooden-handled Mauser and herded the kibbutz sheep down into the wadis above the Sea of Galilee; from the days when you wrote a regular column entitled "From the Diary of a Woman-Member" for your kibbutz newspaper and dreamed of becoming a kibbutz farmer in the Jezreel Valley. The American poet Robert Frost wrote a haunting poem entitled "The Road Not Taken." It ends like this:

> Two roads diverged in a wood and I —
> I took the one less traveled by,
> And that has made all the difference.

The life and career of a politician is never easy on the ego. I imagine this is especially true for someone who has lost five elections. So sometimes, in the dead of night, do you feel in a corner of your heart a pang of regret for the road you didn't take — for the kibbutz farmer you didn't become?

S.P. I don't know what one can do with regrets. I feel sorry for a lot of things I didn't do, but I don't regret all the things I did.

I think this was what was required at the time and, accidentally or otherwise, that brought me into it. I don't think a person can be master of his life. He must also be a servant of circumstances. And unless you want to be a revolutionary by profession, which means doing nothing but making revolutions — and this, too, is a very difficult profession — you have to submit to different circumstances and different calls. So I really don't know. I mean, probably I contributed, probably I gained.

I feel deep in my heart that I tried to be honest to the challenges. And if I made mistakes it was probably due to a moment of weakness or a moment of blindness. And those are not scarce in your life. You may become weak or tired or blind. I was blessed with extraordinary health. When I was born the doctors decided I didn't need any inoculations against sickness, and I have passed my entire life without having any inoculations. And I carry with great pride the title that I believe I'm entitled to — that I feel like a human being, with weaknesses and strengths, mistaken but not corrupted, a work in progress but not completed.

R.L. That was pretty much your description of the Jewish people.

S.P. Well, I'm basically Jewish.

R.L. In 1923, the year you were born, Robert Frost wrote another poem entitled "Stopping by Woods on a Snowy Evening." The last stanza reads:

> The woods are lovely, dark and deep.
> But I have promises to keep,
> And miles to go before I sleep,
> And miles to go before I sleep.

The poem seems curiously appropriate to your predicament. You, too, have promises to keep before you can seek the sanctuary of the dark deep woods — one could interpret this as death. You, too, have miles to go before you can sleep. Do you feel frustrated — bitter even — when you contemplate the distance that remains to be traveled before you can finally rest?

s.p. Philosophically, you have to live in peace with the shortcomings [of life]. You know, the other day I was talking with a friend of mine and I asked him if he'd like to live forever. He said yes. I said, You're wrong — maybe there is great wisdom in the fact that the Lord decided to give you a small portion of time. You wouldn't know what to do with eternity. There are limits to everything. The mere fact that you were born to live a limited period of time has its advantages. And even if you know that you are going through your life like seasons, spring and summer and fall and winter, there is great wisdom in the changing seasons. So when my day arrives I won't complain. And nobody should be so ambitious as to think that with him everything can be achieved. It's a long road. All of us are entitled to take some steps on it. Even if you're wrong, at least be wrong in the right direction. The only real thing is that when my day comes, I would like to think that we will hand over to our children a somewhat improved world, a somewhat improved country, over the one we inherited.

R.L. When you landed in Jaffa in 1934 — you described it as landing on the moon — the Jewish state was a gleam in the eye of a handful of pioneers.

s.p. Yes. No doubt the Jewish people are better off now.

R.L. There's a wonderful Canadian novelist by the name of Nancy Huston. In a novel entitled *The Goldberg Variations,* she wrote this: "I wonder if there's an exact borderline between waking and sleeping, speaking and singing, youth and old age." At seventy-three, do you feel you've crossed the border into old age?

S.P. Maybe partly so. Anyway, I did not have to pay customs! But no, not really, because I feel curious. I would like to work. I would like to do things. And I can still hear good music and read good poetry and meet nice people. And continue to be engaged in so many battles. So what is life but music to your ears and sight to your eyes, walking to your legs and thinking to your mind?

R.L. Once you and Moshe Dayan were caught in a cross-fire north of Jerusalem. You both escaped without injury. You asked Mr. Dayan, "Don't you know fear?" And he answered, "When I find myself facing death, I feel as though I am in a sort of fog. And I'm not afraid of fog." In 1989 you were in this fog—you came close to dying from a rare type of blood poisoning. Does the fog hold dread for you today?

S.P. No. None at all. It doesn't occupy my mind at all. I know for sure that no one has the right to forget that he will die one day, but even if you forget it, you won't escape it. So why do it?

R.L. I once came across an inscription on the tomb of someone named Leonatto Segre Amar in the Jewish cemetery on the Lido of Venice. It reads, in Italian:

> Pensare
>
> Pensare
>
> Pensare
>
> Amare
>
> Sognare
>
> Lottare
>
> Temere
>
> Tremere
>
> Sperare
>
> Capire

Soffrire

Morire

In English, it reads: Think, Think, Think, Love, Dream, Struggle, Fear, Tremble, Hope, Understand, Suffer, Die. The first thing that drew me to this tombstone was the curious repetition of the word "Think" — it sounded suspiciously like an Old Testament injunction, which is to say that this emphasis on the role of the intellect struck me as being very Jewish. Do you agree?

s.p. I do. I do because you cannot have full joy unless you are able to digest it intellectually. People say love is blind, but when you are blind at love you miss a great deal. Even love should be understood intellectually, not only physically and sensually. The highest degree of pleasure is wisdom. And even in love there is wisdom. As far as I'm concerned, the love of wisdom is the highest degree of love. Because all other experiences in life age and disappear. They say that two things never age — foolishness and wisdom. And for that reason I like the emphasis on thinking. It adds to everything you possess, to everything you have experienced, to everything you can hope for. When you say love is blind, you have to compromise. When you say working is a must, you are compromising. And I do not feel the need for so many compromises. Even if I have to compromise, I would like to do it intellectually so that I will enjoy it.

r.l. Each life obviously has its own inventory. What did Leonatto Segre Amar put in his list that you would leave out of yours?

s.p. I don't like his *trembling*. Why should one tremble?

r.l. I thought that Jews were supposed to tremble before the Lord.

s.p. I'm not sure that the Lord is impressed by it. So it's a waste of movement.

R.L. What did Leonatto Segre Amar leave out of his inventory that you would put in yours?

S.P. Tolerance . . . and patience. And never die. Pass away, but never die.

SHIMON PERES was born in Belorussia in 1923 and immigrated to Palestine with his family as a child. After conscription into the Haganah Defense Forces in 1947, he was responsible for manpower and arms in the early War of Independence.

A member of the Knesset since 1959, he served as Israeli minister of defense (1974–77, a period that included the Entebbe rescue operation, as well as the signing of the second interim agreement with Egypt), prime minister (1984–86), vice premier and minister of foreign affairs (1986–88), and deputy prime minister and minister of finance (1988–92). In his second term as foreign affairs minister, he initiated and conducted the Oslo agreements, which led to his sharing the 1994 Nobel Peace Prize with Yitzhak Rabin and Yasir Arafat.

On November 5, 1995, following the assassination of Prime Minister Rabin, Peres was again sworn in as prime minister and defense minister. After the Likud election victory in May 1996, he served as chairman of the opposition Labour Party. In 1997 he established the Peres Center for Peace in Tel Aviv. Included among the ten books he has written are *Entebbe Diary, The New Middle East,* and *Battling for Peace.*

ROBERT LITTELL, a former *Newsweek* journalist, is the author of a dozen of novels, including *The Revolutionist, The Visiting Professor,* and *Walking Back the Cat.*

LIBRARY OF CONGRESS CATALOGING-IN-PUBLICATION DATA

Peres, Shimon, 1923–
    For the future of Israel / Shimon Peres and Robert Littell.
        p.   cm.
    Issued in French as: Conversations avec Shimom Peres.
    ISBN 0-8018-5928-X (alk. paper)
    1. Peres, Shimon,—1923- —Interviews.   2. Statesmen—Israel—
Interviews.   3. Israel—Politics and government.   4. Arab-Israeli
conflict.   I. Littell, Robert, 1935-   .   II. Title.
DS126.6.P47A5   1998
956.9405'092—dc21   97-47041
                                                                    CIP